PENGUIN CLASSICS

THE TWELVE CAESARS

GAIUS SUETONIUS TRANQUILLUS was born into a family of equestrian rank, probably in AD 70; his father had served as a military tribune under the emperor Otho. The place of his birth is unknown (possibly Hippo Regius in North Africa), but he was in Rome by the 90s. He practised as an advocate, perhaps for only a brief time, and embarked on a public career under the patronage of Pliny the Younger; he may have served on his staff when Pliny was governor of the province of Pontus and Bithynia in AD 110–11. Suetonius also devoted himself to scholarship from an early age, producing a number of learned works that are now almost entirely lost; the most important of these was *On Illustrious Men*, a collection of over 100 brief lives of notable Roman writers, parts of which still survive. He served as imperial secretary 'for studies' and 'for libraries', probably under the emperor Trajan, and as imperial secretary in charge of correspondence under the emperor Hadrian, a post from which he was dismissed in AD 122. He was at that time at work on his magnum opus, *The Twelve Caesars*, the only one of his works to survive virtually complete. He died perhaps sometime after the year AD 130.

The poet and novelist ROBERT GRAVES was born in 1895, the son of the poet Alfred Graves and his wife Amy, the great-niece of the historian Leopold von Ranke. He was educated at Charterhouse (1909–14), where he began publishing poetry. After leaving school, he served in the army during the First World War, and was severely wounded in the Battle of the Somme (1916). His first book of poetry appeared later that same year, but it was his autobiography of the war years, *Good-bye to All That* (1929), that first made him famous. Among the most notable of the more than 135 books that he published in his lifetime are the best-selling novels *I, Claudius* (1934) and *Claudius the God* (1935); *The White Goddess* (1948), an original and highly personal study of myth and poetic inspiration; and his *Collected Poems* (1975). He died in Majorca, his home since 1928, in 1985.

J. B. RIVES received his PhD in Classics from Stanford ⟨⟩ (1990), and taught at Columbia University and York Universi⟨⟩ in Toronto before moving to the University of North Carolina at Chapel Hill, where he is currently Kenan Eminent Professor of Classics. He is the author of *Religion and Authority in Roman Carthage* (1995) and *Religion in the Roman Empire* (2006) as well as numerous articles on aspects of religion in the Roman world; he has also published a translation, with introduction and commentary, of Tacitus' *Germania* (1999).

GAIUS SUETONIUS TRANQUILLUS

The Twelve Caesars

Translated by ROBERT GRAVES
Revised with an Introduction and Notes by J. B. RIVES

PENGUIN BOOKS

PENGUIN CLASSICS

Published by the Penguin Group
Penguin Books Ltd, 80 Strand, London WC2R ORL, England
Penguin Group (USA) Inc., 375 Hudson Street, New York, New York 10014, USA
Penguin Group (Canada), 90 Eglinton Avenue East, Suite 700, Toronto, Ontario, Canada M4P 2Y3
(a division of Pearson Penguin Canada Inc.)
Penguin Ireland, 25 St Stephen's Green, Dublin 2, Ireland
(a division of Penguin Books Ltd)
Penguin Group (Australia), 250 Camberwell Road, Camberwell, Victoria 3124, Australia
(a division of Pearson Australia Group Pty Ltd)
Penguin Books India Pvt Ltd, 11 Community Centre, Panchsheel Park, New Delhi – 110 017, India
Penguin Group (NZ), 67 Apollo Drive, Rosedale, North Shore 0632, New Zealand
(a division of Pearson New Zealand Ltd)
Penguin Books (South Africa) (Pty) Ltd, 24 Sturdee Avenue, Rosebank, Johannesburg 2196, South Africa

Penguin Books Ltd, Registered Offices: 80 Strand, London WC2R ORL, England

www.penguin.com

This translation first published 1957
This revised edition published in Penguin Classics 2007

3

Set in 10.25/12.25 pt PostScript Adobe Sabon
Typeset by Rowland Phototypesetting Ltd, Bury St Edmunds, Suffolk
Printed in England by Clays Ltd, St Ives plc

ISBN: 978-0-140-45516-8

www.greenpenguin.co.uk

Contents

Abbreviations

SUETONIUS' LIVES

Aug.	Divus Augustus	*Nero*	Nero
Calig.	Gaius Caligula	*Otho*	Otho
Claud.	Divus Claudius	*Tib.*	Tiberius
Dom.	Domitian	*Tit.*	Divus Titus
Galba	Galba	*Vesp.*	Divus Vespasian
Jul.	Divus Julius	*Vit.*	Vitellius

ROMAN PRAENOMINA

A.	Aulus	Mam.	Mamercus
Ap.	Appius	P.	Publius
C.	Gaius	Q.	Quintus
Cn.	Gnaeus	Ser.	Servius
D.	Decimus	Sex.	Sextus
L.	Lucius	T.	Titus
M.	Marcus	Ti.	Tiberius
M'.	Manius		

ROMAN MAGISTRACIES

aed.	aedile	pr.	praetor
cos.	consul	q.	quaestor
cos. suff.	suffect consul	tr.	tribune

Chronology

BC

133 Tribunate and death of Ti. Sempronius Gracchus.

122 Second tribunate of C. Sempronius Gracchus; opposition of M. Livius Drusus.

112–106 War with Jugurtha; C. Marius elected consul in 107 to take command of the war.

104–100 Marius consul five times in a row; defeats the invading Germanic tribes of the Teutones and Cimbri in 102 and 101.

100 Legislation and death of L. Appuleius Saturninus. Birth of Julius Caesar.

91 Assassination of the younger M. Livius Drusus.

91–87 Social (Marsic) War between Rome and its Italian allies.

88–85 First war with Mithridates under the command of L. Cornelius Sulla; in Rome, Marius and L. Cornelius Cinna take control and kill the supporters of Sulla.

84 Caesar marries Cornelia.

83–82 Sulla returns to Italy; civil war between partisans of Sulla and partisans of Cinna; Sulla's victory followed by proscriptions. In Asia, second war with Mithridates.

82–79 Sulla dictator; Q. Sertorius begins guerrilla war in Spain, which lasts until 72.

80 Caesar's military service in Asia and Bithynia.

78–77 Revolt of M. Aemilius Lepidus in Italy.

75 Caesar travels to Rhodes and is kidnapped by pirates.

74–66 Third war with Mithridates.

72 Caesar military tribune.

70 Cn. Pompeius (Pompey) and L. Licinius Crassus consuls for the first time.

69 Caesar quaestor in Rome and Further Spain; his wife Cornelia dies.

67 Caesar marries Pompeia.

65 Caesar aedile.

63 Caesar elected pontifex maximus; conspiracy of L. Sergius Catilina. Birth of C. Octavius, the future emperor Augustus (23 September).

62 Caesar praetor; divorces Pompeia.

61 Caesar governor of Further Spain.

60 Caesar stands for consulship; forms so-called 'First Triumvirate' with Pompey and Crassus.

59 Caesar consul; marries Calpurnia. Pompey marries Caesar's daughter Julia.

58–50 Caesar's command in Gaul.

56 Renewal of 'First Triumvirate' at Luca.

55 Pompey and Crassus consuls for the second time. Caesar crosses Rhine; invades Britain.

54 Caesar's second invasion of Britain. Death of Julia, daughter of Caesar and wife of Pompey.

52 P. Clodius killed by supporters of T. Annius Milo; Pompey sole consul; Caesar exempted from standing for consulship in person. Battle of Gergovia in Gaul. Parthians defeat Crassus at Carrhae.

49 Senate decrees that Caesar must dismiss his army and disallows the tribunes' veto; Caesar crosses the Rubicon; Pompey leaves Italy for Greece. Caesar besieges Massilia and defeats the Pompeian forces in Spain; returns to Rome.

48 Caesar crosses Adriatic; besieges Pompey at Dyrrhachium, then defeats him at Pharsalus. Pompey flees to Alexandria and is murdered; Caesar follows; war with Ptolemy.

47 Caesar defeats Ptolemy, has affair with Cleopatra; marches to Asia Minor and defeats Pharnaces; returns to Rome; sails to North Africa.

46 Caesar defeats Q. Caecilius Metellus Scipio and Juba in Africa; returns to Rome and reforms calendar; sails to Spain.

45 Caesar defeats the sons of Pompey at Munda in Spain;
returns to Rome and receives exceptional honours.

44 Caesar made dictator for life; refuses crown at Lupercalia
in February; assassinated (15 March). He posthumously
adopts his grandnephew C. Octavius, who takes the name
C. Julius Caesar Octavianus (Octavian, the future Augustus).

43 War of Mutina: Octavian and the Senate against M. Antonius (Mark Antony); Octavian's first consulship. Octavian,
Antony and M. Aemilius Lepidus establish the triumvirate.

42 War of Philippi: Octavian and Antony against M. Junius
Brutus and C. Cassius Longinus. Birth of Tiberius (16
November).

41–40 War of Perusia: Octavian against L. Antonius.

40 Execution of Q. Salvidienus Rufus. Antony marries Octavia.

38 Octavian marries Livia.

38–36 Naval war off Sicily: Octavian against Sextus Pompey.

36 Octavian defeats Sextus Pompey, strips Lepidus of power.

35–33 Octavian campaigns against the Dalmatae in Illyricum.

32 Octavian breaks with Antony.

31 Octavian's third consulship. Battle of Actium: Octavian
against Antony and Cleopatra.

30 Octavian's fourth consulship; death of Antony and Cleopatra.

29 Octavian's fifth consulship; triple triumph.

28 Octavian's sixth consulship; first census and purge of the
Senate.

27 Octavian's seventh consulship; adopts the name Augustus.
Disgrace and suicide of C. Cornelius Gallus.

26–25 Augustus' eighth and ninth consulships; campaigns in
Spain against the Cantabri.

23 Augustus' eleventh consulship. Augustus seriously ill, but
recovers. Conspiracy of A. Terentius Varro Murena and
Fannius Caepio. Augustus receives tribunician power for life;
death of his nephew Marcellus.

21 M. Vipsanius Agrippa marries Julia the elder, Augustus'
daughter.

20 Parthians return Roman standards; Tiberius installs
Tigranes III as king of Armenia.

18 Second purge of the Senate; laws on adultery, marriage and luxury.

17 Augustus adopts his grandsons Gaius and Lucius; celebrates the Saecular Games.

16 Germans cross Rhine and defeat M. Lollius.

16–15 Tiberius and Drusus campaign in the Alps.

13 Tiberius' first consulship.

12 Augustus elected pontifex maximus. Death of Agrippa.

12–9 Campaigns of Tiberius in Pannonia and Drusus in Germany.

11 Tiberius marries Julia the elder.

10 Birth of Claudius (1 August).

9 Tiberius' first consulship; death of Drusus.

9–7 Campaigns of Tiberius in Germany.

8 Augustus' second census.

7 Tiberius' second consulship; given tribunician power for five years.

6 Tiberius retires to Rhodes.

5 Augustus' twelfth consulship; introduction of Gaius to public life.

3 Birth of Galba (24 December).

2 Augustus' thirteenth consulship; introduction of Lucius to public life. Augustus proclaimed 'Father of His Country'. Dedication of Temple of Mars Ultor. Exile of Julia the elder.

1 Gaius sent to the east as commander.

AD

2 Death of Lucius at Massilia; Tiberius returns to Rome.

4 Death of Gaius in Lycia. Augustus adopts Tiberius and Agrippa Postumus; Tiberius adopts Germanicus.

4–6 Campaigns of Tiberius in Germany.

6 Disinheritance of Agrippa Postumus.

6–9 Revolt in Illyricum; campaigns of Tiberius.

8 Exile of Julia the younger.

9 Revolt in Germany; massacre of Roman troops under P. Quinctilius Varus. Birth of Vespasian (17 November).

10–12 Campaigns of Tiberius in Germany.

12 Germanicus' first consulship; Tiberius' Illyrian triumph. Birth of Gaius (31 August). Birth of Vitellius (7 September?).

13–16 Campaigns of Germanicus in Germany.

14 Augustus' third census. Death of Augustus (19 August); Tiberius becomes emperor. Death of Agrippa Postumus. Mutinies in Pannonia and Germany. L. Aelius Sejanus made praetorian prefect.

16 Trial and suicide of M. Scribonius Libo Drusus.

17 Cn. Calpurnius Piso made governor of Syria. Germanicus' German triumph; sent to the east. Cappadocia made a Roman province.

18 Tiberius' third consulship, with Germanicus; Germanicus visits Egypt.

19 Expulsion of Jews from Rome. Death of Germanicus.

20 Trial and suicide of Cn. Calpurnius Piso.

21 Tiberius' fourth consulship, with his son Drusus.

23 Death of Tiberius' son Drusus.

27 Tiberius retires to Capreae.

29 Death of Livia; exile of Agrippina the elder.

31 Tiberius' fifth consulship, with Sejanus. Tiberius summons Gaius to Capreae. Death of Germanicus' son Nero (?). Fall and death of Sejanus.

32 Birth of Otho (28 April).

33 Deaths of Germanicus' son Drusus and Agrippina the elder. First consulship of Galba.

37 Death of Tiberius (16 March); Gaius becomes emperor. Gaius' first consulship, with Claudius. Death of the younger Antonia. Gaius seriously ill in the autumn. Death of Tiberius Gemellus. Birth of Nero (15 December).

38 Deaths of Q. Sutorius Macro and Gaius' sister Drusilla; Gaius visits Sicily.

39 Gaius' second consulship; birth of his daughter and marriage to Caesonia. Conspiracy of Cn. Cornelius Lentulus Gaetulicus; trial of M. Aemilius Lepidus and exile of Gaius' sisters Agrippina and Livilla. Birth of Titus (30 December).

39–40 Gaius campaigns in Gaul and Germany.

40 Gaius' third consulship; death of Ptolemy of Mauretania.

41 Gaius' fourth consulship. Assassination of Gaius (24 January); Claudius becomes emperor. Gaius' sisters Agrippina and Livilla brought back from exile; death of Livilla.

42 Claudius' second consulship. Death of C. Appius Junius Silanus; attempted coup of Furius Camillus Scribonianus.

43 Claudius' third consulship, with L. Vitellius. Invasion of Britain.

44 Claudius' triumph for the conquest of Britain.

47 Claudius' fourth consulship, with L. Vitellius; celebrates Saecular Games. Claudius' censorship, with L. Vitellius. Death of Cn. Pompeius Magnus.

48 'Marriage' of Messalina and C. Silius; execution of Messalina. Consulship of Vitellius.

49 Claudius marries Agrippina the younger. Death of L. Junius Silanus.

50 Claudius adopts Nero.

51 Claudius' fifth consulship, with Vespasian as suffect consul. Birth of Domitian (24 October).

52 Nero acts as prefect of the city during the Latin Festival.

53 Marriage of Nero and Octavia; trial and execution of Domitia Lepida.

54 Death of Claudius (13 October); Nero becomes emperor.

55 Nero's first consulship. Death of Britannicus.

57–8 Nero's second and third consulships.

59 The Great Games. Death of Agrippina. Otho becomes governor of Lusitania.

60 Nero's fourth consulship; first celebration of the Neronia. Galba becomes governor of Tarraconensian Spain.

60–61 Revolt in Britain.

62 Roman defeat in Armenia. Deaths of Octavia and Sex. Afranius Burrus. Nero marries Poppaea.

64 Nero's first stage appearance, in Neapolis; second celebration of the Neronia. Great fire in Rome; persecution of Christians; construction of the Golden House.

65 Discovery of the Pisonian conspiracy. Deaths of Poppaea, Claudius' daughter Antonia and Seneca.

66 Nero marries Statilia Messalina. Coronation of Tiridates in Rome. Beginning of the revolt in Judaea.

66–7 Nero tours Greece. Vespasian sent to command the Roman forces in Judaea.

68 C. Julius Vindex raises a revolt against Nero (March); Galba joins the revolt and is acclaimed emperor by his troops (April); Vindex defeated by L. Verginius Rufus (May); Galba is recognized as emperor by the Senate (8 June?); Nero commits suicide (9 or 11 June). Vitellius becomes governor of Lower Germany (December).

69 Galba's second consulship. Army in Upper Germany withholds allegiance from Galba (1 January); Vitellius acclaimed emperor by his troops (2 January); Galba adopts L. Calpurnius Piso (10 January). Otho's coup; death of Galba (15 January). Otho sets out to meet the army of Vitellius (mid-March). Battle of Betriacum between the armies of Otho and Vitellius (14 April); Otho commits suicide (16 April?); Vitellius recognized as emperor by the Senate (19 April). Vespasian proclaimed as emperor by the army in Egypt (1 July), followed by the armies in Judaea, Syria and Moesia (July–August). Burning of the Capitol (19 December); death of Vitellius (20 or 21 December); Vespasian recognized as emperor by the Senate.

69–70 Vespasian in Egypt.

70 Vespasian's second consulship, with Titus. Domitian marries Domitia Longina. Birth of Suetonius (?).

71 Vespasian's third consulship, with the future emperor Nerva. Judaean triumph of Vespasian and Titus.

72–8 Vespasian's fourth to eighth consulships (72, 75–8) and censorship (73–4), all with Titus.

79 Vespasian's ninth consulship, with Titus. Death of Vespasian (23 June); Titus becomes emperor. Eruption of Mount Vesuvius.

80 Titus' eighth consulship, with Domitian. Dedication of the Flavian Amphitheatre.

81 Death of Titus (13 September); Domitian becomes emperor.

82–8 Domitian's eighth to fourteenth consulships.

83 Triumph over the Chatti; Domitian divorces and remarries Domitia.

86 Triumph over the Dacians. Celebration of Capitoline Games.

88 Celebration of the Saecular Games.

89 Attempted revolt by L. Antonius Saturninus. Double triumph over the Chatti and the Dacians.

90 Domitian's fifteenth consulship.

92 Domitian's sixteenth consulship; campaigns against the Sarmatians.

93 Expulsion of philosophers from Rome. Deaths of Q. Junius Arulenus Rusticus and the younger Helvidius.

95 Domitian's seventeenth consulship. Death of T. Flavius Clemens.

96 Assassination of Domitian (18 September); Nerva becomes emperor.

97 First mention of Suetonius in the letters of Pliny the Younger.

98 Death of Nerva (end of January); Trajan becomes emperor.

112 Death of Pliny the Younger (?).

117 Death of Trajan; Hadrian becomes emperor.

119 Hadrian appoints Suetonius' patron C. Septicius Clarus as praetorian prefect, and (?) Suetonius as imperial secretary in charge of correspondence; Suetonius at work on *The Twelve Caesars*.

122 Hadrian dismisses both Septicius Clarus and Suetonius (?).

after 130 Death of Suetonius (?).

Introduction

Modern readers with an interest in Roman history are apt to think of Suetonius' *The Twelve Caesars* either as a major historical work, comparable to the histories of Tacitus, or as the ancient equivalent of an exposé, filled with titillating titbits about the imperial families. Both perceptions are understandable, although both are misleading. *The Twelve Caesars* is neither history nor exposé, but instead biography, and rather unusual biography at that. In order to appreciate it for what it is, it is helpful to know something about Suetonius' background and to understand the distinctive format that he employs in *The Twelve Caesars*.

1. SUETONIUS' LIFE AND WORKS

Our information about the life and works of Suetonius is relatively meagre, even though we have more and better sources for him than for many ancient authors. Three of these are contemporary with Suetonius himself: a few personal comments in his own writings, several letters of the younger Pliny, and a fragmentary inscription discovered in 1950 in the city of Hippo Regius, on the coast of what is now eastern Algeria. In addition, there are three brief notices about his career in later writers, as well as numerous references to his writings.

Suetonius himself reveals something of his family background. He reports that his grandfather knew the story that those close to Caligula told about one of that emperor's more extravagant displays (*Calig.* 19), which suggests that he had some connections with the court. He provides more specific information about his father, Suetonius Laetus: since he served as a military tribune in the army of the emperor Otho in the spring of AD 69 (*Otho* 10), he must have belonged to the equestrian order, the second tier of the Roman elite, and had a public career.

Suetonius' full name was Gaius Suetonius Tranquillus. Although we do not know the year of his birth, he tells us that he was a young man in the year AD 88 (*Nero* 57), and it is generally thought that he was born around AD 70; one scholar has suggested that his cognomen Tranquillus, 'Peaceful', would have been very appropriate to a child born after the civil wars of AD 68–9. The place of his birth is uncertain. One possibility is Hippo Regius: the inscription found there, an honorific dedication to Suetonius erected at public expense in one of the main squares of the city, suggests that he may have been a native of the city who achieved notable success in the wider world. Wherever he was born, he was in Rome by the 90s, since he records an incident from the reign of Domitian that he himself witnessed (*Dom.* 12). It was presumably in Rome that he embarked on the scholarly studies that became one of his chief occupations. It was also surely in Rome that he acquired as his patron and benefactor Gaius Plinius Secundus, conventionally known as Pliny the Younger. Pliny was one of the leading figures of his day, a noted orator and writer who had a very successful public career, and who is now known chiefly through a surviving collection of his letters. Suetonius makes his first appearance in this collection in two letters written around the year AD 97, when he was probably in his late twenties. From one of these (*Epistles* 1.18), it appears that he was practising as an advocate, that is, a professional speaker who represented people in court cases; in the other (*Epistles* 1.24), Pliny writes to a friend about a small property outside Rome that Suetonius was hoping to buy as a country retreat.

Pliny continued to act as Suetonius' benefactor for some fifteen years, as we can tell from the four further letters that refer to him. From Pliny's letters we can deduce two things. First, Suetonius had an interest in pursuing a public career. At

some point in the period AD 101–103 Pliny in fact obtained
for him a position as military tribune, the same sort of position
his father had held, with a legion in Britain (*Epistles* 3.8); unlike
his father, however, Suetonius did not take up this post, but
asked for it to be transferred to a cousin. Whatever his reasons
for making this request, Pliny was apparently not offended by
it, and continued to act as his patron. Suetonius may in fact
have been on Pliny's staff when Pliny served as governor of the
province of Pontus and Bithynia on a special appointment by
the emperor Trajan. It was from here that Pliny wrote to Trajan
asking him to grant Suetonius the privileges granted to fathers
of three children, a favour that Trajan granted (*Epistles*
10.94–5; see further 'Papian–Poppaean Law' in the Glossary
of Terms). This exchange of letters dates to the second year of
Pliny's governorship, AD 110–11; since Pliny then disappears
from the historical record, it is usually assumed that he died
shortly thereafter. Suetonius would accordingly have needed to
find another patron if he wished to continue advancing in his
public career, and he seems to have found one in Pliny's circle:
C. Septicius Clarus, the dedicatee of the first volume of Pliny's
collected letters (*Epistles* 1.1).

The second fact about Suetonius that emerges from Pliny's
letters is his interest in scholarly and literary pursuits. In one
of the earliest letters to mention him, Pliny describes him as
scholasticus, 'scholarly' (*Epistles* 1.24.4). Somewhat later,
probably around AD 105 or 106, Pliny writes to encourage
Suetonius to publish some work that he has completed but not
yet made public (*Epistles* 5.10). A year or so after that, he
writes to get Suetonius' opinion about a public reading of some
of his own verse (*Epistles* 9.34), and in his letter to Trajan he
describes Suetonius as not only highly respectable and honourable, but also as *eruditissimus*, 'extremely learned' (*Epistles*
10.94.1). For Pliny, a public career and literary pursuits went
hand in hand, as his letters attest. He was not alone in this: his
uncle, Pliny the Elder, had combined a very successful career as
an equestrian official with extensive literary activity, of which
the younger Pliny proudly provided a detailed catalogue (*Epistles*
3.5). The esteem for literary and scholarly pursuits that Pliny

displays seems in fact to have been widespread among the men of his set, which included among others the historian Tacitus.

We have the fullest account of the scholarly side of Suetonius' career from a work entitled *Suda*, a Byzantine encyclopedia dating to the late tenth century AD. The entry on Suetonius (under 'Tranquillus', T 895 in the standard edition of Eve Adler), reads as follows:

> Tranquillus, called Suetonius, Roman *grammaticus*. He wrote *On Greek Pastimes*, one volume; *On Roman Spectacles and Contests*, two volumes; *On the Roman Year*, one volume; *On Critical Marks in Books*, one volume; *On Cicero's Republic*, one volume, in response to Didymus; *On the Correct Names and Form of Clothes and Sandals and Other Things that People Wear; On Abusive Words or Insults and their Derivation; On Rome and its Customs and Usages*, two volumes; *Family Tree of the Caesars*, which covers their lives and successions from Julius to Domitian, eight volumes; *On Illustrious Roman Men*.

Other sources preserve additional titles: *On Notable Prostitutes, On Bodily Defects, On the Institution of Offices, On Kings, On Varied Topics* and *The Meadow* (*Pratum* or *Prata*, a miscellany). Almost all these works are lost, although they were much used by later scholars, to whose references and citations we owe most of our information about them.

What can we deduce from this material about Suetonius' activities as a scholar? The *Suda* entry describes him as a *grammaticus*, a teacher of literature, one who specialized in the meaning and usage of particular words and the explication of obscure names and references. This approach to literary studies had developed in the Greek world in the last few centuries BC, and by the first century BC had become established in Rome as well. It is unlikely, however, that Suetonius was a professional teacher, since as an *eques* he would not have needed to earn a living in this way; he was no doubt instead what we would now call an independent scholar. In describing Suetonius as a *grammaticus*, therefore, the *Suda* was merely indicating his field of accomplishment.

The tradition of 'grammatical' scholarship was what underlay and united Suetonius' varied writings. Some of his works focused precisely on the meaning and usage of words, such as those on insults and clothes. Others were apparently antiquarian in nature, such as those on Greek games, Roman spectacles, the Roman year and the institution of offices. Lastly, some were biographical, such as those on notable prostitutes, illustrious Roman men and, of course, the Caesars. Apart from *The Twelve Caesars*, only parts of the work on illustrious Roman men survive intact; for most of the rest we have only scattered and brief citations. Of two works, however, those on insults and on Greek games, we have brief summaries produced in the Byzantine period. These are very helpful in giving us some sense of what Suetonius' lexicographical and antiquarian works were like. Suetonius composed both works in Greek, a useful reminder of his close familiarity with the Greek literary and intellectual tradition. That on insults, at least in its current form, consists of a historical preface followed by fourteen chapters that group the insults in various categories (terms for boasters, gossips, dimwits and so forth; insults derived from the names of cities or numbers); within the chapters, each word is given a definition and an etymology, and illustrated by citations from various authors. The overall impression is of a work that Pliny would no doubt have described as 'extremely learned', organized almost as a series of index cards.

The only writings of Suetonius to which we can assign even approximate dates are his two major biographical works, *On Illustrious Men* and *The Twelve Caesars*. The former probably appeared sometime between AD 107 and 118, and was a major work comprising brief lives of probably well over 100 Latin men of letters. Its format was much like the one Suetonius used in his work on insults: the biographies were grouped into separate sections according to the field for which the subject was known (poets, orators, historians, philosophers, *grammatici* and rhetors, teachers of rhetoric); each section consisted of a preface, discussing the origin, history and nature of the genre in question, and then a series of entries on the individual writers in chronological order. A range of evidence gives us a fairly good idea of its scope and nature: the section on *gram-matici* and rhetors has survived largely intact; a few other lives preserved in various sources derive from it (certainly those of Terence, Horace, Lucan, Pliny the Elder and Crispus Passienus; probably those of Virgil, Tibullus and Persius); and the *Chron-icle* of St Jerome, who mined it for data, provides a reasonable guide to its remaining contents. These lives were on a much smaller scale than those of the Caesars; the lives of *grammatici* and rhetors rarely exceed 200 words, and the life of Terence, the longest of the surviving lives of poets, is barely more than a third as long as the shortest of the lives of the Caesars. Even so, *On Illustrious Men* must when complete have been a major work of scholarship, and it clearly served as an authoritative reference for centuries afterwards.

Although Suetonius' scholarly productions may seem remote from his public career, it would be a mistake to see these as sharply distinct spheres of his life. As I noted above, the leading men of the day often combined literary interests and scholarly pursuits with public careers. Even the soldierly Trajan valued this sort of learning, or so at least Pliny asserts in his encomium of that emperor: 'How you honour the teachers of rhetoric and the professors of philosophy! Under you scholarly pursuits have regained their breath and lifeblood and native country' (*Pan-egyric* 47.1). Although Pliny's praise may well reflect an ideal rather than reality, the ideal itself is significant: since elite Romans like Pliny placed a high value on literature and learn-ing, it was important that the emperor be seen to patronize these pursuits. It was in fact Trajan who probably appointed Suetonius to the first of his major offices in the imperial bureaucracy, as secretary 'for studies' (*a studiis*) and 'for lib-raries' (*a bibliothecis*). Although the duties of these two pos-itions are not entirely certain, the latter presumably included oversight of the public libraries in Rome, while the former perhaps involved acting as a sort of combined research assistant and cultural adviser to the emperor. Certainly Suetonius, as we have seen, would have been eminently qualified for all these roles.

Since it is only from the Hippo inscription that we know

about these two posts, the chronology is not clear; it is possible that Suetonius held them not under Trajan, but early in the reign of Trajan's successor Hadrian. At any rate, it was certainly under Hadrian that Suetonius held his most important position, that of secretary in charge of the emperor's correspondence (*ab epistulis*). And it was in the same period that he embarked on his magnum opus, *The Twelve Caesars* (this is the title that has become conventional in English; a more literal translation of the Latin title, *De vita Caesarum*, is *On the Life of the Caesars*). Although its preface has perished, the sixth-century Byzantine writer John the Lydian (*On Magistracies* 2.6) reports that Suetonius dedicated it to his new patron, C. Septicius Clarus, whom Hadrian appointed praetorian prefect around the year AD 119 (*Augustan History, Hadrian* 9.5). Suetonius was thus at the peak of his public career as well as his scholarly achievement, working in close proximity to the emperor at the very centre of power. But it was not to last for very long. According to the *Augustan History*, which dates probably from the late fourth century AD, Hadrian 'assigned successors to Septicius Clarus, the praetorian prefect, and Suetonius Tranquillus, the minister for correspondence, and many others, because they had without permission been conducting themselves before his wife Sabina in a more familiar fashion than court etiquette required' (*Augustan History, Hadrian* 11.3). What actually happened remains a mystery. Even the date is uncertain: the *Augustan History* mentions the dismissal immediately after Hadrian's visit to Britain, which can be securely dated to AD 122, but its accuracy in details like this is by no means unimpeachable.

Thereafter, we have no further evidence for Suetonius, as either a public official or a learned writer. At the end of his life of Titus he refers to Domitian's wife Domitia Longina in the past tense, as if she were dead (*Tit.* 10); since she seems to have been still alive at the end of the 120s, Suetonius may have continued to work on *The Twelve Caesars* for a number of years after his dismissal.

2. THE TWELVE CAESARS

An awareness of Suetonius' life and career should make it clear that his *The Twelve Caesars* is not simply the ancient equivalent of a scandal sheet. Suetonius was a serious scholar, who had already made his reputation with several major works. Serious scholars are of course perfectly capable of writing scandalous exposés: the early Byzantine writer Procopius, for example, a major historian and government official of the sixth century AD, did exactly that in his *Secret History*, a scurrilous account of the emperor Justinian and his consort Theodora. But a comparison with Procopius' other writings, notably the eight-volume *History of the Wars of Justinian*, makes it immediately obvious that *Secret History* was little more than a diversion. *The Twelve Caesars*, in contrast, was apparently by far the most substantial of Suetonius' works: it filled eight volumes, whereas *On Illustrious Men* extended perhaps to five, and the others only to one or two.

Not only is *The Twelve Caesars* Suetonius' longest work, but it also clearly involved extensive and careful research. For example, Suetonius argues that, contrary to received opinion, Augustus had a favourable view of Tiberius, and quotes in support several extracts from Augustus' letters (*Tib.* 21); he has a detailed discussion about the birthplace of the emperor Gaius, drawing on a letter of Augustus as well as public records to refute the views of two earlier writers (*Calig.* 8); he insists that 'my own careful researches have turned up no evidence whatsoever' to substantiate allegations about the low origins of Vespasian's family (*Vesp.* 1). He certainly drew on a range of material, including various documentary sources: he made use of the public records for information about the birthplaces of Tiberius and Caligula (*Tib.* 5, *Calig.* 8) and of *The Achievements of the Divine Augustus*, Augustus' official account of his reign, for the number of Augustus' spectacles (*Aug.* 43). He also cites personal documents of the emperors, from which he often, contrary to the normal practice of ancient historians, quotes passages verbatim. Among the most interesting are letters of Augustus, which he quotes extensively (for example, *Aug.* 51, 64, 71, 76, 86; *Tib.* 21; *Calig.* 8; *Claud.* 4); he saw the originals, since he comments on Augustus' handwriting and spelling (*Aug.* 87–8). In addition, he made use of Julius Caesar's will (*Jul.* 83), Augustus' autobiography and will (*Aug.* 2, 101), Tiberius' autobiography and will (*Tib.* 61, 76), Claudius' memoirs (*Claud.* 41), Nero's poems in the original working manuscripts (*Nero* 52) and Domitian's essay on the care of hair (*Dom.* 18). He also drew on other primary sources like the letters of Mark Antony (for example, *Aug.* 7, 16, 69) and, intriguingly, anonymous lampoons and popular songs, which he often records verbatim (for example, *Aug.* 70, *Tib.* 59, *Calig.* 6 and 8, *Nero* 39, *Galba* 6, *Otho* 3, *Dom.* 14). All in all, then, *The Twelve Caesars* gives every sign of being a careful and substantial piece of work by a serious and established scholar; to the extent that Suetonius included gossip and scandal (and even a cursory reading shows that much of what he included is not scandalous at all), he presumably did so for some larger purpose.

But if it is not simply gossip, it is not formal history either. In the Graeco-Roman tradition, history was a recognized literary genre with well established features: it was a dramatic prose narrative with a focus on military and political events and an elevated style. In none of these respects does *The Twelve Caesars* fit the bill. Although most of the lives do contain a certain amount of narrative, the arrangement is more often topical than chronological, and even when it is chronological it rarely constitutes a dramatic narrative. As for subject matter, Suetonius often alludes to major military and political events, but omits a great deal that we would expect to find in a proper history. We would know little of Caesar's wars in Gaul, for example, if we had only *The Twelve Caesars*, and would be completely unaware of major figures like Cn. Domitius Corbulo, the greatest Roman general of the mid first century AD, whose name Suetonius never even mentions. When Suetonius is our only source for a significant historical event, as he is, for example, for the Vinician conspiracy against Nero (*Nero* 36), it becomes frustratingly obvious how little information he actually provides. Lastly, Suetonius' style of writing is a far cry from that of Latin historians like Livy and Tacitus: although generally efficient and at times quite effective, it by no means observes the normal conventions of literary prose. *The Twelve Caesars* abounds in the sort of technical vocabulary and every-day expressions that Livy and Tacitus avoided; Suetonius like-wise does not hesitate to introduce Greek words and phrases as needed (something regarded as inappropriate in formal Latin: see *Tib.* 71), and at times is so keen to pack in data that his writing becomes overly compressed and difficult to understand.

Many of these features can be explained by the fact that Suetonius wrote *The Twelve Caesars* as a work of scholarly biography, and not history at all. Suetonius rigorously excludes everything that does not directly pertain to the person on whom he is focusing, and includes everything that does: hence the absence of major historical events and figures, and hence the presence of so much personal and domestic detail. Yet the simple fact that he was writing biography does not fully account for the distinctive format that he employed. A person's life, after all, consists in large part of a chronological series of events, and an obvious way to recount that life is by means of a dramatic narrative. The other great biographer of antiquity, the Greek writer Plutarch, an older contemporary of Suetonius, did pre-cisely that; as a result, although he too maintains a tight focus on the individual, his biographies often read very much like history. Suetonius, by contrast, seems deliberately to have made his biographies as unlike history as possible.

All the lives share the same basic format: an initial chrono-logical section recounting the emperor's birth and life up to his accession, preceded by a section on ancestry and parentage; then an account of his reign, organized topically; then another chronological section describing his death. Within this basic framework there is considerable variation. Some lives contain a high proportion of narrative: that of Caesar, for example, who never really reigned at all, and those of Galba, Otho and Vitellius, about whose short reigns there was much less to say than about their rise and fall. There are also several different arrangements of topics within the section on the reign. In the life of Augustus, for example, Suetonius divides his material into two main blocks dealing respectively with his public and private life; the same basic pattern occurs in the life of Claudius, although there Suetonius includes in the section on private life a lengthy discussion of Claudius' vices and failings. In contrast, the arrangement in the central sections of the lives of Tiberius, Caligula, Nero and Domitian is fundamentally different: in the lives of these 'bad' emperors Suetonius first deals with the positive or neutral aspects of their reigns, and then goes on to discuss at greater length the negative aspects. Following this introduction I have provided analyses of the individual lives so that readers can see at a glance Suetonius' various principles of organization.

But, in virtually all the lives, the topical sections tend to dominate. The longest life, that of Augustus, has very little real narrative at all. Suetonius reports the main events of Augustus' life up to his first position of power in a single short paragraph (*Aug.* 8), and then announces that 'the story will be more readable and understandable if, instead of keeping chronological order, I use a topical arrangement' (*Aug.* 9). As it happens, there is a sort of narrative in the next section, which deals with Augustus' civil wars in more or less chronological order. But Suetonius, by prefacing this section with a preliminary summary, makes it explicit that the underlying principle of organization is in fact topical: '[Augustus] fought five civil wars, associated respectively with the geographical names Mutina, Philippi, Perusia, Sicily and Actium' (*Aug.* 9). This sort of prospective summary is very common in *The Twelve Caesars*, although it is not always immediately obvious. For example, after describing Nero's tour of Greece and triumphant return to Italy, Suetonius says that 'his insolence, lust, extravagance, greed and cruelty he at first revealed only gradually and secretly' (*Nero* 26). To the unwary, this might appear simply as a general observation about Nero's character; those familiar with Suetonius' method, however, will suspect that such a list is in fact serving as a summary of what is to come, and rightly so: in the thirteen chapters that follow, Suetonius goes on to provide examples of each vice, following the precise order that he indicates in his initial comment.

Suetonius' use of a topical arrangement is in certain respects not only non-historical but even anti-historical, since it obliges him to pull apart individual episodes and file their various component parts under separate headings. We may take as an example one of the most famous events from the reign of Nero, the Great Fire of AD 64, during which the emperor is proverbially said to have 'fiddled' ('played the lyre' would be more historically accurate). Suetonius duly includes this story, as an example of Nero's cruelty towards the people of Rome (*Nero* 38), and also records some events that, as we know from other sources, were linked to the fire: Nero's persecution of Christians, his new regulations on urban construction (both in *Nero* 16) and the construction of his massive Golden House (*Nero* 31). But Suetonius' presentation completely obscures the historical connection between these events: he lists the first two among Nero's useful acts of public policy, with no mention of their relation to the fire, and discusses the Golden House in connection with his extravagance; in the latter case, even though he notes that Nero began construction after his first palace had burned down, he completely fails to mention that it did so in the Great Fire. The latter fact was simply not relevant to his topic of extravagance, and so is omitted.

Why did Suetonius choose this non-historical, even anti-historical, format for his biographies, especially when the example of Plutarch shows that a very different format was possible? One influential theory, first propounded by the German scholar Friedrich Leo (*Die griechisch-römische Biographie nach ihrer literarischen Form* (Leipzig: B. G. Teubner, 1901)), holds that Suetonius and Plutarch represent two fundamentally different traditions of ancient biography: the quasi-historical sort employed by Plutarch was developed by political philosophers to tell the lives of statesmen, whereas the topical sort employed by Suetonius was developed by *grammatici* to provide concise biographical information about poets and writers. Leo argued that Suetonius, who was himself a *grammaticus*, had first used this format appropriately in *On Illustrious Men*, but had then automatically employed it in *The Twelve Caesars* as well, even though it was not at all suitable for the biographies of rulers.

Leo was certainly right to stress the links between *The Twelve Caesars* and the traditions of 'grammatical' scholarship. The topical arrangement of material in *The Twelve Caesars* is very similar to the format of Suetonius' more strictly grammatical works like *On Insults*; much of the work can be analysed as a series of headings and subheadings, each illustrated by a number of examples. We may illustrate this by two paragraphs from the section in the life of Julius Caesar that deals with his clemency (*Jul.* 73–4). The first begins with the statement that 'when given the chance, he would always cheerfully come to terms with his bitterest enemies', a virtual subheading that is duly illustrated by three examples (Gaius Memmius, Gaius Calvus, Valerius Catullus); the effect of a list is even stronger in the original Latin, in which each sentence begins with the name of the person. The second paragraph opens with another subheading ('even when he did take action, it was his nature to show restraint'), followed this time by four examples, each again beginning with a name (the pirates, Cornelius Phagites, Philemon, Publius Clodius). The organization here is almost identical to that which we find in *On Insults*, and occurs throughout *The Twelve Caesars*: the reader is constantly being confronted with what Andrew Wallace-Hadrill has called 'the unremitting tidiness of the scholar's mind' (*Suetonius: The Scholar and His Caesars* (1983; reprinted Bristol: Bristol Classical Press, 1995), p. 201).

Nevertheless, Leo's general thesis about two distinct types of ancient biography is now generally rejected. Many of the reasons have to do with the details of ancient literary history, but one is of importance for any reader of Suetonius' *The Twelve Caesars*. This is the observation that, far from being unsuited to the biographies of rulers and statesmen, the topical arrangement employed by Suetonius was both traditional and widely familiar. We find it, for example, in the encomium, a speech in praise of a notable figure, particularly a ruler or political leader. Thus the Greek writer Xenophon, in the encomium of the Spartan king Agesilaus that he wrote about 360 BC, divides his material into two main parts: first, a chronological narrative of Agesilaus' accomplishments, and then an account of his virtues arranged by category (piety, justice, temperance and so forth). Whether or not this work constitutes an actual biography, in organization it is clearly not far removed from, say, Suetonius' life of Julius Caesar.

The Romans, for their part, had a tradition of commemorating the achievements of eminent men in a type of inscription known as an *elogium*, a summary of accomplishments. One of the earliest extant *elogia* is the following, which dates to the third century BC: 'Lucius Cornelius Scipio Barbatus, the child of his father Gnaeus, a brave and wise man, whose appearance matched his abilities perfectly, who was consul, censor and aedile among you; he took Taurasia and Cisauna in Samnium; he subdued all Lucania and took hostages' (*Inscriptiones Latinae Selectae* no. 1). Later examples are more elaborate, such as this one honouring one of the emperor Tiberius' most illustrious ancestors: 'Appius Claudius Caecus, son of Gaius, censor, twice consul, dictator, three times *interrex*, twice praetor, twice curule aedile, quaestor, three times military tribune. He captured many forts from the Samnites; he routed the army of the Sabines and Tuscans; he forbade peace from being concluded with King Pyrrhus. In his censorship he built the Appian Way and constructed an aqueduct into Rome; he built the Temple of Bellona' (*Inscriptiones Latinae Selectae* no. 54). The tradition of *elogia* was taken to its furthest extreme by Augustus, in the monumental account of his achievements that he composed at the end of his life and had erected outside his tomb (see *Aug.* 101). Despite its considerable length (it runs to some nine pages in modern editions), the main categories that it employs are much the same as those of earlier *elogia*: public offices and honours (sections 4–14); benefactions to the Roman people, including distributions of money (15–18), building projects (19–21) and public entertainments (22–23); and military accomplishments (25–33). As a comparison with the analyses of Suetonius' lives will reveal, many of these categories regularly feature in *The Twelve Caesars*.

Even Suetonius' practice of discussing the emperors' personal qualities and private lives has its parallel in this tradition; the *elogium* of Scipio Barbatus, we may note, mentions not only his bravery and wisdom, but also his imposing appearance. Similarly, Suetonius' friend and benefactor Pliny the Younger, in the encomium of the emperor Trajan that he delivered in AD 100, covers not only the expected topics, such as Trajan's military achievements (*Panegyricus* 12–19), financial generosity (25–9), public entertainments (33), policy reforms (34–43) and building projects (51), but also his hospitality and behaviour at dinner (49.4–8), his pastimes of hunting and sailing (81), and the virtue and modesty of his wife and sister (83–4). These aspects of the emperor's private life, Pliny insists, have significance for his public role: the way an emperor lives his life serves as a model for others (46.6), and the way he spends his leisure time is the best guide to his true character – 'For who is so dissolute that he does not maintain some appearance of sobriety in his public affairs? It is by the activities of our leisure time that we are betrayed. Is it not the case that many previous emperors spent this part of their lives on gambling, fornication and extravagance, thereby substituting the strain of pursuing vice for true relaxation?' (82.9).

If *The Twelve Caesars* is biography, then, it is biography of a very distinctive sort. Whereas Plutarch came close to writing history, Suetonius, building on the traditions of the Greek encomium and the Latin *elogium*, was aiming at providing something very different: a sort of balance sheet, an analytical framework that would allow for a clear assessment of each emperor's relative success or failure. We should remember that, in his career as imperial secretary, Suetonius would have had ample occasion to evaluate the successes and failures of emperors at first hand, and this personal experience no doubt played a part in his choice of format for *The Twelve Caesars*. Contrary to the arguments of Leo, it was a format particularly well suited to accounts of Roman emperors. It was also, perhaps coincidently, one particularly well suited to Suetonius' distinctive talents as a *grammaticus*.

Although Suetonius wrote his lives as a series, they vary not

only in format but also in substance. We can identify three
distinct groups. The lives of Caesar and Augustus are by far the
longest and most detailed. Suetonius uses numerous specific
examples to illustrate his topics, supplies an abundance of
names and circumstantial details, and regularly cites his sources
by name. It is also in these lives that we most clearly observe
him assessing his sources critically and forming his own judge-
ments; as an example we may note his balanced discussion of
the charges of vice brought against Augustus, in which he draws
on a variety of evidence both pro and con (*Aug.* 68–71). The
next four lives, in contrast, Tiberius to Nero, are noticeably
less rich. References to specific sources are fewer and largely
limited to the Augustan period, and, although anecdotes are
duly supplied to illustrate the various subtopics, precise details
are often lacking. At times we can catch Suetonius apparently
making a broad generalization on the basis of a single known
incident (see for example his comment on virgins being raped
before being executed at *Tib.* 61). He also seems to rely more
heavily on received opinion and be less concerned with forming
an independent judgement. The last six lives, Galba to Domitian, are much shorter and at times almost perfunctory. This is
perhaps to be expected in the case of the short-lived emperors
of the year AD 69, but it is surprising in the case of such a major
figure as Vespasian; as for the life of Titus, it hardly counts as
a biography at all. That of Domitian provides something of a
return to the standards of the middle lives, but is still far less
vivid and detailed than we might expect, especially given that
Suetonius is writing about the events of his own lifetime; it is
worth noting that he devotes only slightly more space to the
fifteen-year reign of Domitian than he does to the seven-month
reign of Galba.

This steady decline has provoked considerable discussion.
One hypothesis explains it in terms of Suetonius' own career:
Suetonius wrote the first two lives and did incidental research
for the next four while he was in charge of the emperor's
correspondence and had access to the imperial archives; after
his dismissal by Hadrian, he was cut off from this resource but
carried on with his project as best he could, even though he

understandably lost some of his enthusiasm for it. As attractive as this hypothesis is, it is probably not correct. Close study of Suetonius' sources shows that most of them would have been readily available in the public libraries of Rome. The documentary source most frequently exploited by Suetonius, the correspondence of Augustus, must not have been difficult to access, since Quintilian also cites it (*Institutio Oratoria* 1.6.19, 1.7.22) and Pliny the Elder implies that documents in Augustus' own hand were fairly commonplace (*Natural History* 13.83). In fact it appears that Suetonius was simply more interested in the life and times of Julius Caesar and Augustus. An examination of *On Illustrious Men* indicates that he included in that work numerous figures from the period of Caesar and Augustus, significantly fewer from the early empire, and fewer still from the Flavian period; for example, the section on poets had entries for very minor writers of the first century BC such as Furius Bibaculus, Cornificius and Quintius Atta, but apparently omitted even such important Flavian poets as Statius, Silius Italicus and Martial. It is therefore likely that the varying quality of the lives of the emperors reflects not so much the availability of material as a bias in Suetonius' scholarly interests.

How should we assess the overall value of *The Twelve Caesars*? Most historians of the nineteenth and early twentieth centuries, who were chiefly interested in constructing a narrative of major political and military events, tended to dismiss Suetonius' work with scorn. There is good reason for this. As I discussed above, his particular style of biography led him to ignore much that was relevant to these topics; moreover, such details as he does provide are often wrenched from their context and thus stripped of historical significance. Apart from establishing the emperors' dates of birth and death, on which he often lavished considerable care, he had little interest in precise chronology, so that his chronological indications are usually vague and sometimes downright misleading. Obscurities and distortions like these, however, are simply the by-products of Suetonius' chosen approach to his topic. In terms of specific data, Suetonius maintains a fairly high level of accuracy, at least insofar as we can check them against other sources; actual mistakes are surprisingly few. Yet, even taken on its own terms, *The Twelve Caesars* is not always satisfactory. The problem is not so much that Suetonius can be wrong in his facts as that he can be very partial in his assessments. For example, he presents Tiberius' alleged miserliness in the worst possible light (*Tib.* 46–8), even though he incidentally reveals that his economy allowed him to avoid an increase in taxes (*Tib.* 32), something for which he sharply criticizes Caligula (*Calig.* 40), Nero (*Nero* 44) and even Vespasian (*Vesp.* 16). If Suetonius' goal in *The Twelve Caesars* was to provide a balance sheet for weighing the good and bad qualities of each emperor, he was not always as scrupulous as he might have been in 'laying out both sides of the ledger' (Wallace-Hadrill, *Suetonius*, p. 170).

Nevertheless, *The Twelve Caesars* remains a uniquely valuable resource. Paradoxically, the very partiality of Suetonius' accounts of 'good' and 'bad' emperors is useful, because it allows us to see how the received view of a given emperor was shaped by the agenda of that emperor's successors. It is no accident that the two emperors whom Suetonius rates most highly (setting aside his adulatory account of Titus) are Augustus and Vespasian, both founders of dynasties, whose prestige must have constantly been evoked by their successors. Likewise, the legend of Germanicus the ideal prince, as presented in the opening chapters of the life of Gaius, was no doubt carefully tended by his son Gaius and younger brother Claudius, who both clearly capitalized on his popularity when they became emperors (see for example *Calig.* 13 and *Claud.* 11). In contrast, emperors exaggerated the failings of unpopular predecessors in order to make themselves look better: thus Gaius would have emphasized the miserliness and cruelty of Tiberius, Claudius the extravagance and insanity of Gaius, Nero the stupidity and subservience of Claudius. We can even speculate on the origins of specific stories. For example, given that Gaius' grandmother Antonia died only six weeks after he became emperor, it seems highly unlikely that he would have had time to hound her to her grave, as Suetonius suggests he did (*Calig.* 23), even if he had been so inclined (in fact Suetonius himself notes that at his accession Gaius awarded her many lofty honours: *Calig.* 15).

But Antonia was also the mother of Gaius' successor Claudius, and represented Claudius' only blood tie to the family of Augustus. Claudius would thus have wanted to dissociate her as far as possible from his loathed predecessor, and so would have been keen to circulate stories of Gaius' hostility towards her.

The Twelve Caesars is also uniquely valuable because it contains so much material of a sort not commonly found in other sources. The very fact that Suetonius was not writing history meant that he was not constrained by the normal conventions of ancient historiography. In many respects *The Twelve Caesars* actually prefigures the historiography of today, especially in its verbatim quotations from documentary sources such as letters, popular songs and anonymous lampoons. For the same reason, *The Twelve Caesars* is a goldmine of information on topics that were ignored by the serious historians of the time: public games and spectacles, the pastimes and domestic relations of the emperors, their sexual tastes and manner of dress. Suetonius' willingness to include material of this sort makes his work a crucial resource for present-day social and cultural historians.

It is also what accounts for the enduring popularity of his work. Although, as I have argued, *The Twelve Caesars* was by no means the ancient equivalent of a behind-the-scenes celebrity exposé, there is little question that its mixture of personal detail and outrageous scandal has had a steady appeal to readers interested in the private lives of princes – an appeal that we can trace down to our own day.

3. THE INFLUENCE OF SUETONIUS

Although Suetonius' contemporary Tacitus may in the long run have acquired a loftier reputation, in the short run it was Suetonius who proved more influential. Indeed, after Tacitus we find no further serious historians writing in Latin until the solitary figure of Ammianus Marcellinus at the end of the fourth century AD. Historiography of the traditional sort was instead displaced by imperial biography, for which Suetonius provided the great model. In the early third century AD, at the same time

as the Greek writer Dio Cassius was at work on his massive
history of Rome, a man named Marius Maximus produced
what was in effect a sequel to Suetonius' work: the lives of
twelve more Caesars, from Domitian's immediate successor
Nerva (AD 96–8) down to M. Aurelius Antoninus, better
known as Elagabalus (AD 218–22). This work itself has not
survived, but references to it suggest that Maximus followed
the Suetonian model fairly closely: in the use of a topical
arrangement, the quotation of documents, and, of course, the
inclusion of gossipy personal details. Ammianus had a dismiss-
ive attitude towards Marius Maximus and those who read his
work: the degenerate nobles of his day, he complains (28.4.14),
'hate learning like poison, and can be bothered to read only
Juvenal and Marius Maximus' – two writers whom he links,
we must suppose, because of their propensity for the lurid and
sensational.

One of Ammianus' contemporaries, however, apparently
took a more tolerant view. This was the unknown author of
the curious work known as the *Augustan History*, a collection
of imperial biographies extending from Hadrian to Carinus and
Numerian (AD 117–284). Although the individual biographies
are presented as the products of various writers working in the
late third and early fourth centuries AD, the collection as a
whole is now regarded as the work of a single author active at
the very end of the fourth century. His purpose in concocting
this work, however, has been much debated, with some scholars
suggesting that it was little more than an elaborate literary
prank. Like both Suetonius and Marius Maximus, the author
included scandal and gossip, and like them he often quoted
generously from documents; unlike Suetonius, however, he
seems to have invented the documents that he quoted. Also
unlike Suetonius, he organized the material in his biographies
chronologically, with only occasional and inconsistent use of a
topical arrangement. But he nevertheless certainly presented
himself as working within the Suetonian tradition. 'As for me,'
he says, writing under the name Flavius Vopiscus, 'it has been
my purpose in treating of the life and times of emperors not to
imitate the likes of Sallust, Livy, Tacitus, Trogus and other such

eloquent writers, but Marius Maximus, Suetonius Tranquillus
. . . and the rest, who have handed down to history this sort
of material not so much with eloquence as with honesty'
(*Augustan History, Probus* 2.7).

At the same time, some people continued to appreciate
Suetonius' achievements from a more scholarly viewpoint.
St Jerome mined *On Illustrious Men* for data to include in his
Chronicle, a timeline of events from the creation of the world
down to his own day; it is from Jerome's *Chronicle*, as I noted
above, that we get most of our information about the lost
portions of Suetonius' work. Jerome also took it as the model
for his own treatise *On Illustrious Men*; in the preface, he says
that his friend Dexter had urged him to 'follow Tranquillus'
and do for Christian men of letters what the earlier scholar had
done for pagans. Yet it was not long after this that the works
of Suetonius, along with those of many other classical Greek
and Roman authors, began to disappear; the last western writer
to quote from them is Isidore of Seville, in the early seventh
century.

Apart from part of the section on *grammatici* and rhetors
from *On Illustrious Men*, only *The Twelve Caesars* survived
into the Middle Ages, and even it did not survive intact: the
only manuscript available by the time of Charlemagne had lost
its first few pages, which contained the preface and the beginning of the life of Julius Caesar. Although that manuscript itself
no longer survives, it was the source of all later copies, which
consequently also lack the opening sections of the work. The
earliest extant manuscript dates to the early ninth century, a
time when *The Twelve Caesars* enjoyed a certain vogue. The
most striking evidence for this is the *Life of Charlemagne* by
Einhard, which is clearly modelled on Suetonius' life of Augustus. After the Carolingian period evidence for *The Twelve
Caesars* again becomes scarce: from the tenth century nothing
survives, from the eleventh only three manuscripts, from the
twelfth only two. But with the advent of humanism interest in
Suetonius increased exponentially. *The Twelve Caesars* was one
of Petrarch's favourite books; he owned two copies, one of which
he commissioned himself, while his younger contemporary

Boccaccio made extensive extracts in his own hand. By the
fifteenth century, a copy of Suetonius had come to be regarded
as an essential component of any learned man's library, to the
point that over 100 manuscripts survive from this period.

By this time the popularity of *The Twelve Caesars* had begun
to spread beyond the circles of those able to read the Latin
original. The earliest translation into a vernacular language is
a French version dating to 1381, and the first English translation
appeared in 1606, the work of the great Elizabethan translator
Philemon Holland. In the twentieth century the person most
responsible for ongoing interest in Suetonius was the English
poet and novelist Robert Graves, whose best-selling novels *I,
Claudius* (1934) and *Claudius the God* (1935) drew extensively
on *The Twelve Caesars*. Some twenty years later, when Graves
was approaching the height of his career, he returned to Suetonius:
his translation of *The Twelve Caesars*, first published by
Penguin Classics in 1957, has become by far the most familiar
and widely available English translation.

4. READING SUETONIUS

Despite the great interest that *The Twelve Caesars* has held for
readers over the centuries, it is not necessarily an easy work to
read: Suetonius assumes a great deal of knowledge on the part
of his readers. In part this was simply because he was writing
for his contemporaries, who could be expected to be familiar
with all the details of everyday life in Rome that so often crop
up in his text. But the same thing was true of Tacitus, for
example, and Tacitus' works by and large present fewer difficulties for modern readers. The difference is that Tacitus was
explicitly writing history, and so presents complete narratives
that provide most of the necessary background information.
Suetonius, in contrast, who was writing biography rather than
history, and moreover biography of a particular sort, takes it
for granted that the reader already knows all the events and
people to which he alludes, and so gets on with the business of
slotting the data into the appropriate categories without bring-

ing in unnecessary explanations. As a result, the casual reader
with little or no knowledge of Roman history and culture can
quickly become baffled by the steady barrage of unfamiliar
names and unexplained references.

Graves was well aware of this problem, and tried to circum-
vent it by recourse to two tactics. First, he replaced a number
of Roman terms with what he regarded as suitable contemporary
equivalents. Thus the Roman toga became a 'gown', all senatorial business was transacted in 'the House', the people (*populus*
or *plebs*) became 'the commons', military tribunes became
'colonels', sums of money were expressed in terms of 'gold
pieces' (deliberately meant to evoke the old British 'sovereigns'),
and so forth. Secondly, whenever the Suetonian original
included a reference that Graves felt required more detailed
explanation, he simply introduced additional information into
his translation. For example, where Suetonius says merely that
Thermus awarded Caesar the civic crown, Graves translated,
'Thermus awarded him the civic crown of oak-leaves . . . for
saving a fellow-soldier's life' (*Jul.* 2); and where Suetonius mentions the rumour that Publius Clodius disguised himself as a
woman and seduced Julius Caesar's wife at a public religious
ceremony, Graves noted that this was 'the Feast of the Good
Goddess, from which all men are excluded' (*Jul.* 6). Through
these two devices, the substitution of contemporary terms for
ancient ones and the incorporation of supplementary information, Graves dispensed with introductory essays and notes,
and sought instead to provide the modern reader with the
same sort of unmediated experience of the text that Suetonius'
original readers would have had.

In my revision of the translation, I have deliberately undone
much of what Graves did along these lines. My reasons are
twofold: both practical and methodological. The practical
reason is that the contemporary equivalents that Graves used
for translating Roman terms are no longer contemporary. He
had originally developed these for his Claudius novels of the
1930s, and they tend in fact to reflect the world of the late-
nineteenth- and early-twentieth-century British empire; some
of them, I imagine, must have seemed rather old-fashioned to

many readers even in 1957. Certainly for most readers today, 'colonels' and 'gold pieces' are every bit as remote as 'military tribunes' and 'sesterces', and a reference to Caesar's 'gown' is more likely to require explanation than one to his 'toga'. It would of course be possible to retain Graves's strategy in updated form by devising equivalents taken from the early twenty-first century, but here the methodological reason comes into play. The world of the Roman empire was simply not the same as our own world, and to translate *The Twelve Caesars* as if it were is to give a very misleading impression of what Suetonius was saying. Moreover, I suspect that for many people one of the things that makes the Roman world so interesting is the very fact that it was indeed very different from our own. It thus seems useful, in order not to gloss over that difference, to allow the original terms and references to remain in the translation and, when needed, to provide explanations and clarifications elsewhere.

In my revision, therefore, I have tried to alter the spirit of Graves's approach while retaining the texture of his translation. That is, I have avoided merely pedantic changes that would dampen its lively quality, for which it has been widely and deservedly praised. I have instead limited changes to four categories, listed here in decreasing order of frequency: (1) streamlining and updating the punctuation and spelling; (2) substituting the original Latin terms for Graves's equivalents; (3) removing from the translation explanatory material not found in the original text; (4) modifying the translation in the few places where it seemed to me seriously misleading about substantive issues. These changes, I hope, will render Graves's now classic translation both more accessible and more useful to current and future generations of readers.

To compensate for the removal of Graves's updated terminology and inserted explanations, I have supplied a range of supplementary material, and have here followed the lead of Michael Grant, my predecessor in revising Graves's translation. The Glossary of Terms provides brief definitions of most of the Roman customs and institutions mentioned in the text, including short discussions of Roman names and time-reckoning. The

Glossary of Place Names in Rome, which is keyed to the map of central Rome, identifies the various buildings and areas mentioned in the text; the remaining maps of Italy and the Roman empire have a separate Key to Maps that will allow readers to locate cities, provinces and peoples. I have provided four family trees (three for the Julio-Claudians and one for the Flavians) in order to clarify relationships that Suetonius mentions only in passing or not at all. In the Notes, I have provided supplementary information on a range of issues not covered elsewhere, although I have made no attempt to cover every detail. In particular, I have identified the sources of all Suetonius' quotations from extant texts; where a source is not identified, this is because the text in question has not survived. Lastly, the Index of Historical Persons also functions as a glossary, providing the full names and brief identifications of all the persons mentioned in the text about whom anything is known.

Analyses of the 'Lives'

DIVUS JULIUS

A. Background

  1. Ancestry (now lost)
  2. Birth (now lost) and life up to end of civil wars (1–36)

B. Public life (37–44)

  1. Aftermath of civil wars: triumphs, largesse to soldiers and people (37–8)
  2. Games and spectacles (39)
  3. Public policy: actual (40–43) and planned (44)

C. Character and conduct (45–80)

  1. Appearance and personal habits (45–54)
    (a) Appearance and health (45)
    (b) Household economy (46–8)
    (c) Sexual life (49–52)
    (d) Drinking and eating (53)
    (e) Greed (54)
  2. Literary accomplishments (55–6)
  3. Military character (57–70)
    (a) Personal attributes (57–64)
    (b) Treatment of his soldiers (65–70)
  4. Personal relations (71–5)
    (a) Loyalty to dependants and friends (71–2)
    (b) Clemency towards enemies (73–5)
  5. Arrogance in public life (76–80)

D. Assassination, funeral and aftermath (80–89)

DIVUS AUGUSTUS

A. Background (1–8)
   1. Ancestry (1–4)
   2. Birth and life up to gaining power (5–8)

B. Public life (9–60)
   1. War (9–25)
      (a) Civil wars (9–19)
      (b) Foreign wars (20–25)
   2. Peace (26–60)
      (a) Public offices (26–8)
      (b) Public policy (28–34)
      (c) Senate, *equites*, people (35–42)
      (d) Games and spectacles (43–5)
      (e) Italy and the provinces (46–9)
      (f) Signet ring (50)
      (g) Public virtues (51–6)
      (h) Esteem by Senate, people and kings (57–60)

C. Private life (61–96)
   1. Personal relations (61–7)
      (a) Family (61–5)
      (b) Friends (66)
      (c) Dependants (67)
   2. Appearance and personal habits (68–83)
      (a) Sexual life, charges of luxury and greed, fondness for
          gambling (68–71)
      (b) Houses, entertaining, food and drink, sleep (72–8)
      (c) Appearance, personal care, pastimes (79–83)
   3. Literary accomplishments (84–9)
   4. Religion and superstition (90–96)
      (a) Personal beliefs and attitudes (90–93)
      (b) Omens of his rule and victories (94–6)

D. Death and aftermath (97–101)

   1. Omens (97)
   2. Death (98–9)
   3. Burial, honours and will (100–101)

TIBERIUS

A. Background (1–25)

   1. Ancestry (1–4)
   2. Birth and life up to accession (5–25)
     (a) Birth and childhood (5–6)
     (b) Public life under Augustus (7–9)
     (c) Retirement to Rhodes (10–13)
     (d) Omens of his rule (14)
     (e) Return to public life under Augustus (15–21)
     (f) Accession (22–5)

B. Positive and neutral aspects of his reign (26–37)

   1. Modesty and restraint (26–32)
   2. Public policy (33–7)

C. Negative aspects of his reign (38–67)

   1. Residence (38–41)
     (a) Initial unwillingness to leave Rome (38)
     (b) Withdrawal to Capreae (39–40)
     (c) Subsequent neglect of public affairs (41)
   2. Vices (42–67)
     (a) Indulgence in food and drink (42)
     (b) Sexual excess (43–5)
     (c) Stinginess and greed (46–9)
     (d) Hostility to family (50–54)
     (e) Hostility to friends (55–6)
     (f) Cruelty (57–65)
     (g) Hatred of Tiberius and his own self-loathing (66–7)

GAIUS CALIGULA

NERO

GALBA

A. Background (1–11)

   1. The end of the Julio-Claudians (1)
   2. Ancestry (2–3)
   3. Birth and omens of rule (4)
   4. Life and career up to governorship of Spain (5–9)
   5. Revolt against Nero and accession (9–11)

B. Reign (12–15)

   1. Vices (12)
   2. Popular reaction (13)
   3. Influence of his associates (14)
   4. Public policy (14–15)

C. Fall and death (16–20)

   1. Hostility of army (16)
   2. Adoption of Piso (17)
   3. Omens (18)
   4. Death (19–20)

D. Personal characteristics: appearance, dining habits, sexual life (21–2)

E. Aftermath of death (23)

OTHO

A. Background (1–6)

   1. Ancestry (1)
   2. Birth and life up to reign of Galba (2–4)
   3. Coup against Galba (5–6)

B. Reign (7)

C. Fall and death (8–11)

    1. Revolt of Vitellius and Otho's response (8–9)
    2. Suicide (9–11)

D. Appearance and personal habits; reactions to death (12)

VITELLIUS

A. Background (1–10)

    1. Ancestry (1–3)
    2. Birth and early career (3–6)
    3. Governorship of Germany, revolt and accession (7–10)

B. Reign (11–14)

    1. Inauspicious opening (11)
    2. Influence of freedman (12)
    3. Vices: gluttony (13) and cruelty (14)

C. Fall and death (15–18)

DIVUS VESPASIAN

A. Background (1–7)

    1. Ancestry (1)
    2. Birth and career up to command of army in Judaea (2–4)
    3. Omens of rule (5)
    4. Revolt and accession; healing miracles (6–7)

B. Public life (8–19)

    1. Public offices (8)
    2. Public policy (8–11)
    3. Virtues and vices (12–19)
        (a) Modesty and restraint (12)
        (b) Clemency (13–15)
        (c) Greed (16) and liberality (17–19)

Further Reading

SUETONIUS AND HIS WRITINGS

The best introduction to Suetonius and his work is Andrew Wallace-Hadrill, *Suetonius: The Scholar and his Caesars* (1983; reprinted Bristol: Bristol Classical Press, 1995). A number of useful studies are collected in *Aufstieg und Niedergang der römischen Welt*, vol. II.33.5 (Berlin and New York: De Gruyter, 1991), especially R. G. Lewis, 'Suetonius' "Caesares" and their Literary Antecedents', pp. 3623–74, and K. R. Bradley, 'The Imperial Ideal in Suetonius' "Caesares"', pp. 3701–32. On the ancient biographical tradition, see Arnaldo Momigliano, *The Development of Greek Biography* (expanded edn: Cambridge, Mass.: Harvard University Press, 1993).

The surviving lives from *On Illustrious Men* are most easily available in the Loeb edition of Suetonius, ed. and trans. J. C. Rolfe (Cambridge, Mass.: Harvard University Press, 1914; rev. edn by K. R. Bradley, 1997–8); the section on *grammatici* and rhetors has recently been edited, with an English translation and extensive commentary, by Robert Kaster (*Suetonius: De grammaticis et rhetoribus*, Oxford: Oxford University Press, 1995). The remains of Suetonius' lost works have not been translated.

Commentaries on individual lives contain a wealth of information on points of detail, especially historical; although based on the Latin text (the chief exception is that of Jones and Milns on the Flavian emperors), they can generally be used with profit by anyone.

*

Butler, H. E., and M. Cary, C. *Suetoni Tranquilli Divus Iulius* (Oxford: Oxford University Press, 1927; rev. G. B. Townend, Bristol: Bristol Classical Press, 1982)

Carter, John M., *Suetonius: Divus Augustus* (Bristol: Bristol Classical Press, 1982)

Lindsay, Hugh, *Suetonius: Tiberius* (Bristol: Bristol Classical Press, 1995)

Hurley, Donna W., *An Historical and Historiographical Commentary on Suetonius' Life of C. Caligula* (Atlanta: Scholars Press, 1993)

Lindsay, Hugh, *Suetonius: Caligula* (Bristol: Bristol Classical Press, 1993)

Hurley, Donna W., *Suetonius: Divus Claudius* (Cambridge: Cambridge University Press, 2001)

Mottershead, J., *Suetonius: Claudius* (Bristol: Bristol Classical Press, 1986)

Bradley, Keith R., *Suetonius' Life of Nero: An Historical Commentary* (Brussels: Latomus, 1978)

Warmington, B. H., *Suetonius: Nero* (2nd edn, Bristol: Bristol Classical Press, 1999)

Murison, Charles, *Suetonius: Galba, Otho, Vitellius* (Bristol: Bristol Classical Press, 1992)

Shotter, David, *Suetonius: Lives of Galba, Otho and Vitellius* (Warminster: Aris & Phillips, 1993)

Jones, Brian W., *Suetonius: Vespasian* (Bristol: Bristol Classical Press, 2000)

Jones, Brian W., *Suetonius: Domitian* (Bristol: Bristol Classical Press, 1996)

Jones, Brian, and Robert Milns, *Suetonius: The Flavian Emperors* (Bristol: Bristol Classical Press, 2002)

HISTORICAL BACKGROUND

Many modern histories are available; the following, differing widely in scope, can be recommended.

Boatwright, Mary T., Daniel J. Gargola and Richard J. A. Talbert, *A Brief History of the Romans* (Oxford: Oxford University Press, 2006)

Goodman, Martin, *A History of the Roman World, 44 BC–AD 180* (London and New York: Routledge, 1997)

Le Glay, Marcel, Jean-Louis Voisin and Yann Le Bohec, *A History of Rome* (3rd edn, Oxford: Blackwell, 2005)

Scullard, H. H., *From the Gracchi to Nero* (5th edn, London: Methuen, 1982) – a more detailed account of the period 133 BC–AD 68

Syme, Ronald, *The Roman Revolution* (Oxford: Oxford University Press, 1939) – a very detailed account of the period 60 BC–AD 14, and a classic of modern historiography

Wellesley, Kenneth, *The Year of the Four Emperors* (3rd edn, London and New York: Routledge, 2000) – a detailed study of the civil wars in AD 68–9

Virtually all the ancient writers and texts mentioned in the introduction and notes are available in English translation: the Loeb Classical Library provides the most extensive collection, but many can also be found in the Penguin Classics and Oxford World's Classics series. Translations of important documentary texts (those preserved in inscriptions or papyrus) are also available. Robert K. Sherk, ed. and trans., *The Roman Empire: Augustus to Hadrian* (Cambridge: Cambridge University Press, 1988) includes among much other material the inscription recording Augustus' celebration of the Saecular Games and his *Res gestae*. The latter is also translated, with introduction and extensive notes, in P. A. Brunt and J. M. Moore (eds.), *Res gestae Divi Augusti: The Achievements of the Divine Augustus* (Oxford: Oxford University Press, 1967). The recently discovered copy of the senatorial decree regarding Cn. Calpurnius

Piso, accused of murdering Germanicus, is translated by Cynthia Damon in a special issue of the *American Journal of Philology*: 120/1 (spring 1999): *The Senatus Consultum de Cn. Pisone Patre*, ed. Cynthia Damon and Sarolta Takács.

The lives and reigns of the Roman emperors have continued to attract the attention of scholars. The following studies (some closer to traditional biographies than others) are only a selection of those available, but can be recommended as judicious and reliable; I have also included a few studies of other figures who played important roles in this period.

Gelzer, Matthias, *Caesar: Politician and Statesman*, trans. Peter Needham (Cambridge, Mass.: Harvard University Press, 1968)

Goldsworthy, Adrian, *Caesar: Life of a Colossus* (New Haven: Yale University Press, 2006)

Meier, Christian, *Caesar*, trans. David McLintock (New York: HarperCollins, 1995)

Huzar, Eleanor, *Mark Antony: A Biography* (rev. edn, London: Croom Helm, 1986)

Jones, H. M., *Augustus* (New York and London: W. W. Norton, 1970)

Shotter, David, *Augustus Caesar* (2nd edn, London and New York: Routledge, 2005)

Wallace-Hadrill, Andrew, *Augustan Rome* (Bristol: Bristol Classical Press, 1993)

Barrett, Anthony A., *Livia: First Lady of Imperial Rome* (New Haven: Yale University Press, 2002)

Levick, Barbara, *Tiberius the Politician* (London and New York: Routledge, 1976)

Seager, Robin, *Tiberius* (2nd edn, Oxford: Blackwell, 2005)

Kokkinos, Nikos, *Antonia Augusta: Portrait of a Great Roman Lady* (rev. edn, London: Libri, 2002)

Barrett, Anthony A., *Caligula: The Corruption of Power* (London: B. T. Batsford, 1989)

Levick, Barbara, *Claudius* (New Haven: Yale University Press, 1990)

Momigliano, Arnaldo, *Claudius: The Emperor and his Achievements*, trans. W. D. Hogarth (2nd edn, Cambridge: Heffer, 1961)

Ginsburg, Judith, *Representing Agrippina*, ed. Erich Gruen (Oxford: Oxford University Press, 2005)

Champlin, Edward, *Nero* (Cambridge, Mass.: Harvard University Press, 2003)

Griffin, Miriam T., *Nero: The End of a Dynasty* (London: B. T. Batsford, 1984)

Griffin, Miriam T., *Seneca: A Philosopher in Politics* (Oxford: Oxford University Press, 1976)

Murison, Charles L., *Galba, Otho, Vitellius: Careers and Controversies* (Hildesheim and New York: Georg Olms, 1993)

Levick, Barbara, *Vespasian* (London and New York: Routledge, 1999)

Jones, Brian W., *The Emperor Titus* (London: Croom Helm, 1984)

Jones, Brian W., *The Emperor Domitian* (London and New York: Routledge, 1992)

A Note on the Text

Graves's translation, and my revision, are based on the standard modern edition of *De vita Caesarum* by Maximilian Ihm (Leipzig: Teubner, 1907). The text is usually cited by life and section number; the numbering system within the lives derives not from Suetonius himself, but from an early modern edition of the text.

DIVUS JULIUS

1. He lost his father at the age of fifteen.[1] During the next consulship, after being nominated to be the next flamen of Jupiter, he broke an engagement, made for him while he was still a boy, to marry one Cossutia, for, though rich, she came of only equestrian family. Instead, he married Cornelia, daughter of that Cinna who had been consul four times, and later she bore him a daughter named Julia. The dictator Sulla tried to make Caesar divorce Cornelia, and when he refused he stripped him of the priesthood, his wife's dowry and his own inheritance, treating him as if he were a member of the opposing party.[2] Caesar disappeared from public view and, though suffering from a virulent attack of quartan fever, was forced to find a new hiding place almost every night and bribe householders to protect him from Sulla's secret police. Finally he won Sulla's pardon through the intercession of the Vestal Virgins and his near relatives Mamercus Aemilius and Aurelius Cotta. It is well known that, when the most devoted and eminent men pleaded Caesar's cause and would not let the matter drop, Sulla at last gave way. Whether he was divinely inspired or showed peculiar foresight is an arguable point, but these were his words: 'Very well then, you win! Take him! But never forget that the man whom you want me to spare will one day prove the ruin of the party of optimates which you and I have so long defended. There are many Mariuses in this fellow Caesar.'[3]

2. Caesar first saw military service in Asia, where he went as aide-de-camp to Marcus Thermus, the praetorian governor of the province. When Thermus sent Caesar to raise a fleet in Bithynia, he wasted so much time at King Nicomedes' court

that a homosexual relationship between them was suspected, and suspicion gave place to scandal when, soon after his return to headquarters, he revisited Bithynia, ostensibly collecting a debt incurred there by one of his freedmen. However, Caesar's reputation improved later in the campaign, when Thermus awarded him the civic crown at the storming of Mytilene.[4]

3. He also campaigned in Cilicia under Servilius Isauricus, but not for long, because the news of Sulla's death sent him hurrying back to Rome, where a revolt headed by Marcus Lepidus[5] seemed to offer prospects of rapid advancement. Nevertheless, though Lepidus made him very advantageous offers, Caesar turned them down; he had small confidence in Lepidus' capacities, and found the political atmosphere less promising than he had been led to believe.

4. After this revolt was suppressed, Caesar brought a charge of extortion against Cornelius Dolabella, a man of consular rank who had once been awarded a triumph; but he failed to secure a sentence, so he decided to visit Rhodes until the resultant ill feeling had time to die down, meanwhile taking a course in rhetoric from Apollonius Molon, the best living exponent of the art. Winter had already set in when he sailed for Rhodes and was captured by pirates off the island of Pharmacussa. They kept him prisoner for nearly forty days, to his intense annoyance; he had with him only a physician and two valets, having sent the rest of his staff away to borrow the ransom money. As soon as the stipulated fifty talents arrived and the pirates duly set him ashore, he raised a fleet and went after them. He had often smilingly sworn, while still in their power, that he would soon capture and crucify them, and this is exactly what he did. Then he continued to Rhodes, but Mithridates was now ravaging the nearby coast; so, to avoid the charge of showing inertia while the allies of Rome were in danger, he raised a force of auxiliaries and drove Mithridates' deputy from the province – which confirmed the timorous and half-hearted cities of Asia in their allegiance.

5. On Caesar's return to Rome, the people voted him the rank of military tribune, and he vigorously helped their leaders to undo Sulla's legislation by restoring the tribunes of the people

to their ancient powers. Then one Plotius introduced a bill for the recall from exile of Caesar's brother-in-law, Lucius Cinna, and the others who had supported Lepidus and then joined Sertorius[6] after Lepidus' death. Caesar himself spoke in support of the bill, which was passed.

6. During his quaestorship he made the customary funeral speeches from the Rostra in honour of his aunt Julia and his wife Cornelia, and while eulogizing Julia's maternal and paternal ancestry he did the same for his own ancestry too. 'Her mother', he said, 'was a descendant of kings, since her family, the Marcii Reges, was founded by Ancus Marcius; and her father, of gods – since the Julii (of which we Caesars are a branch) reckon descent from the goddess Venus.[7] Thus Julia's stock can claim both the sanctity of kings, who reign supreme among mortals, and the reverence due to gods, who hold even kings in their power.' He next married Pompeia, Quintus Pompeius' daughter, who was also Sulla's granddaughter, but divorced her on a suspicion of adultery with Publius Clodius; indeed, so persistent was the rumour of Clodius' having disguised himself as a woman and seduced her at a public religious ceremony that the Senate ordered a judicial inquiry into the alleged desecration of these sacred rites.[8]

7. As quaestor, Caesar was appointed to Further Spain, where the praetorian governor sent him off on an assize circuit. At Gades he saw a statue of Alexander the Great in the Temple of Hercules, and was overheard to sigh impatiently – vexed, it seems, that at an age when Alexander had already conquered the whole world, he himself had done nothing in the least epoch-making. Moreover, when on the following night, much to his dismay, he had a dream of raping his own mother, the soothsayers greatly encouraged him by their interpretation of it, namely that he was destined to conquer the earth, our universal mother.

8. At all events, he laid down his quaestorship at once, bent on performing some notable act at the first opportunity that offered. He visited the Latin colonies, which were bitterly demanding Roman citizenship,[9] and might have persuaded them to revolt, had not the consuls realized the danger and

garrisoned the district with the legions recently raised for the Cilician campaign.

9. Undiscouraged, Caesar soon made an even more daring attempt at revolution in Rome itself. A few days before taking up his aedileship he was suspected of plotting with Marcus Crassus, a man of consular rank; also with Publius Sulla and Lucius Autronius, who had jointly been elected to the consulship but been found guilty of bribery and corruption. These four had agreed to wait until the new year, and then attack the Senate House, killing as many senators as convenient. Crassus would then proclaim himself dictator and Caesar his master of the horse; the government would be reorganized to suit their pleasure; Sulla and Autronius would be appointed consuls. Tanusius Geminus mentions their plot in his history; more information is given in Marcus Bibulus' edicts and in the speeches of Gaius Curio the elder. Another reference to it may be detected in a letter of Cicero to Axius, where Caesar is said to have 'established in his consulship the monarchy which he had planned while only an aedile'. Tanusius adds that Crassus was prevented, either by scruples or by nervousness, from appearing at the appointed hour, and that Caesar therefore did not give the agreed signal, which, according to Curio, was letting his toga fall and expose the shoulder. Both Curio and Marcus Actorius Naso state that Caesar also plotted with Gnaeus Piso, a young nobleman suspected of raising a conspiracy in Rome and for that reason appointed governor of Spain, although he was not qualified for the position. Caesar, apparently, was to lead a revolt in Rome as soon as Piso did so in Spain; the Ambrani and the Latins who lived beyond the Po would have risen simultaneously. But Piso's death cancelled the plan.[10]

10. During his aedileship, Caesar filled the Comitium, the Forum, its adjacent basilicas and the Capitol itself with a display of the material which he meant to use in his public shows, building temporary colonnades for the purpose. He exhibited wild-beast hunts and stage plays, some at his own expense, some in cooperation with his colleague Marcus Bibulus – but took all the credit in either case, so that Bibulus remarked openly, 'The temple of the heavenly twins in the Forum is

always simply called "Castor's";[11] and I always play Pollux to Caesar's Castor when we give a public entertainment together.' Caesar also put on a gladiatorial show, but had collected so immense a troop of combatants that his terrified political opponents rushed through a bill limiting the number of gladiators that anyone might keep in Rome; consequently far fewer pairs fought than had been advertised.

11. After thus securing the goodwill of the people, Caesar worked through the tribunes to be put in charge of Egypt by popular vote. His excuse for demanding so unusual an appointment was an outcry against the Alexandrians who had just deposed their king, although the Senate had recognized him as an ally and friend of Rome.[12] However, the optimate party opposed the measure; so Caesar took vengeance by replacing the public monuments – destroyed by Sulla many years ago – that had commemorated Marius' victories over Jugurtha, the Cimbri and the Teutones. Further, as president of the court concerned with murder, he prosecuted men who had earned public bounties for bringing in the heads of Roman citizens during the proscriptions, although they had been exempted by the Cornelian laws.[13]

12. He also bribed a man to bring a charge of high treason against Gaius Rabirius, who some years previously had earned the Senate's gratitude by checking the seditious activities of Lucius Saturninus, a tribune of the people. Caesar, chosen by lot to try Rabirius, pronounced the sentence with such satisfaction that, when Rabirius appealed to the people, the greatest argument in his favour was the judge's obvious prejudice.

13. Obliged to abandon his ambitions concerning Egypt, Caesar stood for the office of pontifex maximus, and used the most flagrant bribery to secure it. The story goes that, reckoning up the enormous debts thus contracted, he told his mother, as she kissed him goodbye on the morning of the poll, that if he did not return to her as pontifex he would not return at all. However, he defeated his two prominent rivals, both of whom were much older and more distinguished than himself, and the votes he won from their own tribes exceeded those cast for them in the entire poll.

14. When the Catilinarian conspiracy[14] came to light, the whole Senate, with the sole exception of Caesar, then praetor-elect, demanded the death of those involved. Caesar proposed merely that they should be imprisoned, each in a different town, and their estates confiscated. What was more, he so browbeat those senators who took a sterner line, by suggesting that the people would conceive an enduring hatred for them if they persisted in their view, that Decimus Silanus, as consul-elect, felt obliged to interpret his own proposal – which, however, he could not bring himself to recast – in a more liberal sense, begging Caesar not to misread it so savagely. And Caesar would have gained his point, since many senators (including the consul Cicero's brother) had been won over to his view, had Marcus Cato not kept the irresolute Senate in line. Caesar continued to block proceedings until a body of Roman *equites*, serving as a defence force, threatened to kill him unless he ceased his violent opposition. They even unsheathed their swords and made such passes at him that most of his companions fled and the remainder huddled around, protecting him with their arms or their togas. He was sufficiently impressed not only to leave the Senate House, but to keep away from it for the rest of that year.

15. On the first day of his praetorship, Caesar ordered Quintus Catulus to appear before the people and explain why he had made so little progress with the restoration of the Capitol, demanding that Catulus' commission should be taken from him and entrusted to someone else. However, the senators of the optimate party, who were escorting the newly elected consuls to their inaugural sacrifice in the Capitol, heard what was afoot and came pouring downhill in a body to offer obstinate resistance. Caesar withdrew his proposal.

16. Caecilius Metellus, a tribune of the people, then proposed some highly inflammatory bills despite his colleagues' veto, and Caesar stubbornly championed them until at last they were both suspended by a senatorial decree. Nevertheless, he had the effrontery to continue holding his court, until warned that he would be removed by force. Thereupon he dismissed the lictors, took off his praetorian toga, and went quickly home, where he had decided to live in retirement because the times allowed him

no other alternative. On the following day, however, a crowd of people made a spontaneous move towards Caesar's house, riotously offering to put him back on the tribunal; but he restrained their ardour. The Senate, who had hurriedly met to deal with this demonstration, were so surprised by his unexpectedly correct attitude that they sent a deputation of high officials to thank him publicly; they then summoned him to the Senate House, where with warm praises they revoked their decree and confirmed him in his praetorship.

17. The next danger that threatened Caesar was the inclusion of his name in a list of Catilinarian conspirators handed to the special commissioner, Novius Niger, by an informer named Lucius Vettius, and also in another list laid before the Senate by Quintus Curius, who had been voted a public bounty as the first person to betray the plot. Curius claimed that this information came directly from Catiline, and Vettius went so far as to declare that he could produce a letter written to Catiline in Caesar's own hand. Caesar would not lie down under this insult, and appealed to Cicero's testimony that he had voluntarily come forward to warn him about the plot and that Curius was not therefore entitled to the bounty. As for Vettius, who had been obliged to produce a bond when he made his revelations, this was declared forfeit and his goods were seized; the people, crowding around the Rostra, nearly tore him in pieces. Caesar thereupon sent Vettius off to jail, and Novius Niger, the commissioner, as well, for having let a magistrate of superior rank to himself be indicted at his tribunal.

18. The province of Further Spain was now allotted to Caesar. He relieved himself of the creditors who tried to keep him in Rome until he had paid his debts by providing sureties for their eventual settlement. Then he took the illegal and unprecedented step of hurrying off before the Senate had voted him the necessary funds. He may have been afraid of being taken to court while still a private citizen, or he may have been anxious to respond as quickly as possible to the appeals of our Spanish allies for help against aggression. At any rate, he rapidly pacified the province and returned to Rome with equal haste – not waiting until he had been relieved – to demand a triumph

and stand for the consulship. But the day of the consular elections had already been announced. His candidacy could therefore not be admitted unless he entered the city as a civilian, and
when a general outcry arose against his intrigues to be exempted
from the regulations governing candidatures, he was forced to
forgo the triumph so as not to be excluded from the consulship.

19. There were two other candidates: Lucius Lucceius and
Marcus Bibulus. Caesar now approached Lucceius and suggested that they should join forces; since Lucceius had more
money and Caesar greater influence, it was agreed that Lucceius
should finance their joint candidacy by bribing the voters. The
optimates got wind of this arrangement and, fearing that if
Caesar were elected consul with a pliant colleague by his side
he would stop at nothing to gain his own ends, they authorized
Marcus Bibulus to bribe the voters as heavily as Lucceius had
done. Many men contributed funds, and Cato himself admitted
that this was an occasion when even bribery might be excused
for the sake of the commonwealth. Caesar and Bibulus were
elected consuls, but the optimates continued to restrict Caesar's
influence by ensuring that, when he and Bibulus had completed
their term, neither should govern a province of any significance;
they would be put in charge of the forests and public pas-
turelands in Italy. Infuriated by this slight, Caesar exerted his
charm on Gnaeus Pompey, who had quarrelled with the Senate
because it was so slow in approving the steps that he had taken
to defeat Mithridates. He also succeeded in conciliating Pompey
and Marcus Crassus – they were still at odds after their failure
to agree on matters of policy while sharing the consulship.
Pompey, Caesar and Crassus now formed a triple pact,[15] jointly
swearing to oppose all public policies of which any one of them
might disapprove.

20. Caesar's first act as consul was to rule that a daily record
of proceedings in the Senate and before the people should be
taken and published; he also revived the obsolete custom of
having an orderly walk before him, during the months in which
his colleague held the fasces, while the lictors followed behind.
Next he introduced an agrarian law, and when Bibulus delayed
its passage by announcing that the omens were unfavourable

he drove him from the Forum by force of arms. On the following day Bibulus lodged a complaint in the Senate, and when
nobody dared move a vote of censure or make any observation
on this scandalous event – though decrees condemning minor
breaches of the peace had often been passed – he felt so frustrated that from then on he stayed at home, satisfying his
resentment with further edicts about unfavourable omens.

Caesar was thus enabled to govern alone and do very much
as he pleased. It became a joke to sign documents 'in the consulship of Julius and Caesar' rather than 'Bibulus and Caesar',
naming the same man twice, with nomen and cognomen. And
this lampoon went the rounds:

> The event occurred, as I recall, when Caesar governed Rome –
> Caesar, not Marcus Bibulus, who kept his seat at home.

Caesar partitioned two districts of Campania, a plain called
Stellas that our ancestors had consecrated and an agricultural
district that was farmed on behalf of the commonwealth, among
citizens with three or more children, selecting the candidates
through commissioners rather than by lots. When the publicans
asked for relief, he cancelled one-third of their obligations, but
gave them frank warning not to bid too high for their contracts
in future. He freely granted all other pleas whatsoever, and
either met with no opposition or intimidated anyone who dared
intervene. Marcus Cato once tried to delay proceedings by
talking out the debate, but Caesar had him forcibly ejected by
a lictor and led off to prison. Lucius Lucullus went a little too
far in opposing Caesar's policy, whereupon Caesar so terrified
him by threats of legal proceedings that Lucullus fell on his
knees and begged his pardon. Hearing that Cicero had been
making a doleful speech in court about the evils of his times,
Caesar at once granted the long-standing request of Cicero's
enemy Publius Clodius to be transferred from patrician to
plebeian rank,[16] rushing the measure through at the ninth hour
of the very same day. Finally, he began an attack on the opposing faction by bribing Vettius to announce that some of them
had tried to make him assassinate Pompey. As had been

arranged, Vettius was brought before the Rostra and mentioned a few names, but the whole affair was so suspicious that it led to nothing, and Caesar, realizing that he had been too hasty, is said to have poisoned his agent.

21. Caesar then married Calpurnia, daughter of Lucius Piso, his successor in the consulship, and at the same time betrothed his own daughter Julia to Gnaeus Pompey, thus breaking her previous engagement to Servilius Caepio, who had recently given him a great deal of support in the struggle against Bibulus. He now always called on Pompey to open debates in the Senate, though having hitherto reserved this honour for Crassus, thereby flouting the tradition that a consul should continue, throughout the year, to preserve the order of precedence established for speakers on the Kalends of January.

22. Having thus secured the goodwill of his father-in-law Piso and his son-in-law Pompey, Caesar surveyed the many provinces open to him and chose Gaul as being the likeliest to supply him with wealth and triumphs. True, he was at first appointed governor only of Cisalpine Gaul and Illyricum – the proposal came from Vatinius – but afterwards the Senate added Transalpine Gaul to his jurisdiction, fearing that if this were denied him the people would insist that he should have it. His elation was such that he could not refrain from boasting to a packed Senate House, some days later, that having now gained his dearest wish, to the annoyance and grief of his opponents, he would proceed to 'stamp upon their persons'. When someone interjected with a sneer that a *woman* would not find this an easy feat, he answered amicably, 'Why not? Semiramis was supreme in Syria, and the Amazons once ruled over a large part of Asia.'[17]

23. At the close of his consulship the praetors Gaius Memmius and Lucius Domitius demanded an inquiry into his official conduct during the past year. Caesar referred the matter to the Senate, which would not discuss it, so after three days had been wasted in idle recriminations he left for Gaul. His quaestor was at once charged with various irregularities, as a first step towards his own impeachment. Then Lucius Antistius, a tribune of the people, arraigned Caesar, who, however, appealed to

the whole college of tribunes, pleading absence on business of national importance, and thus staved off the trial. To prevent a recurrence of this sort of trouble he made a point of putting the chief magistrates of each new year under some obligation to him, and refusing to support any candidates or allow them to be elected unless they promised to defend his cause while he was absent from Rome. He had no hesitation in holding some of them to their promises by an oath or even a written contract.

24. But eventually Lucius Domitius stood for the consulship and openly threatened that, once elected, he would remove Caesar from his military command, having failed to do this while praetor. So Caesar called upon Pompey and Crassus to visit Luca, which lay in his province, and there persuaded them to prolong his governorship of Gaul for another five years and to oppose Domitius' candidature by seeking the consulship themselves. This success encouraged Caesar to expand his regular army with legions raised at his own expense – one even recruited in Transalpine Gaul and called by the Gallic word 'Alauda', which he trained and equipped in Roman style. Later he made every Alauda legionary a full citizen. He now lost no opportunity of picking quarrels – however flimsy the pretext – with allies as well as hostile and barbarous tribes, and marching against them. At first the Senate set up a commission of inquiry into the state of the Gallic provinces, and some speakers went so far as to recommend that Caesar should be handed over to the enemy. But the more successful his campaigns, the more frequent were public thanksgivings voted for him, and they lasted more days than those which any general before him had ever earned.

25. Briefly, his nine years' governorship produced the following results.[18] He reduced to the form of a province the whole of Gaul enclosed by the Pyrenees, the Alps, the Cevennes, the Rhine and the Rhône – about 32,000 miles in circumference – except for certain allied states which had given him useful support, and exacted an annual tribute of 40 million sesterces. Caesar was the first Roman to build a military bridge across the Rhine and cause the Germans on the further bank heavy losses. He also invaded Britain, a hitherto unknown country,

and defeated the natives, from whom he exacted a large sum of money as well as hostages for future good behaviour. He met with only three serious reverses: in Britain, when his fleet was all but destroyed by a gale; in Gaul, when one of his legions was routed at Gergovia; and on the German frontier, when his legates Titurius and Aurunculeius were ambushed and killed.

26. During this time Caesar lost, one after the other, his mother, his daughter and his grandson. Meanwhile, the assassination of Publius Clodius had caused such an outcry that the Senate voted for the appointment of only a single consul, naming Pompey as their choice. When the tribunes of the people wanted Caesar to stand as Pompey's colleague, Caesar asked whether they would not persuade the people to let him do so without visiting Rome; his governorship of Gaul, he wrote, was nearly at an end, and he preferred not to leave until his conquests had been completed. Their granting of this concession so fired Caesar's ambitions that he neglected no expense in winning popularity, both as a private citizen and as a candidate for his second consulship. He began building a new forum with the spoils taken in Gaul, and paid more than 100 million sesterces for the site alone. Then he announced a gladiatorial show and a public banquet in memory of his daughter Julia – an unprecedented event – and to create as much excitement as possible he had the banquet catered for partly by his own household, partly by the market contractors. He also issued an order that any well-known gladiator who failed to win the approval of the spectators should be forcibly rescued from execution and reserved for the coming show. New gladiators were also trained, not by the usual professionals in the schools, but in private houses by Roman *equites* and even senators who happened to be skilled at arms. Letters of his survive, begging these trainers to give their pupils individual instruction in the art of fighting. He fixed the daily pay of the regular soldiers at double what it had been. Whenever the granaries were full he would make a lavish distribution to the army, without measuring the amount, and occasionally gave every man a Gallic slave.

27. To preserve Pompey's friendship and renew the family ties, he offered him the hand of his sister's granddaughter

Octavia, though she had already married Gaius Marcellus, and in return he asked leave to marry Pompey's daughter,[19] who was betrothed to Faustus Sulla. Having now won all Pompey's friends and most of the Senate to his side with loans at a low rate of interest or interest free, he endeared himself to persons of less distinction too by handing out valuable presents, whether or not they asked for them. His beneficiaries included even the favourite slaves and freedmen of prominent men. Caesar thus became the one reliable source of help to all who were in legal difficulties, or in debt, or living beyond their means, and he refused help only to those whose criminal record was so black, or whose purse so empty, or whose tastes so expensive, that even he could do nothing for them. He frankly told such people, 'What you need is a civil war.'

28. Caesar took equal pains to win the esteem of kings and provincial authorities by offering them gifts of prisoners, a thousand at a time, or lending them troops whenever they asked and without first obtaining official permission from the Senate and People. He also presented the principal cities of Asia and Greece with magnificent public works, and did the same for those of Italy, Gaul and Spain. Everyone was amazed by this liberality, and wondered what the sequel would be.

At last Marcus Claudius Marcellus, the consul, announced in an edict that he intended to raise a matter of vital public interest; he then proposed to the Senate that, since the war had now ended in victory, Caesar should be relieved of his command before his term as governor expired, that a successor should be appointed, and that the armies in Gaul should be disbanded. He further proposed that Caesar should be forbidden to stand for the consulship without appearing at Rome in person, since Pompey had not subsequently annulled the decree of the people. Pompey, when he introduced a bill regulating the privileges of magistrates, had forgotten to make a special exception for Caesar in the clause debarring absentees from candidacy, and had corrected this oversight only after the law had been engraved on a bronze tablet and registered at the public treasury.[20] Nor was Marcellus content to oust Caesar from his command and cancel the privilege already voted him, namely to stand for the consulship *in absentia*. He also asked that the colonists whom Caesar had settled at Novum Comum under the Vatinian Act should lose their citizenship. This award, he said, had been intended to further Caesar's political ambitions and lacked legal sanction.

29. The news infuriated Caesar, but he had often been reported as saying, 'Now that I am the leading Roman of my day, it will be harder to put me down a peg than degrade me to the ranks.' So he resisted stubbornly, persuading the tribunes of the people to veto Marcellus' bills and at the same time enlisting the help of Servius Sulpicius, Marcellus' colleague. When, in the following year, Marcellus was succeeded in office by his cousin Gaius, who adopted a similar policy, Caesar again won over the other consul, Aemilius Paulus, with a heavy bribe, and also bought Gaius Curio, the most energetic tribune of the people. Realizing, however, that his opponents had made a determined stand and that both the new consuls-elect were unfriendly to him, he appealed to the Senate, begging them in a written address not to cancel a privilege voted him by the people without forcing all other military leaders to resign their commands at the same time as he did. But this was read as meaning that he counted on mobilizing his veteran troops sooner than Pompey could his raw levies. Next, Caesar offered to resign command of eight legions and quit Transalpine Gaul if he might keep two legions and Cisalpine Gaul, or at least Illyricum and one legion, until he became consul.

30. Since the Senate did not intervene and his opponents refused to make any deal where the public good was concerned, Caesar crossed into Cisalpine Gaul, where he held his regular assizes, and halted at Ravenna. He was resolved to defend the rights of the tribunes by war if the Senate took any serious action against the ones who were working in his interests. And this was in fact Caesar's pretext for launching the civil war. Additional motives are suspected, however. Pompey's comment was that, because Caesar had insufficient capital to carry out his grandiose schemes or give the people all that they had been encouraged to expect on his return, he chose to throw everything into confusion. Another view is that he dreaded

having to account for the irregularities of his first consulship, during which he had disregarded auspices and laws and vetos, for Marcus Cato had often sworn to impeach him as soon as the legions were disbanded. Moreover, people said at the time, frankly enough, that should Caesar return from Gaul as a private citizen he would plead his case like Milo in a court ringed around with armed men.[21] This sounds plausible enough, because Asinius Pollio records that when Caesar, at the battle of Pharsalus, saw his opponents slaughtered and routed, he said, in these very words, 'They brought it on themselves. They would have condemned me regardless of all my victories – me, Gaius Caesar – had I not appealed to my army for help.' It has also been suggested that constant exercise of power gave Caesar a love of it, and that, after weighing his enemies' strength against his own, he took this chance of fulfilling his youthful dreams by making a bid for absolute rule. Cicero seems to have come to a similar conclusion: in the third book of his *On Duties*, he records that Caesar repeatedly quoted some lines of Euripides, which Cicero himself translated as follows:[22]

> Is crime consonant with nobility?
> Then noblest is the crime of tyranny –
> In all things else obey the laws of heaven.

31. Accordingly, when news reached him that the tribunes' veto had been disallowed and that they had fled the city, he at once sent a few cohorts ahead with all secrecy, and disarmed suspicion by attending a public show, inspecting the plans of a school for gladiators which he proposed to build, and dining as usual among a crowd of guests. But at dusk he borrowed a pair of mules from a nearby bakery, harnessed them to a carriage, and set off quietly with a few of his staff. His lights went out, he lost his way, and the party wandered about aimlessly for some hours, but at dawn found a guide who led them on foot along narrow lanes until they came to the right road. Caesar overtook his advanced guard at the river Rubicon, which formed the boundary of his province. Well aware how critical a decision confronted him, he turned to his staff,

remarking, 'We may still draw back but, once across that little bridge, we shall have to fight it out.'

32. As he stood, in two minds, an apparition of superhuman size and beauty was seen sitting on the riverbank playing a reed pipe. A party of shepherds gathered around to listen, and, when some of Caesar's men broke ranks to do the same, the apparition snatched a trumpet from one of them, ran down to the river, blew a thunderous blast, and crossed over. Caesar exclaimed, 'Let us accept this as a sign from the gods and follow where they beckon, in vengeance on our double-dealing enemies. The die is cast.'[23]

33. He led his army to the further bank, where he welcomed the tribunes of the people who had fled to him from Rome. Then he tearfully addressed the troops and, ripping open his tunic to expose his breast, begged them to stand faithfully by him. The belief that he then promised to promote every man present to the equestrian order is based on a misunderstanding. He had accompanied his pleas with the gesture of pointing to his left hand, as he declared that he would gladly reward those who championed his honour with the very ring on his finger; but some soldiers on the fringe of the assembly, who saw him better than they could hear his words, read too much into the gesture and put it about that Caesar had promised them all the right to wear a gold ring and the 400,000 sesterces that went with it.

34. Here follows a brief account of Caesar's subsequent movements.[24] He occupied Picenum, Umbria and Etruria; captured Lucius Domitius, who had been named as his emergency successor in Gaul and was holding Corfinium; let him go free; and then marched along the Adriatic coast to Brundisium, where Pompey and the consuls had fled from Rome with the intention of crossing the straits as soon as possible. When his efforts to prevent this proved ineffective, he marched on Rome, entered it, summoned the Senate to review the political situation, and then hurriedly set off for Spain, where Pompey's strongest forces were stationed under the command of his legates Marcus Petreius, Lucius Afranius and Marcus Varro. Before leaving, Caesar told his household, 'I am off to meet an

army without a leader; when I return I shall meet a leader
without an army.' Though delayed by the siege of Massilia,
which had shut its gates against him, and by a severe lack of
supplies, he won a rapid and overwhelming victory.

35. Caesar returned by way of Rome, crossed over into Macedonia, and after blockading Pompey for nearly four months
behind immense containing works, routed him at Pharsalus.
Pompey fled to Alexandria; Caesar followed, and, when he
found that King Ptolemy had murdered Pompey and was planning to murder him as well, declared war. This proved to be a
most difficult campaign, fought during winter within the city
walls of a well-equipped and cunning enemy; but, though
caught off his guard and without military supplies of any kind,
Caesar was victorious. He then handed over the government of
Egypt to Cleopatra and her younger brother, fearing that, if
it were made a Roman province, some independent-minded
governor might one day launch a bid for power from there.
From Alexandria he proceeded to Syria, and from Syria to
Pontus, news having come that Pharnaces, son of the famous
Mithridates, had taken advantage of the confused situation and
already gained several successes. Five days after his arrival and
four hours after catching sight of Pharnaces, Caesar crushed
him in a single battle, and commented drily on Pompey's good
fortune in having built up his reputation for generalship by
victories over such poor stuff as this. Then he beat Scipio and
Juba in Africa, where they were reorganizing the remnants of
the Pompeian party, and Pompey's sons in Spain.

36. Throughout the civil war Caesar was never defeated
himself, but, of his legates, Gaius Curio died in Africa, Gaius
Antonius was captured in Illyricum, Publius Dolabella lost a
fleet also off Illyricum, and Gnaeus Domitius Calvinus had his
army destroyed in Pontus. Yet, though invariably successful, he
twice came close to disaster: at Dyrrhachium, where Pompey
broke his blockade and forced him to retreat – Caesar remarked
when Pompey failed to pursue him, 'He does not know how to
win wars' – and in the final battle in Spain, where all seemed
lost and he even considered suicide.

37. After defeating Scipio, Caesar celebrated four triumphs

in one month with a few days' interval between them, and, after defeating Pompey's sons, a fifth. These triumphs were the Gallic – the first and most magnificent – the Alexandrian, the Pontic, the African and lastly the Spanish. Each differed completely from the others in its presentation. As Caesar rode through the Velabrum on the day of his Gallic triumph, the axle of his chariot broke, and he nearly took a toss; but afterwards he ascended to the Capitol between two lines of elephants, forty in all, which acted as his torch-bearers. In the Pontic triumph one of the decorated wagons carried a simple three-word inscription:

CAME, SAW, CONQUERED!

This referred not, like the rest, to the deeds of the war, but to the speed with which he had won it.

38. Every infantryman of Caesar's veteran legions earned a reward of 24,000 sesterces, in addition to the 2,000 paid at the outbreak of hostilities, and a farm as well. These farms could not be grouped together without evicting the current owners, but were scattered all over the countryside. Every citizen received ten pecks of grain and ten pounds of oil, besides the 300 sesterces which Caesar had promised at first and now raised to 400, by way of interest on the delay in payment. He also waived the annual rent: in Rome, up to 2,000 sesterces; in Italy, no more than 500. He added a public banquet and a distribution of meat, and also a dinner to celebrate his Spanish victory; but he decided that this had not been splendid enough, and five days later he served a second, more succulent, one.

39. His public shows were of great variety. They included a gladiatorial contest, stage plays for every quarter of Rome performed in several languages, chariot races in the Circus, athletic competitions, and a mock naval battle. At the gladiatorial contest in the Forum, a man named Furius Leptinus, of praetorian family, fought Quintus Calpenus, an advocate and former senator. The sons of petty kings from Asia and Bithynia danced the Pyrrhic war dance. In the theatrical performances, Decimus Laberius, a Roman *eques*, acted in his own play; but

afterwards, having been given 500,000 sesterces and a gold ring, he walked straight from the stage through the orchestra to sit in the first fourteen rows.[25] The racecourse at the Circus was extended at either end, and a broad ditch was dug around it; the contestants were young noblemen who drove four-horse and two-horse chariots or rode pairs of horses, jumping from back to back. The Troy Game was performed by two troops of boys, one younger than the other. Wild-beast hunts took place five days running, and the entertainment ended with a battle between two armies, each consisting of 500 infantry, 20 elephants and 30 cavalry. To let the camps be pitched facing each other, Caesar removed the central barrier of the Circus, around which the chariots ran. Athletic contests were held in a temporary stadium on the Campus Martius, and lasted for three days. The naval battle was fought between heavily manned Tyrian and Egyptian biremes, triremes and quadriremes on an artificial lake dug in the Lesser Codeta. Such huge numbers of visitors flocked to these shows from all directions that many of them had to sleep in tents pitched along the streets or roads, and the pressure of the crowd often crushed people to death. The victims included two senators.

40. Caesar next turned his attention to domestic reforms. First he reorganized the calendar, which the pontifices had allowed to fall into such disorder, by intercalating days or months as it suited them, that the harvest and vintage festivals no longer corresponded with the appropriate seasons. He linked the year to the course of the sun by lengthening it to 365 days, abolishing the intercalary month[26] and adding an entire day every fourth year. But to make the next Kalends of January fall at the right season, he drew out this particular year by two extra months, inserted between November and December, so that it consisted of fifteen, including the intercalary one inserted in the old style.

41. He brought the Senate up to strength, created new patricians, and increased the yearly quota of praetors, aediles and quaestors, as well as of minor officials; he reinstated those degraded by the censors or condemned for corruption by a jury. Also, he arranged with the people that, apart from the consuls,

half the magistrates should be popularly elected and half nominated by himself. Allowing even the sons of proscribed men to
stand, he circulated brief directions to the voters. For instance,
'Caesar the dictator to such-and-such a tribe of voters: I recommend so-and-so to you for office.' He limited jury service
to *equites* and senators, disqualifying the treasury tribunes.[27]
Caesar conducted a census in a novel way: he made landlords
help him to complete the list, street by street, and reduced from
320,000 to 150,000 the number of householders who might
draw free grain. To do away with the nuisance of having to
summon everyone periodically for enrolment in the register, he
made the praetors keep it up to date by replacing the names of
dead men with those of others not yet listed.

42. Since the population of Rome had been considerably
diminished by the transfer of 80,000 men to overseas colonies,
he forbade any citizen between the ages of twenty and forty
who was not on military service to absent himself from Italy
for more than three years in succession. Nor might any senator's
son travel abroad unless as a member of some magistrate's
household or staff, and at least a third of the cattlemen employed by ranchers had to be freeborn. Caesar also granted the
citizenship to all medical practitioners and professors of liberal
arts resident in Rome, thus inducing them to remain and tempting others to follow suit. He disappointed popular agitators by
cancelling no debts, but in the end he decreed that every debtor
should have his property assessed according to pre-war valu-
ation and, after deducting the interest already paid directly or
by way of a banker's guarantee, should satisfy his creditors
with whatever sum that might represent; as a result, creditors
lost about a fourth of what they had lent. Caesar dissolved all
private associations except the ancient ones, and increased the
penalties for crime; and since wealthy men had less compunction about committing major offences, because they could
simply go into exile with their property intact, he punished
murderers of close relatives (as Cicero records) by the seizure
of their entire property, and others by seizure of half.

43. In his administration of justice he was both conscientious
and severe, and went so far as to degrade senators found guilty

of extortion. Once, when a man of praetorian rank married a woman on the day after her divorce from her husband, he annulled the union, although adultery between them was not suspected. He imposed a tariff on foreign manufactures; he forbade the use of litters, except on stated occasions, and the wearing of either purple robes[28] or pearls by those below a certain rank and age. To implement his laws against luxury he placed inspectors in different parts of the market to seize delicacies offered for sale in violation of his orders; sometimes he even sent lictors and guards into dining rooms to remove illegal dishes, already served, which his watchmen had failed to intercept.

44. Caesar was continually planning great new works for the embellishment of the city and for the empire's protection and enlargement. His most notable projects were a temple of Mars, the biggest in the world, to build which he would have had to fill up and pave the lake where the naval sham fight had been staged, and an enormous theatre sloping down from the Tarpeian Rock. Another task he set himself was the reduction of the civil law to manageable proportions, by selecting from the unwieldy mass of statutes only the most essential, and publishing them in a few volumes. Still another was to provide public libraries, by commissioning Marcus Varro to collect and classify Greek and Latin books on a comprehensive scale. His engineering schemes included the draining of the Pomptine Marshes and of the Fucine Lake, the building of a highway from the Adriatic across the Apennines to the Tiber, and the cutting of a canal through the Isthmus of Corinth. In the military field he planned an expulsion of the Dacians from Pontus and Thrace, which they had recently occupied, and then an attack on Parthia by way of Lesser Armenia; but he decided not to risk a pitched battle until he had familiarized himself with Parthian tactics.

All these schemes were cancelled by his assassination. Before describing that, I should perhaps give a brief description of his appearance, personal habits, dress, character, and conduct in peace and war.

45. Caesar is said to have been tall, fair and well built, with

a rather broad face and keen, dark eyes. His health was sound, apart from sudden fainting spells and a tendency to nightmares which troubled him towards the end of his life, but he twice had epileptic fits while on campaign. He was something of a dandy, so that he not only kept himself carefully trimmed and shaved but also, as some people have charged, depilated with tweezers. His baldness was a disfigurement which his enemies harped upon, much to his exasperation, but he used to comb the thin strands of hair forward from the crown of his head, and of all the honours voted him by the Senate and People none pleased him so much as the privilege of wearing a laurel wreath on all occasions – he constantly took advantage of it. His dress was, it seems, unusual: he had added wrist-length sleeves with fringes to his purple-striped senatorial tunic, which he wore not only belted but loosely belted at that – hence Sulla's warning to the optimates: 'Beware of that boy with the loose clothes!'

46. Caesar's first home was a modest house in the Subura quarter, but later, as pontifex maximus, he used the official residence on the Sacred Way. Contemporary literature contains frequent references to his fondness for luxurious living. Having built a country mansion near Aricia from the foundations up, one story goes, he was not entirely satisfied with it and so, although poor at the time and heavily in debt, he tore the whole place down. It is also recorded that he carried tessellated and mosaic pavements with him on his campaigns.

47. Pearls seem to have been the lure that prompted his invasion of Britain, and he would sometimes test them in the palm of his hand to determine their weight; he was also a keen collector of gems, carvings, statues and paintings of ancient workmanship. So high were the prices he paid for slaves of good character and attainments that even he became ashamed of his extravagance and would not allow the sums to be entered in his accounts.

48. I find also that, while stationed abroad, he always had dinner served in two separate rooms: one for his officers and Greek friends, the other for Roman citizens and the more important provincials. He paid such strict attention to his domestic economy, however small the detail, that he once put his

baker in irons for giving him a different sort of bread from that served to his guests, and he executed a favourite freedman for committing adultery with the wife of an *eques*, although no complaint had been lodged by the husband.

49. The only charge ever brought against him regarding his sexual tastes was that he had been King Nicomedes' bedmate – always a dark stain on his reputation, and frequently quoted by his enemies. Licinius Calvus published the notorious verses:

> The riches of Bithynia's King
> Who Caesar on his couch abused.

Dolabella called him 'the Queen's rival and inner partner of the royal bed', and the elder Curio 'Nicomedes' Bithynian brothel'. Bibulus, Caesar's colleague in the consulship, described him in an edict as 'the Queen of Bithynia, who once wanted to sleep with a monarch, but now wants to be one'. And Marcus Brutus recorded that, about the same time, one Octavius, a scatter-brained creature who would say the first thing that came into his head, walked into a packed assembly where he saluted Pompey as 'King' and Caesar as 'Queen'. All this can be discounted as mere slander, but Gaius Memmius directly charges Caesar with having joined a group of Nicomedes' toy boys at a banquet, where he acted as the royal cupbearer, and adds that certain Roman merchants, whose names he supplies, were present as guests. Cicero too not only wrote in several letters that 'Caesar was led by Nicomedes' attendants to the royal bedchamber, where he lay on a golden couch dressed in a purple robe, and so this descendant of Venus lost his virginity in Bithynia,' but also once interrupted Caesar while he was addressing the Senate in defence of Nicomedes' daughter Nysa and listing his obligations to Nicomedes himself. 'Enough of that,' Cicero shouted, 'if you please! We all know what he gave you, and what you gave him in return.' Lastly, when Caesar's own soldiers followed his decorated chariot in the Gallic triumph, chanting ribald songs, as they were privileged to do, this was one of them:

> Gaul was brought to shame by Caesar;
>   By King Nicomedes he.
> Here comes Caesar, wreathed in triumph
>   For his Gallic victory!
> Nicomedes wears no laurels,
>   Though the greatest of the three.

50. His affairs with women are commonly described as numerous and extravagant: among those of noble birth whom he is said to have seduced were Servius Sulpicius' wife Postumia, Aulus Gabinius' wife Lollia, Marcus Crassus' wife Tertulla, and even Gnaeus Pompey's wife Mucia. Be this how it may, both the elder and the younger Curio reproached Pompey with being led by his desire for power to marry the daughter of the man on whose account he had divorced the mother of his three children and whom he had often despairingly called 'Aegisthus'.[29] But Marcus Brutus' mother Servilia was the woman whom Caesar loved best, and in his first consulship he bought her a pearl worth 6 million sesterces. He gave her many presents during the civil war, as well as knocking down certain valuable estates to her at a public auction for a song. When surprise was expressed at the low price, Cicero made a clever remark: 'It was even cheaper than you think, because a third [*tertia*] had been discounted.' Servilia, you see, was also suspected at the time of having prostituted her daughter Tertia to Caesar.

51. That he had love affairs in the provinces too is suggested by another of the ribald verses sung during the Gallic triumph:

> Home we bring our bald whoremonger;
>   Romans, lock your wives away!
> All the bags of gold you lent him
>   Went his Gallic tarts to pay.

52. Among his mistresses were several queens – including Eunoë, wife of Bogud of Mauretania, whom, according to Marcus Actorius Naso, he loaded with presents; Bogud is said to have profited equally. The most famous of these queens was

Cleopatra. He often feasted with her until dawn, and they would have sailed together in her state barge nearly to Ethiopia had his soldiers consented to follow him. He eventually summoned Cleopatra to Rome, and would not let her return home without high titles and rich presents. He even allowed her to give his own name to the son whom she had borne him.[30] Some Greek historians say that the boy closely resembled Caesar in features as well as in gait. Mark Antony informed the Senate that Caesar had in fact acknowledged his paternity, and that other friends of Caesar, including Gaius Matius and Gaius Oppius, were aware of this. Oppius, however, seems to have felt the need to clear his friend's reputation, because he published a book to prove that the boy whom Cleopatra had fathered on Caesar was not his at all. A tribune of the people named Helvius Cinna informed a number of people that, following instructions, he had drawn up a bill for the people to pass during Caesar's absence from Rome, legitimizing his marriage with any woman, or women, he pleased – 'for the procreation of children'. And, to emphasize the bad name Caesar had won for both easy virtue and adultery, the elder Curio refers to him in a speech as 'every woman's husband and every man's wife'.

53. Yet not even his enemies denied that he drank abstemiously. An epigram of Marcus Cato's survives: 'Caesar was the only sober man who ever tried to overturn the republic.' And Gaius Oppius relates that he cared so little for good food that when once he attended a dinner party where scented oil had been served by mistake and all the other guests refused it, Caesar helped himself more liberally than usual, to show that he did not consider his host either careless or boorish.

54. He was not particularly honest in money matters, either while a provincial governor or while holding office at Rome. Several memoirs record that as consular governor of Further Spain he not only begged his allies for money to settle his debts, but wantonly sacked several Lusitanian towns, though they had accepted his terms and opened their gates to receive him. In Gaul he plundered large and small temples of their votive offerings, and more often gave towns over to pillage because their

inhabitants were rich than because they had offended him. As a result, he collected larger quantities of gold than he could handle, and began selling it in Italy and the provinces at 3,000 sesterces to the pound. In the course of his first consulship he stole 3,000 pounds of gold from the Capitol and replaced it with the same weight of gilded bronze. He sold alliances and thrones for cash, making Ptolemy give him and Pompey nearly 6,000 talents, and later he paid his civil-war army, and the expenses of his triumphs and entertainments, by open extortion and sacrilege.

55. Caesar equalled, if he did not surpass, the greatest orators and generals the world had ever known. His prosecution of Dolabella unquestionably placed him in the first rank of advocates. Cicero, discussing the matter in his *Brutus*, confesses that he knew no more eloquent speaker than Caesar, and calls his style chaste and pellucid, not to say grand and noble; he also wrote to Cornelius Nepos, 'Very well, then! Do you know any man who, even if he has concentrated on the art of oratory to the exclusion of all else, can speak better than Caesar? Or anyone who makes so many witty remarks? Or whose vocabulary is so varied and yet so exact?'[31] Caesar seems to have modelled his style, at any rate when a beginner, on Caesar Strabo – part of whose *Defence of the Sardinians* he borrowed verbatim for use in a courtroom speech of his own. It is said that he pitched his voice high in speaking, and used impassioned gestures which far from displeased his audience.

Several of Caesar's undoubted speeches survive, and he is credited with others that are hardly genuine. Augustus said that the *Defence of Quintus Metellus* could hardly have been published by Caesar himself, and that it appeared to be a version taken down by shorthand writers who could not keep up with his delivery. He was probably right, because on examining several manuscripts of the speech I find that even the title is given as *What He Composed for Metellus* – although it is written in the character of Caesar defending Metellus and himself against a joint accusation. Augustus also doubted the authenticity of Caesar's *Address to the Soldiers in Spain*. It is written in two parts, one speech supposedly delivered before the first battle, the other before the second – though on the latter occasion, at least, according to Asinius Pollio, the enemy's attack gave Caesar no time to address his troops at all.

56. He left memoirs of his war in Gaul and of his civil war against Pompey, but no one knows who wrote those of the Alexandrian, African and Spanish campaigns. Some say that it was his friend Oppius; others that it was Hirtius, who also finished *The Gallic War*, left incomplete by Caesar, adding a final book.[32] Cicero, also in the *Brutus*, observes, 'Caesar wrote admirably; his memoirs are cleanly, directly and gracefully composed, and divested of all rhetorical trappings. And while his sole intention was to supply historians with factual material, the result has been that several fools have been pleased to primp up his narrative for their own glorification; but every writer of sense has given the subject a wide berth.' Hirtius says downrightly, 'These memoirs are so highly rated by all judicious critics that the opportunity of enlarging and improving on them, which he purports to offer historians, seems in fact withheld from them. And, as his friends, we admire this feat even more than strangers can: they appreciate the faultless grace of his style, we know how rapidly and easily he wrote.' Asinius Pollio, however, believes that the memoirs show signs of carelessness and inaccuracy: Caesar, he holds, did not always check the truth of the reports that came in, and was either disingenuous or forgetful in describing his own actions. Pollio adds that Caesar must have planned a revision.[33]

Among his literary remains are two books of *An Essay on Analogy*, two more of *Answers to Cato* and a poem, *The Journey*.[34] He wrote *An Essay on Analogy* while coming back over the Alps after holding assizes in Cisalpine Gaul, *Answers to Cato* in the year that he won the battle of Munda, and *The Journey* during the twenty-four days he spent on the road between Rome and Further Spain. Many of the letters and dispatches sent by him to the Senate also survive, and he seems to have been the first statesman to reduce such documents to book form; previously, consuls and generals had written right across the page, not in neat columns. Then there are his letters to Cicero and his private letters to friends, the more confidential passages of which he wrote in cipher: to understand their apparently incomprehensible meaning one must substitute each letter that Caesar wrote with the one which occurs three places before – for instance, D stands for A. It is said that in his boyhood and early youth he also wrote pieces called *In Praise of Hercules* and *The Tragedy of Oedipus* and *Collected Sayings*, but nearly a century later the emperor Augustus sent a brief, frank letter to Pompeius Macer, whom he had appointed to oversee the libraries, forbidding him to circulate these minor works.

57. Caesar was a most skilful swordsman and horseman, and showed surprising powers of endurance. He always led his army, more often on foot than in the saddle, went bareheaded in sun and rain alike, and could travel lightly in a carriage for long distances at incredible speed, a hundred miles in a single day. If he reached an unfordable river he would either swim or propel himself across it on an inflated skin, and often arrived at his destination before the messengers whom he had sent ahead to announce his approach.

58. It is a disputable point which was the more remarkable when he went to war: his caution or his daring. He never exposed his army to ambushes, but made careful reconnaissances, and he refrained from crossing over into Britain until he had collected reliable information about the harbours there, the best course to steer, and the navigational risks. On the other hand, when news reached him that his camp in Germany was being besieged, he disguised himself as a Gaul and picked his way through the enemy outposts to take command on the spot. He ferried his troops from Brundisium to Dyrrhachium in the winter season, through the enemy fleet. And one night, when the reinforcements that he had ordered were delayed, despite his repeated pleas, Caesar muffled his head with a cloak, secretly put to sea alone in a small boat, and refused either to reveal his identity or to allow the helmsman to turn back before a storm until he was almost shipwrecked.

59. Religious scruples never deterred him for a moment. When the victim escaped from him at the sacrifice before he set off to fight with Scipio and Juba in Africa, he did not delay but sailed at once. He also slipped and fell as he disembarked on

his arrival, but turned this into a favourable omen by clasping the ground and shouting, 'Africa, I have tight hold of you!' Then, to ridicule the prophecy according to which the Scipios were destined to be perpetually victorious in that province, he took about with him a contemptible member of the Cornelian family who was given the nickname 'Salvito' because of his disgraceful life.[35]

60. Sometimes he fought after careful tactical planning, sometimes on the spur of the moment – at the end of a march, often, or in miserable weather, when he would be least expected to make a move. Towards the end of his life, however, he took fewer chances, having come to the conclusion that his unbroken run of victories ought to sober him, now that he could not possibly gain more by winning yet another battle than he would lose by a defeat. It was his rule never to let enemy troops rally when he had routed them, and always therefore to assault their camp at once. If the fight was a hard fought one he used to send the chargers away – his own among the first – as a warning that those who feared to stand their ground need not hope to escape on horseback.

61. This charger of his, an extraordinary animal with feet that looked almost human – each of its hoofs was cloven in five parts, resembling human toes – had been foaled on his private estate. When the haruspices pronounced that its master would one day rule the world, Caesar carefully reared and was the first to ride the beast; nor would it allow anyone else to do so. He later raised a statue to it before the Temple of Venus Genetrix.

62. If Caesar's troops gave ground he would often rally them single-handedly, catching individual fugitives by the throat and forcing them round to face the enemy again, even if they were panic-stricken – as when one standard bearer threatened him with the sharp butt of his Eagle and another, whom he tried to detain, ran off leaving the standard in his hand.

63. Caesar's reputation for presence of mind is fully borne out by the instances quoted. After the battle at Pharsalus, he had sent his troops ahead of him into Asia and was crossing the Hellespont in a small ferry boat when Lucius Cassius with ten naval vessels approached. Caesar made no attempt to escape

but rowed towards the flagship and demanded Cassius' surrender, which in fact he received.

64. Again, while attacking a bridge at Alexandria, Caesar was forced by a sudden enemy sortie to jump into a rowing boat. So many of his men followed him that he dived into the sea and swam 200 yards until he reached his nearest ship – holding his left hand above water the whole way, to keep certain documents dry, and towing his general's cloak behind him with his teeth, to save this trophy from his opponents.

65. He judged his men by their fighting record, not by their morals or social position, treating them all with equal severity – and equal indulgence, since it was only in the presence of the enemy that he insisted on strict discipline. He never gave forewarning of a march or a battle, but kept his troops always on the alert for sudden orders to go wherever he directed. Often he made them turn out when there was no need at all, especially in wet weather or on public holidays. Sometimes he would say, 'Keep a close eye on me!' and then steal away from camp at any hour of the day or night, expecting them to follow. It was certain to be a particularly long march, and hard on stragglers.

66. If rumours about the enemy's strength were causing alarm, his practice was to heighten morale not by denying or belittling the danger, but on the contrary by further exaggerating it. For instance, when his troops were in a panic at the news of Juba's approach, he called them together and announced, 'You may take it from me that the king will be here within a few days, at the head of ten infantry legions, thirty thousand cavalry, a hundred thousand lightly armed troops and three hundred elephants. This being the case, you may as well stop asking questions and making guesses. I have given you the facts, with which I familiar. Any of you who remain unsatisfied will find themselves aboard a leaky hulk and being carried across the sea wherever the winds may decide to blow them.'

67. Though turning a blind eye to much of their misbehaviour and never laying down any fixed scale of penalties, he allowed no deserter or mutineer to escape severe punishment. Sometimes, if a victory had been complete enough, he relieved the troops of all military duties and let them carry on as wildly as

they pleased. One of his boasts was 'My men fight just as well when they are stinking of perfume.' He always addressed them not as 'soldiers' but as 'comrades', which put them into a better humour, and he equipped them splendidly. The silver and gold inlay of their weapons both improved their appearance on parade and made them more careful not to get disarmed in battle. Caesar loved his men dearly; when news came that Titurius' command had been massacred, he swore neither to cut his hair nor to trim his beard until they had been avenged.

68. By these means he won the devotion of his men as well as making them extraordinarily brave. At the outbreak of the civil war every centurion in every legion volunteered to equip a cavalryman from his savings, and the private soldiers unanimously offered to serve under him without pay or rations, pooling their money so that nobody should go short. Throughout the entire struggle not a single man deserted, and many of them, when taken prisoner, preferred death to the alternative of fighting against him. Such was their fortitude in facing starvation and other hardships, both as besiegers and as besieged, that when at the siege of Dyrrhachium Pompey was shown the substitute for bread, made from a herb, on which they were feeding, he exclaimed, 'I am fighting wild beasts!' Then he ordered the loaf to be hidden at once, not wanting his men to find out how tough and resolute the enemy were and so lose heart.

Their stout-heartedness in fighting is attested by the fact that after their only reverse, at Dyrrhachium, they themselves demanded to be punished; whereupon Caesar felt called upon to console rather than upbraid them. In other battles, they easily beat enormously superior forces. A single cohort of the Sixth Legion held a fort against four Pompeian legions for hours, though almost every man had been repeatedly wounded by arrow shot – 130,000 arrows were afterwards collected at the scene of the engagement. This high level of courage is less surprising when individual examples are considered. For example, the centurion Cassius Scaeva, blinded in one eye, wounded in thigh and shoulder, and with no fewer than 120 holes in his shield, continued to defend the approaches to the fort. Nor was his by any means an exceptional case. At the

naval battle of Massilia, a private soldier named Gaius Acilius
grasped the stern of an enemy ship and, when someone lopped
off his right hand, nevertheless boarded her and drove the
enemy back with the boss of his shield only – a feat rivalling
that of Cynegirus among the Greeks.[36]

69. Caesar's men did not mutiny once during the Gallic
war, which lasted ten years. In the civil wars they were less
dependable, but whenever they made insubordinate demands
he faced them boldly and always brought them to heel again –
not by appeasement, but by sheer exercise of personal authority.
At Placentia, although Pompey's armies were as yet undefeated,
he disbanded the entire Ninth Legion with ignominy, later
reinstating them in response to their abject pleas – this with
great reluctance, and only after executing the ringleaders.

70. At Rome too, when the Tenth Legion agitated for their
discharge and bounty and were terrorizing the city, Caesar
defied the advice of his friends and at once confronted the
mutineers in person. Again he would have disbanded them
ignominiously, though the African war was still being hotly
fought, but by addressing them as 'citizens' he readily regained
their affections. A shout went up: 'We are your soldiers, Caesar,
not civilians!', and they clamoured to serve under him in Africa
– a demand which he nevertheless disdained to grant. He
showed his contempt for the more disaffected soldiers by withholding a third part of the prize money and land which had
been set aside for them.

71. Even as a young man Caesar was well known for the
loyalty he showed his dependants. He protected a nobleman's
son named Masintha against King Hiempsal with such devotion
that in the course of the quarrel he caught Juba, the king's son,
by the beard. Masintha, being then declared the king's vassal,
was arrested, but Caesar immediately rescued him and harboured him in his own quarters for a long while. At the close
of his praetorship Caesar sailed for Spain, taking Masintha
with him. The lictors carrying the fasces and the crowds who
had come to say goodbye acted as a screen; nobody realized
that Masintha was hidden in Caesar's litter.

72. He showed consistent affection to his friends. Gaius

Oppius, travelling by his side once through a wild forest, suddenly fell sick, and Caesar insisted on his using the only shelter that offered while he and the rest of his staff slept outside on the bare ground. Having attained supreme power, he raised some of his friends, even men of humble birth, to high office and brushed aside criticism by saying, 'If bandits and cutthroats had helped to defend my honour, I should have shown them gratitude in the same way.'

73. Moreover, when given the chance, he would always cheerfully come to terms with his bitterest enemies. He supported Gaius Memmius' candidature for the consulship, though they had both spoken most damagingly against each other. When Gaius Calvus, after his cruel lampoons of Caesar, made a move towards reconciliation through mutual friends, Caesar met him more than halfway by writing him a friendly letter. Valerius Catullus had also libelled him in his verses about Mamurra, yet Caesar, while admitting that these were a permanent blot on his name, accepted Catullus' apology and invited him to dinner that same afternoon, and never interrupted his friendship with Catullus' father.[37]

74. Yet, even when he did take action, it was his nature to show restraint; if he crucified the pirates who had held him to ransom, this was only because he had sworn in their presence to do so, and he first mercifully cut their throats. He could never bring himself to take vengeance on Cornelius Phagites, even though in his early days, while he was sick and a fugitive from Sulla, Cornelius had tracked him at night and demanded hush money. On discovering that Philemon, the slave who served as his secretary, had been induced by his enemies to poison him, Caesar ordered a simple execution, without torture. When Publius Clodius was accused of adultery with Caesar's wife Pompeia in sacrilegious circumstances, and both his mother Aurelia and his sister Julia had given the court a detailed and truthful account of the affair, Caesar himself refused to offer any evidence. When asked why, in that case, he had divorced Pompeia, he replied, 'Because I cannot have members of my household suspected, even when they are innocent.'

75. Nobody can deny that during the civil war, and after,

he behaved with wonderful restraint and clemency. Whereas Pompey declared that all who were not actively with him were against him and would be treated as public enemies, Caesar announced that all who were not actively against him were with him. He allowed every centurion whom he had appointed on Pompey's recommendation to join the Pompeian forces if he pleased. At Ilerda, when the articles of capitulation were being discussed and the rival armies were fraternizing, Afranius and Petreius suddenly decided not to surrender and massacred every Caesarian soldier found in their camp; yet Caesar did not stoop to imitate this treachery.³⁸ During the battle of Pharsalus he shouted to his men, 'Spare your fellow Romans!', and then allowed them to save one enemy soldier apiece, whoever he might be. My researches show that not a single Pompeian died except in battle, apart from Afranius and Faustus Sulla and young Lucius Caesar. It is thought that not even these three were killed by his own command, though Afranius and Faustus had taken up arms again after he had spared their lives, and Lucius Caesar had cruelly cut the throats of his slaves and freedmen, even butchering the wild beasts that he had obtained for a public show. At last, towards the end of his career, Caesar invited back to Italy all exiles whom he had not yet pardoned, permitting them to hold magistracies and command armies; he even went so far as to restore the statues of Sulla and Pompey, which the crowd had thrown down and smashed. He also preferred to discourage rather than punish any plots against his life or any slanders on his name. All that he would do, when he detected such plots or became aware of secret nocturnal meetings, was to announce openly that he knew about them. As for slanderers, he contented himself with warning them in public to keep their mouths shut, and good-naturedly took no action either against Aulus Caecina for his most libellous pamphlet or against Pitholaus for his scurrilous verses.

76. Yet other deeds and sayings of Caesar's may be set to the debit account, so that he is judged to have abused his rule and been justly assassinated. Not only did he accept excessive honours, such as continual consulships, a life dictatorship, a perpetual censorship, the title Imperator put before his name

and the title Father of His Country after it, a statue among those of the ancient kings, and a raised seat in the orchestra of the theatre, but he took other honours which, as a mere mortal, he should certainly have refused. These included a golden throne in the Senate House and another on the tribunal, a ceremonial wagon and litter for carrying his statue in the religious procession around the Circus, temples, altars, divine images, a couch for his image at religious festivals, a flamen, a new college of Luperci, and the renaming of a month after him.[39] Few, in fact, were the honours which he was not pleased to accept or assume.

His third and fourth consulships were merely titular; the dictatorship conferred on him at the same time supplied all the authority he needed. And in both years he substituted two new consuls for himself during the last quarter, meanwhile letting only tribunes and aediles of the people be elected, and appointing prefects with praetorian rank to govern the city during his absence. One of the consuls died suddenly the day before the Kalends of January, and when someone asked to hold office for the remaining few hours Caesar granted his request.[40] He showed equal scorn of ancestral tradition by choosing magistrates several years ahead, decorating ten former praetors with the emblems of consular rank, and admitting to the Senate men of foreign birth, including semi-civilized Gauls who had been granted Roman citizenship. He placed his own slaves in charge of the mint and the public revenues, and sent his toy boy Rufio, the son of one of his freedmen, to command the three legions stationed at Alexandria.

77. Titus Ampius has recorded some of Caesar's public statements which reveal a similar presumption: that the republic was nothing – a mere name without form or substance; that Sulla had proved himself a dunce by resigning his dictatorship; and that, now his own word was law, people ought to be more careful how they approached him. Once, when a haruspex reported that a sacrificial beast had been found to have no heart – an unlucky omen indeed – Caesar told him arrogantly, 'The omens will be as favourable as I wish them to be; nor should it be considered a portent if a beast lacks a heart.'

78. But what provoked particularly bitter hostility was that when one day the entire Senate, armed with an imposing list of honours that they had just voted him, came to where he sat in front of the Temple of Venus Genetrix, he did not rise to greet them. According to some accounts, he would have risen had not Cornelius Balbus prevented him; according to others, he made no such move and grimaced angrily at Gaius Trebatius, who suggested this courtesy. The case was aggravated by a memory of Caesar's behaviour during one of his triumphs: he had ridden past the benches reserved for the tribunes of the people, and was so furious at a certain Pontius Aquila for keeping his seat that he shouted, 'Hey, there, Aquila the tribune! Do you want me to restore the republic?' For several days after this incident he added to every undertaking he gave, 'With the kind consent of Pontius Aquila.'

79. This open insult to the Senate was emphasized by an even more arrogant action. As he returned to Rome from the Latin Festival, a member of the crowd set a laurel wreath bound with a white fillet on the head of his statue.[41] Two tribunes of the people, Epidius Marullus and Caesetius Flavus, ordered the fillet to be removed at once and the offender imprisoned. But Caesar reprimanded and summarily degraded them both: either because the suggestion that he should be made king had been so rudely rejected, or else because – this was his own version – they had given him no chance to reject it himself and so earn deserved credit. From that day forward, however, he lay under the odious suspicion of having tried to revive the title of king, though, indeed, when the people greeted him as 'king' he now protested, 'No, I am Caesar, not king,'[42] and though, again, when at the Lupercalia Mark Antony, the consul, made several attempts to crown him in front of the Rostra he refused the offer each time and at last sent the crown to the Capitol for dedication to Jupiter Optimus Maximus. What made matters worse was a persistent rumour that Caesar intended to move the seat of government to Troy or Alexandria, carrying off all the national resources, drafting every available man in Italy for military service, and letting his friends govern what was left of the city. At the next meeting of the Senate (it was further

whispered), Lucius Cotta would announce a decision of the
Quindecimviri who had charge of the Sibylline Books that,
since these prophetic writings stated clearly 'Only a king can
conquer the Parthians,' the title of king must be conferred on
Caesar.

80. Because his enemies shrank from agreeing to this proposal, they pressed on with their plans for his assassination.
Several groups, each consisting of two or three malcontents,
now united in a general conspiracy. Even the people had come
to disapprove of how things were going, and no longer hid
their disgust at Caesar's tyrannical rule but openly demanded
champions to protect their ancient liberties. When foreigners
were admitted to the Senate, someone put up a poster which
read, 'Good Fortune! If any newly appointed senator enquires
the way to the Senate House, let nobody direct him there!' And
the following popular song was sung everywhere:

> Caesar led the Gauls in triumph,
> Led them uphill, led them down,
> To the Senate House he took them,
> Once the glory of our town.
> 'Pull those breeches off,' he shouted,
> 'Change into a purple gown!'[43]

As Quintus Maximus, one of the three-month suffect consuls,
entered the theatre, the lictor called out as usual, 'Make way
for the consul!' Cries of protest went up: 'What? For him? He's
no consul!' The deposition of Caesetius and Marullus caused
such widespread annoyance that at the next consular elections
people cast a great many votes in their favour. Someone then
wrote on the pedestal of Lucius Brutus' statue, 'If only you
were alive now!', and on that of Caesar himself:

> Brutus[44] was elected consul
> When he sent the kings away;
> Caesar sent the consuls packing,
> Caesar is our king today.

More than sixty conspirators banded together against him, led by Gaius Cassius and Marcus and Decimus Brutus. A suggested plan was to wait until the elections in the Campus Martius, when Caesar would take his stand on the wooden bridge along which voters walked to the poll; one group of conspirators would then topple him over, while another waited underneath with daggers drawn. An alternative was to attack him in the Sacred Way or at the entrance to the theatre. The conspirators wavered between these plans until Caesar called a meeting of the Senate in the Assembly Hall of Pompey[45] for the Ides of March; they then decided at once that this would be by far the most convenient time and place.

81. Unmistakable signs forewarned Caesar of his assassination. A few months previously the veterans who had been sent to colonize Capua under the Julian Law were breaking up some ancient tombs in search of stone for their new farmhouses – all the more eagerly when they came across a large hoard of ancient vases. One of these tombs proved to be that of Capys, the founder of the city, and there they found a bronze tablet with a Greek inscription to this effect: 'When the bones of Capys are disturbed, a descendant of his[46] will be murdered by his kindred and later avenged at great cost to Italy.' This story should not be dismissed as idle fiction or a lie, because our authority for it is none other than Cornelius Balbus, a close friend of Caesar. Soon afterwards a herd of horses which Caesar had dedicated to the river Rubicon, after fording it, and allowed to roam untended in the valley, were beginning to show a repugnance for the pasture and shedding bucketfuls of tears. Again, during a sacrifice the haruspex Spurinna warned Caesar to beware of a danger that would not pass until the Ides of March; and on the day before the Ides a little bird called the king wren flew into the Assembly Hall of Pompey with a sprig of laurel in its beak – pursued by a swarm of different birds from a nearby copse, which tore it to pieces there and then. Furthermore, on his last night Caesar dreamed that he was soaring above the clouds and then shaking hands with Jupiter, while his wife Calpurnia dreamed that the pediment of their house[47] collapsed and that her husband was stabbed in her

arms; and suddenly the bedroom door burst open of its own accord.

These warnings, and a touch of ill health, made him hesitate for some time whether to go ahead with his plans or whether to postpone the meeting. Finally Decimus Brutus persuaded him not to disappoint the Senate, who had been in full session for an hour or more waiting for him to arrive. It was just about the fifth hour of the day when he set off. As he went, someone handed him a note containing details of the plot against his life, but he merely added it to the bundle of petitions in his left hand, which he intended to read later. Several victims were then sacrificed, and, despite consistently unfavourable omens, he entered the Assembly Hall, deriding Spurinna as a false prophet. 'The Ides of March have come,' he said. 'Aye, they have come,' replied Spurinna, 'but they have not yet gone.'

82. As soon as Caesar took his seat the conspirators crowded around him as if to pay their respects. Tillius Cimber, who had taken the lead, came up close, pretending to ask a question. Caesar made a gesture of postponement, but Cimber caught hold of his shoulders. 'This is violence!' Caesar cried, and at that moment one of the Casca brothers slipped behind and with a sweep of his dagger stabbed him just below the throat. Caesar grasped Casca's arm and ran it through with his stylus; he was leaping away when another dagger caught him in the breast. Confronted by a ring of drawn daggers, he drew the top of his toga over his face and at the same time ungirded the lower part, letting it fall to his feet so that he would die with his lower body decently covered. Twenty-three dagger thrusts went home as he stood there. Caesar did not utter a sound after Casca's blow had drawn a groan from him, though some say that when he saw Marcus Brutus about to deliver a blow he reproached him in Greek with 'You too, my son?'[48] The entire Senate then dispersed in confusion, and Caesar was left lying dead for some time until three of his household slaves carried him home in a litter, with one arm hanging over the side. The physician Antistius came to the conclusion that none of the wounds had been mortal except the second one in the breast. The conspirators had decided to drag the dead man down to the

Tiber, confiscate his property, and revoke all his edicts, but fear of Mark Antony, the consul, and Lepidus, the master of horse, kept them from making their plans good.

83. At the request of Lucius Piso, Caesar's father-in-law, his will, which he had drafted on the previous Ides of September at his villa near Lavicum and entrusted to the safekeeping of the Chief Vestal, was unsealed and read in Antony's house. From the time of his first consulship until the outbreak of the civil war (according to Quintus Tubero) Caesar's principal heir had been Gnaeus Pompey, and he used to read out this part of his will to the assembled troops. But in the final version of his will he left three-quarters of his estate to Gaius Octavius and one-eighth each to Lucius Pinarius and Quintus Pedius, these being the three grandsons of his sisters; at the close of the will he also adopted Gaius Octavius into the family name. He appointed several of the assassins as guardians to his son, in the case that he should have one; Decimus Brutus even figured among his heirs in the second degree.[49] Caesar left the people his gardens on the banks of the Tiber and 300 sesterces a man.

84. When the funeral arrangements had been announced, his friends raised a pyre on the Campus Martius near his daughter Julia's tomb and a gilded shrine on the Rostra resembling that of Venus Genetrix. In it they set an ivory couch, spread with purple and gold cloth, and from a pillar at its head hung the clothing in which he had been murdered. Since it was thought that a procession of mourners, filing past the pyre in orderly fashion and laying funeral gifts on it, would probably take more than a day, everyone was invited to come there by whatever route he pleased, regardless of precedence. Emotions of pity and indignation were aroused at the funeral games by a line from Pacuvius' play *Contest for the Arms of Achilles*, 'What, did I save these men that they might murder me?', and by a similar sentiment from Atilius' *Electra*. Mark Antony dispensed with a formal eulogy; instead, he instructed a herald to read, first, the recent decree simultaneously voting Caesar all divine and human honours, and then the oath by which the entire Senate had pledged themselves to watch over his safety. Antony added a few short words of comment. When the ivory

funeral couch had been carried down into the Forum by a group of magistrates and former magistrates, and a dispute arose as to whether the body should be cremated in the Temple of Jupiter Capitolinus or in the Assembly Hall of Pompey, two figures suddenly appeared, javelin in hand and sword at thigh, and set fire to the couch with torches. Immediately the spectators assisted the blaze by heaping on it dry branches and the judges' chairs along with the court benches, as well as whatever else came to hand. Thereupon the musicians and the theatrical performers took off the clothes which had been used in his triumphs and which they had put on for the present occasion, tore them into pieces, and flung them on the flames, and his veterans added the arms which they were wearing to honour his funeral. Many women in the audience similarly sacrificed their jewellery together with their children's golden amulets and embroidered tunics. Public grief was enhanced by crowds of foreigners lamenting in their own fashion – especially Jews, who came flocking to the Forum for several nights in succession.

85. As soon as the funeral was over, the people, snatching brands from the pyre, ran to burn down the houses of Brutus and Cassius, and were repelled with difficulty. Mistaking Helvius Cinna for the Cornelius Cinna who had delivered a bitter speech against Caesar on the previous day and whom they were out to kill, they murdered him and paraded the streets with his head stuck on the point of a spear. Later they raised a twenty-foot-high column of Numidian marble in the Forum, and inscribed on it, 'To the Father of His Country'. For a long time afterwards they used to offer sacrifices at the foot of this column, make vows there, and settle disputes by oaths taken in Caesar's name.

86. Some of his friends suspected that, having no desire to live much longer because of his failing health, he had taken no precautions against the conspiracy and neglected the omens and warnings of well-wishers. It has also been suggested that he placed such confidence in the Senate's last decree and in their oath of loyalty that he dispensed even with the armed Spaniards who had hitherto acted as his permanent escort. A contrary view is that, as a relief from taking constant precautions, he

deliberately exposed himself to all the plots against his life which he knew had been formed. Also, he is quoted as having often said, 'It is more important for the commonwealth than for myself that I should survive. I have long been sated with power and glory; but, should anything happen to me, the commonwealth will enjoy no peace. A new civil war will break out under far worse conditions than the last.'

87. Almost all authorities, at any rate, believe that he welcomed the manner of his death. He had once read in Xenophon about the funeral instructions given by Cyrus on his deathbed,[50] and said how much he loathed the prospect of a lingering end – he wanted a sudden one. And on the day before his murder he had dined at Marcus Lepidus' house, where the topic discussed happened to be 'the best sort of death' – and 'Let it come swiftly and unexpectedly,' cried Caesar.

88. He was fifty-five years old when he died, and his immediate deification, formally decreed in the Senate, convinced the city as a whole, if only because, on the first day of the games given by his successor Augustus in honour of this apotheosis, a comet appeared about an hour before sunset and shone for seven days running. This was held to be Caesar's soul, elevated to heaven; hence the star now placed above the forehead of his divine image. It was decided that the Assembly Hall where he fell should be walled up, that the Ides of March should be known ever afterwards as 'The Day of Parricide', and that the Senate should never again meet on that day.

89. Very few, indeed, of the assassins outlived Caesar for more than three years, or died naturally. All were condemned to death, and all met it in different ways – some in shipwreck, some in battle, some using the very daggers with which they had treacherously murdered Caesar to take their own lives.

DIVUS AUGUSTUS

1. The Octavii, by all accounts, were famous in ancient Velitrae. An 'Octavian Street' runs through the busiest part of the city, and an altar is shown there consecrated by one Octavius, a local commander. Apparently news of an attack by a neighbouring city reached him while he was sacrificing a victim to Mars; snatching the intestines from the fire, he offered them only half-burned, and hurried away to win the battle. The Velitraean records include a decree that all future offerings to Mars must be made in the same fashion, the carcass of every victim becoming a perquisite of the Octavii.

2. King Tarquinius Priscus admitted the Octavii, among other plebeian families, to the Roman Senate, and, though Servius Tullius awarded them patrician privileges, they later reverted to plebeian rank until eventually Divus Julius made them patricians once more. Gaius Rufus was the first Octavius elected to office by the popular vote – he won a quaestorship. His sons Gaius and Gnaeus fathered two very different branches of the family. Gnaeus' descendants held all the highest offices of state in turn, but Gaius' branch, either by accident or by choice, remained simple *equites* until the entry into the Senate of Augustus' father. Augustus' great-grandfather had fought as a military tribune under Aemilius Papus in Sicily during the Second Punic War.[1] His grandfather, who enjoyed a comfortable income, was apparently content with municipal magistracies, and lived to an advanced age. These historical details are not derived from Augustus' own memoirs, which merely record that he came of a rich old equestrian family, and that his father had been the first Octavius to enter the Senate. Mark Antony wrote

scornfully that Augustus' great-grandfather had been only a freedman, a rope maker from the neighbourhood of Thurii, and his grandfather a money-changer. This is as much information as I have managed to glean about Augustus' paternal family.

3. Gaius Octavius, his father, was from the beginning of his life a man of considerable wealth and reputation; consequently I cannot believe that he was also a money-changer who distributed bribes among the voters in the Campus and undertook other electioneering services. He was certainly born rich enough to achieve office without having to engage in such practices, and he proved a capable administrator. After his praetorship he became governor of Macedonia, and the Senate commissioned him to pass through Thurii on his way there and disperse a group of runaway slaves who, having fought under Spartacus and Catiline, were now terrorizing the district. He governed Macedonia courageously and justly, winning a big battle in Thrace, mainly against the Bessi, and letters survive from Cicero reproaching his brother Quintus, who was consular governor of Asia at the same time, for inefficiency, and advising him to make Octavius his model in all diplomatic dealings with allies.²

4. Gaius died suddenly on his return to Rome, before he could stand as a candidate for the consulship. He left three children: Octavia the elder, Octavia the younger and Augustus. The mother of Octavia the elder was Ancharia; the other two were his children by Atia, daughter of Marcus Atius Balbus and Julius Caesar's sister Julia. Balbus' paternal family originated in Aricia, and could boast of many ancestral busts of senators; his mother was also closely related to Pompey the Great. Balbus served first as praetor, and then with a commission of twenty appointed under the Julian Law to divide estates in Campania among the people. Mark Antony likewise tried to belittle Augustus' maternal line by alleging that his great-grandfather Balbus had been born in Africa, and kept first a perfumery and then a bakehouse at Aricia. Cassius Parmensis similarly sneers at Augustus as the grandson of a baker and a money-changer, writing in one of his letters, 'Your mother's flour came from

a miserable Arician bakery, and the coin-stained hands of a Nerulian money-changer kneaded it.'

5. Augustus was born just before sunrise on 23 September, while Marcus Tullius Cicero and Gaius Antonius were consuls, at Ox Heads, in the Palatine district;[3] a shrine to him, built soon after his death, marks the spot. The case of a young patrician, Gaius Laetorius by name, figures in the published book of *Proceedings of the Senate*. Pleading his youth and position to escape the maximum punishment for adultery, he further described himself as 'the occupant and, one might even say, temple warden of the place first touched at his birth by Divus Augustus'. Laetorius begged for pardon in the name of his 'own special god'. The Senate afterwards consecrated that part of the building by decree.

6. In the country mansion near Velitrae which belonged to Augustus' grandfather, a small room, not unlike a food pantry, is still shown and described as Augustus' nursery; the local people firmly believe that he was also born there. Religious scruples forbid anyone to enter except for some necessary reason and after purification. It had long been believed that casual visitors would be overcome by a sudden awful terror, and recently this was proved true when, one night, a new owner of the mansion, either from ignorance or because he wanted to test the truth of the belief, went to sleep in the room. A few hours later he was hurled out of bed by a supernatural agency and found lying half-dead against the door, bedclothes and all.

7. I can prove pretty conclusively that as a child Augustus was called Thurinus ['the Thurian'], perhaps because his ancestors had once lived at Thurii, or because his father had defeated the slaves in that neighbourhood soon after he was born; my evidence is a bronze statuette which I once owned. It shows him as a boy, and a rusty, almost illegible inscription in iron letters gives him this name. I have presented the statuette to the emperor,[4] who has placed it among the household gods in his bedroom. Moreover, Augustus was often sneeringly called 'the Thurian' in Antony's correspondence. Augustus answered by confessing himself puzzled: why should his former name be thrown in his face as an insult? Later he adopted the name

Gaius Caesar to comply with the will of his mother's uncle, and then the title Augustus, after a motion to that effect had been introduced by Munatius Plancus.[5] Some senators wished him to be called Romulus, as the second founder of the city, but Plancus had his way. He argued that 'Augustus' was both a more original and a more honourable title, since sanctuaries and all places consecrated by the augurs are known as 'august' – the word being either from *auctus* or from the phrase *avium gestus* (or *gustus*).[6] Plancus supported his point by a quotation from Ennius' *Annals*: 'When glorious Rome had founded been, by augury august.'

8. At the age of four Augustus lost his father. At twelve he delivered a funeral oration in honour of his grandmother Julia. At sixteen, having now come of age, he was awarded military decorations when Caesar celebrated his African triumph, though he had been too young to take part in the war. Caesar then went to fight Pompey's sons in Spain; Augustus followed with a very small escort, along roads held by the enemy, after a shipwreck too, and in a state of semi-convalescence from a serious illness. This energetic action delighted Caesar, who soon formed a high estimate of Augustus' character.

Having recovered possession of Spain, Caesar planned a war against the Dacians and Parthians, and sent Augustus ahead to Apollonia, where he spent his spare time studying. News then came that Caesar had been assassinated after naming him his heir, and Augustus was tempted, for a while, to put himself under the protection of the troops quartered nearby. However, deciding that this would be rash and injudicious, he returned to Rome and there entered upon his inheritance, despite his mother's doubts and the active opposition of his stepfather, Marcius Philippus, a man of consular rank. Augustus now took command of the army and governed the commonwealth: first with Mark Antony and Lepidus and then only with Antony, for nearly twelve years; finally by himself, for another forty-four years.[7]

9. After this summary of Augustus' life, I shall fill in its various parts; but the story will be more readable and understandable if, instead of keeping chronological order, I use a topical arrangement.

He fought five civil wars, associated respectively with the geographical names Mutina, Philippi, Perusia, Sicily and Actium. The first and the last were against Mark Antony, the second against Brutus and Cassius, the third against Antony's brother Lucius, and the fourth against Sextus Pompey, son of Pompey the Great.

10. The underlying motive of every campaign was that Augustus felt it his duty, above all, to avenge Caesar and keep his decrees in force. On his return from Apollonia, he decided to punish Brutus and Cassius immediately; but they foresaw the danger and escaped, so he had recourse to the law and prosecuted them for murder. Finding that the officials who should have celebrated Caesar's victory with public games did not dare to carry out their commission, he undertook the task himself. Because stronger authority was needed to implement his other plans, Augustus announced his candidature for a tribuneship of the people – death had created a vacancy – although he was a patrician but not yet a senator.[8] Mark Antony, one of the two consuls, on whose assistance Augustus had particularly counted, opposed this action and denied him even his ordinary legal rights, except on payment of a heavy bribe. Augustus therefore went over to the optimates, well aware that they hated Antony, especially because he was now besieging Decimus Brutus at Mutina and trying to expel him from the province to which he had been appointed by Caesar with the Senate's approval. At the urging of certain people, Augustus actually engaged assassins to murder Antony and, when the plot came to light, spent as much money as he could raise on enlisting a force of veterans to protect himself and the commonwealth. The Senate awarded him praetorian rank, gave him the command of this army, and instructed him to join Hirtius and Pansa, the two new consuls, in the relief of Decimus Brutus. Augustus brought the campaign to a successful close within three months, after fighting a couple of battles. According to Antony, he ran away from the first of these and did not reappear until the next day, having lost both his charger and his general's cloak. But it is generally agreed that in the second engagement he showed not only skill as

a commander but courage as a soldier: when, at a crisis in the fighting, the standard bearer of his legion was seriously wounded, Augustus himself shouldered the Eagle and carried it for some time.

11. Because Hirtius fell in battle and Pansa later succumbed to a wound, a rumour went about that Augustus had engineered both deaths with the object of gaining sole control over their victorious armies after Antony's defeat. Pansa certainly died in such suspicious circumstances that Glyco, his physician, was arrested on a charge of poisoning the wound, and Aquilius Niger goes so far as to assert that in the confusion of battle Augustus dispatched Hirtius with his own hand.

12. However, when Augustus heard that Mark Antony had been taken under Lepidus' protection and that the other military commanders, supported by their troops, were coming to terms with these two, he at once deserted the optimates. His excuse was that some of them had contemptuously called him 'the boy', while others had sneered that he should be honoured and then removed⁹ – to avoid making the due return to his veterans and himself. Augustus showed regret for this temporary defection from his former allegiance by imposing a heavier fine on the people of Nursia than they could possibly meet, and then exiling them from their city; they had offended him by erecting a monument to fellow citizens killed at Mutina, with the inscription 'Fallen in the Cause of Freedom'.

13. Having formed an alliance with Antony and Lepidus,¹⁰ Augustus defeated Brutus and Cassius at Philippi, though in ill health at the time. In the first of the two battles fought he was driven out of his camp and escaped with some difficulty to Antony's command. After the second and decisive one he showed no clemency to his beaten enemies, but sent Brutus' head to Rome for throwing at the feet of Caesar's statue and insulted the more distinguished of his prisoners. When one of these humbly asked for the right of decent burial, he got the cold answer 'That must be settled with the carrion birds.' And when a father and his son pleaded for their lives, Augustus, it is said, told them to decide which of the two should be spared by casting lots. The father sacrificed his life for the son, and

was executed; the son then committed suicide; Augustus watched them both die. His conduct so disgusted the remainder of the prisoners, including Marcus Favonius, a well-known disciple of Cato, that while being led off in chains they courteously saluted Antony as *imperator*, but abused Augustus to his face with the vilest epithets.

The victors divided between them the responsibilities of government. Antony undertook to pacify the eastern provinces if Augustus led the veterans back to Italy and settled them on municipal lands. However, Augustus failed to satisfy either the landowners, who complained that they were being evicted from their estates, or the veterans, who felt entitled to better rewards for their service.

14. At this point Lucius Antonius felt strong enough, as consul and brother of the powerful Mark Antony, to raise a revolt. Augustus forced him to take refuge in the city of Perusia, which he starved into surrender, but only after being twice exposed to great danger. On the first occasion, before the revolt broke out, he had found a private soldier watching the games from one of the seats reserved for *equites* and ordered his removal by an attendant; when Augustus' enemies then circulated a rumour that the offender had been tortured and executed, an angry crowd of soldiers began to demonstrate at once and Augustus would have lost his life had not the missing soldier suddenly reappeared, safe and unhurt. On the second occasion Augustus was sacrificing close to the walls of Perusia, during the siege, when a party of gladiators made a sortie and nearly cut off his retreat.

15. After the fall of the city, Augustus took vengeance on crowds of prisoners and returned the same answer to all who sued for pardon or tried to explain their presence among the rebels: it was simply 'You must die.' According to some people, he chose 300 prisoners of equestrian or senatorial rank, and offered them on the Ides of March at the altar of Divus Julius, as human sacrifices. There are those who say that Augustus fought because he wished to offer his secret enemies, and those whom fear rather than affection kept with his party, a chance to declare themselves by joining Lucius Antonius; he would

then crush them, confiscate their estates, and thus manage to
pay off his veterans.

16. The Sicilian war,[11] one of his first enterprises, lasted a long
time. It was interrupted by two storms that wrecked his fleets –
in the summer too – and obliged him to rebuild them, and by a
successful blockade of his grain supplies, which forced him to
grant a popular demand for an armistice. At last, however, he
got his new ships into fighting condition, with 20,000 freed
slaves trained as oarsmen, and formed the Julian harbour at
Baiae by letting the sea into the Lucrine and Avernan lakes. Here
he exercised his crews all one winter, and when the sailing season
opened he defeated Sextus Pompey between Mylae and Nau-
lochus, even though on the eve of the battle he fell so fast asleep
that his friends had to wake him and ask for the signal to begin
hostilities. This, I think, must have been the occasion of Mark
Antony's taunt 'He could not even stand up to review his fleet
when the ships were already at their fighting stations, but lay on
his back and gazed up at the sky, never rising to show that he was
alive until Marcus Agrippa had routed the enemy.' Augustus has
also been taken to task for allegedly crying out, when he heard
that his fleets were sunk, 'I will win this war, whatever Neptune
may do!', and for removing the god's image from the sacred
procession at the next celebration of games in the Circus.

It would be safe to say that the Sicilian was by far his most
dangerous campaign. He once landed an army in Sicily and was
sailing back to Italy, where the bulk of his forces were stationed,
when Demochares and Apollophanes, Sextus Pompey's ad-
mirals, suddenly appeared and he just managed to escape them
with a single ship. He was also nearly captured in Italy itself:
as he walked along the road to Rhegium by way of Locri, he
saw a flotilla of biremes heading for the shore and, not realizing
that they were Pompeians, went down to greet them on the
beach. Afterwards, while hurriedly escaping inland by narrow,
winding paths, he faced a new danger. Some years previously
he had proscribed the father of Aemilius Paulus,[12] an officer of
his staff, one of whose slaves, now seeing a good opportunity
to pay off an old score, tried to murder him.

Lepidus, the third member of the triumvirate, whom Augustus had summoned from Africa to his support, thought himself so important as the commander of twenty legions that, when Sextus Pompey had been beaten, he violently demanded the highest place in the government. Augustus deprived him of his legions, and Lepidus, though successfully pleading for his life, spent what was left of it in permanent exile at Circeii.

17. Eventually Augustus broke his friendship with Mark Antony, which had always been a tenuous one and in continual need of patching, and proved that his rival had failed to conduct himself as befitted a Roman citizen by ordering the will he had deposited at Rome to be opened and publicly read. It listed among Antony's heirs the illegitimate children fathered by him on Cleopatra. Nevertheless, when the Senate outlawed Antony, Augustus allowed all his relatives and friends to join him under safe conduct, including Gaius Sosius and Titus Domitius,[13] the consuls of the year. He also excused Bononia, a city traditionally dependent on the Antonii, from joining the rest of Italy in taking an oath to support him. Shortly thereafter he defeated Antony in a sea battle off Actium, where the fighting went on so long that he spent the whole night aboard his ship.

In winter quarters on Samos, after this victory, Augustus heard the alarming news of a mutiny at Brundisium among troops whom he had picked from every unit in the army; they were demanding the bounties due to them and an immediate discharge. He returned to Italy, but ran into two storms: the first between the headlands of the Peloponnese and Aetolia, and the second off the Ceraunian Mountains. Some of his galleys went down on both occasions; the rigging of his own vessel was carried away, and her rudder split. He stayed no more than twenty-seven days at Brundisium, just long enough to pacify the mutineers, then took a roundabout route to Egypt by way of Asia and Syria, besieged Alexandria, where Antony had fled with Cleopatra, and soon reduced it. At the last moment Antony sued for peace, but Augustus ordered him to commit suicide, and inspected the corpse. He was so anxious to save Cleopatra as an ornament for his triumph that he actually summoned Psylli to suck the poison from her wound, supposedly the bite of an asp.[14] Though he allowed them honourable burial in the same tomb and gave orders that the mausoleum which they had begun to build should be completed, he had the elder of Antony's sons by Fulvia dragged from the image of Divus Julius, to which he had fled with vain pleas for mercy, and executed. Augustus also sent cavalry in pursuit of Caesarion, whom Cleopatra claimed to be the son of Caesar, and killed him when captured. However, he spared Cleopatra's children by Antony, brought them up no less tenderly than if they had been members of his own family, and gave them the education which their rank deserved.

18. About this time he had the sarcophagus containing Alexander the Great's mummy removed from the mausoleum at Alexandria and, after a long look at its features, showed his veneration by crowning the head with a golden diadem and strewing flowers on the trunk. When asked, 'Would you now like to visit the mausoleum of the Ptolemies?' he replied, 'I came to see a king, not a row of corpses.' Augustus turned the kingdom of Egypt into a Roman province, and then, to increase its fertility and its yield of grain for the Roman market, set troops to clean out the irrigation canals of the Nile, which had silted up after many years' neglect. To perpetuate the glory of his victory at Actium, he founded a city close to the scene of the battle and named it Nicopolis, and made arrangements for the celebration of games there every five years.[15] He also enlarged an ancient local temple of Apollo, and embellished his camp with trophies taken from Antony's fleet, consecrating the site jointly to Neptune and Mars.

19. Next he suppressed a series of sporadic riots and revolts, besides certain conspiracies, all of them detected before they became dangerous. The leaders of the conspiracies were, in historical sequence, young Lepidus, Varro Murena and Fannius Caepio, Marcus Egnatius, and Plautius Rufus and Lucius Paulus, the husband of Augustus' granddaughter.[16] In addition to these, there were Lucius Audasius, a feeble old man who had been indicted for forgery, and Asinius Epicadus, a half-breed from the tribe of the Parthini, and lastly Telephus, a slave whose task was to remind his noble mistress of her engagements: attempts against Augustus' life were made by men from even

the lowest walks of life. Audasius and Epicadus planned to rescue Augustus' daughter Julia and his grandson Agrippa from the islands where they were confined and forcibly take them to the legions; Telephus nursed a delusion that he was fated to become emperor and planned an armed attack on the Senate as well as Augustus.[17] Then an Illyrian camp orderly, who had managed to sneak by the porters, was caught one night near his bedroom, armed with a hunting knife; but since no statement could be extracted from him it is doubtful whether he was really insane or merely pretending to be.

20. Augustus commanded armies in only two foreign wars: against the Dalmatae while he was still in his teens,[18] and against the Cantabri after defeating Antony. In one of the Dalmatian battles his right knee was struck by a sling stone; in another, he had one leg and both arms severely crushed when a bridge collapsed. The remainder of his foreign wars were conducted by his legates, though during some of the Pannonian and German campaigns he either visited the front or kept in close touch by moving up to Ravenna, Mediolanum or Aquileia.

21. Either as a local commander or as commander-in-chief at Rome, Augustus conquered Cantabria, Aquitania, Pannonia, Dalmatia and the whole of Illyricum, besides Raetia and the Alpine tribes known as Vindelici and Salassi. He also checked the raids of the Dacians, inflicting heavy casualties on them – three of their generals fell in action; drove all the Germans back across the Elbe, except the Suebi and Sigambri, who surrendered and agreed to settle in Gallic territory near the Rhine; and pacified other tribes who gave trouble.

Yet Augustus never wantonly invaded any country, and felt no temptation to increase the boundaries of the empire or enhance his military glory; indeed, he made certain barbarian chieftains swear in the Temple of Mars Ultor that they would faithfully keep the peace for which they sued. In some instances he tried to bind them to their oaths by demanding an unusual kind of hostage, namely women, well aware that barbarians do not feel bound to respect treaties secured only by male hostages. But he let them send acceptable substitutes as often as they pleased. Even when tribes rebelled frequently or showed particular ill faith, Augustus' most severe punishment was to sell as slaves the prisoners he took, ordering them to be kept at some distance from their own country and not to be freed until thirty years had elapsed. Such was his reputation for courage and clemency that the very Indians and Scythians – nations of whom we then knew by hearsay alone – voluntarily sent ambassadors to Rome, pleading for his friendship and that of the Roman people. The Parthians also were ready to grant Augustus' claims on Armenia and, when he demanded the surrender of the Eagles captured from Marcus Crassus and Mark Antony,[19] not only returned them but offered hostages into the bargain; and once, because several rival princes were claiming the Parthian throne, they announced that they would elect whichever candidate he chose.

22. The gates of the Temple of Janus Quirinus, which had been closed no more than twice since the foundation of Rome, he closed three times during a far shorter period, as a sign that the empire was at peace on land and at sea. He enjoyed an ovation after Philippi, and again after his Sicilian successes – and celebrated three full triumphs in a row for his victories won in Dalmatia, off Actium and at Alexandria.

23. He suffered only two heavy and disgraceful defeats, both in Germany, the generals concerned being Lollius and Varus. Lollius' defeat was ignominious rather than of strategic importance, but Varus' nearly wrecked the empire, since three legions with their general and officers and auxiliaries were massacred to a man.[20] When the news reached Rome, Augustus ordered guards to patrol the city and prevent any rising, and then prolonged the terms of the provincial governors, so that the allies should have men of experience, whom they trusted, to confirm their allegiance. He also vowed to celebrate games in honour of Jupiter Optimus Maximus as soon as the situation improved; similar vows had been made during the Cimbric and Marsic wars.[21] Indeed, it is said that he took the disaster so deeply to heart that he left his hair and beard untrimmed for months; he would often beat his head on a door, shouting 'Quinctilius Varus, give me back my legions!', and always kept the anniversary as a day of deep mourning.

24. Augustus introduced many reforms into the army, besides reviving certain obsolete practices, and exacted the strictest discipline. He grudged even his legates leave to visit their wives, and granted this only during the winter. When a Roman *eques* cut off the thumbs of his two young sons to incapacitate them for army service, Augustus had him and his property publicly auctioned; but, realizing that a group of publicans were bidding for the man, knocked him down to an imperial freedman, with instructions that he should be sent away and allowed a free existence in some country place. He gave the entire Tenth Legion an ignominious discharge because of their insolent behaviour, and when some other legions also demanded their discharge in a similarly riotous manner, he disbanded them, withholding the bounty which they would have earned had they continued loyal. If a cohort broke in battle, he decimated it and fed the survivors on barley.[22] Centurions found absent from their posts were sentenced to death, like other ranks, and any lesser dereliction of duty earned them one of several degrading punishments – such as being made to stand all day long in front of general headquarters, sometimes wearing tunics without sword belts, sometimes carrying ten-foot poles or even sods of turf.

25. When the civil wars were over, Augustus no longer addressed the troops as 'comrades' but as 'soldiers', and had his sons and stepsons follow suit. He thought 'comrades' too flattering a term, consonant neither with military discipline nor with peacetime service nor with the respect due to himself and his family. Apart from the city fire brigades and militia companies raised to keep order during food shortages, he enlisted freedmen in the army only on two occasions. The first was when the colonies on the borders of Illyricum needed protection; the second when the Roman bank of the Rhine had to be held in force.[23] These soldiers were recruited as slaves from the households of well-to-do men and women and then immediately freed; but he kept them segregated in their original companies, not allowing them either to mix with men of free birth or to carry arms of standard pattern.

Most of the decorations with which Augustus rewarded distinguished conduct in the field were valuable silver and gold medallions or collars rather than the vallar or mural garlands[24] which brought greater distinction. These garlands he awarded as rarely as possible and with due regard to merit; private soldiers sometimes won them. Marcus Agrippa earned the right to fly a blue banner in recognition of his naval victory off Sicily. The only fighting men whom Augustus held ineligible for decorations were generals who had already celebrated triumphs, even though they might have fought beside him and shared in his victories; he explained that they themselves had the right to confer such awards at their discretion. The two faults which he condemned most strongly in a military commander were haste and recklessness, and he constantly quoted such Greek proverbs as 'More haste, less speed' and 'Give me a safe commander, not a rash one,' and the Latin tag 'Well done is quickly done.' It was a principle of his that no campaign or battle should ever be fought unless more could clearly be gained by victory than lost by defeat, and he would compare those who took great risks in the hope of gaining some small advantage to a man who fishes with a golden hook, though aware that nothing he can catch will be valuable enough to justify its loss.

26. Of the public appointments and honours conferred on Augustus, some he assumed before he was officially old enough and some were extraordinary ones granted him for life. At the age of twenty he usurped the consulship, marching on Rome as though it were an enemy city and sending messengers ahead in the name of his army to demand the appointment. When the Senate hesitated to obey, the centurion Cornelius, the leader of the legation, opened his military cloak, displayed the hilt of his sword, and boldly said, 'If you do not make him consul, this will!' Nine years later Augustus undertook his second consulship, and his third after another two years. Having held the next nine in sequence, he declined any more for as many as seventeen years, then sought a twelfth term and two years later a thirteenth – but only because he wanted to be holding the highest available office when his sons, Gaius and Lucius, successively came of age.[25] He held his sixth, seventh, eighth, ninth and tenth consulships for a full year each, and the remainder

for nine months, or six, or four, or three – except for the second: that was the occasion of his seating himself on a curule chair in front of the Temple of Jupiter Capitolinus early on the Kalends of January and resigning his office to a suffect consul a few hours later. He was absent from Rome at the beginning of his fourth consulship, which found him in Asia; of his fifth, which found him in Samos; and of his eighth and ninth when he was visiting Tarraco.

27. For ten years Augustus remained a member of the triumvirate commissioned to organize the commonwealth, and, though at first opposing his colleagues' plan for a proscription, yet once this had been decided upon he carried it out more ruthlessly than either of them. They often relented under the pressure of political influence or when the intended victims appealed for pity; Augustus alone demanded that no one be spared, and even added to the list of proscribed persons the name of his guardian Gaius Toranius, who had been an aedile at the same time as his father Octavius. Julius Saturninus has more to say on this subject: when the proscription was over and Marcus Lepidus, in an address to the Senate, justified the severe measures that had been taken but encouraged the hope that greater leniency would now be shown, since enough blood had been shed, Augustus spoke in a quite opposite sense. 'I consented to close the list', he said, 'on condition that I should be allowed a free hand in future.' Later, however, he emphasized his regret for this rigorous attitude by creating Titus Vinius Philopoemen an *eques* – Philopoemen had, it appears, secretly harboured his patron, who was on the list of the proscribed.[26]

Under the triumvirate, many of Augustus' acts won him people's hatred. Once, for instance, while addressing a soldiers' assembly at which a crowd of civilians were also present, he saw a Roman *eques* named Pinarius transcribing his speech, and had him stabbed there and then as taking too close an interest in the proceedings. Again, a spiteful comment by Tedius Afer, the consul-elect, on some act of Augustus provoked him to such frightful threats that Afer committed suicide by jumping from a height. There was also the case of Quintus Gallius the praetor who, while paying Augustus his respects, clutched a set

of writing tablets underneath his robe. Augustus suspected that
he had a sword, but dared not have him searched on the spot,
for fear of being mistaken, so a little later he ordered some
centurions and soldiers to drag him away from the tribunal.
Gallius was tortured as if he were a slave, and, though he
confessed to nothing, Augustus himself tore out his eyes and
sentenced him to death. In his own account of the incident,
however, Augustus records that Gallius asked for an audience,
attacked him unexpectedly, and was removed to prison; that,
being then banished from Italy, he disappeared on the way to
his place of exile, but whether he was shipwrecked or ambushed
by bandits nobody knew.

The people awarded Augustus lifelong tribunician power,
and once or twice he chose a colleague to share it with him
for a five-year period. The Senate also voted him the task of
supervising public morals and scrutinizing the laws – another
lifelong appointment. Thus, although he did not adopt the title
of censor, he was privileged to hold a public census, and did so
three times, assisted by a colleague on the first and third
occasions, though not the second.

28. Twice Augustus seriously thought of restoring the republic: immediately after the fall of Antony, when he remembered
that Antony had often accused him of being the one obstacle
to such a change, and again when he could not shake off
an exhausting illness. He then actually summoned the chief
magistrates and the Senate to his house and gave them a faithful
account of the military and financial state of the empire. On
reconsideration, however, he decided that to divide the responsibilities of government among several hands would be to
jeopardize not only his own life but also national security; so
he did nothing. The results were almost as good as his intentions, which he expressed from time to time and even published
in an edict: 'May I be privileged to build firm and lasting
foundations for the commonwealth. May I also achieve the
reward to which I aspire: that of being known as the author of
the best possible constitution, and of carrying with me, when I
die, the hope that these foundations will abide secure.' And,
indeed, he achieved this success, having taken great trouble

to prevent his political system from causing any individual distress.

Aware that the city was architecturally unworthy of its position as capital of the empire, besides being vulnerable to fire and river floods, Augustus so improved its appearance that he could justifiably boast, 'I found Rome built of bricks; I leave it clothed in marble.' He also used as much foresight as could have been expected in guarding against future disasters.

29. Among his larger public works, three must be singled out for mention: the Forum dominated by the Temple of Mars Ultor, the Temple of Apollo on the Palatine, and the Temple of Jupiter Tonans on the Capitoline. He built his Forum because the two already in existence could not deal with the recent great increase in the number of lawsuits caused by a corresponding increase in population; this was why he hurriedly opened it even before the Temple of Mars had been completed. Public prosecutions and the casting of lots for jury service took place only in this Forum. Augustus had vowed to build the Temple of Mars during the Philippi campaign of vengeance against his father Caesar's assassins. He therefore decreed that the Senate should meet here whenever declarations of war or claims for triumphs were considered, and that this should be both the starting point for military governors, when escorted to their provinces, and the repository of all triumphal tokens when they returned victorious. The Temple of Apollo was erected in the part of his house on the Palatine to which, the haruspices said, the god had drawn attention by having it struck with lightning. The colonnades running out from it housed Latin and Greek libraries, and in his declining years Augustus frequently held meetings of the Senate in the nave, or revised jury lists there. A lucky escape on a night march in Cantabria prompted him to build the Temple of Jupiter Tonans: a flash of lightning had scorched his litter and killed the slave who was going ahead with a torch.

Some of Augustus' public works were undertaken in the names of relatives, such as the portico and basilica of his grandsons Gaius and Lucius, the porticos of his wife Livia and his sister Octavia, and the theatre of his nephew Marcellus. He also often urged leading citizens to embellish the city with new public monuments or to restore and improve ancient ones, according to their means. Many responded: thus the Temple of Hercules and the Muses was taken on by Marcius Philippus, that of Diana by Lucius Cornificius, the Atrium of Liberty by Asinius Pollio, the Temple of Saturn by Munatius Plancus, a theatre by Cornelius Balbus, an amphitheatre by Statilius Taurus, and a variety of magnificent buildings by Marcus Agrippa.

30. Augustus divided the city into districts and wards, placing the districts under the control of magistrates annually chosen by lot and the wards under supervisors locally elected. He organized stations of nightwatchmen to watch for fires; as a precaution against floods, he cleared the Tiber channel, which had been choked with an accumulation of rubbish and narrowed by projecting houses. Also, he improved the approaches to the city, repaving the Via Flaminia as far as Ariminum at his own expense, and calling upon men who had won triumphs to spend their share of the plunder on putting the other main roads into good condition. Furthermore, he restored ruined or burned temples, beautifying these and others with the most lavish gifts – for instance, a single donation to Jupiter Capitolinus of 16,000 pounds of gold, besides pearls and precious stones to the value of 50 million sesterces.

31. Finally, on assuming the office of pontifex maximus vacated by the death of Lepidus – he could not bring himself to divest his former colleague of it while he was alive – Augustus collected all the copies of Greek and Latin prophetic verse then current, the work of either anonymous or unsuitable authors, and burned more than 2,000. He kept only the Sibylline Books, and edited even these before depositing them in two gilded cases under the pedestal of Palatine Apollo's image. Since official negligence had allowed the calendar, reformed by Divus Julius, to fall into confusion, he put it straight again, and while doing so he renamed the month of Sextilis after himself (although he had been born in September), because it was during Sextilis that he had won his first consulship and his most decisive victories.[27] He increased the priesthoods in number and dignity

and in privileges too, being particularly generous to the college of Vestal Virgins. When a death caused a vacancy in this college and many citizens busily tried to keep their daughters' names off the list of candidates, Augustus took a solemn oath that if any of his granddaughters had been of eligible age he would have proposed her. He also revived certain obsolescent rites and appointments: the Augury of Safety, the office of the flamen of Jupiter, the Lupercalia, the Saecular Games and the Compitalia. But at the Lupercalia he forbade any boys to run who had not yet shaved off their first beards, and at the Saecular Games no young people might attend a night performance unless accompanied by an adult relative. The images of the Lares Compitales were to be crowned twice a year, with wreaths of spring and summer flowers.[28]

Next to the immortal gods, Augustus most honoured the memory of those citizens who had raised the Roman people from small beginnings to their present glory; this was why he restored many public buildings erected by men of this calibre, complete with their original dedicatory inscriptions, and raised statues to them, wearing triumphal dress, in the twin colonnades of his Forum. Then he proclaimed, 'This has been done to make my fellow citizens insist that both I (while I live) and the leaders of following ages shall not fall below the standard set by those great men of old.' He also transferred Pompey's statue from the hall in which Julius Caesar had been assassinated to a marble arch facing the main entrance of the theatre.

32. Many of the antisocial activities that endangered public peace were a legacy of lawlessness from the civil wars, but some were of more recent origin. For example, bandits infested the roads armed with swords, supposedly worn in self-defence, which they used to overawe travellers – whether freeborn or not – and force them into slave barracks built by the landowners. Numerous so-called 'workmen's guilds', in reality organizations for committing every sort of crime, had also been formed. Augustus now stationed armed police in bandit-ridden districts, had the slave barracks inspected, and dissolved all workmen's guilds except those that had been established for some time and were carrying on legitimate business. Since the records of old

debts to the public treasury had become by far the most profitable means of blackmail, Augustus burned them, also granting
title deeds to the occupants of city sites wherever public claim
to ownership was disputable. When persons had long been
awaiting trial on charges that were not pressed, and therefore
continued to wear mourning in public – with advantage to
nobody except their gleeful enemies – Augustus struck the cases
off the lists and forbade any such charge to be renewed unless
the plaintiff agreed to suffer the same penalty, if he lost the
case, as the defendant would have done. To prevent actions for
damages or disputed claims from either not being heard or
being delayed, he increased the legal term by another thirty
days, which had hitherto been devoted to supplementary public
games sponsored by magistrates. He added a fourth, inferior,
division of jurors to the three already existing; these *ducenarii*,
as they were called, judged cases which involved only small
monetary claims.[29] The minimum age for enrolment in a jury
was reduced from thirty-five to thirty years; but, observing a
general movement to evade jury service, he grudgingly granted
each of the four divisions in turn one year's exemption and
closed all courts throughout the months of November and
December.

33. Augustus proved assiduous in his administration of justice, often remaining in court until nightfall, and if he happened
to be unwell he would have his litter carried up to the tribunal.
Sometimes he even judged cases from his sickbed at home. As
a judge, he was both conscientious and lenient: once, to save a
man who had obviously committed parricide from being sewn
up in a sack[30] – because no one can be punished in this way
unless he has confessed – he is said to have asked the accused,
'I may assume, of course, that you did not kill your father?' On
another occasion the witnesses to a forged will were punishable
under the Cornelian Law but, besides the usual two tablets
for recording their verdict of 'guilty' or 'not guilty', Augustus
handed the jurors a third, for acquitting any of the accused
whose signature had, in their opinion, either been obtained by
false pretences or attached in error. Every year he referred to
the urban praetor cases in which Roman citizens had exercised

their right of appeal; the appeals of provincials would be handled by men of consular status whom he had appointed to oversee the affairs of the province concerned.

34. The existing laws that Augustus revised and the new ones that he enacted dealt, among other matters, with extravagance, adultery and unchastity, bribery, and the encouragement of marriage in the senatorial and equestrian orders. His marriage law being more rigorously framed than the others, he found himself unable to make it effective because of an open revolt against several of its clauses. He was therefore obliged to withdraw or amend certain penalties exacted for a failure to marry, to increase the rewards he offered for large families, and to allow a widow or widower three years' grace before having to marry again. Even this did not satisfy the *equites*, who demonstrated against the law at a public entertainment, demanding its repeal; whereupon Augustus sent for the children of Germanicus and publicly displayed them, some sitting on his own knee, the rest on their father's – and made it quite clear by his affectionate looks and gestures that it would not be at all a bad thing if the *eques* imitated that young man's example. When he then discovered that bachelors were getting betrothed to little girls, which meant postponing the responsibilities of fatherhood, and that married men were frequently changing their wives, he dealt with these evasions of the law by shortening the permissible period between betrothal and marriage and by limiting the number of lawful divorces.

35. The number of senators had been swollen by a coarse and ungainly crowd: there were more than a thousand – some of them wholly unworthy and enrolled through backroom deals after the death of Caesar, who were popularly known as 'Orcus Men'.[31] Augustus restored the order to its former size and repute by two new acts of enrolment. First, each member was allowed to nominate one other; then Augustus and Agrippa together reviewed the list and announced their own choice. When Augustus presided on this second occasion he is said to have worn a sword and a steel corselet beneath his tunic, with ten burly senatorial friends crowding around him. According to Cremutius Cordus, the senators were not even then permitted

to approach Augustus' chair except singly and after the folds of their robes had been carefully searched. Though shaming some of them into resignation, he did not deny them the right to wear senatorial dress, or to watch public shows from the orchestra seats, or to attend the order's public banquets. He then encouraged those selected for service to a more pious and less inconvenient discharge of their duties by ruling that, before taking his seat, each member should offer incense and wine at the altar of whatever temple had been selected for a meeting, that regular meetings should not be held more than twice a month – on the Kalends and the Ides – and that during September and October no member need attend apart from the few whose names were drawn by lot to provide a quorum for the passing of decrees. He also arranged that personal counsellors should be chosen by lot every six months to assist him in reviewing business which would later be laid before the Senate as a whole. During debates of critical importance Augustus shelved the custom of calling on members in order of seniority, and instead singled out speakers arbitrarily; this was intended to make all present take an alert interest in proceedings and feel responsible for constructive thought, instead of merely rising to remark, 'I agree with the last speakers.'

36. Among Augustus' other innovations were a ban on the publication of the *Proceedings of the Senate*; a statutory interval between the conclusion of magistracies and their holders' departure to provincial appointments; a fixed mule-and-tent allowance to provincial governors, replacing the system by which they contracted for these necessities and charged them to the public treasury; the transfer of the treasury from the control of city quaestors to that of praetors or men of praetorian status; and the ruling that a board of ten, instead of men of quaestorian status, should convoke the centumviral court.

37. To give more men some experience in the administration of public affairs, he created new offices dealing with the upkeep of public buildings, roads and aqueducts, the clearing of the Tiber channel, and the distribution of grain to the people. He also established the office of prefect of the city, a board of three for choosing new senators, and another for reviewing the troops

of *equites*, whenever this was needed. He also revived the long
obsolete custom of appointing censors, increased the number
of praetors, and requested not one colleague but two whenever
he held a consulship. The Senate, however, refused this last
plea, everyone shouting that it was sufficient detraction from
his supreme dignity to acknowledge even a single colleague.

38. Augustus showed equal generosity in recognizing strategic skill, by letting full triumphs be voted to more than thirty
of his generals and triumphal decorations to an even larger
number. Senators' sons were now encouraged to familiarize
themselves with public administration; they might wear purple-
striped togas immediately upon coming of age, and attend
meetings of the Senate. When their military careers began, they
were made not only military tribunes in regular legions but
also commanders of cavalry squadrons, and Augustus usually
appointed two to the command of each squadron, thus ensuring
that no one lacked military experience. He frequently reviewed
the troops of *equites*, and revived the long-forgotten custom of
making them ride in procession. Yet he withdrew the spectators'
right of challenging *equites* to dismount while the parade was in
progress, and those who were so old or infirm that they would
look ridiculous if they took part might now send their riderless
mounts to the starting point and report to Augustus on foot.
Later, all *equites* over thirty-five years of age who did not wish to
retain their chargers were excused the embarrassment of publicly
surrendering them.

39. With the assistance of ten senators, Augustus cross-
examined every *eques* on his personal affairs. Some, whose lives
proved to have been scandalous, were punished, others were
degraded, but in most cases he was content to reprimand cul-
prits with greater or less severity. The luckiest were those whom
he obliged merely to take the tablets handed them and read his
censure in silence where they stood. *Equites* who had borrowed
money at a low rate of interest, in order to invest it at a higher,
earned his particular displeasure.

40. If insufficient candidates of senatorial rank presented
themselves for election as tribunes of the people, Augustus nominated *equites* to fill the vacancies, but allowed them, when their

term of office had expired, either to remain members of the equestrian order or to become senators, whichever they preferred. Since many *equites* had lost so much money during the civil wars that they no longer possessed the property qualification of their rank, and therefore refrained from taking their seats in the fourteen rows reserved for the order, he announced that anyone who had once been a *eques* or was the son of an *eques* was not liable to punishment under the law governing theatres.

Augustus revised the roll of citizens, ward by ward. He tried to obviate the frequent interruptions of their trades which the public grain distribution entailed by handing out vouchers for a four months' supply three times a year; but he was implored to resume the former custom of monthly distributions, and consented. He also revived the traditional privilege of elections, and attempted to suppress bribery by imposing various penalties and by distributing on election day 1,000 sesterces from his own funds to every member of his own tribes, the Fabian and the Scaptian,[32] in order to protect candidates against demands for further emoluments.

Augustus thought it most important not to let the native Roman stock be tainted with foreign or servile blood, and was therefore very unwilling to create new Roman citizens or permit the manumission of more than a limited number of slaves. Once, when Tiberius requested that a Greek dependant of his should be granted the citizenship, Augustus wrote back that he could not assent unless the man put in a personal appearance and convinced him that he was worthy of the honour. When Livia made the same request for a Gaul from a tributary province, Augustus turned it down, saying that he would do no more than exempt the fellow from tribute – 'I would far rather forfeit whatever he may owe the imperial exchequer than cheapen the value of the Roman citizenship.' Not only did he make it extremely difficult for slaves to be freed, and still more difficult for them to attain full independence, by strictly regulating the number, condition and status of freedmen, but he ruled that no slave who had ever been in irons or subjected to torture could become a citizen, even after the most honourable form of manumission.

Augustus even set himself to revive the ancient Roman dress, and once, on seeing a group of men in dark cloaks among the crowd, burst out indignantly, 'Behold them, conquerors of the world, the toga clad race of Romans!',[33] and he instructed the aediles that no one should ever again be admitted to the Forum or its environs unless he wore a toga and no cloak.

41. His generosity to all classes was displayed on many occasions. For instance, when he brought the treasures of the Ptolemies to Rome at his Alexandrian triumph, so much cash passed into private hands that the interest rate on loans dropped sharply, while real-estate values soared. Later he made it a rule that, whenever estates were confiscated and the funds realized by their sale exceeded his requirements, he would grant interest-free loans for fixed periods to anyone who could offer security for twice the amount. He increased the property qualification for senators from 800,000 to 1.2 million sesterces, and made good the shortfall for those who could not meet it. His awards of largesse to the people were frequent, but differed in size: sometimes it was 400 sesterces a head, sometimes 300, sometimes 250; and even little boys benefited, though hitherto eleven years had been the minimum age for a recipient. In times of food shortage he often supplied grain to every man on the citizen list at a very cheap rate, or occasionally even free, and doubled the number of vouchers.

42. However, to show that he did all this not to win popularity but to improve public health, he once sharply reminded the people, when they complained of the scarcity and high price of wine, that 'Marcus Agrippa, my son-in-law, has made adequate provision for thirsty citizens by building several aqueducts.' Again, he replied to a demand for largesse which he had in fact promised, 'I always keep my word.' But when they demanded largesse for which no such promise had been given, he issued a proclamation in which he called them a pack of shameless rascals, and added that, though he had intended to make a distribution, he would now tighten his purse strings. Augustus showed equal dignity and strength of character on another occasion when, after announcing a distribution of largesse, he found that the list of citizens had been swelled by a

considerable number of recently freed slaves. He gave out that those to whom he had promised nothing were entitled to nothing, and that he refused to increase the total sum; thus the original beneficiaries must be content with less. In one period of exceptional scarcity he found it impossible to cope with the public distress except by expelling every useless mouth from the city, such as the slaves in the slave market, all members of gladiatorial schools, all foreign residents with the exception of physicians and teachers, and a huge crowd of household slaves. He writes that, when at last the grain supply improved, 'I had a good mind to discontinue permanently the supply of grain to the city, reliance on which had discouraged Italian agriculture, but refrained because some politician would be bound one day to revive the dole as a means of ingratiating himself with the people.' Nevertheless, in his handling of the food problem he now began to consider the interests of farmers and grain merchants as much as the needs of city dwellers.

43. No one before had ever provided so many, so different, or such splendid public shows. He records the presentation of four games in his own name and twenty-three in the names of other magistrates who were either absent or could not afford the expense.[34] Sometimes plays were shown in all the various city districts and on several stages, the actors speaking a variety of languages; and gladiators fought not only in the Forum or the amphitheatre, but in the Circus and Saepta as well; or the show might, on the contrary, be limited to a single wild-beast hunt. He also held athletic competitions in the Campus Martius, for which he put up tiers of wooden seats, and dug an artificial lake beside the Tiber, where the present Grove of the Caesars stands, for a mock sea battle. On these occasions he posted guards in different parts of the city to prevent ruffians from turning the emptiness of the streets to their own advantage. Chariot races and foot races and wild beast hunts took place in the Circus, and among the participants were several youths of distinguished family. Augustus also ordered frequent performances of the Troy Game by two troops, of older and younger boys; it was an admirable tradition, he held, that the scions of noble houses should make their public debut in this

way. When Nonius Asprenas fell from his horse at one performance and broke a leg, Augustus comforted him with a golden
torc and the hereditary surname of 'Torquatus'. Soon afterwards, however, he discontinued the Troy Game, because
Asinius Pollio the orator attacked it bitterly in the Senate, his
grandson Aeserninus having broken a leg too.

Even Roman *equites* sometimes took part in stage plays and
gladiatorial shows, until a senatorial decree put an end to the
practice. After this, no person of good family appeared in any
show, with the exception of a young man named Lycius: he
was a dwarf, less than two feet tall and weighing only seventeen
pounds, but had a tremendous voice. At one of the games
Augustus allowed the people a sight of the first group of
Parthian hostages ever sent to Rome by leading them down the
middle of the arena and seating them two rows behind himself.
And whenever a strange or remarkable animal was brought to
the city, he used to exhibit it in some convenient place on
days when no public shows were being given: for instance, a
rhinoceros in the Saepta, a tiger on the stage, and a serpent
some seventy-five feet long in front of the Comitium.

Once Augustus happened to be ill on the day that he had
vowed to hold games in the Circus, and was obliged to lead the
sacred procession lying in a litter; and when he opened the
games celebrating the dedication of the Theatre of Marcellus
and sat down in his curule chair it gave way and sent him
sprawling on his back. A panic started in the theatre during a
public performance in honour of his grandsons; the audience
feared that the walls might collapse. Augustus, finding that he
could do nothing else to pacify or reassure them, left his own
box and sat in what seemed to be the most threatened part of
the auditorium.

44. He issued special regulations to prevent the disorderly
and haphazard system by which spectators secured seats for
these shows, having been outraged by the insult to a senator
who, on entering the crowded theatre at Puteoli, was not offered
a seat by a single member of the audience. The consequent
senatorial decree provided that at every public performance,
wherever held, the front row of benches must be reserved for

senators. At Rome, Augustus would not admit the ambassadors of independent or allied peoples to seats in the orchestra, on learning that some were mere freedmen. Other rules of his included the separation of soldiers from civilians; the assignment of special seats to married plebeian men, to boys not yet come of age, and, close by, to their tutors; and a ban on the wearing of dark cloaks except in the back rows. Also, whereas men and women had hitherto always sat together, Augustus confined women to the back rows even at gladiatorial shows; the only ones exempt from this rule were the Vestal Virgins, for whom separate accommodation was provided facing the praetor's tribunal. No women at all were allowed to witness the athletic contests; indeed, when the audience clamoured at the pontifical games for a special boxing match, Augustus postponed this until early the next morning, and issued a proclamation to the effect that women should not attend the theatre before the fifth hour.[35]

45. He had a habit of watching the games from the upper rooms of houses overlooking the Circus which belonged to his friends or freedmen; but occasionally he used the gods' platform,[36] and even took his wife and children there with him. Sometimes he did not appear until the show had been running for several hours, or even for a day or more, but always excused his absences and appointed a substitute president. Once in his seat, however, he watched the proceedings intently, either to avoid the bad reputation earned by Julius Caesar for reading or answering letters and petitions during such performances, or just to enjoy the fun, as he frankly admitted doing. This enjoyment led him to offer special prizes at games provided by others or to give the victors valuable presents from his private funds; and he never failed to reward, according to their merits, the competitors in any Greek contests that he attended. His chief delight was to watch boxing, particularly when the fighters were Italians – and not merely professional bouts, in which he often used to pit Italians against Greeks, but slogging matches between untrained roughs in narrow city alleys.

In short, Augustus honoured all sorts of professional entertainers by his friendly interest in them: he maintained and even increased the privileges enjoyed by athletes; banned gladiatorial contests if the defeated fighter were forbidden to plead for mercy; and amended an ancient law empowering magistrates to punish stage players wherever and whenever they pleased, so that they were now competent to deal only with misdemeanours committed at games or theatrical performances. Nevertheless, he insisted on a meticulous observance of regulations during athletic matches and gladiatorial contests, and was exceedingly strict in checking the licentious behaviour of stage players. When he heard that Stephanio, an actor in Roman tragedies, went about attended by a page boy who was really a married woman with her hair cropped, he had him flogged through all three theatres and then exiled. Acting on a praetor's complaint, he had the pantomime performer Hylas publicly scourged in the hall of his own residence; and he expelled Pylades not only from Rome, but from Italy too, because when a spectator started to hiss, he called the attention of the whole audience to him by giving him the finger.

46. After thus improving and reorganizing Rome, Augustus increased the population of Italy by personally founding twenty-eight veteran colonies. He also supplied country towns with municipal buildings and revenues, and even gave them, to some degree at least, privileges and honours equalling those enjoyed by the city of Rome. This was done by granting the city councillors of colonies the right to vote for candidates in the city elections; their ballots were to be placed in sealed containers and counted at Rome on polling day. To maintain the number of *equites*, he allowed any township to nominate men capable of taking up army commands reserved for equestrians; to encourage the birth rate of the Roman people, on his tours of the districts of Italy he offered 1,000 sesterces for every son or daughter whom a citizen could produce.

47. Augustus kept for himself all the more vigorous provinces – those that could not be safely administered by an annual governor; the remainder went to senatorial governors chosen by lot. Yet, as occasion arose, he would change the status of provinces from imperial to senatorial, or contrariwise, and paid frequent visits to both sorts. Finding that certain cities which

had treaties of alliance with Rome were ruining themselves through political irresponsibility, he took away their right of self-governance; but he also granted subsidies to others crippled by public debts, rebuilt some cities which had been devastated by earthquakes, and even awarded partial or full citizenship to those that could show a record of faithful service in the Roman cause. So far as I know, Augustus inspected every province of the empire, except Sardinia and Africa, and would have toured these too, after his defeat of Sextus Pompey in Sicily, had not a sequence of gales prevented him from sailing; later, he had no particular reason, nor any opportunity, for visiting either province.

48. He nearly always either restored the kingdoms which he had conquered to their defeated dynasties or combined them with others, and he followed a policy of linking together his royal allies by mutual ties of friendship or intermarriage, which he was never slow to propose. Nor did he treat them otherwise than as imperial functionaries, showing them all consideration and finding guardians for those who were not yet old enough to rule, until they came of age – and for those who suffered from mental illness, until they recovered. He also brought up many of their children with his own, and gave them the same education.

49. His military dispositions were as follows. The legions and their auxiliaries were distributed among the various provinces, one fleet being stationed at Misenum and another at Ravenna, to command respectively the western and eastern Mediterranean. The rest of his armed forces served partly as a police force in Rome, partly as a personal bodyguard, for he had disbanded a company of Calagurritani after Antony's defeat and a company of Germans after the Varus disaster – both of which had served as his bodyguard. However, he never kept more than three cohorts on duty at Rome, and even these had no permanent camp; the remainder he stationed in nearby towns, changing them regularly from summer to winter quarters. Augustus also standardized the pay and allowances of the entire army – at the same time fixing the period of service and the bounty due on its completion – according to military rank;

this would discourage them from revolting, when back in civil life, on the excuse that they were either too old or had insufficient capital to earn an honest living. In order to have sufficient funds always in hand for the upkeep of his military establishment and for pensioning off veterans, he formed a military treasury maintained by additional taxation. In order to keep in close touch with provincial affairs, he organized relays of runners strung out at short intervals along the highways, and later a stage-coach – which has proved the more satisfactory arrangement, because messengers can be cross-examined on the situation as well as delivering letters.

50. The first seal Augustus used for official documents, petitions and letters was a sphinx; next came a head of Alexander the Great; lastly, his own head, cut by Dioscurides, the seal which his successors continued to employ. He not only dated every letter, but entered the exact hour of the day or night when it was composed.

51. There are numerous positive proofs of Augustus' clemency and unassuming behaviour. To supply a full list of the political enemies whom he pardoned and allowed to hold high office would be tedious. It will be enough to record that a fine was the sole punishment he awarded Junius Novatus, a plebeian, for circulating a most damaging libel on him under the name of Agrippa Postumus, and that Cassius Patavinus, another plebeian, who openly boasted at a large banquet that he would enjoy assassinating him and had the courage too, escaped with a mild form of exile. Then again, hearing at an inquiry into the case of Aemilius Aelianus of Corduba that the most serious of the many charges brought against him was one of 'vilifying Caesar', Augustus pretended to lose his temper and told the prosecutor, 'I wish you could prove that charge! I'll show Aelianus that I have a nasty tongue too, and vilify him even worse!' He then dropped the whole inquiry and never resumed it. When Tiberius mentioned the matter in a letter, with violent expostulations against Aelianus, Augustus replied, 'My dear Tiberius, you must not give way to youthful emotion or take it to heart if anyone speaks ill of me; let us be satisfied if we can make people stop short at unkind words.'

52. Although the voting of temples to popular governors was a commonplace, he would not accept any such honour in the provinces unless his name were coupled with that of Rome. He even more vigorously opposed the dedication of a temple to himself at home, and went so far as to melt down the silver statues previously erected and spend the silver coined from them on golden tripods for Apollo Palatine. When the people would have forced a dictatorship on him he fell on his knee and, throwing back his toga to expose his naked breast, implored their silence.

53. He always felt horrified and insulted when called 'Lord'.[37] Once, while he was watching a comedy, one of the players spoke the line 'O just and generous Lord!', whereupon the entire audience rose to their feet and applauded, as if the phrase referred to Augustus. An angry look and a peremptory gesture soon quelled this gross flattery, and the next day he issued an edict of stern reprimand. After this he would not let even his children or grandchildren use the obsequious word, though it might be only in joke, either when talking to him or about him.

Augustus did his best to avoid leaving or entering any city in broad daylight, because that would have obliged the authorities to give him a formal welcome or send-off. During his consulships he usually went on foot through the streets of Rome, and on other occasions in a closed litter. His morning audiences were open even to the common people, and he behaved very sociably to all who came with requests – once a petitioner showed such nervousness that Augustus laughed and said, 'Anyone would think you were offering a penny to an elephant!' On days when the Senate was in session he would not allow the senators to pay their customary call at his home, but would himself enter the Senate House and greet each of them in turn by name, unprompted; and after the conclusion of business he said goodbye in the same fashion, not requiring them to rise. He exchanged social calls with many men and always attended their family celebrations, until he grew elderly and had an uncomfortable experience at a crowded betrothal party. When a senator named Cerrinius Gallus, whom Augustus knew only slightly, went suddenly blind and decided to starve himself to death, he paid him a visit and spoke so consolingly that Gallus changed his mind.

54. Augustus' speeches in the Senate would often be interrupted by such remarks as 'I don't understand you!' or 'I'd dispute your point if I got the chance.' And it happened more than once that, exasperated by recriminations which lowered the tone of the debates, he left the Senate House in angry haste, and was followed by shouts of 'You ought to let senators say exactly what they think about matters of public importance!' When everyone was required to nominate one other during the reform of the Senate, Antistius Labeo chose Augustus' old enemy Marcus Lepidus, then living in exile. Augustus asked, 'Surely there are others more deserving of this honour?'; Labeo answered, 'A man is entitled to his own opinion.' Yet Augustus never punished anyone for showing independence of mind on such occasions, or even for behaving insolently.

55. He remained unmoved by the lampoons on him which were posted up in the Senate House, but took trouble to prove their pointlessness; and instead of trying to discover their authors he merely moved that henceforth it should be a criminal offence to publish any defamatory libel, either in prose or verse, signed with another's name.

56. Though replying in an edict to various ugly and damaging jokes current at his expense, he vetoed a law that would have suppressed free speech in wills. Whenever he took part in the elections, he used to take his favoured candidates with him on a tour of the wards and canvass for them in the traditional manner. He would also cast a vote himself in his own tribe, like an ordinary citizen. If called upon to give evidence in court, he answered questions patiently and did not even mind being contradicted. He made his Forum somewhat narrow because he could not bring himself to evict the owners of nearby houses. He never nominated his sons for office without adding, 'If they deserve this honour'. Once, while they were still boys and the entire theatre audience stood up to cheer them, he expressed his annoyance in no uncertain terms. Although anxious that his friends should take a prominent share in the administration, he expected them to be bound by the same laws as their fellow

citizens and equally liable to public prosecution. When Cassius
Severus had brought a charge of poisoning against Augustus'
close friend Nonius Asprenas, Augustus asked the Senate what
they wished him to do. 'I find myself in a quandary,' he said,
'because to appear on his behalf might be construed as an
attempt to shield a criminal, whereas my silence would suggest
that I was treacherously prejudicing a friend's chance of acquit-
tal.' With universal consent, he sat quietly for several hours
among the advocates and witnesses, but abstained even from
testifying to Nonius' character. He did, however, appear for
some of his own dependants, among them a former staff officer
named Scutarius, who had been accused of slander. Yet he
actively intervened in only one case, and then by a personal
appeal to the plaintiff; this concerned Castricius, who had
disclosed the conspiracy of Murena.

57. The degree of affection that Augustus won by such
behaviour can easily be gauged. The grateful senatorial decrees
may, of course, be discounted as to a certain extent inspired by
a sense of obligation. But the equestrian order voluntarily and
unanimously decided to celebrate his birthday, spreading the
festivities over two days, and once a year men of all classes
would throw into the Curtian Lake the coins which they previously vowed for his continued well-being. They would also
place good luck coins in the Capitol on the Kalends of January,
even if he happened to be out of town. With the sum that thus
accrued, Augustus bought valuable images of the gods, which
he set up in the city wards, among them Apollo of Sandal Maker
Street and Jupiter of the Tragedians. When his home on the
Palatine burned down, a fund for its rebuilding was started by
the veterans, the guilds of minor officials, and the citizen tribes,
to which people of every sort made further individual contributions according to their means. Augustus, to show his gratitude for the gift, took a token coin from each heap, but no
more than a single denarius. His homecomings after tours of
the provinces were always acclaimed with respectful good
wishes and songs of joy as well, and it became a custom to
cancel all punishments on the day he set foot in Rome.

58. In a universal movement to confer on Augustus the title

Father of His Country, the first approach was made by the people, who sent a deputation to him at Antium; when he declined this honour, a huge crowd met him on his return to Rome with laurel wreaths. Finally, the Senate followed suit, but, instead of issuing a decree or acclaiming him with shouts, chose Valerius Messala to speak for them all when Augustus entered the Senate House. Messala's words were 'Caesar Augustus, good fortune and divine blessings to you and your family! For this is the best way we know to pray for perpetual joy and prosperity for this commonwealth of ours. The Senate agree with the People of Rome in saluting you as Father of your Country.' With tears in his eyes, Augustus answered – again I quote his exact words – 'Gentlemen of the Senate, I have at last achieved my highest ambition. What more can I ask of the immortal gods than that they may permit me to enjoy your approval until my dying day?'

59. Augustus' private physician, Antonius Musa, who had pulled him through a serious illness, was honoured with a statue, bought by public subscription and set up beside Aesculapius'.[38] The will of more than one householder directed that his heirs should take sacrificial victims to the Capitol and carry a placard before them as they went, inscribed with an expression of their gratitude for Augustus' having been allowed to outlive the testator. Some Italian cities voted that their official year should commence on the anniversary of his first visit to them, and several provinces not only erected temples and altars to him and the Roman people, but arranged for most of their cities to hold games in his honour at five-year intervals.

60. Each of the allied kings who enjoyed Augustus' friendship founded a city called 'Caesarea' in his own dominions; and all clubbed together to provide funds for completing the temple of Olympian Jupiter at Athens,[39] which had been begun centuries before, and dedicating it to his *genius*. These kings would often leave home, dressed in the togas of their Roman citizenship, without any emblems of royalty whatsoever, and visit Augustus at Rome or even while he was visiting the provinces; they would attend his morning audiences with the simple devotion of dependants.

61. This completes my account of Augustus' civil and military career, and of how he governed his wide empire in peace and war. Now follows a description of his private life, his character and his domestic fortunes, from his youth down to the last day of his life.

Augustus lost his mother while he was consul for the first time, and his sister Octavia when he was fifty-four. He had been a devoted son and brother while they lived, and conferred the highest posthumous honours on them at their deaths.

62. As a young man he was betrothed to the daughter of Publius Servilius Isauricus, but on his reconciliation with Mark Antony, after their first disagreement, the troops insisted that they should become closely allied by marriage; so, although Antony's stepdaughter Claudia – borne by his wife Fulvia to her ex-husband Publius Clodius – was barely of age, Augustus married her; however, he quarrelled with Fulvia and divorced Claudia before the union had been consummated. Soon afterwards he married Scribonia, both of whose previous husbands had been men of consular rank, and by one of whom she had a child. Augustus divorced her too, 'because', as he wrote, 'I could not bear the way she nagged at me' – and immediately took Livia Drusilla away from her husband, Tiberius Nero, though she was pregnant at the time. Livia remained the one woman whom he truly loved until his death.

63. Scribonia bore him a daughter, Julia, but to his great disappointment the marriage with Livia proved childless, apart from a premature birth. Julia's first husband was Marcellus, his sister Octavia's son, then hardly more than a child, and when he died Augustus persuaded Octavia to let her become Marcus Agrippa's wife – though Agrippa was at the time married to one of Marcellus' two sisters and had fathered children on her. At Agrippa's death, Augustus cast about for a new son-in-law, even if he were only an *eques*, eventually choosing Tiberius, his stepson; this meant, however, that Tiberius must divorce his wife, who had already given him an heir. According to Mark Antony, Julia was betrothed first to his own son Antonius and then to Cotiso, king of the Getae, whose daughter Augustus himself proposed to marry in exchange.[40]

64. Julia bore Agrippa three sons, Gaius, Lucius and Agrippa, and two daughters, Julia and Agrippina. Augustus married this Julia to the son of Lucius Paulus the censor, and Agrippina to his sister's grandson Germanicus. He adopted Gaius and Lucius and brought them up in his home, after buying them from Agrippa in a symbolic sale.[41] He trained his new sons in the business of government while they were still young, sending them as commanders-in-chief to the provinces when only consuls-elect. The education of his daughter and granddaughters included even spinning and weaving; they were forbidden to say or do anything, either publicly or in private, that could not decently figure in the imperial daybook. He took severe measures to prevent them forming friendships without his consent, and once wrote to Lucius Vinicius, a young man of good family and conduct, 'You were very ill mannered to visit my daughter at Baiae.' Augustus gave his grandsons reading, writing and other simple lessons, for the most part acting as their tutor himself, and was at pains to make them model their handwriting on his own. Whenever they dined in his company he had them sit on the lowest couch, and while accompanying him on his travels they rode either ahead of his carriage or one on each side of it.

65. His satisfaction with the success of this family training was, however, suddenly dashed. He found out that both the elder and the younger Julia had been indulging in every sort of vice, and banished them. When Gaius then died in Lycia and Lucius eighteen months later at Massilia, Augustus adopted his third grandson, Agrippa Postumus, and at the same time his stepson Tiberius by means of a curiate law.[42] Yet he soon disinherited Agrippa, whose behaviour had lately been vulgar and brutal, and packed him off to Surrentum in disgrace.

When members of his family died, Augustus bore his loss with far more resignation than when they disgraced themselves. The deaths of Gaius and Lucius did not break his spirit, but after discovering his daughter Julia's adulteries he refused to see visitors for some time. He made the matter known to the Senate through a letter, staying at home while a quaestor read it to them. He may even have considered her execution; at any rate, hearing that one Phoebe, a freedwoman in Julia's confidence, had hanged herself, he cried, 'I should have preferred to be Phoebe's father!' Julia was forbidden to drink wine or enjoy any other luxury during her exile, and was denied all male company, whether free or servile, except by Augustus' special permission and after he had been given full particulars of the applicant's age, height and complexion, and of any distinguishing marks on his body – such as moles or scars. He kept Julia for five years on an island before moving her to the mainland, where she received somewhat milder treatment. Yet nothing would persuade him to recall his daughter from exile, and when the Roman people interceded several times on her behalf, he stormed at a popular assembly, 'May the gods curse you with daughters as lecherous as mine, and with wives as adulterous!' While in exile the younger Julia gave birth to a child, which Augustus refused to let the father acknowledge; it was exposed at his orders. Because Agrippa Postumus' conduct, so far from improving, grew daily more irresponsible, he was transferred to an island and held there under military surveillance; Augustus then asked the Senate to pass a decree making Postumus' banishment permanent. And whenever his name or that of either Julia came up in conversation he would sigh deeply and cry out, 'Ah, never to have married, and childless to have died!',[43] referring to them as 'my three boils' or 'my three running sores'.

66. Though slow in making friends, once Augustus took to a man, he showed great constancy and not only rewarded him as his qualities deserved, but even condoned his minor shortcomings. Indeed, it would be hard to recall an instance when one of Augustus' friends fell from favour, apart from Salvidienus Rufus and Cornelius Gallus, two nobodies whom he promoted, respectively, to a consulship and the governorship of Egypt. Rufus, who had taken part in a plot, was handed over to the Senate and sentenced to death; Gallus, who had shown ingratitude and an envious nature, was at first merely denied access to Augustus' home and the imperial provinces, but prosecutions and senatorial decrees eventually drove him to suicide.[44] Augustus commended the loyal Senate for feeling as

strongly as they did on his behalf, but complained with tears of the unfortunate position in which he was placed: the only man in Rome who could not punish his friends merely by an expression of disgust for them – the matter must always be taken further. However, as I say, the cases of Rufus and Gallus were exceptional. Augustus' other friends all continued rich and powerful so long as they lived, despite occasional coolnesses, each ranking among the leaders of his order. It will be enough to mention in this context his annoyance at Marcus Agrippa's show of impatience and at Maecenas' inability to hold his tongue. Agrippa had felt that Augustus was not behaving as warmly towards him as usual, and when Marcellus, not himself, became the second man at Rome he resigned all his offices and went off to Mytilene; Maecenas was guilty of confiding a secret to his wife Terentia – namely that Murena's conspiracy had been disclosed.[45]

Augustus expected the affection that he showed his friends to be warmly reciprocated even in the hour of death. For, although nobody could call him a legacy-hunter – indeed, he could never bear to benefit under the will of a man personally unknown to him – yet he was almost morbid in his careful weighing of a friend's deathbed tributes. His disappointment if they economized in their bequests to him or failed to make at least some highly complimentary mention of his name was only too apparent, nor could he repress his satisfaction if they remembered him with loving gratitude. But whenever any testator of whatever order left him either legacies or shares in promised inheritances, Augustus at once resigned his rights in favour of the man's children, if he had any, or in the case of minors kept the money until the boys came of age or the girls married, whereupon he handed it over, increased by the accumulated interest.

67. Augustus behaved strictly but kindly towards his dependants and slaves, and honoured some of his freedmen, such as Licinus, Celadus and others, with his close intimacy.[46] A slave named Cosmus, who had complained of him in the vilest terms, was punished merely by being put in shackles. Once, when Augustus and his steward Diomedes were out walking together

. and a wild boar suddenly charged them, Diomedes took fright
and dodged behind his master. Augustus later made a joke
of the incident, though he had been in considerable danger,
preferring to accuse Diomedes of cowardice than anything
worse – after all, his action had not been premeditated. Yet,
when one Polus, a favourite freedman, was convicted of adultery with freeborn Roman matrons, Augustus ordered him to
commit suicide; and he sentenced his secretary Thallus to have
his legs broken for divulging the contents of a dispatch – his
fee had been 500 denarii. And because his son Gaius' tutor and
attendants used their master's sickness and subsequent death
as an excuse for arrogant, greedy behaviour in the province of
Asia, Augustus had them flung into a river with weights tied
around their necks.

68. As a young man Augustus was accused of various improprieties. For instance, Sextus Pompey jeered at his effeminacy;
Mark Antony alleged that Julius Caesar made him submit to
intercourse as the price of adoption; Antony's brother Lucius
added that, after sacrificing his virtue to Caesar, Augustus had
sold his favours to Aulus Hirtius, the governor of Spain, for
300,000 sesterces, and that he used to soften the hairs on his
legs by singeing them with red-hot walnut shells. One day at
the theatre, when an actor came on the stage representing a
eunuch priest of the Mother of the Gods and, as he played his
drum, another actor exclaimed, 'Do you see how this *cinaedus*
regulates the sphere with his finger?',[47] the audience mistook
the line for a hint at Augustus and broke into enthusiastic
applause.

69. Not even his friends could deny that he often committed
adultery, though of course they said in justification that he did
so for reasons of state, not simple passion – he wanted to
discover what his enemies were at by getting intimate with their
wives. Mark Antony accused him not only of indecent haste in
marrying Livia, but of hauling a former consul's wife from her
husband's dining room into the bedroom – before his eyes too!
He brought the woman back, says Antony, blushing to the ears
and with her hair in disorder. Antony also writes that Scribonia
was divorced for having said a little too much when a rival got

her claws into Augustus, and that his friends used to behave
like the slave-dealer Toranius in arranging his pleasures for him
– they would strip mothers of families or grown girls of their
clothes and inspect them as though they were up for sale. A
racy letter of Antony's survives, written before he and Augustus
had quarrelled privately or publicly: 'What has come over you?
Do you object to my screwing Cleopatra? She's my wife, and
it's not even as though this were anything new – the affair
started nine years ago. And what about you? Is Livia Drusilla
the only woman you screw? My congratulations if, when this
letter arrives, you haven't screwed Tertulla or Terentilla or
Rufilla or Salvia Titisenia or all of them. Does it really matter
so much where or with whom you get off?'

70. Then there was Augustus' private banquet, known as
'The Feast of the Twelve Gods', which caused a public scandal.
The guests came dressed as gods or goddesses, Augustus himself
representing Apollo, and our authority for this is not only a
spiteful letter of Antony's, which names all the twelve, but the
following well-known anonymous lampoon:

> Those rogues engaged the services
>   Of a stage manager;
> So Mallia found six goddesses
>   And six gods facing her!
>
> Apollo's part was lewdly played
>   By impious Caesar; he
> Made merry at a table laid
>   For gross debauchery.
>
> Such scandalous proceedings shocked
>   The Olympians. One by one
> They quit and Jove, his thunders mocked,
>   Vacates the golden throne.

What made the scandal even worse was that the banquet took
place at a time of food shortage, and on the next day people
were shouting, 'The gods have gobbled all the grain!' or 'Caesar

is Apollo, true – but he's Apollo of the Torments' – this being
the god's epithet in one city district. Some found Augustus a
good deal too fond of expensive furniture, Corinthian bronzes[48]
and the gaming table. While the proscriptions were in progress,
someone had scrawled on the base of his statue:

> I do not take my father's line;
> His trade was silver coin, but mine
> Corinthian vases –

the belief being that he enlarged the proscription lists with
names of men who owned vases of this sort. And during the
Sicilian war another rhyme was current:

> He took a beating twice at sea,
> And threw two fleets away.
> So now to achieve one victory
> He tosses dice all day.

71. Augustus easily disproved the accusation (or slander, if
you like) of prostituting his body to men by the decent nor-
mality of his sex life, then and later, and that of having over-
luxurious tastes by his conduct at the capture of Alexandria,
where the only loot he took from the royal palace was a single
agate cup – he melted down all the golden dinner services.
However, the charge of being a womanizer stuck, and as an
elderly man he is said to have still harboured a passion for
deflowering girls – who were collected for him from every
quarter, even by his wife. Augustus did not mind being called
a gambler; he diced openly, in his old age too, simply because
he enjoyed the game – not only in December, but on other
holidays as well, and actually on working days. That this is
quite true a letter in his own handwriting proves: 'I dined, my
dear Tiberius, with the same men, except that Vinicius and the
elder Silius were also invited; we gambled like old men all
through the meal, and until yesterday turned into today. Anyone who threw the dog or the six put a denarius in the pool for
each of the dice, and anyone who threw Venus scooped the

lot.'[49] And another letter runs, 'We spent the Quinquatrus very pleasantly, my dear Tiberius, keeping the gaming table warm by playing all day long. Your brother made fearful complaints about his luck, yet in the long run was not much out of pocket. He went down heavily at first, but we were surprised to see him slowly recouping most of his losses. I lost 20,000 sesterces; however, that was because, as usual, I behaved with excessive sportsmanship. If I had demanded all the stakes which I forgave people or kept all those which I gave up to others, I should have been at least 50,000 to the good. Well, that is how I like it: my generosity will gain me immortal glory, you may be sure!' And to his daughter he wrote, 'Enclosed please find 250 denarii, which is the sum I give each of my dinner guests in case they feel like dicing or playing "odd and even" at table.'

72. Augustus' other personal habits are generally agreed to have been moderate and unexceptionable. His first house, once the property of Calvus the orator, stood close to the Roman Forum at the top of the Ringmakers' Stairs; from there he moved to what had been Hortensius' house on the Palatine Hill. But his new house was neither larger nor more elegant than the first, the low colonnades having columns of peperino stone, and the rooms innocent of marble or elaborately tessellated floors. There he slept in the same bedroom all the year round for over forty years, although the winter climate of Rome did not suit his health. Whenever he wanted to be alone and free of interruptions he could retreat to a study at the top of the house, which he called 'Syracuse' or 'my little workshop'. He would hide himself away either here or else in a suburban villa owned by one of his freedmen, but if he fell ill he always took refuge in Maecenas' house. He spent his holidays at seaside resorts and islands of Campania, or in country towns near Rome, such as Lanuvium or Praeneste or Tibur – where he often administered justice in the colonnades of Hercules' temple. Such was his dislike of all large pretentious mansions that he went so far as to demolish one built by his granddaughter Julia on too lavish a scale. His own were modest enough and remarkable less for their statuary and pictures than for their landscape gardening and the rare antiques on display: for example, at

Capreae he had collected the huge skeletons of sea and land monsters, popularly known as 'Giants' Bones', and the weapons of ancient heroes.

73. How simply Augustus' home was furnished may be deduced by examining the couches and tables still preserved, many of which would now hardly be considered fit for a private citizen. He is said to have always slept on a low bed, with a very ordinary coverlet. On all but special occasions he wore house clothes woven and sewn for him by his sister, wife, daughter and granddaughters. His togas were neither tight nor full, and the purple stripe on them was neither narrow nor broad; but his shoes had rather thick soles to make him look taller. And he always kept a change of better shoes and clothes at hand: he might be unexpectedly called upon to appear in an official capacity.

74. He gave frequent dinner parties, and very formal ones too, paying strict attention to social precedence and personal character. Valerius Messala writes that the sole occasion on which Augustus ever invited a freedman to dine was when he honoured Menas for delivering Sextus Pompey's fleet into his power, and even then Menas was first enrolled on the list of freeborn citizens. However, Augustus himself records that he once invited a former member of his bodyguard, the freedman whose villa he used as a retreat. At such dinner parties he would sometimes arrive late and leave early, letting his guests start and finish without him. The meal usually consisted of three courses, though in expansive moods Augustus might serve as many as six. There was no great extravagance, and a most cheerful atmosphere, because of his talent for making shy guests, who either kept silent or muttered to their neighbours, join in the general conversation. He also enlivened the meal with performances by entertainers, actors or even men who gave turns at the Circus – but more often by professional storytellers.

75. Augustus spared no expense when celebrating holidays, and behaved very light-heartedly on occasion. At the Saturnalia, for instance, or whenever else the fancy took him, he whimsically varied the value of his gifts. They might consist of rich

clothing and gold or silver plate; or every sort of coin, including specimens from the days of the early monarchy and foreign pieces; or merely lengths of goat-hair cloth, sponges, pokers or tongs – all given in return for tokens inscribed with misleading descriptions of the objects concerned. At some dinner parties he would also auction tickets for prizes of most unequal value. and paintings with their faces turned to the wall, for which the guests would bid by table, so that the loss or gain was shared among them; they might either pick up most satisfactory bargains or throw away their money.

76. In this character sketch I need not omit his eating habits. He was frugal and, as a rule, preferred the food of the common people, especially the coarser sort of bread, whitebait, fresh hand-pressed cheese, and green figs of the second crop; and he would not wait for dinner, if he felt hungry, but ate anywhere. The following are verbatim quotations from his letters: 'I had a snack of bread and dates while out for my drive today'; and 'On the way back home in my litter from the Regia, I munched an ounce of bread and a few hard-skinned grapes'; and again 'Not even a Jew, my dear Tiberius, fasts so scrupulously on his sabbaths as I have done today; not until dusk had fallen did I touch a thing, and that was at the baths, before I had my oil rub, when I swallowed two mouthfuls.' This failure to observe regular mealtimes often resulted in his dining alone, either before or after his guests; but he came to the dining hall nevertheless, and watched them eat.

77. Augustus was also a habitually abstemious drinker. During the siege of Mutina, according to Cornelius Nepos, he never took more than three cups of wine at dinner. In later life his limit was a pint; if he ever exceeded this he would deliberately vomit. Raetian was his favourite, but he seldom touched wine during the day; instead, he would moisten his throat with a morsel of bread dunked in cold water, or a slice of cucumber, or the heart of a young lettuce, or a fresh or dried sour apple.

78. After lunch he used to rest for a while without removing clothes or shoes, one hand shading his eyes, his feet uncovered. When dinner was over he would retire to a couch in his study, where he worked late, until all or most of the outstanding

business of the day had been cleared off. Then he went to bed and slept seven hours at the outside, with three or four breaks of wakefulness. If he found it hard to fall asleep again on such occasions, as frequently happened, he sent for readers or storytellers, and on dropping off would not wake until the sun was up; he could not bear lying sleepless in the dark with no one by his side. If he had to officiate at some official or religious ceremony that involved early rising – which he also loathed – he would spend the previous night at a friend's house as near the venue as possible. Even so, he often needed more sleep than he got, and would doze off during his litter journeys through the city if anything delayed his progress and the bearers set the litter down.

79. Augustus was remarkably handsome and very graceful even as an old man, but negligent of his personal appearance. He cared so little about his hair that, to save time, he would have two or three barbers working hurriedly on it together, and meanwhile read or write something, whether they were giving him a haircut or a shave. He always wore so serene an expression, whether talking or in repose, that a Gallic chief once confessed to his compatriots, 'When granted an audience with Augustus during his passage across the Alps I would have carried out my plan of hurling him over a cliff had not the sight of that tranquil face softened my heart; so I desisted.' Augustus' eyes were clear and bright, and he liked to believe that they shone with a sort of divine radiance: it gave him profound pleasure if anyone at whom he glanced keenly dropped his head as though dazzled by looking into the sun. In old age, however, his left eye had only partial vision. His teeth were small, few and decayed; his hair blondish and rather curly; his eyebrows met above the nose; he had ears of normal size, a nose that was prominent at the bridge and curved downward at the tip, and a complexion intermediate between dark and fair. Julius Marathus, Augustus' freedman and record-keeper, makes his height five and three-quarters feet; this is an exaggeration, although his body and limbs were so beautifully proportioned that one did not realize how small a man he was unless someone tall stood close to him.

80. His body is said to have been marred by blemishes of various sorts – a constellation of seven birthmarks on his chest and stomach, exactly corresponding with the Great Bear, and a number of hard, dry patches suggesting ringworm, caused by an itching of his skin and a too vigorous use of the scraper at the baths. He had a weakness in his left hip, thigh and leg, which occasionally gave him the suspicion of a limp, but this was improved by the sand-and-reed treatment. Sometimes the forefinger of his right hand would be so numbed by cold that it hardly served to guide a pen, even when strengthened with a long horn fingerstall. He also suffered from bladder pains – which, however, ceased to trouble him once he had passed gravel in his urine.

81. Augustus survived several dangerous illnesses at different periods. The worst was after his Cantabrian conquest, when abscesses on the liver reduced him to such despair that he consented to try a remedy which ran counter to all medical practice: because hot fomentations afforded him no relief, his physician Antonius Musa successfully prescribed cold ones. He was also subject to certain seasonal disorders: right before his birthday he was often under the weather; in early spring he was bothered by a tightness of the diaphragm, and when the sirocco blew by a head cold. These so weakened his constitution that either hot or cold weather caused him great distress.

82. In winter he wore no fewer than four tunics and a heavy woollen toga above his under-tunic, and below that a woollen chest protector and wrappings around his thighs and legs. In summer he slept with the bedroom door open or in the court-yard beside a fountain, having someone to fan him; he could not bear the rays even of the winter sun, but always wore a broad-rimmed hat to protect himself against glare, whether at home or elsewhere. He preferred to travel by litter, at night, and his bearers kept so leisurely a pace that they were two days in arriving at Praeneste or Tibur, and whenever it was possible to reach his destination by sea he did so. Indeed, he pampered his health, especially by not bathing too often and being usually content with an oil rub or a sweat bath, after which he rinsed off with water either warmed over a fire or allowed to stand in

the sun until it had lost its chill. When hot brine or sulphur water from the Albula springs was prescribed for his rheumatism he did no more than sit on a wooden bath seat – calling it by the Spanish name *dureta* – and alternately dip his hands and feet into the bath.

83. As soon as the civil wars were over, Augustus discontinued his riding and fencing exercises on the Campus Martius and instead used to play catch or handball. But soon he was content to go riding or take walks, muffled in a cloak or blanket, that ended with a sharp sprint and some jumping. Sometimes he went fishing as a relaxation; sometimes he played at dice, marbles or nuts in the company of little boys, and he was always on the lookout for ones with cheerful faces and cheerful chatter, especially Syrians and Mauretanians – he loathed people who were dwarfish or in any way deformed, regarding them as freaks of nature and bringers of bad luck.

84. Even in his boyhood Augustus had studied rhetoric with great eagerness and industry, and during the Mutina campaign, busy though he was, he is said to have read, written and declaimed daily. He kept up his interest by carefully drafting every address intended for delivery to the Senate, the people or the troops, although gifted with quite a talent for extempore speech. What is more, he avoided the embarrassment of forgetting his words or the drudgery of memorizing them by always reading from a manuscript. All important statements made to individuals, even to his wife Livia, were first committed to notebooks and then repeated aloud, so that he would avoid saying either too much or too little in speaking offhand. His articulation of words, constantly practised under an elocution teacher, was pleasant and rather unusual, but sometimes, when his voice proved inadequate for addressing a large crowd, he called a herald.

85. Augustus wrote numerous prose works on a variety of subjects, some of which he read aloud to a group of his closer friends as though in a lecture hall: the *Reply to Brutus' Eulogy of Cato,* for instance. In this case, however, he tired just before the end – being then already an old man – and handed the last roll to Tiberius, who finished it for him. Among his other

works were *An Encouragement to the Study of Philosophy* and thirteen books of *My Autobiography,* which took the story only up to the time of the Cantabrian war. He made occasional attempts at verse composition, including *Sicily,* a short poem in hexameters, and an equally short collection of *Epigrams,* most of them composed at the baths. Both these books survive; but growing dissatisfied with the style of his tragedy, *Ajax,* which he had begun in great excitement, he destroyed it. When friends asked, 'Well, what has Ajax been doing lately?', he answered, 'Ajax has not fallen on his sword,[50] but wiped himself out on my sponge.'

86. He cultivated a simple and easy oratorical style, avoiding overly contrived epigrams, affected rhythms, and 'the stink of far-fetched phrases', as he called it; his main object was to say what he meant as plainly as possible. An anxiety not to let his audience or his readers lose their way in his sentences explains why he put prepositions before the names of cities, where common usage omits them, and why he often repeated the same conjunction several times where a single appearance would have been less awkward, if more confusing. He expressed contempt for both innovators and archaizers as equally mischievous, and would occasionally attack them sharply – especially his friend Maecenas, whose 'perfume-drenched ringlets' he parodied mercilessly. Even Tiberius, who sometimes sought out obsolete and difficult words, did not escape Augustus' ridicule, and Antony was for him a madman who wrote 'as though he wanted to be wondered at rather than understood'. He made fun of Antony's bad taste and inconsistent literary style: 'Your use of antique diction borrowed by Sallust from Cato's *Origins* suggests that you are in two minds about imitating Annius Cimber or Veranius Flaccus. But at other times it looks as though you were trying to acclimatize in Latin the nonsensicalities of those garrulous Asiatic orators.' And to a letter praising the intelligence of his granddaughter Agrippina he adds, 'But please take great care to avoid affectation in writing or talking.'

87. Augustus' everyday language must have contained many whimsical expressions of his own coinage, to judge from autograph letters. Thus he often wrote 'they will pay on the Greek

Kalends', meaning 'never'. Another of his favourite remarks was 'Let us be satisfied with *this* Cato!'[51] He also had a favourite metaphor for swift and sudden actions: 'Quicker than boiled asparagus.' Here is a list of unusual synonyms which constantly appear in Augustus' letters: *baceolus* for *stultus*, *pulleiaceus* for *pullus*, *vacerrosus* for *cerritus*, *vapide se habere* for *male se habere*, *betizare* for *languere* – on the analogy of the colloquial form *lachanizare*.[52] Among his grammatical peculiarities occur the forms *simus* for *sumus* and *domos* in the genitive singular for *domus*, to which he invariably clung as a sign that they were his considered choice and not simply a mistake. I have noticed one particular habit of his: rather than break a long word at the end of a line and carry forward to the next whatever letters were left over, he would write these underneath the first part of the word and draw a loop to connect them with it.

88. Instead of paying a strict regard to orthography as formulated by the grammarians, he inclined towards phonetic spelling. Since most writers make such slips as transposing or omitting not only letters but whole syllables, I should not have mentioned that Augustus often did the same but for my surprise on finding, in more than one book of memoirs, the story that he once retired a consular governor for being ill-educated enough to write *ixi* for *ipsi*. When Augustus wrote in cipher he simply wrote B for A, C for B, and so on throughout the alphabet, except that he wrote AA for X.

89. He had ambitions to be as proficient in Greek as in Latin, and did very well under the tutorship of Apollodorus of Pergamum, who accompanied him to Apollonia, though a very old man, and taught him elocution. Afterwards Augustus spent some time with the philosopher Areius and his sons Dionysius and Nicanor, who broadened his general education; but he never learned to speak Greek with real fluency, and never ventured on any Greek literary composition. Indeed, if he ever had occasion to use the language he would write down whatever it might be in Latin and get someone to make a translation. Yet nobody could describe him as ignorant of Greek poetry, because he greatly enjoyed Old Comedy[53] and often put plays of that period on the stage. His chief interest in the literature of both

languages was the discovery of moral precepts, with suitable anecdotes attached, capable of public or private application, and he would transcribe passages of this sort for the attention of his household, generals and provincial governors, and city magistrates whenever he thought it necessary. He even read whole volumes aloud to the Senate, and issued proclamations commending them to the people – such as Quintus Metellus' *On the Need for Larger Families* and Rutilius' *On Restricting the Height of Buildings* – just to prove that he had been anticipated in his recommendations by far earlier thinkers.

Augustus gave all possible encouragement to intellectuals: he would politely and patiently attend readings not only of their poems and historical works, but of their speeches and dialogues. Yet he objected to being made the theme of any work unless the author were known as a serious and reputable writer, and often warned the praetors not to let his name be vulgarized by its constant occurrence in prize orations.

90. As for Augustus' superstitions: he is recorded to have been scared of thunder and lightning, against which he always carried a piece of sealskin as an amulet, and he took refuge in an underground vault whenever a heavy storm threatened – because, as I have already mentioned, he had once narrowly escaped being struck by lightning on a night march.

91. Warnings conveyed in dreams, either his own or those of others, were not lost on him: for example, before the battle of Philippi, when so ill that he decided not to leave his tent, he changed his mind on account of a friend's dream – most fortunately too, as it proved. The camp was captured, and a party of the enemy, breaking into the tent, plunged their swords through and through his camp bed under the impression that he was still in it, tearing the bedclothes to ribbons. Every spring he had a series of ugly dreams, but none of the horrid visions seen in them came true, whereas the few dreams he had at other seasons were more reliable. One day, after he had paid frequent visits to the Temple of Jupiter Tonans, founded by himself on the Capitoline Hill, Jupiter Capitolinus approached him in a dream with a complaint that the newcomer was stealing his worshippers. He replied, 'I put Tonans so close to your temple

because I had decided to give you a doorkeeper.' When Augustus awoke, he hung a set of bells from the gable of the new building to make it look like a front door. Because of another dream, he used to sit in a public place once a year holding out his hand for the people to give him change, as though he were a beggar.

92. Augustus had absolute faith in certain premonitory signs, considering it bad luck to thrust his right foot into the left shoe as he got out of bed, but good luck to start a long journey or voyage during a drizzle of rain, as a sign of success and a speedy return. Prodigies made a particularly strong impression on him. Once, when a palm tree pushed its way between the paving stones in front of his home he had it transplanted to the inner court beside his household gods, and lavished care on it. When he visited Capreae, the drooping branches of a moribund old oak suddenly regained their vigour, which so delighted him that he arranged to buy the island from the city of Neapolis in exchange for Aenaria. He also had a superstition against starting a journey on the day after a market day, or undertaking any important task on the Nones – although in this case, as he explained to Tiberius in a letter, it was merely the unlucky 'no' sound of the word that affected him.

93. Augustus showed great respect towards all ancient and long-established foreign rites, but despised the rest. Once, for example, after becoming an initiate at Athens, he judged a case in which the privileges of the Attic Ceres' priests were questioned. Since certain religious secrets had to be quoted in the evidence, he cleared the court, dismissed his legal advisers, and settled the dispute *in camera*. On the other hand, during his journey through Egypt he would not go out of his way, however slightly, to honour Apis,[54] and he praised his grandson Gaius for not offering prayers at Jerusalem when he was travelling near Judaea.

94. At this point it might be well to list the omens occurring before, on, and after the day of Augustus' birth, from which his future greatness and lasting good fortune could clearly be prognosticated.

In ancient days, part of the city wall of Velitrae had been

struck by lightning, which was interpreted to mean that a native Velitraean would one day rule the world. Confidence in this prediction led the citizens to declare immediate war against Rome, and to keep on fighting until they were nearly wiped out; only centuries later did the world ruler appear in the person of Augustus.

According to Julius Marathus, a public portent warned the Roman people some months before Augustus' birth that nature was making ready to provide them with a king, and this caused the Senate such consternation that they issued a decree which forbade the rearing of any male child for a whole year. However, a group of senators whose wives were expecting prevented the decree from being filed at the public treasury and thus becoming law – for each of them hoped that the prophesied king would be his own son.

Then there is a story which I found in Asclepiades of Mendes' *Theologumena*. Atia, with certain married women friends, once attended a solemn midnight service at the Temple of Apollo, where she had her litter set down and presently fell asleep, as the others also did. Suddenly a serpent crept in to her and after a while glided away again. On awakening, she purified herself as if after sleeping with her husband. An irremovable coloured mark in the shape of a serpent, which then appeared on her body, made her ashamed to visit the public baths any more, and the fact that Augustus was born nine months later suggested that he was the son of Apollo. Before she gave birth, Atia also dreamed that her internal organs were carried up to heaven and overhung all lands and seas; similarly, Augustus' father Octavius dreamed that the sun rose from her womb.

Augustus' birth coincided with the Senate's debate on the Catilinarian conspiracy, and it is widely known that when Octavius arrived late, because of Atia's confinement, Publius Nigidius, hearing at what hour the child had been delivered, cried out, 'The ruler of the world is now born.'[55] Octavius, during a subsequent expedition through the wilder parts of Thrace, reached a grove sacred to Liber Pater, where he consulted the priests about his son's destiny. After performing certain barbaric rites, they gave him the same response, for the wine they had poured over the altar caused a pillar of flame to shoot up far above the roof of the shrine – a sign never before granted except to Alexander the Great when he sacrificed at that very altar. That night Octavius had another dream: his son appeared in superhuman majesty, armed with the thunderbolt, sceptre and ornaments of Jupiter Optimus Maximus, crowned with a solar diadem, and riding in a belaurelled chariot drawn by twelve dazzlingly white horses.

Gaius Drusus records that, one evening, the infant Augustus was placed by the nurse in his cradle on the ground floor, but had vanished by daybreak; at last a search party found him lying on the top of a lofty tower, his face turned towards the rising sun. Once, when he was just learning to talk at his grandfather's suburban estate, the frogs broke into a loud chorus of croaking; he told them to stop, and it is locally claimed that no frog has croaked there since. On a later occasion, as he sat lunching in a copse beside the Campanian road, close to the fourth milestone, an eagle, to his great surprise, swooped at him, snatched a crust from his hand, carried it aloft – and then, to his even greater surprise, glided gently down again and restored what it had stolen.

Quintus Catulus, after rededicating the Capitol, dreamed two dreams on successive nights. In the first, Jupiter Optimus Maximus drew aside one of several boys who were playing near his altar and slipped into the fold of the boy's toga the image of the commonwealth that he held in his hand. Then Catulus dreamed that he saw the same boy sitting in the lap of Jupiter Capitolinus; he tried to have him removed, but the god countermanded the order because the boy was being reared as the saviour of the commonwealth. Next day, Catulus met Augustus, looked at him with startled eyes – they had never met before – and pronounced him the identical boy of his dreams. Another version of Catulus' first dream is that a crowd of boys were begging Jupiter for a guardian; the god then pointed to one of them, saying, 'Whatever you need, ask him!', lightly touched the boy's mouth, and conveyed a kiss from it to his own lips.

When Cicero escorted Julius Caesar to the Capitol, he hap-

pened to tell his friends what he had dreamed the night before:
a boy of noble features, let down from heaven by a golden
chain, stood at the temple door and was handed a whip by
Jupiter. At that moment Cicero's eye caught Augustus, whom
his grand-uncle Caesar had brought to the ceremony but whom
few of those present knew by sight. He cried, 'There goes the
very boy!'

When Augustus celebrated his coming of age, the seams of
his senatorial tunic split and it fell at his feet. Some people
interpreted the accident as a sign that the senatorial order itself
would some day be brought to his feet.

As Divus Julius was felling a wood near Munda to clear a
site for his camp, he noticed a palm tree and ordered it to be
spared, palm fronds being a presage of victory. The tree then
suddenly put out a new shoot which, a few days later, had
grown so tall as to overshadow it. What was more, a flock of
doves began to nest in the fronds, although doves notoriously
dislike hard, spiny foliage. This prodigy was the immediate
reason, they say, for Caesar's desire that his grand-nephew, and
no one else, should succeed him.

At Apollonia, Augustus and Agrippa together visited the
house of Theogenes the astrologer, and climbed upstairs to his
observatory; they both wished to consult him about their future
careers. Agrippa went first and was prophesied such almost
incredibly good fortune that Augustus expected a far less
encouraging response, and felt ashamed to disclose his nativity.
Yet when at last, after a good deal of hesitation, he grudgingly
supplied the information for which both were pressing him,
Theogenes rose and flung himself at his feet; and this gave
Augustus so implicit a faith in the destiny awaiting him that he
even ventured to publish his horoscope, and struck a silver coin
stamped with Capricorn, the sign under which he had been
born.

95. When he returned to Rome from Apollonia at news
of Caesar's assassination, the sky was clear of clouds, but a
rainbow-like halo formed around the sun, and suddenly lightning struck the tomb of Caesar's daughter Julia. Then, when
he first took the auspices as consul, twelve vultures appeared

to him just as they had to Romulus, and the livers of all the sacrificial victims were seen to be doubled inwards at the bottom – an omen which, experts agreed, presaged a wonderful future for him.

96. Augustus even foresaw the successful conclusion of all his wars. At Bononia, where the army of the triumvirs had assembled, an eagle perched on Augustus' tent and defended itself vigorously against the converging attack of two ravens, bringing both of them down. This augury was understood by the troops as portending a rupture between their three leaders, the outcome of which would be obvious. On Augustus' way to Philippi, a Thessalian stopped him to report that he had been assured of victory by Caesar's ghost, whom he met on a lonely road. Sacrificing one day before the walls of Perusia, Augustus had failed to secure a satisfactory omen, and sent for more victims; at this point the enemy made a sudden sortie from the beleaguered city and carried off the entire sacrificial apparatus, including the carcasses. The haruspices unanimously reassured him that whatever disasters had been threatened by the omens would fall upon their present possessors, and this proved to be true. On the eve of the naval battle off Sicily, Augustus was walking along the shore when a fish leaped from the sea and fell at his feet. Before Actium, he was about to board his ship and give the signal for hostilities to begin when he met a peasant driving an ass, and asked his name. The peasant replied, 'I am Eutychus and my ass is called Nicon.'⁵⁶ To commemorate the victory, Augustus set up bronze statues of Eutychus and his ass on the camp site, which he now dedicated to Mars and Neptune.

97. Next we come to Augustus' death and subsequent deification, both of which were predicted by evident signs. While he was closing a census period with a purificatory ceremony in the crowded Campus Martius, an eagle circled around him several times, then flew to the nearby temple and perched above the first 'A' of Agrippa's name. As soon as Augustus noticed this, he ordered Tiberius, who was acting as his colleague, to read out the usual vows for the next census period, because, though having composed and recorded them on a tablet, he would not make himself responsible for vows payable after his

death. At about the same time lightning melted the initial letter
of his name on the inscription below one of his statues. This
was interpreted to mean that he would live only another hundred days, which the letter 'C' signifies, and that he would be
enrolled among the gods, since the remainder of the word,
namely AESAR, is the Etruscan for 'god'.

Again, when sending Tiberius off to Illyricum and planning
to accompany him as far as Beneventum, Augustus got held up
by a long list of court cases and cried, 'I will stay here no longer,
whoever tries to detain me!' These words were subsequently
recalled as prophetic. He started off for Beneventum, but on
reaching Astura he met with a favourable breeze and decided
to take ship that evening – although night voyages were against
his usual habits – and so contracted an illness, the first symptom
of which was diarrhoea.

98. After coasting past Campania, with its islands, he spent
the next four days in his villa on Capreae, where he rested and
amused himself. As he had sailed through the bay of Puteoli,
the passengers and crew of a recently arrived Alexandrian ship
had put on white robes and garlands, burned incense, and
wished him the greatest of good fortune: it was to him, they
said, that they owed their lives and their liberty to sail the seas,
to him they owed their entire freedom and prosperity. This
incident gratified Augustus so deeply that he gave each member
of his staff forty aurei, making them promise under oath to
spend them only on Alexandrian trade goods. What was more,
he made the last two or three days of his stay on Capreae the
occasion for distributing among other presents Roman togas
and Greek mantles, insisting that the Romans should speak and
dress like Greeks, and that the Greeks should do the opposite.
He sat for a long time watching the athletic training of the many
local ephebes, Capreae being a very conservative settlement.[57]
Afterwards he invited these young men to a banquet at which
he presided, and not merely allowed but expected them to
play jokes and freely scramble for the tokens which he threw,
entitling the holders to fruit, sweetmeats and the like. In short,
he indulged in every form of fun.

Augustus called Capreae 'Lubberland', because some of his

staff, now settled on the island, were growing so lazy. One of his friends, Masgaba by name, he always used to call by the Greek word for 'Founder', as though he were the founder of the settlement. This fellow had died the year before, and when Augustus noticed from his dining room window that a crowd of torch-bearers were attending his tomb he improvised this Greek line, 'I see the Founder's tomb ablaze with fire,' then asked Tiberius' friend Thrasyllus, who was reclining opposite him and did not understand the reference, 'What poet wrote that?' Thrasyllus hesitated, and Augustus capped his own line, reciting, 'With torches, look, they honour Masgaba!', and again asked, 'Who wrote that?' Thrasyllus, unable to divine the authorship, mumbled, 'Both lines are very good, whoever the poet was.' Augustus burst out laughing and made great fun of Thrasyllus.

He next crossed over to Neapolis, although his stomach was weak from an intermittent recurrence of the same trouble, and watched an athletic competition which was held in his honour every five years. Finally he started off with Tiberius and said goodbye to him at Beneventum. Feeling worse on the homeward journey, he took to his bed at Nola, and sent messengers to recall Tiberius from his journey. At his arrival Augustus had a long talk with him in private, after which he attended to no further important business.

99. On the day that he died, Augustus frequently enquired whether rumours of his illness were causing any popular disturbance. He called for a mirror, and had his hair combed and his lower jaw, which had fallen from weakness, propped up. Presently he summoned a group of friends and asked, 'Have I played my part in the farce of life creditably enough?', adding the theatrical tag:

> If I have pleased you, kindly signify
> Appreciation with a warm goodbye.

Then he dismissed them, but when fresh visitors arrived from Rome he wanted to hear the latest news of Drusus' daughter, who was ill. Finally he kissed his wife with 'Goodbye, Livia;

remember our marriage!', and died almost at once. He must have longed for such an easy exit, for whenever he had heard of anyone having passed away quickly and painlessly he used to pray, 'May Heaven grant the same *euthanasia* to me and mine!' The only sign that his wits were wandering, just before he died, was his sudden cry of terror 'Forty young men are carrying me off!' But even this may be read as a prophecy rather than a delusion, because forty praetorians were to form the guard of honour that conveyed him to his lying-in-state.

100. Augustus died in the same room as his father Octavius. That was 19 August at about the ninth hour, the consuls of the year being Sextus Pompeius and Sextus Appuleius,[58] when he was just thirty-five days short of his seventy-sixth year. City councillors from the neighbouring municipalities and colonies bore the body in stages all the way from Nola to Bovillae – but at night, owing to the hot weather – laying it during the day in the town hall or principal temple of every halting place. From Bovillae, a party of Roman *equites* carried it to the vestibule of his house at Rome.

The senators vied with one another in proposing posthumous honours for Augustus. Among the motions introduced were the following: that his funeral procession should pass through the Triumphal Gate preceded by the image of Victory from the Senate House, and that the sons and daughters of leading citizens should sing his dirge; that on the day of his cremation iron rings should be worn instead of gold ones; that his ashes should be gathered by priests of the leading colleges; that the name August should be transferred to September, because Augustus had been born in September but had died in the month now called August; and that the period between his birth and death should be officially entered in the calendar as 'the Augustan Age'. But such excessive proposals were kept in check, and he was given two funeral eulogies, by Tiberius before the Temple of Divus Julius and by Tiberius' son Drusus from the original Rostra; afterwards a party of senators shouldered the body and took it to a pyre on the Campus Martius, where it was burned. Furthermore, a man of praetorian rank actually swore that he had seen Augustus' spirit soaring up to heaven through the flames. Leading *equites*, barefoot and wearing unbelted tunics, then collected his ashes and placed them in the family Mausoleum. He had built this himself during his sixth consulship, between the Via Flaminia and the Tiber, at the same time converting the neighbourhood into a public park.

101. Augustus' will, composed on 3 April of the previous year, when Lucius Plancus and Gaius Silius were consuls, occupied two notebooks, written partly in his own hand, partly in those of his freedmen Polybius and Hilarion. The Vestal Virgins, to whose safekeeping he had entrusted these documents, now produced them, as well as three rolls also sealed by him. All were opened and read in the Senate. It proved that he had appointed Tiberius and Livia as heirs in the first degree, with Tiberius taking two-thirds of his estate and Livia one-third, and both adopting his name; as heirs in the second degree he named Tiberius' son Drusus, taking one-third of the estate, and Germanicus and his three male children, taking the remainder; as heirs in the third degree,[59] many of his relatives and friends.

He also left a bequest of 40 million sesterces to the Roman people, 3.5 million to the tribes, 1,000 to every praetorian guard, 500 to every member of the urban cohorts, 300 to every legionary soldier. These legacies were to be paid at once, because he had always kept enough cash for the purpose. There were other minor bequests, some as large as 2 million sesterces, which were not to be settled until a year after his death because 'my estate is not large; indeed, my heirs will not receive more than 150 million sesterces; for, although my friends have bequeathed me some 1,400 million in the last twenty years, nearly the whole of this sum, besides what came to me from my father, from my adoptive father, and from others, has been used in the public interest.'

He had given orders that if anything happened to his daughter Julia or his granddaughter of the same name their bodies must be excluded from the Mausoleum. One of the three sealed rolls contained directions for his own funeral; another a record of his accomplishments,[60] which he wished to have engraved on bronze and posted at the entrance to the Mausoleum; the third an account book of the whole empire, with statements of how many troops were stationed and in what places, what money reserves were held by the public treasury and the imperial exchequer, and what revenues were due for collection. He also supplied the names of freedmen and slave secretaries who could furnish details under all these heads on demand.

TIBERIUS

1. The patrician branch of the Claudian family – there was a plebeian branch too, of equal influence and distinction – came to Rome, which had then been only recently founded, from the Sabine town of Regillae, bringing with them a large train of dependants. They did so at the instigation of either Titus Tatius, Romulus' co-ruler, or (according to the more widely held story) Atta Claudius, the head of the family, about six years after the expulsion of the kings.[1] The Claudii were enrolled among the patricians, and were also publicly decreed an estate beyond the Anio for their dependants to farm, and a family burial ground at the foot of the Capitoline Hill. In the course of time they amassed twenty-eight consulships, five dictatorships, seven censorships, six triumphs and two ovations. Many different praenomina and cognomina were used by members of the family, but they unanimously decided to ban the praenomen Lucius, because one Lucius Claudius had been convicted as a highwayman and another as a murderer, and added the cognomen Nero, which is Sabine for 'strong and energetic'.

2. History records many distinguished services and equally grave injuries done to the commonwealth by Claudii. Let me quote only a few instances. Appius Caecus prudently advised the Senate that an alliance with King Pyrrhus would not be in the national interest. Claudius Caudex was the first to take a fleet across the straits, and expelled the Carthaginians from Sicily. Tiberius Nero intercepted Hasdrubal as he arrived in Italy from Spain with powerful reinforcements for his brother Hannibal, and defeated him before a junction could be effected. On the debit side of the ledger must be set Claudius Regillianus'

attempt, while one of the ten commissioners for codifying the laws, to enslave and seduce a freeborn girl – a wicked act which made the plebeians desert Rome in a body for the second time, leaving the patricians to their own devices.[2] Then there was Claudius Russus, who set up a crowned image of himself at the town called Forum Appii and attempted to conquer Italy with the help of his armed dependants. And Claudius Pulcher, who, as consul, took the auspices before a naval battle off Sicily and, finding that the sacred chickens had refused their feed, cried, 'If they will not eat, let them drink!' He threw them into the sea, fought the battle in defiance of religious scruples, and lost it. When the Senate then ordered Claudius to appoint a dictator, he made a joke of the critical military situation by choosing one Glycias, his dispatch rider.

An equal disparity may be found between the records of the Claudian women. There was a Claudia who, when the ship that was bringing the sacred emblems of the Idaean Mother Goddess to Rome grounded on a Tiber mudbank, publicly prayed that she might be allowed to refloat it in proof of her perfect chastity, and did so.[3] Against her achievement may be set that of Claudius Pulcher's sister. She was riding through the crowded streets in a carriage, and making such slow progress that she shouted, 'If only my brother were alive to lose another fleet! That would thin out the population a little.' She was consequently tried for treason before the people, as had happened to no woman before her. It is well worth noting that all the Claudii were optimates and keen advocates of patrician powers and prerogatives, with the sole exception of Publius Clodius, who found he could best expel Cicero from Rome by becoming the adoptive son of a plebeian – as it happened, a man younger than himself. Moreover, they were so rude and violent in their attitude towards the plebeians that not even when tried on a capital charge would any of them condescend to wear suppliant dress or sue for mercy; and some, in their constant quarrels with the tribunes of the people, actually dared to strike them. Once, when a Claudius was about to celebrate a triumph without first obtaining the people's consent, his sister, a Vestal Virgin, mounted the chariot and rode with him all the way to the

Capitol, thus making it sacrilege for the tribunes of the people to halt the procession.

3. Tiberius was doubly a Claudius, his father having been descended from the original Tiberius Nero and his mother from Appius Pulcher, both of them sons of Appius Caecus.[4] His maternal grandfather had, however, been adopted into the Livian family. The Livii were originally plebeians, but had also achieved great distinction, winning eight consulships, two censorships, three triumphs, and the titles of dictator and master of the horse. Among the best known members of this family were Livius Salinator and the Drusi. Livius Salinator had been convicted of malpractices after his first consulship, yet was re-elected to a second term and even appointed censor – whereupon he set a mark of censure against the names of every single tribe, to register his disapproval of their fickleness. The first Drusus gained his cognomen by killing an enemy chieftain called Drausus in single combat, and it became hereditary. He is also said to have brought back from Gaul, where he was a governor of praetorian rank, the gold which his ancestors had paid to the Senones in ransom for captured Rome; this contradicts the tradition that the treasure had already been redeemed by the dictator Camillus.[5] His great-great-grandson, known as 'the Senate's patron' because of his stalwart opposition to the reforms of the Gracchi, left a son who was treacherously murdered by his opponents while pursuing a complex policy in similar circumstances.[6]

4. Tiberius' father Nero as a quaestor commanded Julius Caesar's fleet during the Alexandrian war and contributed a great deal to his eventual victory. Caesar showed his appreciation by making him a pontifex in place of Publius Scipio, and sent him to plant colonies in Gaul, including those of Narbo and Arelate. Yet at Caesar's death, when, to prevent further rioting, all the other senators voted for an amnesty, Nero moved that rewards should be conferred on the assassins. Later he was elected praetor; but when towards the end of his term the triumvirs quarrelled among themselves, he retained the emblems of office longer than was his legal right and followed Mark Antony's brother Lucius, then consul, to Perusia. When

Perusia fell, only Nero scorned to capitulate. He stood loyally by his convictions, and escaped to Praeneste, thence to Neapolis, and after a vain attempt at enlisting a force of slaves with a promise of freedom he took refuge in Sicily. There Sextus Pompey was slow to grant him an audience and refused to allow him the use of the fasces. Taking offence, Nero crossed over to Achaia, where he joined Mark Antony. On the conclusion of peace he presently returned in Antony's train to Rome, and with him came his wife Livia Drusilla, who had borne him one son and was pregnant with another. Yet when Augustus wanted to marry Livia, Nero surrendered her to him, and died soon afterwards. The elder son was named Tiberius Nero, the younger, Drusus.[7]

5. Some believe that Tiberius was born at Fundi, but their only evidence is that his maternal grandmother originated there, and that a statue of Prosperity has since been set up in the town by senatorial decree. The bulk of trustworthy opinion makes him born on the Palatine in the course of the civil war which was to be decided at Philippi, the date being given as 16 November, and the consuls as Marcus Aemilius Lepidus (his second term) and Lucius Munatius Plancus.[8] This is what is reported in the calendar and the public records, yet some writers still insist that he was born in the previous year, during the consulship of Hirtius and Pansa, or in the following year, during that of Servilius Isauricus and Lucius Antonius.

6. His childhood and youth were beset with hardships and difficulties, since his parents took him wherever they went in their flight. When the enemy broke into the city of Neapolis and the couple secretly slipped down to the port, their companions tried to assist them by snatching little Tiberius first from his nurse's breast and then from Livia's arms – but he bawled out so loud that he nearly betrayed the whole party. He was next hurried all over Sicily, where Sextus Pompey's sister Pompeia gave him a cloak, a brooch and some gold charms; these are still on show at Baiae. His parents finally fled to Achaia, and entrusted him to the public care of the Spartans, who happened to be under the patronage of the Claudii. He then had a narrow escape: while the party were departing from

Sparta by night, they ran into a sudden forest fire which so surrounded them that it scorched Livia's hair and part of her robe. On their return to Rome, a senator named Marcus Gallius made a will adopting Tiberius; he accepted the inheritance, but soon dropped the name, Gallius having been one of Augustus' political opponents.[9]

At the age of nine Tiberius mounted on the Rostra to deliver his father's funeral eulogy, and four or five years later he took part in Augustus' triumph after Actium, mounted on the left trace horse of his chariot, while Marcellus, Octavia's son, rode the right. He also presided at the city games and led the detachment of older boys in the Troy Game at the Circus.

7. The principal events between Tiberius' coming of age and his accession to the throne may be summarized as follows. He staged a gladiatorial contest in memory of his father, and another in memory of his grandfather Drusus. The first took place in the Forum, the second in the amphitheatre, and he persuaded some retired gladiators to appear with the rest, by paying them 100,000 sesterces each. There were theatrical performances too, but Tiberius did not attend them; Livia and Augustus financed these lavish entertainments.

Tiberius married Vipsania Agrippina, daughter of Marcus Agrippa and granddaughter of Caecilius Atticus,[10] the Roman *eques* to whom Cicero addressed many of his letters. It proved a happy marriage; but when Vipsania had already borne him a son, Drusus, and was pregnant again, he was required to divorce her and hurriedly marry Augustus' daughter Julia. Tiberius took this very ill. He loved Vipsania and strongly disapproved of Julia, realizing like everyone else that she had felt a passion for him while still married to her previous husband. Tiberius continued to regret the divorce so heartily that, when he one day accidentally caught sight of Vipsania and followed her with tears in his eyes and intense unhappiness written on his face, precautions were taken against his ever seeing her again. At first he lived on good terms with Julia and dutifully reciprocated her love, but gradually he conceived such a loathing for her that, after their child had died in infancy at Aquileia, he broke off marital relations. On the death in Germany of his brother

Drusus, Tiberius brought the body back to Rome, walking in front of the coffin all the way.

8. Tiberius' civil career began with his defence, against various charges, of King Archelaus, the Trallians and the Thessalians, at a court presided over by Augustus. Next he appeared before the Senate as advocate of the Laodiceans, Thyatirans and Chians who had appealed for relief because of losses incurred in an earthquake. When Fannius Caepio plotted against Augustus with Varro Murena, Tiberius acted as prosecutor and secured their condemnation on a charge of treason. Meanwhile he had undertaken two special commissions: to reorganize the defective grain supply and to inquire into the state of slave barracks throughout Italy – the owners having made a bad name for themselves by confining lawful travellers in them, and by harbouring men who would rather pass as slaves than be drafted for military service.

9. He first saw military service in the Cantabrian campaign, as a military tribune; next he took an army to the east, where he restored the kingdom of Armenia to Tigranes, personally crowning him in front of his tribunal; then he proceeded to collect the standards which the Parthians had captured from Marcus Crassus.[11] After this Tiberius governed Transalpine Gaul, where barbarian raids and feuds between the chieftains had caused considerable unrest. After that he fought consecutively in the Alps, Pannonia and Germany. The first of these campaigns brought about the subjugation of the Raeti and Vindelici; the second that of the Breuci and Dalmatae; and in the third he took some 40,000 German prisoners, whom he brought across the Rhine and settled in new homes on the Gallic bank. Tiberius' exploits were rewarded with an ovation, followed by a regular triumph, and it seems that what was then a novel honour had previously been conferred on him, namely triumphal decorations. He became in turn quaestor, praetor and consul, and always before he was old enough to qualify officially as a candidate. A few years later he held another consulship, and was given the tribunician power for a five-year period.

10. Yet, though in the prime of life, in excellent health, and

at the height of his career, Tiberius suddenly decided to retire
as completely as possible from public affairs. His motive may
have been an inveterate dislike of Julia, whom he dared not
charge with adultery or divorce but could no longer endure, or
it may have been a decision not to bore his fellow countrymen
by remaining too long in the public eye – perhaps he even hoped
to increase his reputation by a prolonged absence, so that the
need of his services might at some point be felt. Another view
is that, since Augustus' children Gaius and Lucius had recently
come of age, Tiberius voluntarily resigned his established position as second man in the empire and left the political field
open for them; Marcus Agrippa had done much the same when
Marcellus began his official career – retiring to Mytilene so as
not to overshadow Marcellus by his great reputation or be
mistaken for a rival. This was, in fact, the reason which Tiberius
afterwards gave. At the time, however, he applied for leave of
absence merely on the ground that he was weary of office and
needed a rest; nor would he consider either Livia's express pleas
for him to stay or Augustus' open complaints in the Senate that
this was an act of desertion. On the contrary, he defeated their
vigorous efforts to blunt his resolution by a four days' hunger
strike. In the end he sailed off; leaving his wife and son behind
at Rome, he hurried down to Ostia without saying a word to
any of the friends who came to say goodbye, and kissing only
very few of them before he went aboard his ship.

11. As Tiberius coasted past Campania, news reached him
that Augustus was ill; so he cast anchor for a while. But when
tongues began to wag, accusing him of standing by in the hope
of seizing power, he at once made the best of his way to Rhodes,
though the wind was almost dead against him; he had cherished
pleasant memories of that beautiful and healthy island since
touching there during his return voyage from Armenia. Contenting himself with a modest town house and a nearby country
villa, which was not on a grand scale either, he behaved most
unassumingly: after dismissing his lictors and runners he would
often stroll about the gymnasium, where he greeted and chatted
with ordinary Greeks almost as if they were his social equals.

It happened once that, in arranging the next day's pro-

gramme, he had expressed a wish to visit the local sick. His
staff misunderstood him. Orders went out that all the patients
in town should be carried to a public colonnade and there
arranged in separate groups according to their ailments.
Tiberius was shocked; for a while he stood at a loss, but at last
he went to see the poor fellows, apologizing even to the
humblest and least important for the inconvenience he had
caused them. He exercised his tribunician power on a single
recorded occasion only. It should be explained that he constantly
attended the schools and halls where professors lectured, and
listened to the ensuing discussions. Once, when two sophists had
started a violent argument, an impudent member of the audience dared abuse him for joining in and appearing to support
one sophist at the expense of the other. Tiberius slowly retired
to his house, from which he all at once reappeared with a group
of lictors; then, instructing a herald to summon the scurrilous
wretch before his tribunal, he ordered him off to jail.

Soon afterwards, Tiberius learned that Julia had been
banished for immoral and adulterous behaviour, and that his
name had been used by Augustus on the bill of divorce sent
her. The news delighted him, but he felt obliged to send a
stream of letters urging a reconciliation between Augustus and
her, and, though well aware that Julia deserved all she got, he
allowed her to keep whatever presents she had at any time
received from him. When the term of his tribunician power
expired he asked Augustus' leave to return and visit his family,
whom he greatly missed, and confessed at last that he had
settled in Rhodes only because he wished to avoid the suspicion
of rivalry with Gaius and Lucius. Now that both were fully
grown and the acknowledged heirs, he explained, his reasons
for keeping away from Rome were no longer valid. Augustus,
however, turned down the plea, telling him to abandon all
concern for his family, whom he had been so eager to desert.

12. Thus Tiberius remained, most unwillingly, in Rhodes,
and could hardly persuade Livia to wheedle him the title of
legate from Augustus, as an official cloak for his disfavour. His
days were now clouded with anxiety. Although he lived a quiet
private life in the country, avoiding contact with all important

men who landed, unwelcome attentions continued to be paid him, because no general or magistrate sailing anywhere in the vicinity ever failed to break his journey at Rhodes. The anxiety was well founded. When Tiberius had visited Samos to greet his stepson Gaius, commander of the east, the slanders spread by Marcus Lollius, Gaius' guardian, ensured him a chilly welcome. Again, some centurions of Tiberius' creation, who had returned to camp from leave, were said to have circulated mysterious messages, apparently incitements to treason, emanating from him. When Augustus informed Tiberius of this suspicion, he answered with reiterated demands that some responsible person, of whatever rank, should be detailed to visit Rhodes and there keep unceasing watch on what he did and said.

13. Tiberius discontinued his usual exercise on horseback and with weapons, wore a Greek cloak and slippers instead of the Roman dress suitable to a man of his standing, and for two years or longer grew daily more despised and shunned – until the people of Nemausus were encouraged to overturn his statues and busts. One day, at a private dinner party attended by Gaius, Tiberius' name cropped up, and a guest rose to say that if Gaius gave the order he would sail straight to Rhodes and 'fetch back the Exile's head' – for he had come to be known simply as 'the Exile'. This incident brought home to Tiberius the extreme danger of his situation, and he pleaded most urgently for a recall to Rome; Livia supported him with equal warmth, and Augustus at last gave way. But this was partly due to a fortunate chance: Augustus had left the final decision on Tiberius' case to Gaius, who happened at the time to be on rather bad terms with Lollius and was therefore amenable to his stepfather's pleas. With Gaius' permission, then, Tiberius was recalled, although on condition that he take no part and renounce all interest in public affairs.

14. So Tiberius returned to Rome after an absence of more than seven years, with a great unshaken belief in a glorious future that certain presages and prophecies had fixed in his mind since early childhood. Just before his birth, for instance, Livia had tried various means of foretelling whether her child would be male or female; one was to take an egg from under-

neath a brooding hen and warm it alternately in her own hands and in those of her women – and she successfully hatched a cock chick which already had a fine comb. Also, while Tiberius was a mere infant, Scribonius the astrologer prophesied for him an illustrious career and a crownless kingship – though, of course, nobody in those days knew that the Caesars would soon become kings in all but name. Again, when he first commanded an army and was marching through Macedonia into Syria, the altars consecrated by the victorious legions at Philippi were suddenly crowned with spontaneous fires. Later, on his way to Illyricum, he stopped near Patavium to visit Geryon's oracle; there he drew a lot which advised him to throw golden dice into the fountain of Aponus, if he wished his enquiries to be answered. He did so, and made the highest possible cast; one can still see the same dice shining through the water. Finally, a few days before the letter arrived recalling him from Rhodes, an eagle – a bird never previously seen in the island – perched upon the roof of his house, and on the very eve of this welcome news the tunic into which he was changing seemed to be ablaze. When the ship hove in sight, Tiberius happened to be strolling along the cliffs with Thrasyllus the astrologer, whom he had made a member of his household on account of his learning. Now Tiberius was losing faith in Thrasyllus' powers of divination and regretted having rashly confided secrets to him, for, despite his rosy predictions, everything seemed to be going wrong. Thrasyllus was, indeed, in immediate danger of being pushed over the cliff when he pointed out to sea and announced that the distant ship brought good news – a lucky stroke which persuaded Tiberius of his trustworthiness.

15. On his return to Rome, Tiberius introduced his son Drusus to public life, but immediately afterwards moved from Pompey's house in the Carinae to another residence in the Gardens of Maecenas, also on the Esquiline Hill, where he lived in strict retirement, attending only to his private affairs and taking no part in public life. Before three years had passed, however, Gaius and Lucius were both dead; Augustus then adopted Tiberius as a son, along with Agrippa Postumus, their only surviving brother; and Tiberius was himself obliged to

adopt his nephew Germanicus. He thereupon ceased to act as the head of a household, surrendering all the privileges which this position entailed; he made no more gifts, freed no more slaves, and even refunded all inheritances and legacies which could not be entered in his *peculium*.[12] From that time on Augustus did everything possible to advance Tiberius' reputation, especially after having to disown Agrippa Postumus, for that made it pretty clear who his heir must be.

16. Tiberius was given another five years of tribunician power, with the task of pacifying Germany, and the Parthian envoys who visited Augustus at Rome with messages from their king were instructed to present themselves before Tiberius too, in Germany. There followed the Illyrian revolt, which he was sent to suppress, and which proved to be the most bitterly fought of all foreign wars since Rome had defeated Carthage. Tiberius conducted it for three years at the head of fifteen regular legions and a correspondingly large force of auxiliaries. Supplies were always short, and conditions arduous, but, though often called back to Rome, he never allowed the powerful and active enemy forces to assume the offensive. Tiberius was well paid for his stubbornness by finally reducing the whole of Illyricum – an enormous stretch of country enclosed by Italy, Noricum, the Danube, Thrace, Macedonia and the Adriatic Sea – to complete submission.

17. This feat appeared in a still more glorious light when Quinctilius Varus fell in Germany with his three legions: but for the timely conquest of Illyricum, most people realized, the victorious Germans would have made common cause with the Pannonians. Tiberius was therefore voted a triumph and many other distinctions. Proposals were made for decreeing him the cognomen Pannonicus or Invictus or Pius, but Augustus vetoed all these in turn, promising on each occasion that Tiberius would be satisfied with the one he would acquire after he himself had died.[13] Tiberius himself postponed his triumph because of the public mourning for Varus, but nevertheless entered Rome dressed in a senatorial toga and wreathed with laurel. A tribunal had been built in the Saepta; on it were four curule chairs, behind which the Senate stood, ranged in a

semicircle. Tiberius mounted the steps and took his seat at Augustus' side, the two outer chairs being occupied by the consuls. From this place of honour he acknowledged the popular cheers, and was then escorted around the appropriate temples.

18. In the following year Tiberius visited Germany and, finding that the disaster there had been due to Varus' rashness and neglect of precautions against surprise, refrained from taking any strategic decisions without the assent of his general staff. This was a notable departure from habit; hitherto he had always had complete confidence in his own judgement, but he was now relying on a large military council. His attention to detail increased. At every crossing of the Rhine he strictly limited the amount of permissible baggage, and would not signal the advance unless he had first inspected every transport wagon, to make sure that none carried anything but necessities. Once across the river, he made it his practice to eat on the bare turf, to sleep in the open as often as not, and always to commit his daily and emergency orders to writing. Moreover, any officer who did not understand his instructions was required to consult him personally at any hour of the day or night.

19. Tiberius imposed the severest discipline on his men, reviving obsolete methods of punishment or branding them with ignominy for misbehaviour. He even officially censured a legionary commander because he had sent a few soldiers across the river as escort for one of his freedmen who was hunting there. Although leaving so little to chance, Tiberius would enter a battle with far greater confidence if, on the previous night, the lamp by which he was working went out inexplicably all of a sudden: he used to say that he and his ancestors had always found this a reliable omen of good luck while on campaign. At the conclusion of this campaign a Bructeran assassin gained admittance to headquarters, disguised as an attendant, but betrayed himself by nervousness and confessed under torture.

20. Two years after going to Germany, Tiberius returned and celebrated the postponed Illyrian triumph; with him went those generals whom he had recommended for triumphal decorations. Before proceeding up the Capitoline Hill, he descended

from his chariot and knelt at the feet of his adoptive father, who was presiding over the ceremonies. Tiberius showed gratitude to the Pannonian leader Bato, who had allowed the Roman army to escape when trapped in a gorge, by giving him rich presents and a home at Ravenna. Then he provided a thousand-table public banquet and gave 300 sesterces to every male guest. The money fetched by the sale of his spoils went to restore the Temple of Concord and that of Castor and Pollux, both buildings being rededicated in his own name and that of his dead brother Drusus.

21. Soon afterwards the consuls introduced a measure which gave Tiberius joint control of the provinces with Augustus and the task of assisting him to carry out the next five-year census. When the usual purificatory sacrifices had completed the census, Tiberius set off for Illyricum, but was immediately recalled by Augustus, whom he found in the throes of his last illness. They spent a whole day together in confidential talk. I am well aware of the story that, when Tiberius finally took his departure, Augustus gasped to his attendants, 'Poor Rome, doomed to be ground by those slow-moving jaws!' I am also aware that, according to some writers, he so frankly disliked Tiberius' dour manner as to interrupt his own careless chatter whenever he entered; and that, when begged by Livia to adopt her son, he is suspected of having agreed the more readily because he foresaw that, with a successor like Tiberius, his death would be increasingly regretted as the years went by. Yet how could so prudent and far-sighted a leader have acted as blindly as this in a matter of such importance? My belief is that Augustus weighed Tiberius' good qualities against the bad, and decided that the good tipped the scale; he had, after all, publicly sworn that his adoption of Tiberius was in the public interest, and had often referred to him as an outstanding general and the only one capable of defending Rome against her enemies. In support of my contention let me quote the following passages from Augustus' correspondence:

Goodbye, my very dear Tiberius, and the best of luck go with you in your battles on my behalf – and the Muses! Goodbye, dearest and bravest of men and the most conscientious general alive! If anything goes wrong with you, I shall never smile again!

Your summer campaigns, dear Tiberius, deserve my heartiest praise; I am sure that no other man alive could have conducted them more capably than yourself in the face of so many difficulties and the war-weariness of the troops. All those who served with you agree with me that the well-known line should be amended in your favour, from 'Alone he saved us by his cautious ways'[14] to 'Alone he saved us by his watchful eye.'

If any business comes up that demands unusually careful thought, or that annoys me, I swear by the God of Truth that I miss my dear Tiberius more than I can say. And the Homeric verses run in my head: 'If he came with me, such his wisdom is, we should escape the fury of the fire.'[15]

When I hear or read that constant campaigning is wearing you out, damnation take me if I don't get gooseflesh in sympathy! I beg you to take things easy, because if you were to fall ill the news would kill your mother and me, and the whole empire of the Roman people would be in jeopardy.

My state of health is of little importance compared with yours. I pray that the gods will always keep you safe and sound for us, if they have not taken an utter aversion to the Roman people.

22. Tiberius revealed Augustus' death only after young Agrippa Postumus had been put to death. The military tribune appointed as his guard killed him, after receiving a written order to that effect. So much is known, but some doubt remains whether this order was left by Augustus at his death, in order to eliminate any pretext for a civil war, or whether Livia wrote it in his name, or, if so, whether Tiberius knew anything of the matter. At all events, when the tribune arrived to report that he had done his duty, Tiberius replied that he had given no such order and that the man would have to account for his actions to the Senate. He was, it seems, trying to avoid

immediate unpopularity, for he soon allowed the incident to be forgotten.

23. Tiberius used his tribunician power to convene the Senate and break the news of Augustus' death. After reading a few words of a prepared speech, he suddenly groaned aloud and, protesting that grief had robbed him of his voice and that he wished his life would also be taken, handed the scroll to his son Drusus, who finished the task. A freedman then read Augustus' will aloud, all senators present who had witnessed the document being first called upon to acknowledge their seals – witnesses of lower rank would do the same outside the Senate House. The preamble to the will ran as follows: 'Since fate has cruelly carried off my sons Gaius and Lucius, Tiberius Caesar is to inherit two-thirds of my property.' This wording strengthened the suspicion that Augustus had nominated Tiberius as his successor only for want of any better choice.

24. Tiberius did not hesitate to exercise power immediately by calling on the praetorians to provide him with a bodyguard, which was to rule in fact and in appearance. Yet a long time elapsed before he assumed the position of *princeps*. When his friends urged him to accept it, he went through the farce of scolding them for the suggestion, saying that they did not realize what a monstrous beast power was, and he kept the Senate guessing by his carefully evasive answers and hesitations, even when they threw themselves at his feet imploring him to change his mind. This made some of them lose patience, and in the confusion a voice was heard shouting, 'Oh, let him either take it or leave it.' And another senator openly taunted him with 'Some people are slow to do what they promise; you are slow to promise what you have already done.' Finally, with a great show of reluctance, and complaints that they were forcing him to become a miserable and overworked slave, Tiberius accepted the principate; but even then he hinted that he might later resign it. His actual words were 'until I grow so old that you may be good enough to grant me a respite'.

25. His hesitation was caused by threats of danger from many quarters, so that he often said, 'I'm holding a wolf by the ears.' A slave of Agrippa Postumus named Clemens had recruited a

fairly large force of his fellows, sworn to avenge their dead
master; Lucius Scribonius Libo, a nobleman, was secretly planning a revolt; and camp mutinies now broke out in Illyricum
and Germany.[16] Both bodies of mutineers demanded very large
concessions, particularly that they should be paid at the same
rate as the praetorians. The army in Germany also refused to
acknowledge a *princeps* whom they had not chosen themselves,
and did all they could to make their commander Germanicus
seize power, despite his flat refusal. A fear that they might
succeed was the main reason for Tiberius' plea to the Senate:
'Pray assign me any part in the government you please; but
remember that no single man can bear the whole burden of
empire – I need a colleague, or perhaps several colleagues.' He
then gave out that he was dangerously ill, so that Germanicus
would be more patient, expecting to succeed him shortly or at
least be given a share in the rule. However, both mutinies were
suppressed; Tiberius tricked Clemens into surrender, and in the
following year he convicted Libo before the Senate – though
hitherto he had merely kept on his guard, not feeling powerful
enough to take active measures against him. Thus, when Libo
took part in a pontifical sacrifice, Tiberius, who was with him,
had substituted a leaden knife for the sharp double-bladed steel
one which Libo would use, and he later refused his plea for a
private audience unless Drusus were present, and even then
pretended to need the support of Libo's arm as they walked up
and down together, and clung tightly to it.

26. These immediate anxieties past, Tiberius at first behaved
with great discretion and almost as modestly as if he had never
held public office. Of the many high honours voted him, he
accepted none but a few unimportant ones, and could hardly
be persuaded to let his birthday, which fell on a day of the
Plebeian Games,[17] be honoured by the addition of a two-horse
chariot race to those held in the Circus. He vetoed all bills for
the dedication of temples and priests to his divinity, and
reserved the right to sanction even the setting up of his statues
and busts – which were not to be placed among the images of
the gods, but only amid the temple decor. Proposals that all
citizens should swear to approve his past and future actions,

and that the months of September and October should be renamed respectively Tiberius and Livius (after his mother), met with his veto. He also declined to use Imperator as a praenomen or Father of His Country as a title, or to let the civic crown be fixed in his entry hall; and he even refrained from using the name Augustus, though his by right of inheritance, in any letters except those addressed to foreign monarchs. While *princeps*, he held no more than three consulships:[18] one for a few days, the next for three months, and the third – during his absence – until 15 May.

27. Such was his hatred of flatterers that he refused to let senators approach his litter, whether in greeting or on business; and one day, when a man of consular rank came to apologize for some fault and tried to embrace his knees in suppliant fashion, Tiberius retreated so hurriedly that he tumbled over backwards. And if anyone, either in conversation or in a speech, spoke of him in too fulsome terms, Tiberius would interrupt and sternly correct the phrase. Once, when addressed as 'My Lord', he gave warning that no such insult must ever again be thrown at him. Another man referred to 'your sacred occupations', and a third said that he had 'approached the Senate on Tiberius' authority'; Tiberius made them change these words to 'your laborious occupations' and 'on Tiberius' recommendation'.

28. He was, moreover, quite unperturbed by abuse, slander, or lampoons on himself and his family, and would often say that liberty to speak and think as one pleases is the test of a free country. When the Senate asked that those who had offended in this way should be brought to book, he replied, 'We cannot spare the time to undertake any such new enterprise. Open that window, and you will let in such a rush of denunciations as to waste your whole working day; everyone will take this opportunity of airing some private feud.' A remarkably modest statement of his is recorded in the *Proceedings of the Senate*: 'If so-and-so challenges me, I shall lay before you a careful account of what I have said and done; if that does not satisfy him, I shall reciprocate his dislike of me.'

29. Tiberius showed an almost excessive courtesy when addressing both individual senators and the Senate as a whole.

Once, on the floor of the Senate House, he found himself disagreeing with Quintus Haterius, and said, 'You will, I hope, forgive me if I trespass on my rights as a senator by speaking rather more plainly than I should.' Then he turned to the House, saying, 'Let me repeat, gentlemen of the Senate, that a right-minded and true-hearted *princeps*, who has had as much power placed in his hands as you have placed in mine, should regard himself as the servant of the Senate, and often of the people as a whole, and sometimes even of private citizens. I do not regret this view, because I have always found you to be generous, just and indulgent masters.'

30. He even gave the appearance of restoring popular liberties by seeing that the Senate and magistrates enjoyed their former dignity and authority. He referred all public business, however important or unimportant, to the senators, asking for advice in every matter that concerned the national revenue, the allocation of monopolies, and the construction or repair of public buildings; he even consulted them about the drafting or disbanding of troops, the stationing of legions and auxiliaries, the extension of military commands, the choice of generals to conduct particular campaigns, and how to answer letters from foreign rulers. When a cavalry commander was accused of robbery with violence, Tiberius ordered him to plead his case before the Senate. He always entered the Senate House unattended, except for one day when he was sick and carried in on a litter – and even then he dismissed his bearers immediately.

31. If decrees were passed in defiance of his wishes, he abstained from complaint – for example, when he had insisted that magistrates-elect should stay at home and attend to business, but the Senate allowed a praetor-elect to travel overseas with free use of official transport and lodging. And on expressing the opinion that a road could rightfully be made at Trebiae with a legacy bequeathed to the city for the building of a new theatre, he was overruled and the testator's intentions were respected. Once it happened that the Senate put a motion to the vote; Tiberius sided with the minority, and not a soul followed him. He left a great deal of public business to the magistrates and the ordinary processes of law; the consuls grew

so important again that an African embassy came before them, complaining that they could make no headway with Caesar, to whom they had been sent. Nor was this at all remarkable; everyone knew that he even stood up when the consuls appeared, and made way on meeting them in the streets.

32. Some generals of consular rank earned a rebuff by addressing their dispatches to Tiberius rather than the Senate and asking him to approve awards of military honours, as though they were not entitled to give these at their own discretion. He also congratulated a praetor who, when he assumed office, revived the ancient custom of publicly eulogizing his own ancestors, and he attended the funerals of important citizens to the extent of witnessing their cremation. Tiberius displayed a like moderation in dealing with men of lesser rank. He summoned to Rome the Rhodian magistrates who had sent him a public report without adding the usual complimentary formula of prayers for his health, yet did not reprimand them when they appeared; he merely instructed them to repair the omission and sent them home again. During his stay at Rhodes a *grammaticus* named Diogenes used to lecture every sabbath, and when Tiberius wanted to hear him some other day of the week he sent a slave out to say, 'Come back on the seventh day.' Diogenes now turned up at Rome and waited at his door to pay Tiberius his respects; Tiberius' only revenge was a mild message: 'Come back in the seventh year.' He answered some governors, who had written to recommend an increase in the burden of provincial taxation, with 'A good shepherd shears his flock; he does not flay them.'

33. Very gradually Tiberius showed that he was indeed *princeps*, and though at first his policy was not always consistent, he nevertheless took considerable pains to further the national interest. At first, too, he intervened only when things were not done properly, revoking certain orders published by the Senate, and sometimes offering to sit on the tribunal beside the magistrates, or at one end of the curved dais, in an advisory capacity. And if it came to his ears that influence was being used to acquit a criminal in some court or other, he would suddenly appear and address the jury either from the floor or

from the tribunal, asking them to remember the sanctity of the law and their oath to uphold it, and the serious nature of the crime on which their verdict was required. He also undertook to arrest any decline in public morality due to negligence or licence.

34. Tiberius cut down the expenses of public entertainments by lowering the pay of actors and setting a limit to the number of gladiatorial combats on any given occasion. Once he protested violently against an absurd rise in the cost of Corinthian vases and high-quality fish – three mullets had been offered for sale at 10,000 sesterces each! His proposal was that a ceiling should be imposed on the prices of household furnishings, and that market values should be annually regulated by the Senate. At the same time the aediles were to restrict the amount of food offered for sale in cookshops and eating houses, even banning bakery items. And, to set an example in his campaign against waste, he often served at formal dinner parties half-eaten dishes left over from the day before, or only one side of a wild boar – which, he said, contained everything that the other side did.

He issued an edict against promiscuous kissing, and likewise against the giving of good-luck gifts after the Kalends of January. On the receipt of such a gift he had formerly always returned one four times as valuable, and presented it personally; but he discontinued this practice when he found the whole of January becoming spoilt by a stream of gift-givers who had not been able to get an audience on the actual Kalends.

35. An ancient Roman custom revived by Tiberius was the punishment of married women guilty of improprieties by the decision of a family council, in cases when no one had brought a public prosecution. When a Roman *eques* had sworn that he would never divorce his wife whatever she did, but then found her in bed with their son-in-law, Tiberius absolved him from his oath. Married women of good family but bad reputation were beginning to declare themselves professional prostitutes, and so escape punishment for their adulteries by renouncing the privileges of their rank, and wastrels of both the senatorial and equestrian orders purposely got themselves reduced in status so as to evade the law forbidding their appearance on

the stage or in the arena. All such offenders were now exiled, which discouraged any similar sheltering behind the letter of the law. Tiberius demoted a senator on hearing that he had moved to his country estate right before the Kalends of July in order to rent a house in the city more cheaply later on. He cancelled the quaestorship of another man who had married a woman the day before he cast lots for a province, but divorced her the next day.

36. He abolished foreign cults at Rome, particularly the Egyptian and Jewish, forcing all those who had embraced these superstitions to burn their religious vestments and other accessories. Jews of military age were removed to unhealthy regions on the pretext of drafting them into the army; those too old or too young to serve – including non-Jews who had adopted similar practices – were expelled from the city and threatened with slavery if they defied the order. Tiberius also banished all astrologers except such as asked for his forgiveness and undertook to abandon that art.

37. Tiberius safeguarded the country against banditry and local revolts by decreasing the distance between military posts, and at Rome he provided the praetorian guards, who had hitherto been billeted in scattered lodging houses, with regular barracks and a fortified camp. He also discountenanced city riots, and if any broke out, he crushed them without mercy. The theatre audience had formed factions in support of rival actors, and once when their quarrels ended in bloodshed Tiberius exiled not only the faction leaders but the actors who had been the occasion of the riot; nor would he ever give way to popular entreaties by recalling them. Trouble occurred in Pollentia, where the townsfolk would not let the corpse of a leading centurion be removed from the marketplace until they had extorted money from his heirs for a gladiatorial show. Tiberius detached one cohort from Rome and another from the Cottian Alps to converge on Pollentia, after disguising their destination. They had orders to enter the town simultaneously by opposite gates, suddenly display their weapons, blow trumpets, and arrest most of the people and the magistrates – whom he then sentenced to life imprisonment.

He also abolished the right of sanctuary in temples and holy places, which criminals enjoyed throughout the empire, and punished the people of Cyzicus for their outrageous treatment of certain Roman citizens by withdrawing the right to self-governance conferred on them as a reward for services in the Mithridatic war. Immediately after his accession he delegated the task of dealing with frontier incidents to his legates, but sanctioned aggressive action only if it seemed unavoidable. He disciplined foreign kings suspected of ill will towards Rome by threats and reprimands rather than punitive expeditions, and decoyed some of them with glowing promises to Rome – where they were detained at his pleasure. Among them were Maroboduus the German, Rhascuporis the Thracian and Archelaus the Cappadocian, whose kingdom he reduced to provincial status.

38. In the first two years of his reign Tiberius did not once set foot outside the gates of Rome; after that he went only to nearby towns, no further than Antium, and even that very occasionally and for just a few days. Yet he often announced that he would make a tour of the provinces and inspect the troops there, and almost every year he made preparations for his departure, chartering transport and arranging for provisions in the towns and colonies. At last he even allowed people to make vows for his safe return from the promised tour, which earned him the nickname of 'Callipides' – from the character in the Greek proverb who keeps running without advancing a single foot.

39. After the loss of his son Drusus at Rome and his adopted son Germanicus in Syria, Tiberius retired to Campania – from which almost everyone swore he would not return, but would soon die there. This prediction was not far out, because Rome had in fact seen the last of him, and he narrowly escaped death a few days later. He was dining at a country house called The Cavern, near Tarracina, when some huge rocks fell from the roof and killed several guests and attendants close to him; he miraculously survived.

40. His pretext for the progress through Campania was that he must dedicate a temple to Jupiter Capitolinus at Capua and

a temple to Augustus at Nola. But, these tasks done, he crossed over to the isle of Capreae, which fascinated him by having only one small landing beach – the remainder of its coast consisted of sheer cliffs surrounded by deep water. However, a catastrophe at Fidenae recalled him to the mainland almost at once: the amphitheatre had collapsed during a gladiatorial show, and more than 20,000 people lay dead in the ruins. Tiberius now gave audiences to everyone who demanded them, and was the readier to be gracious because he had given orders on leaving the city some days previously that he must not be disturbed throughout his journey.

41. On his return to Capreae he let all affairs of state slide, neither filling vacancies that occurred in the equestrian order, nor appointing new military tribunes and cavalry officers, nor sending out new provincial governors; Spain and Syria were left without legates of consular rank for several years. He allowed the Parthians to overrun Armenia, the Dacians and Sarmatians to ravage Moesia, and the Germans to invade Gaul – a negligence as dangerous to the empire as it was dishonourable.

42. But having found seclusion at last, and no longer feeling himself under public scrutiny, he rapidly succumbed to all the vicious passions which he had for a long time tried, not very successfully, to disguise. I shall give a faithful account of these from the start. Even as a young officer he was such a hard drinker that his name, Tiberius Claudius Nero, was displaced by the nickname 'Biberius Caldius Mero'.[19] When already *princeps* and busily engaged on the reform of public morals, he spent two whole days and the intervening night in an orgy of food and drink with Pomponius Flaccus and Lucius Piso – at the conclusion of which he made Flaccus the governor of Syria and Piso the prefect of the city – actually eulogizing them in their commissions as 'excellent fellows at all hours of the day or night'. Being invited to dinner by Cestius Gallus, a lecherous old spendthrift whom Augustus had ignominiously removed from the Senate and whom he had himself reprimanded for his ill living only a few days previously, Tiberius accepted on condition that the dinner should follow Gallus' usual routine, and that the serving girls should be naked. At another banquet

a very obscure candidate for the quaestorship drained an amphora of wine at Tiberius' challenge, whereupon he was preferred to rival candidates from the noblest families. Tiberius also paid Asellius Sabinus 200,000 sesterces to show his appreciation of a dialogue in which a mushroom, a fig-pecker, an oyster and a thrush competed for a culinary prize; and he established a new office, Comptroller of Pleasures, first held by an *eques* named Titus Caesonius Priscus.

43. On retiring to Capreae he made himself a private play-house, where sexual extravagances were practised for his secret pleasure. Bevies of girls and toy boys, whom he had collected from all over as adepts in unnatural practices and who were known as *spintriae*, would perform before him in groups of three to excite his waning passions. A number of small rooms were furnished with the most indecent pictures and statuary obtainable, as well as the erotic manuals of Elephantis; the inmates of the establishment would know from these exactly what was expected of them. He furthermore devised little nooks of lechery in the woods and glades of the island, and had boys and girls dressed up as Pans and nymphs posted in front of caverns or grottoes, so that the island was now openly and generally called 'Caprineum'.[20]

44. Some aspects of his criminal obscenity are almost too vile to discuss, much less believe. Imagine training little boys, whom he called his 'minnows', to chase him while he went swimming and get between his legs to lick and nibble him. Or letting babies not yet weaned from their mother's breast suck at his groin instead – such a filthy old man he had become! Then there was a painting by Parrhasius, which had been bequeathed him on condition that, if he did not like the subject, he could have 1 million sesterces instead. Tiberius not only preferred to keep the picture but hung it in his bedroom; it showed Atalanta satisfying Meleager[21] with her mouth. The story goes that once, while sacrificing, he took an erotic fancy to the attendant who carried the incense casket, and could hardly wait for the cere-mony to end before hurrying away him and his brother, the pipe player, and raping them both. When they protested at this dastardly crime he had their legs broken.

45. What nasty tricks he used to play on women, even those of high rank, is clearly seen in the case of a certain Mallonia whom he summoned to his bed. She showed such an invincible repugnance to complying with his aged lusts that he set informers on her track and during her very trial continued to shout, 'Are you sorry?' Finally she left the court and went home; there she stabbed herself to death after a violent tirade against 'that filthy-mouthed, hairy, stinking old beast'. So a joke at his expense, slipped into the next Atellan farce, won a loud laugh and went the rounds at once:

> The old goat goes
> For the does
> With his tongue.

46. Tiberius was close-fisted to the point of miserliness, never paying his staff a salary when on a foreign mission, but merely providing their keep. On the sole occasion that he behaved liberally to these friends of his, Augustus bore the expense. Tiberius then arranged them in three categories according to their rank; the first were given 600,000 sesterces, the second 400,000 sesterces, and the third, whom he described not as 'friends' but as 'Greeks', 200,000.

47. As *princeps*, he was responsible for no magnificent public works: his only two undertakings, the erection of Augustus' Temple and the restoration of Pompey's Theatre, still remained uncompleted at the end of all those years. He gave no public shows at all, and hardly ever attended those given by others, because he did not want to be asked for anything – especially after the crowd forced him, on one of his rare visits to the theatre, to buy the freedom of a slave comedian named Actius. Though relieving the financial distress of a few senators, he avoided having to repeat this generous act by announcing that in future imperial assistance would be restricted to such persons as could prove to the satisfaction of the Senate that they were not responsible for their financial embarrassment. Shame and pride then prevented many impoverished senators from making an application; among these was Hortalus, grandson of the

orator Quintus Hortensius, whose income was very moderate
indeed but whom Augustus' pleas had encouraged to beget four
children.

48. Tiberius showed large-scale generosity no more than
twice. On the first occasion he offered a public loan of 100
million sesterces, free of interest, for three years, because a
decree which he had persuaded the Senate to pass – ordering all
moneylenders to invest two-thirds of their capital in agricultural
land, provided that their debtors at once disbursed in cash
two-thirds of what they owed – failed to relieve the acute
economic crisis. On the second occasion, he paid for the
rebuilding of certain blocks of houses on the Caelian Hill which
had been destroyed in a fire. This too was an emergency measure
during bad times, yet he made such a parade of his open-
handedness as to rename the whole hill the 'Augustan'. After
doubling the legacies bequeathed by Augustus to the army,
Tiberius never gave them anything beyond their pay, except for
the 1,000 denarii a head which the praetorian guard won for
not aligning themselves with Sejanus and some gifts awarded the
legions in Syria for being the only ones not to have set consecrated
statues of Sejanus among their regimental standards. He granted
few veterans their discharge, reckoning that if they died while
serving he would be spared the expense of the discharge bounty.
The only free money grant any province got from him was
when an earthquake destroyed some cities in Asia.

49. As the years went by, this stinginess turned to rapacity.
It is notorious that he forced the fabulously wealthy Gnaeus
Lentulus Augur to name him as his sole heir and then to commit
suicide, by playing on his nervous apprehensions; and that
he gratified Quirinius, an extremely rich and childless former
consul, by executing the noble Aemilia Lepida – he had divorced
her after twenty years of marriage and accused her of having
once attempted to poison him. Tiberius also confiscated the
property of leading Spanish, Gallic, Syrian and Greek provincials on trivial and absurd charges, such as keeping too much of
their wealth in ready cash. He made many states and individuals
forfeit their ancient immunities and mineral rights, and the
privilege of collecting taxes. As for Vonones, the king of Parthia,

whom his subjects had dethroned but who, under the impression that he was confiding himself to Roman protection, escaped to Antioch with a huge treasure, Tiberius treacherously robbed and killed him.

50. Tiberius' first hostile action against his own family was when his brother Drusus wrote to him privately suggesting that they should jointly compel Augustus to restore the republican constitution; Tiberius placed the letter in Augustus' hands. This set the pattern for later behaviour. He showed so little pity for his exiled wife Julia that he did not have the decency to confirm Augustus' decree which merely confined her to a single town, but restricted her to a single house where visitors were forbidden. He even deprived her of the annual sums hitherto paid her by Augustus, on the pretext that no mention of these had appeared in his will and that consequently under common law she was no longer entitled to draw them. Tiberius complained that his mother Livia vexed him by wanting to be his co-ruler; he avoided frequent meetings or long private talks with her so that he would not appear to be directed by her advice, which all the same he occasionally both needed and followed. A senatorial proposal adding 'Son of Livia' as well as 'Son of Augustus' to his honorifics so deeply offended him that he vetoed proposals to confer on her the title Mother of Her Country or any notable public honour. What is more, he often warned Livia to remember that she was a woman and must not interfere in affairs of state. He became especially insistent on this point when a fire broke out near the Temple of Vesta and news reached him that Livia was directing the civilian and military firefighters in person, as she had frequently done when Augustus was still alive, and urging them to redouble their efforts.

51. Afterwards Tiberius quarrelled openly with his mother. The story goes that she repeatedly urged him to enrol in the jurors' list the name of a man who had been granted citizenship. Tiberius agreed to do so on one condition – that the entry should be marked 'forced upon him by his mother'. Livia lost her temper and produced from a strongbox some of Augustus' old letters to her commenting on Tiberius' sour and stubborn character. Annoyance with her for hoarding these documents

so long and then spitefully confronting him with them is said
by some to have been his main reason for retirement to Capreae.
At all events he visited her exactly once in the last three years
of her life, and only for an hour or two at that, and when she
eventually fell sick he made no effort to repeat the visit. Livia
then died, and he spoke of attending her funeral, but did not
come. After several days her corpse grew so corrupt and noi-
some that he sent to have it buried, but vetoed her deification
on the pretext that she had herself forbidden this. He also
annulled her will, and began taking his revenge on all her
friends and confidants – even those whom, as she died, she had
appointed to take charge of her funeral rites – and went so far
as to condemn one of them, an *eques*, to the treadmill.

52. Tiberius had no paternal feelings either for his natural
son Drusus, whose vicious and dissolute habits offended him,
or for his adopted son Germanicus. When Drusus died, Tiberius
appeared to be perfectly unconcerned, and went back to his
usual business almost as soon as the funeral ended, cutting
short the period of official mourning; in fact when a Trojan
delegation arrived with condolences, a month or two later,
Tiberius grinned, having apparently got over his loss, and
replied, 'May I condole with you, in return, on the death of your
eminent fellow citizen Hector?'[22] He described Germanicus'
glorious victories as wholly ineffective and even harmful for
the commonwealth, so little affection did he feel for him. He
actually sent the Senate a letter of complaint when Germanicus,
without consulting him, hurried to Alexandria on account of a
sudden disastrous famine.[23] It is even believed that he arranged
for Gnaeus Piso, the governor of Syria, to poison Germanicus,
and that Piso, when tried on this charge, would have produced
his instructions had they not been taken from him. This is why
'Give us back Germanicus!' was written on the walls throughout Rome and shouted all night. Tiberius later strengthened
popular suspicion by his cruel treatment of Germanicus' wife
Agrippina and her children.

53. When Agrippina, after her husband's death, protested a
little too boldly, Tiberius took her by the hand, quoting the
Greek line 'And if you are not queen, my dear, have I then

done you wrong?'; and this was the last time that he ever condescended to address her. Indeed, since she seemed scared of tasting an apple which he handed her at dinner, the invitation to his table was never repeated; he said that she had charged him with attempted poisoning. Yet the whole scene had been carefully stage-managed: he would offer the apple as a test of her feelings for him, and she would suspect that it carried sudden death and refuse it. At last he falsely accused her of planning to take sanctuary beside the image of her grandfather Augustus or with the army abroad, and exiled her to Pandataria. In punishment for her violent protests he ordered a centurion to give her a good flogging, in the course of which she lost an eye. Then she decided to starve herself to death and, though he had her jaws prised open for forcible feeding, eventually succeeded. So he wickedly slandered her memory, persuading the Senate to decree her birthday a day of ill omen, and boasting of his clemency in not having her strangled and thrown out on the Gemonian Stairs. He even allowed a decree to be passed congratulating him on this pious attitude and voting a golden commemorative gift to Jupiter Capitolinus.

54. Through Germanicus, Tiberius had three adoptive grandsons named Nero, Drusus and Gaius, and through Drusus a natural grandson named Tiberius. After the deaths of Germanicus and Drusus, he recommended Nero and Drusus, the eldest of these, to the Senate, and celebrated their coming-of-age ceremonies by giving the people largesse. But when he found that, at the celebrations for the new year, prayers for their safety were being added to his own, he asked the Senate to decide whether this was a proper procedure, suggesting that such honours should be conferred only on men who had served their country long and meritoriously. His dislike for the young pair having thus been revealed, he rendered them liable to all sorts of accusations: people manipulated them into making abusive complaints and then reported their behaviour in detail. This gave him grounds for writing the Senate so harsh a letter of complaint that both were declared public enemies and put to death – Nero on the island of Pontia, Drusus in a cellar of the Palatine. It is believed that Nero was forced to commit suicide when an executioner,

announcing that he had come with the Senate's warrant, displayed the noose for hanging him and the hooks for dragging his corpse to the Tiber. Drusus, they say, was deprived of food, and was so starved that he tried to eat the stuffing from his mattress; the bodies of both were chopped into so many pieces that they could hardly be collected for burial.

55. To serve as advisers on public issues, in addition to his old friends and associates, Tiberius had asked the Senate to choose twenty of their most prominent members. Of these, barely two or three survived unscathed. All the rest he killed, one way or another, including Aelius Sejanus, who dragged many others to ruin with him. Tiberius felt no affection for Sejanus, but had given him plenary powers as being efficient and cunning enough to do what was required of him – namely to make away with Germanicus' children and ensure that Tiberius' own grandson through Drusus should succeed him in the empire.

56. He acted no less cruelly towards his Greek companions, with whom he most preferred to relax. One day he asked a man named Zeno, who had been discoursing in a rather affected style, 'What damned dialect may that be?' 'It is Doric,' replied Zeno. Tiberius mistook this for a taunting reference to his exile at Rhodes, where Doric is spoken, and banished Zeno to Artichoke Island. At the dinner table he used to pose questions arising from his daily study. The *grammaticus* Seleucus had been finding out from the imperial servants what books he was reading, and was coming prepared with all the answers; hearing of this, Tiberius dismissed him from his company, and later forced him to commit suicide.

57. Some signs of Tiberius' savage and dour character could be distinguished even in his boyhood. Theodorus of Gadara, who taught him rhetoric, seems to have been the first to do so, since, on having occasion to reprove Tiberius, he would call him 'mud, kneaded with blood'. But after he became *princeps*, even when he was still gaining popular favour by a pretence of moderation, there could be no doubt that Theodorus had been right. Once, as a funeral procession was passing, a wit hailed the corpse and asked him to tell Augustus' ghost that his bequests to the people had not yet been duly paid. Tiberius ordered the

man to be arrested and brought before him. 'I will give you your due at once', he said, and ordered his execution, saying, 'Why not go to my father yourself and tell him the truth about those legacies?' Soon afterwards a Roman *eques* named Pompey appeared in the Senate to lodge a strong protest. Tiberius threatened imprisonment, shouting 'You're Pompey, aren't you? I'll make you a Pompeian!' – a harsh pun on the man's name and the fate of Pompey the Great's supporters.

58. About this time a praetor asked Tiberius whether, in his opinion, courts should be convened to try cases of *maiestas*. Tiberius replied that the law must be enforced; and enforce it he did – most savagely too. One man was accused of decapitating an image of Augustus with a view to substituting another head; his case was tried before the Senate and, finding a conflict of evidence, Tiberius had the witnesses examined under torture. The offender was sentenced to death, which provided a precedent for increasingly far-fetched accusations: people could now be executed for beating a slave or changing their clothes close to a statue of Augustus, or for carrying a ring or coin bearing Augustus' image into a privy or a brothel, or for criticizing anything Augustus had ever said or done. The climax came when a man died merely for letting an honour be voted him by his town council on the same day that honours had once been voted to Augustus.

59. Tiberius did so many other wicked deeds under the pretext of reforming public morals – but in reality to gratify his lust for seeing people suffer – that many satires were written against the evils of the day, and expressing gloomy fears about the future:

> You cruel monster! I'll be damned, I will,
> If even your own mother loves you still.

> *

> You are no knight – Caesar's adopted son
> May own no cash to qualify as one;
> And banishment in Rhodes cancelled your right
> To be a citizen – far less a knight.

> *

> Saturn's golden age has passed,[24]
> Saturn's age could never last;
> Now while Caesar holds the stage
> This must be an iron age.
>
> *
>
> He is not thirsty for neat wine
>   As he was thirsty then,
> But warms him up a tastier cup,
>   The blood of murdered men.
>
> *
>
> Here is a Sulla, men of Rome, surnamed
> Sulla the Fortunate – to your misfortune;
> Here is a Marius come back at last
> To capture Rome; here is an Antony
> Uncivilly provoking civil strife,
> His hands thrice dyed in costly Roman blood.
> Confess: 'Rome is no more!'. All who return
> To reign, from banishment, reign bloodily.

At first Tiberius dismissed these verses as the work of bilious malcontents who were impatient with his reforms and did not really mean what they said. He would remark, 'Let them hate me, so long as they approve!'[25] But, as time went on, his conduct justified every line they had written.

60. A few days after he came to Capreae a fisherman suddenly intruded on his solitude by presenting him with an enormous mullet. Tiberius was so terrified that he had managed to clamber up the trackless cliffs at the rear of the island that he ordered his guards to rub the fisherman's face with it. The scales skinned it raw, and the poor fellow shouted in his agony, 'Thank heaven I did not also bring Caesar that huge crab I caught!' Tiberius sent for the crab and had it used in the same way. A praetorian guard once stole a peacock from his garden and was sentenced to death. On another occasion, during a country jaunt, the bearers of Tiberius' litter were held up by a bramble thicket; he had the guards' centurion, whose task it was to choose the right path, stretched on the ground and flogged until he nearly died.

61. Soon Tiberius broke out in every sort of cruelty, and never lacked for victims: these were the friends and even acquaintances first of his mother, then of Agrippina, Nero and Drusus, and finally of Sejanus. With Sejanus out of the way his savageries increased, which proved that Sejanus had not, as some thought, been inciting him to commit them, but had merely been providing the opportunities that he demanded. Nevertheless, in Tiberius' dry, brief autobiography we find him daring to assert that Sejanus had been killed for persecuting Nero and Drusus; the fact was that he had himself put Nero to death when Sejanus was already an object of suspicion, and Drusus after he had fallen from power.

A detailed list of Tiberius' barbarities would take a long time to compile; I shall content myself with sketching out the chief categories. Not a day, however holy, passed without an execution; he even desecrated the beginning of the new year. Many men were accused and condemned with their children – some actually by their children – and the relatives forbidden to go into mourning. Special awards were voted to the informers who had denounced them, and in certain circumstances to the witnesses too. An informer's word was always believed. Every crime became a capital one, even the utterance of a few careless words. A poet found himself accused of slander – he had written a tragedy which presented Agamemnon in a bad light – and a historian had made the mistake of describing Brutus and Cassius as 'the last of the Romans'.[26] Both these authors were executed without delay, and their works – though once publicly read before Augustus and accorded general praise – were called in and destroyed. Tiberius denied those who escaped with a prison sentence not only the solace of reading books, but the privilege of talking to their fellow prisoners. Some of the accused, on being warned to appear in court, felt sure that the verdict would be 'guilty', and to avoid the humiliation of a trial stayed at home and severed an artery; yet Tiberius' men bandaged their wounds and hurried them, half-dead, to prison. Others obeyed their summons and then drank poison in full view of the Senate. The bodies of all executed persons were flung on the Gemonian Stairs and dragged to the Tiber with hooks – as many as twenty a day, including women and children. Tradition forbade the strangling of virgins, so when little girls had been condemned to die in this way, the executioner began by violating them.[27] Tiberius used to punish with life those who wished to die. He regarded death as a comparatively light affliction, and, on hearing that a man named Carnalus had forestalled his execution by suicide, exclaimed, 'Carnalus has got away!' Once, during a jail inspection, a prisoner begged to be put out of his misery; Tiberius replied, 'No; we are not yet friends again.' A man of consular rank has recorded in his memoirs that he attended a banquet at which Tiberius was suddenly asked by a loud-voiced dwarf, standing among a group of jesters near the table, 'What of Paconius? Why is he still alive after being charged with *maiestas*?' Tiberius told him to hold his impudent tongue, but a few days later requested the Senate to make a quick decision about Paconius' execution.

62. On eventually discovering that his son Drusus had died, not as the result of illness and overindulgence, as he had thought, but from poison administered by his wife Livilla in partnership with Sejanus, Tiberius grew enraged and redoubled his cruelties until nobody was safe from torture and death. He spent whole days investigating the Drusus affair, which obsessed him to such a degree that when a man whose guest he had been at Rhodes arrived in response to his own friendly invitation, he mistook him for an important witness in the case and had him put to the torture at once. When the truth came out, he actually executed the man to avoid publicizing the scandal.

In Capreae they still show the place at the clifftop where Tiberius used to watch his victims being thrown into the sea after prolonged and exquisite tortures. A party of marines was stationed below, and when the bodies came hurtling down they whacked at them with oars and boathooks, to make sure that they were completely dead. An ingenious torture of Tiberius' devising was to trick men into drinking huge draughts of wine, and then suddenly to knot a cord tightly around their genitals, which not only cut into the flesh but prevented them from urinating. He would have killed even more people, it is thought, if he himself had not died first, and if Thrasyllus had not cleverly persuaded him to postpone his designs by an assurance that he still had many years of life in hand. These victims would have included his own grandsons Gaius, of whom he was already harbouring suspicions, and Tiberius, whom he hated as having been born from adultery. The story is credible, because he sometimes used to envy Priam for having outlived his entire family.[28]

63. Much evidence is extant, not only of the hatred that Tiberius earned but of the state of terror in which he himself lived and of the insults heaped upon him. He forbade anyone to consult haruspices, except openly and with witnesses present. He even attempted to suppress all oracles in the neighbourhood of Rome, but desisted for fear of the miraculous power shown by the Praenestine lots:[29] although he brought them to Rome in a sealed chest, they vanished and did not become visible again until returned to the temple. Tiberius had assigned provinces to certain men of consular rank, but, not daring to send them out, detained them in Rome for several years until their successors had been appointed. Meanwhile they relayed his frequent instructions to their legates and agents in the provinces which they officially governed yet were unable to visit.

64. After exiling Agrippina and her two sons, he always moved them from one place of confinement to another in closed litters, with their wrists and ankles fettered and a military escort to prevent all persons met on the road from even stopping to watch the litter go by, let alone glance inside.

65. Becoming aware that Sejanus was plotting a usurpation, Tiberius found some difficulty in getting rid of him, even though his birthday was being publicly celebrated and golden statues had been raised to him everywhere, and he did so at last by subterfuge rather than by the exercise of imperial authority. First of all, to detach Sejanus from his own immediate entourage while pretending to honour him, Tiberius appointed him his colleague in a fifth consulship, which he assumed solely for this purpose a long time after the fourth; but he did not visit Rome for his inauguration. Next he made Sejanus believe that he would soon marry into the imperial family and be awarded

tribunician power; and then, taking him off his guard, he sent a shamefully abject message to the Senate begging, among other things, that one of the consuls should fetch him – a poor lonely old man – into their presence under military escort. He also took precautions against the revolt which he feared might yet break out by ordering that his grandson Drusus, who was still in prison at Rome, should be released if necessary and appointed commander. He thought, indeed, of taking refuge with some provincial army and had a naval flotilla standing by to carry him off the island, where he waited on a clifftop for the distant signal (announcing all possible eventualities) which he had ordered to be made in case his couriers might be delayed. Even when Sejanus' conspiracy had been suffocated, Tiberius did not show the least sign of increased confidence, but remained in the so-called Villa Io for the next nine months.

66. His uneasiness of mind was aggravated by a perpetual stream of reproaches from all sides, and every one of his condemned victims either cursed him to his face or arranged for a defamatory notice to be posted in the theatre seats occupied by senators. His attitude to these reproaches varied markedly: sometimes shame made him want nobody to hear about the incident, sometimes he laughed and deliberately publicized it. He even had a scathing letter from Artabanus, king of Parthia, in which he was accused of murdering his family, slaughtering innocent people, neglecting his duties and indulging his lusts, and was urged to satisfy the intense and pardonable loathing of his people by committing suicide as soon as convenient.

67. At last, growing thoroughly disgusted with himself, he as good as confessed his misery. A letter to the Senate began in this strain: 'If I know what to tell you, gentlemen of the Senate, or how to tell it, or what to leave altogether untold for the present, may all the gods and goddesses in heaven bring me to an even worse damnation than I now daily suffer.' According to one body of opinion, his skill in divination allowed him to foresee these things and to know how much hatred and ill repute lay in store for him; this made him refuse, point blank, the title Father of His Country offered by the Senate and also forbid them to swear an oath approving in advance and in

retrospect of whatever he said or did, for fear that his shame would be intensified when he turned out to be unworthy of such honours. This conclusion may, in fact, be deduced from his formal reply to the two proposals: 'So long as my wits do not fail me, you can count on the consistency of my behaviour; but I should not like you to set the precedent of binding your-selves to approve a man's every action, for what if something happened to alter that man's character?' And again: 'If you ever feel any doubts about my character or my devotion to you – but may I die before that happens! – the title Father of His Country will not recompense me for the loss of your regard, and you will be ashamed either of having given me the title without sufficient deliberation, or of having shown fickleness by changing your opinion of me.'

68. Tiberius was strongly and heavily built, and above aver-age height. His shoulders and chest were broad, and his body perfectly proportioned from top to toe. His left hand was more agile than the right, and so strong that he could poke a hole in a sound, newly plucked apple or wound the skull of a boy or young man with a flick of his finger. He had a handsome, fresh-complexioned face, though subject to occasional rashes of pimples. Letting his back hair grow down over the nape seems to have been a family habit of the Claudii. Tiberius' eyes were remarkably large and possessed the unusual power of seeing in the dark, when he first opened them after sleep, although this phenomenon disappeared after a minute or two. His gait was a stiff stride, with the neck poked forward, and if ever he broke his usual stern silence to address those walking with him he spoke with great deliberation and eloquent move-ments of the fingers. Augustus disliked these mannerisms and put them down to pride, but frequently assured both the Senate and the people that they were physical, not moral, defects. Tiberius enjoyed excellent health almost to the end of his reign, although after the age of thirty he never called in a doctor or asked one to send him medicine.

69. He lacked any deep regard for the gods or religious scruples, his belief in astrology having persuaded him that the world was wholly ruled by fate. Yet thunder had a most fright-

ening effect on Tiberius: whenever the sky wore an ugly look he would put on a laurel wreath, which he supposed would make him lightning-proof.

70. Tiberius was deeply devoted to Greek and Latin literature and, while still a young man, modelled his Latin oratorical style on that of old Messala Corvinus; but he ruined it with so many affectations and pedantries that his extempore speeches were considered far better than the prepared ones. He also wrote a lyric poem entitled *Lament on the Death of Lucius Caesar*, and Greek verses in the manner of his favourites Euphorion, Rhianus and Parthenius, whose writings and busts he placed in the public libraries among those of the classics – thus prompting several scholars to publish rival commentaries on these poets and dedicate them to him. However, he had a particular bent for mythology and carried his researches in it to such a ridiculous point that he would test *grammatici* – whose society, as I have already mentioned, he cultivated above all others' – by asking them questions like 'Who was Hecuba's mother?', 'What name did Achilles assume when he was in the girls' quarters?', 'What song did the Sirens sing?'[30] Furthermore, on his first entrance into the Senate after the death of Augustus he showed equal respect for the gods and for his adoptive father's memory by reviving the example set long ago by Minos at the death of his son: he performed a sacrifice with wine and incense as usual, but dispensed with the customary pipe players.[31]

71. Tiberius spoke Greek fluently, but there were occasions when he stuck to Latin, especially in the Senate: indeed, he once apologized, before saying 'monopoly', for having to use a foreign word. And he objected to the Greek word 'emblems' when it appeared in a decree: if a one-word Latin equivalent could not be found, he said, a periphrasis of several words must serve. At another time he gave orders that a soldier who had been asked in Greek to give evidence on oath must answer either in Latin or not at all.

72. During the entire period of Tiberius' retirement from Rome he only twice attempted to return. On the first occasion he sailed up the Tiber in a trireme as far as the gardens near Julius Caesar's artificial lake, having posted troops along both

banks to order away anyone who came to meet him; but after a distant view of the city walls he sailed back, it is not known why. On the second occasion he rode up the Via Appia as far as the seventh milestone, but then retreated because of a frightening portent. This was the death of a pet snake which he used to feed with his own hands. When about to do so as usual, he found it half-eaten by a swarm of ants, and a soothsayer warned him, 'Beware the power of the mob.' He hurried back to Campania, fell ill at Astura, yet felt strong enough to continue with his journey. At Circeii he disguised his ill health by attending the garrison games, and even threw javelins from his president's box at a wild boar let loose in the arena. He twisted the muscles of his side by this effort, and then aggravated his condition by sitting in a draught while overheated. Nevertheless, he resolutely went on to Misenum without any change in daily routine, continuing to enjoy banquets and other diversions – partly because he now never practised self-denial, partly because he wanted nobody to realize how ill he was. Indeed, when the physician Charicles, on leaving the dining table, kissed his hand in farewell, Tiberius suspected a covert attempt to feel his pulse and begged Charicles to sit down again. Then he kept the party going until very late, and when it ended, followed his nightly habit of standing in the middle of the banqueting hall, with a lictor beside him, for a personal goodnight to each of the departing guests.

73. Meanwhile he read in the *Proceedings of the Senate* a paragraph to the effect that some persons whom he had sent for trial merely as 'named by an informer' had been discharged without a hearing. 'This is contempt!' he shouted furiously, and decided to make his way back to Capreae, the only place where he felt safe when issuing a stern order. But bad weather and increasing sickness delayed his voyage, and he died soon afterwards in a country house which had once belonged to Lucullus. He was then seventy-seven years old and had reigned for nearly twenty-three years. It was 16 March, and the consuls of the year were Gnaeus Acerronius Proculus and Gaius Pontius Nigrinus.[32]

Some believe that he had been given a slow, wasting poison by

Gaius; others that, when convalescent after fever, he demanded food but was refused it. According to one account, his seal ring was taken from him when he seemed about to die, and when he revived and demanded it back he was smothered with a pillow. Seneca writes that Tiberius, realizing how near his end was, removed the ring himself, as if as a present for someone, but then clung to it a while before replacing it on his finger; that he afterwards lay quiet for some little time with the fist clenched, until summoning his servants; and that, when no one answered, he got out of bed, collapsed, and died.

74. On his last birthday Tiberius dreamed that the enormous, beautiful statue of Apollo Temenites,[33] which he had brought from Syracuse to erect in the library of Augustus' Temple, came in to announce 'Tiberius will never dedicate me!' A few days before his death the lighthouse on Capreae was wrecked by an earthquake. At Misenum the dead embers of the fire which had been put into a brazier to warm his dining room suddenly blazed up again, early in the evening, and continued to glow until late that night.

75. The first news of his death caused such joy at Rome that some people ran about yelling 'To the Tiber with Tiberius!' and others offered prayers to Mother Earth and the Di Manes[34] to give him no home below except among the impious. There were also loud threats to drag his body off with a hook and fling it on the Gemonian Stairs, for popular resentment against his savage behaviour was now increased by a fresh outrage. It so happened that the Senate had decreed a ten days' stay of execution in the case of all persons sentenced to death, and Tiberius died the very day on which the period of grace expired for some of them. The unfortunate creatures threw themselves on the mercy of the public, but since Gaius was not yet at hand there was no one to whom an appeal could be made, and the jailers, afraid of acting illegally, carried out the sentence of strangling them and throwing their bodies on the Gemonian Stairs. Thus the hatred of Tiberius grew hotter than ever – his cruelty, it was said, continued even after his death – and when the funeral procession left Misenum, the cry went up, 'Take him to Atella! Give him a half-burning in an amphitheatre!'[35]

However, the soldiers carried the corpse on to Rome, where it was cremated with due ceremony.

76. Two years before his death Tiberius had drawn up a will in his own handwriting; an identical copy was also found in the handwriting of a freedman. Both these documents had been signed and sealed by witnesses of the very lowest class. In them, Gaius son of Germanicus and Tiberius son of Drusus were named as Tiberius' co-heirs, and if either should die the survivor was to be the sole heir. Tiberius left legacies to several other persons, including the Vestal Virgins, with a bounty for every serving soldier in the army and every member of the Roman people, and separate bequests to the city wardmasters.

GAIUS CALIGULA

1. Germanicus, father of Gaius Caesar, was the son of Drusus and Antonia the younger, and was eventually adopted by Tiberius, his paternal uncle.[1] He served as quaestor five years before he was legally eligible and became consul without holding any of the intermediary offices, and was then appointed to the command of the forces in Germany. When Augustus' death became known, the legions there were unanimously opposed to Tiberius' succession and would have acclaimed Germanicus emperor, but he showed a remarkable example of filial respect and personal integrity by diverting their attention from this project; he took the offensive in Germany, and won a triumph. As consul for the second time he was hurried to the east, where conditions were unsettled, before being able to take office. There he defeated the king of Armenia and reduced Cappadocia to provincial status, but he succumbed to a protracted illness at Antioch, being only thirty-four years old when he died. Because of the dark stains which covered his body and the foam on his lips, poison was suspected; significantly, they also found the heart intact among the ashes after cremation – a heart steeped in poison is supposedly proof against fire.

2. If we may accept the common verdict, Tiberius craftily arranged Germanicus' death with the advice and assistance of Gnaeus Piso. Piso had been appointed to govern Syria at about the same time, and there, deciding that he must make an enemy either of Germanicus or of Tiberius, took every opportunity to provoke Germanicus, even when on his sickbed, by the meanest acts and speeches – behaviour for which the Senate condemned

him to death on his return to Rome, after he had narrowly escaped a popular lynching.[2]

3. Germanicus is everywhere described as having been of outstanding physical and moral excellence. He was handsome, courageous, a past master of Greek and Latin oratory and learning, conspicuously kind-hearted, and gifted with the ability of winning universal respect and affection. Only his legs were somewhat undeveloped, but he strengthened them by assiduous exercise on horseback after meals. He often fought and killed an enemy in hand-to-hand combat, and did not cease to plead cases in the law courts even when he had gained a triumph. Some of his Greek comedies are extant, besides other literary works. At home or abroad he always behaved modestly, would dispense with lictors when visiting any free or allied town, and offered sacrifices at whatever tombs of famous men he came across. On deciding to bury under one mound all the scattered bones of Varus' fallen legionaries, he led the search party himself and took an active part in the collection. Towards his detractors Germanicus showed such tolerance and leniency, regardless of their identity or motives, that he would not even break with Piso (who was cancelling his orders and plaguing his subordinates) until he found that spells and potions were being used against him. And then he did no more than renounce his friendship in the traditional manner, and leave testamentary instructions for his family to take vengeance on Piso if anything should happen to himself.

4. Such virtuous conduct brought Germanicus rich rewards. He was so deeply respected and loved by all his acquaintances that Augustus – I need hardly mention his other relatives – wondered for a long time whether to make him his successor, but at last ordered Tiberius to adopt him. Germanicus, the records show, had won such intense popular devotion that he was in danger of being mobbed to death whenever he arrived at a place or took his leave again. Indeed, when he came back from Germany after suppressing the native uprising, all the praetorian cohorts marched out in welcome, despite orders that only two were to do so, and the entire people of Rome – all

ages and ranks and both sexes – flocked as far as the twentieth milestone to meet him.

5. But the most spectacular proof of the devotion in which Germanicus had been held appeared on the day of his death and immediately afterwards. The populace stoned temples and upset altars; heads of families threw their household gods into the street and abandoned their newly born children. Even the barbarians who were fighting us or one another are said to have made immediate peace as though a domestic tragedy had afflicted the whole world, some princes shaving their own beards and their wives' heads in token of profound grief. The King of Kings himself cancelled his hunting parties and banquets, which is a sign of public mourning in Parthia.

6. While Rome was still stunned by the first news of his illness and waiting for further bulletins, a rumour that he had recovered went the rounds one evening after dark and sent people rushing to the Capitol with torches and sacrificial victims; so eager were they to fulfil their vows that the temple gates were almost torn down. Tiberius was awakened by the joyful chant:

> All is well again at Rome,
> All is well again at home,
> Here's an end to all our pain:
> Germanicus is well again!

When the news of his death finally broke, neither edicts nor official expressions of sympathy could console the people; mourning continued throughout the festival days of December. The bitterness of their loss was aggravated by the horrors which followed, for everyone believed, and with good reason, that moral respect for Germanicus had alone kept Tiberius from displaying the cruelty of his wicked heart.

7. Germanicus married Agrippina, daughter of Marcus Agrippa and Julia, who bore him nine children. Two died in infancy, and a third, an extremely likeable boy, during early childhood. Livia dedicated a statue of him, dressed as Cupid,

to Venus Capitolina; Augustus kept a replica in his bedroom, and used to kiss it fondly whenever he entered. The other children – three girls, Agrippina, Drusilla and Livilla, born in successive years, and three boys, Nero, Drusus and Gaius Caesar – survived their father; but Tiberius later brought charges against Nero and Drusus, whom he persuaded the Senate to execute as public enemies.

8. Gaius Caesar was born on 31 August, during the consulship shared by his father with Gaius Fonteius Capito.³ His birthplace is disputed. According to Gnaeus Lentulus Gaetulicus he was born at Tibur, but according to Pliny the Elder at the village of Ambitarvium in the territory of the Treveri, just above Confluens; Pliny supports his view by mentioning certain local altars inscribed 'In Honour of Agrippina's *Puerperium*'. A verse which went the rounds at his accession also suggests that he was born in the winter quarters of the legions:

> Born in a barracks,
>   Reared in the arts of war:
> A noble nativity
>   For a Roman emperor!

The public records, however, give his birthplace as Antium, and my researches convince me that this is correct. Pliny shows that Gaetulicus tried to flatter the proud young *princeps* by pretending that he came from Tibur, a city sacred to Hercules, and that he lied with greater confidence because Germanicus did have a son named Gaius Caesar born there the year before, whose sadly premature death I have already mentioned. Nevertheless, Pliny is himself mistaken, since Augustus' biographers agree that Germanicus' first visit to Gaul took place after he had been consul, by which time Gaius was already born. Moreover, the inscriptions on the altars do not prove Pliny's point, since Agrippina bore Germanicus two daughters in Gaul, and any confinement is a *puerperium*, regardless of the child's sex – girls were then still called *puerae* as often as *puellae*, and boys *puelli* as often as *pueri*.⁴ Finally, I have found a letter which Augustus wrote to his granddaughter Agrippina a few months before he died; the Gaius mentioned in it must have been this one, because no other child of that name was alive at the time. It reads, 'Yesterday, I made arrangements for Talarius and Asillius to bring your son Gaius to you on the eighteenth of May, if the gods will. I am also sending with him one of my slaves, a doctor who, as I have told Germanicus in a letter, need not be returned to me if he proves of use to you. Goodbye, my dear Agrippina! Keep well on the way back to your Germanicus.' Clearly, Gaius could not have been born in a country to which he was first taken from Rome at the age of nearly two. These details also weaken my confidence in that anonymous verse about his birth in a barracks. So we are, I think, reduced to accepting the only other authority, namely the public records, especially since Gaius preferred Antium to any other city and treated it as his native place; he even planned, they say, to transfer the seat of imperial government there when he wearied of Rome.

9. He won his cognomen Caligula from an army joke, because he grew up among the troops and wore the miniature uniform of a private soldier.[5] An undeniable proof of the hold on their affections which this early experience of camp life gave him is that when they rioted at the news of Augustus' death and were ready for any madness, the mere sight of little Gaius calmed them down. As soon as they realized that he was being removed to a neighbouring city to protect him from their violence, they were overcome by contrition; some of them seized and stopped his carriage, pleading to be spared this disgrace.

10. Gaius also accompanied Germanicus to Syria. On his return he lived with his mother, and next, after she had been exiled, with his great-grandmother Livia Augusta, whose funeral oration he delivered from the Rostra though he had not yet come of age. He then lived with his grandmother Antonia until Tiberius summoned him to Capreae at the age of nineteen. He assumed the adult toga and shaved his first beard on one and the same day, but this was a most informal occasion compared with his brothers' coming-of-age celebrations. The courtiers tried every trick to force him into making complaints against Tiberius – always, however, without success. He not

only failed to show any interest in the murder of his relatives, but affected an amazing indifference to his own ill treatment, behaving so obsequiously to his adoptive grandfather and to the entire household that someone said of him, very neatly, 'Never was there a better slave, or a worse master.'

11. Yet even in those days he could not control his natural brutality. He loved watching tortures and executions, and, disguised in a wig and a long robe, abandoned himself nightly to the pleasures of feasting and scandalous living. Tiberius was ready enough to indulge a passion which Gaius had for theatrical dancing and singing, on the ground that it might have a civilizing influence on him. With characteristic shrewdness, the old emperor had exactly gauged the young man's vicious inclinations, and would often remark that Gaius' advent portended his own death and the ruin of everyone else. 'I am nursing a viper in Rome's bosom,' he once said; 'I am educating a Phaethon for the whole world.'[6]

12. Gaius shortly thereafter married Junia Claudilla, daughter of the distinguished senator Marcus Silanus. Then he was appointed augur in place of his brother Drusus, but transferred to the pontificate before his inauguration in compliment to his dutiful behaviour and exemplary life. This encouraged him in the hope of becoming Tiberius' successor, because Sejanus' downfall had reduced the court to a shadow of its former self; and when Junia died in childbirth he seduced Ennia, wife of Naevius Macro, the praetorian prefect, not only swearing to marry her if he became emperor, but putting the oath in writing. After Ennia helped him win Macro's support, he assailed Tiberius with poison, as some people think; he issued orders for his ring to be removed while he was still breathing, and when he would not let it go he had him smothered with a pillow. According to one account he throttled Tiberius with his own hands, and when a freedman cried out in protest at this wicked deed he crucified him at once. All this may be true; some writers report that Gaius later confessed to intended if not actual parricide. He would often boast, that is to say, of having carried a dagger into Tiberius' bedroom with the virtuous intention of avenging his mother and brothers; but, accord-

ing to his own account, he found Tiberius asleep and, restrained by feelings of pity, threw down the dagger and went out. Tiberius, he said, was perfectly aware of what had happened, yet never dared question him or take any action in the matter.

13. Gaius' accession seemed to the Roman people – one might almost say to the whole world – like the answer to their prayers. The memory of Germanicus and compassion for a family that had been practically wiped out by successive murders made most provincials and soldiers, many of whom had known him as a child, and the entire population of Rome as well, show extravagant joy that he was now emperor. When he escorted Tiberius' funeral procession from Misenum to Rome he was, of course, dressed in mourning, but a dense crowd greeted him ecstatically with altars, sacrifices and torches, and such endearments as 'star', 'chick', 'baby' and 'pet'.

14. On his arrival in the city the Senate (and a mob of people who had forced their way into the Senate House) immediately and unanimously conferred absolute power upon him. They set aside Tiberius' will, which made his other grandson, then still a child, joint heir with Gaius, and so splendid were the celebrations that 160,000 victims were publicly sacrificed during the next three months, or perhaps even a shorter period. A few days later he visited the prison islands off Campania, and vows were uttered for his safe return – at that time no opportunity of demonstrating a general concern for his welfare was ever disregarded. When he fell ill, anxious crowds besieged the Palatine all night. Some swore that they would fight as gladiators if the gods allowed him to recover; others even carried placards volunteering to die instead of him. To the great love in which he was held by his own people, foreigners added their own tribute of devotion. Artabanus, the king of the Parthians, who had always loathed and despised Tiberius, made unsolicited overtures of friendship to Gaius, attended a conference with the governor of Syria, and, before returning across the river Euphrates, paid homage to the Roman Eagles and standards and the statues of the Caesars.

15. Gaius strengthened his popularity by every possible means. He delivered a funeral speech in honour of Tiberius to

a vast crowd, weeping profusely all the while, and gave him a magnificent burial. But as soon as this was over he sailed for Pandataria and the Pontian Islands to fetch back the remains of his mother and his brother Nero – and during rough weather too, in proof of devotion. He approached the ashes with the utmost reverence, and transferred them to the urns with his own hands. Equally dramatic was his gesture of raising a standard on the poop of the bireme which brought the urns to Ostia, and thence up the Tiber to Rome. He had arranged that the most distinguished *equites* available should carry them to the Mausoleum about noon, when the streets were at their busiest, and also appointed an annual day for commemorative rites, marked by chariot races in the Circus, at which Agrippina's image would be paraded in a covered carriage. He honoured his father's memory by renaming the month of September 'Germanicus', and sponsored a senatorial decree which awarded his grandmother Antonia, at a blow, all the honours won by Livia Augusta in her entire lifetime. As fellow consul he chose his uncle Claudius, who had hitherto been a mere *eques*, and adopted young Tiberius when he came of age, giving him the title of Youth Leader.[7] He included the names of his sisters in the official oath which everyone had to take, which ran, 'I will not value my life or that of my children less highly than I do the safety of Gaius and his sisters,' and in the consular motions, as follows: 'Good fortune attend Gaius Caesar and his sisters!'

A similar bid for popularity was to recall all exiles and dismiss all criminal charges whatsoever that had been pending since the time of Tiberius. The batches of written evidence in his mother's and brothers' cases were brought to the Forum at his orders and burned, to set at rest the minds of such witnesses and informers as had testified against them, but first he swore before heaven that he had neither read nor abstracted a single document. He also refused to examine a report supposedly concerning his own safety, on the ground that nobody could have any reason to hate him, and swore that he would never listen to informers.

16. Gaius drove the spintrian perverts[8] from the city, and could only with difficulty be restrained from drowning the lot.

He gave permission for the works of Titus Labienus, Cremutius Cordus and Cassius Severus,[9] which had been banned by order of the Senate, to be sought out and republished – making his desire known that posterity should be in full possession of all historical facts. In addition, he revived Augustus' practice, discontinued by Tiberius, of publishing an imperial budget, and invested the magistrates with full authority over court cases, not allowing litigants to come to him to appeal their decisions. He scrupulously scanned the list of *equites*, but, though publicly dismounting any who had behaved in a wicked or scandalous manner, was not unduly severe with those guilty of lesser misbehaviour – he merely omitted their names from the list which he read out. His creation of a fifth judicial division aided jurors to keep abreast of their work; his reviving of the electoral system was designed to restore voting rights to the people. He honoured every one of the bequests in Tiberius' will, though this had been set aside by the Senate, and in that of Julia Augusta, which Tiberius had suppressed; he abolished the Italian half-per-cent auction tax; and he paid compensation to a great many people whose houses had been damaged by fire. Any king whom he restored to the throne was awarded the taxes that had accumulated since his deposition – Antiochus of Commagene, for example, got a refund of 100 million sesterces. To show his interest in public morality, he awarded 800,000 sesterces to a freedwoman who, though put to extreme torture, had not revealed her patron's guilt. These acts won him many official honours, among them a golden shield, carried once a year to the Capitol by the colleges of priests marching in procession and followed by the Senate, while the children of the aristocracy chanted an anthem in praise of his virtues. By a senatorial decree, the day of his accession was called the Parilia, as though Rome had now been born again.[10]

17. Gaius held four consulships: the earliest for two months, from the Kalends of July; the next for the whole month of January; the third for the first thirteen days of January; and the fourth for the first seven. Only the last two were in sequence.[11] He assumed his third consulship at Lugdunum, without a colleague – not, as some people think, through arrogance or

indifference, but because the news that his fellow consul-elect had died in Rome just before the Kalends of January had not reached him in time. He twice presented every member of the people with 300 sesterces, and twice invited all the senators and *equites*, with their wives and children, to an extravagant banquet. At the second of these banquets he gave every man a toga and every woman a purple scarf. In order to increase the public rejoicing in Rome for all time, he extended the Saturnalia with an additional day, which he called 'Youth Day'.

18. He held several gladiatorial contests, some in Statilius Taurus' amphitheatre and others in the Saepta, diversifying them with prize fights between the best boxers of Africa and Campania; he occasionally allowed magistrates or friends to preside at these instead of doing so himself. Again, he staged a great number of different theatrical shows in various buildings – sometimes at night, with the whole city illuminated – and would scatter vouchers among the audience entitling them to all sorts of gifts, over and above the basket of food which was everyone's due. At one banquet, noticing with what extraordinary gusto an *eques* seated opposite dug into the food, he sent him his own heaped plate as well, and rewarded a senator, who had been similarly enjoying himself, with a praetorship, though he was not yet qualified to hold this office. Many all-day games were celebrated in the Circus, and between races he introduced panther-baiting and the Troy Game. For certain special games, when all the charioteers were men of senatorial rank, he had the Circus decorated in red and green. Once, while he was inspecting the Circus equipment, from the Gelotian House which overlooks it, a group of people standing in the nearby balconies called out, 'What about a day's racing, Caesar?' So on the spur of the moment he gave immediate orders for games to be held.

19. One of his spectacles was on such a fantastic scale that nothing like it had ever been seen before. He collected all available merchant ships and anchored them in two lines, close together, the whole way from Baiae to the mole at Puteoli, a distance of three miles and some 600 feet. Then he had the ships boarded over, with earth heaped on the planks, and made

a kind of Via Appia along which he trotted back and forth for two consecutive days. On the first day he wore a civic crown, a sword, a shield and a cloth-of-gold cloak, and rode a gaily caparisoned charger. On the second he appeared in charioteer's costume driving a team of two famous horses, with a boy named Dareus, one of his Parthian hostages, triumphantly displayed in the car beside him; behind came a force of praetorians and a group of his friends mounted in Gallic chariots. Gaius is of course generally supposed to have built the bridge as an improvement on Xerxes' famous feat of bridging the much narrower Hellespont.[12] Others believe that he planned this huge engineering feat to terrify the Germans and Britons, on whom he had his eye. But my grandfather used to tell me as a boy that, according to some courtiers in Gaius' confidence, the sole reason for the bridge was this: when Tiberius could not decide whom to appoint as his successor and inclined towards his grandson and namesake, Thrasyllus the astrologer had told him, 'As for Gaius, he has no more chance of becoming emperor than of riding a horse dry-shod across the Gulf of Baiae.'

20. Gaius gave several shows abroad – theatrical performances at Syracuse and mixed games at Lugdunum, where he also held a competition in Greek and Latin oratory. The losers, they say, had to present the winners with prizes and make speeches praising them, while those who failed miserably were forced to erase their entries with either sponges or their own tongues – at the threat of being thrashed and flung into the Rhône.

21. He completed certain projects neglected by Tiberius, namely the Temple of Augustus and Pompey's Theatre, and began the construction of an aqueduct in the Tibur district and an amphitheatre near the Saepta. (His successor Claudius finished the aqueduct, but work on the amphitheatre was abandoned.) Gaius rebuilt the ruinous walls and temples of Syracuse, and among his other projects were the restoration of Polycrates' palace at Samos, the completion of Didymaean Apollo's temple at Miletus, and the building of a city high up in the Alps. But he was most deeply interested in cutting a canal through the Isthmus of Corinth, and sent a *primipilaris* there to survey the site.

22. So much for Gaius the Emperor; the rest of this history must needs deal with Gaius the Monster.

He adopted a variety of titles, such as Pious, Son of the Camp, Father of the Army, Caesar Optimus Maximus.[13] But when once, at the dinner table, some foreign kings who had come to pay homage were arguing which of them was the most nobly descended, he burst out, 'Nay, let there be one master, and one king!'[14] And he nearly assumed a royal diadem then and there, transforming an ostensible principate into an actual kingdom. However, after his courtiers reminded him that he already outranked any king or local ruler, he insisted on being treated as a god – arranging for the most revered or artistically famous statues of the gods, including that of Jupiter at Olympia, to be brought from Greece and have their heads replaced by his own.

Next he extended his Palatine residence as far as the Forum, converted the shrine of Castor and Pollux into a vestibule, and would often stand between these divine brothers to be worshipped by all visitants, some of whom addressed him as 'Jupiter Latiaris'.[15] He established a shrine to his own godhead, with priests, the costliest possible victims, and a life-sized golden image, which was dressed every day in clothes identical with those that he happened to be wearing. All the richest citizens tried to gain priesthoods here, either by influence or by bribery. Flamingos, peacocks, black grouse, guinea hens and pheasants were offered as sacrifices, each on a particular day. When the moon shone full and bright he always invited the moon goddess to his bed, and during the day he would indulge in whispered conversations with Jupiter Capitolinus, pressing his ear to the god's mouth, and sometimes raising his voice in anger. Once he was overheard threatening the god, 'Either you throw me or I will throw you!'[16] Finally he announced that Jupiter had persuaded him to share his home, and therefore connected the Palatine with the Capitol by throwing a bridge across the Temple of Divus Augustus; he next began building a new house inside the precincts of the Capitol itself, in order to live even nearer.

23. Because of Agrippa's humble origin Gaius loathed being

described as his grandson, and would fly into a rage if anyone mentioned him, in speech or song, as an ancestor of the Caesars. He nursed a fantasy that his mother had been born of an incestuous union between Augustus and Julia, and, not content with thus discrediting Augustus' name, cancelled the annual commemorations of his victories at Actium and Sicily, declaring that they had proved the ruin of the Roman people. He called his great-grandmother Livia Augusta a 'Ulysses in petticoats',[17] and in a letter to the Senate he dared describe her as of low birth – 'her maternal grandfather Aufidius Lurco having been a mere town councillor from Fundi' – although the public records showed Lurco to have held high office at Rome.[18] When his paternal grandmother Antonia begged him to grant her a private audience he insisted on taking Macro, the praetorian prefect, as his escort. Unkind treatment of this sort hurried her to the grave, though according to some he accelerated the process with poison; and when she died he showed so little respect that he sat in his dining room and watched the funeral pyre burn. He sent a military tribune to kill young Tiberius without warning, on the pretext that Tiberius had insulted him by taking an antidote against poison – his breath smelled of it – and he forced his father-in-law, Marcus Silanus, to cut his own throat with a razor, the charge being that he had not followed him when he put to sea in a storm, but had stayed on shore to seize power at Rome if anything happened to him. The truth was that Silanus, a notoriously bad sailor, could not face the voyage; and young Tiberius' breath smelled of medicine taken for a persistent cough which was gaining a hold on his lungs. Gaius preserved his uncle Claudius mainly as a butt for practical jokes.

24. It was his habit to commit incest with each of his three sisters in turn, and at large banquets, when his wife reclined above him, placed them all in turn below him.[19] They say that he ravished his sister Drusilla before he came of age: their grandmother Antonia, at whose house they were both staying, caught them in bed together. Later, he took Drusilla from her husband, the former consul Lucius Cassius Longinus, quite unashamedly treating her as his wife; when he fell dangerously

ill, he left her all his property, and the empire too. At her death he made it a capital offence to laugh, to bathe, or to dine with one's parents, wives or children while the period of public mourning lasted, and he was so crazed with grief that he suddenly rushed from Rome by night, drove through Campania, took ship to Sicily, and returned just as impetuously, without having shaved or cut his hair in the meantime. Afterwards, whenever he had to take an important oath, he swore by Drusilla's godhead, even at a public assembly or an army parade. He showed no such extreme love or respect for the two surviving sisters, and often, indeed, let his toy boys sleep with them; and at Aemilius Lepidus' trial he felt no compunction about denouncing them as adulteresses who were party to plots against him – openly producing letters in their handwriting (acquired by trickery and seduction) and dedicating to Mars Ultor the three swords with which, the accompanying placard alleged, they had meant to kill him.[20]

25. It would be hard to say whether the way he got married, the way he dissolved his marriages or the way he behaved as a husband was the most disgraceful. He attended the wedding ceremony of Gaius Piso and Livia Orestilla, but had the bride carried off to his own home. After a few days, however, he sent her away, and two years later he banished her, suspecting that she had returned to Piso in the interval. According to one account, he told Piso, who was reclining opposite him at the wedding feast, 'Hands off my wife!' and took her home with him at once, and announced the next day that he had taken a wife in the style of Romulus and Augustus. Then he suddenly sent to the provinces for Lollia Paulina, wife of Gaius Memmius,[21] the consular army commander, because somebody had remarked that her grandmother was once a famous beauty; but he soon discarded her, forbidding her ever again to sleep with another man. Caesonia was neither young nor beautiful and had three daughters by a former husband, besides being recklessly extravagant and utterly promiscuous, yet he loved her with a passionate faithfulness and often, when reviewing the troops, used to take her out riding in helmet, cloak and shield. For his friends he even paraded her naked, but he would not

allow her the dignified title of wife until she had borne him a child, whereupon he announced the marriage and the birth simultaneously. He named the child Julia Drusilla, and carried her around the temples of all the goddesses in turn before finally entrusting her to the lap of Minerva, whom he called upon to supervise his daughter's growth and education. What he regarded as the surest proof of his paternity was her violent temper: while still an infant, she would try to scratch out her little playmates' eyes.

26. It seems hardly worthwhile to record how Gaius treated such relatives and friends as his cousin King Ptolemy (son of Juba and Mark Antony's daughter Selene) and even Macro and his wife Ennia, by whose help he had become emperor. Their very loyalty and nearness to him earned them cruel deaths. Nor was he any more respectful or considerate in his dealings with the Senate, but made some of the highest officials run for miles beside his chariot, dressed in their togas, or wait in short linen tunics at the head or foot of his dining couch. Often he would send for men whom he had secretly killed, as though they were still alive, and remark offhandedly a few days later that they must have committed suicide. When the consuls forgot to announce his birthday, he dismissed them and left the commonwealth for three days without its chief officers. One of his quaestors was charged with conspiracy; Gaius had his clothes stripped off and spread on the ground, to give the soldiers who flogged him a firmer foothold.

He behaved just as arrogantly and violently towards people of less exalted rank. A crowd bursting into the Circus in the middle of the night to secure free seats angered him so much that he had them driven away with clubs; more than a score of *equites*, as many married women, and numerous others were crushed to death in the ensuing panic. Gaius liked to stir up trouble in the theatre by scattering gift vouchers before the seats were occupied, thus tempting the common people to invade the rows reserved for *equites*. During gladiatorial shows he would have the canopies removed at the hottest time of the day and forbid anyone to leave; or cancel the regular programme and substitute worn-out wild beasts and feeble old fighters; or stage

comic duels between respectable householders who happened
to be physically disabled in some way or other. More than once
he closed down the granaries and let the people go hungry.

27. The following instances will illustrate his cruelty. Having
collected wild animals for one of his shows, he found butcher's
meat too expensive and decided to feed them with criminals
instead. He paid no attention to the charge sheets, but simply
stood in the middle of a colonnade, glanced at the prisoners
lined up before him, and gave the order 'Kill every man between
that bald head and that other one over there.' Someone had
sworn to fight in the arena if he recovered from his illness;
Gaius forced him to fulfil this oath and watched his swordplay
closely, not letting him go until he had won the match and
begged abjectly to be released. Another fellow had pledged
himself on the same occasion to commit suicide; Gaius, finding
that he was still alive, ordered him to be dressed in wreaths and
fillets and driven through Rome by the imperial slaves, who
kept harping on his pledge and finally flung him over the ram-
part. Many men of decent family were branded at his command
and sent down the mines, or put to work on the roads, or
thrown to the wild beasts. Others were confined in narrow
cages, where they had to crouch on all fours like animals, or
were sawn in half – and not necessarily for major offences, but
merely for criticizing his shows, failing to swear by his *genius*,
and so forth.

Gaius made parents attend their sons' executions, and when
one father excused himself on the ground of ill health he provided
a litter for him. Having invited another father to dinner just after
the son's execution, he overflowed with good fellowship in an
attempt to make him laugh and joke. He watched the manager
of his gladiatorial and wild-beast shows being flogged with
chains for several days running, and had him killed only when
the smell of suppurating brains became insupportable. A writer
of Atellan farces was burned alive in the amphitheatre, because
of a single line which had an amusing double entendre. One
eques, on the point of being thrown to the wild beasts, shouted
that he was innocent; Gaius brought him back, removed his
tongue, and then ordered the sentence to be carried out.

28. Once he asked a returned exile how he had been spending his time. To flatter him the man answered, 'I prayed continuously to the gods for Tiberius' death and your accession, and my prayer was granted.' Gaius therefore concluded that the new batch of exiles must be praying for his own death, so he sent agents from island to island and had them all killed. Being anxious that one particular senator should be torn in pieces, he persuaded some of his colleagues to challenge him as a public enemy when he entered the Senate House, stab him with their pens, and then hand him over for lynching to the rest of the Senate; and he was not satisfied until the victim's limbs, organs and guts had been dragged through the streets and heaped up at his feet.

29. His savage crimes were matched by his brutal language. He claimed that no personal trait made him feel prouder than his 'inflexibility' – by which he must have meant 'brazen impudence'. As though mere deafness to his grandmother Antonia's good advice were not enough, he told her, 'Bear in mind that I can do anything I want to anyone I want!' Suspecting that young Tiberius had taken drugs as prophylactics to the poison he intended to administer, Gaius scoffed, 'Can there really be an antidote against Caesar?' And on banishing his sisters he remarked, 'I have swords as well as islands.' One man of praetorian status, taking a cure at Anticyra, made frequent requests for an extension of his sick leave; Gaius had his throat cut, suggesting that if hellebore had been of so little benefit over so long a period, he must need to be bled. When signing the execution list after the ten-day waiting period he used to say, 'I am clearing my accounts.' And one day, after sentencing a number of Gauls and Greeks to die in the same batch, he boasted of having 'subdued Gallograecia'.[22]

30. The method of execution he preferred was to inflict numerous small wounds, avoiding the prisoner's vital organs, and his familiar order 'Make him feel that he is dying!' soon became proverbial. Once, when the wrong man had been killed, owing to a confusion of names, he announced that the victim had equally deserved death, and he often quoted the tragic line 'Let them hate me, so long as they fear me.'[23] He would

indiscriminately abuse the Senate as having been supporters of
Sejanus or informers against his mother and brothers (at this
point producing the papers which he was supposed to have
burned), and exclaim that Tiberius' cruelty had been quite
justified since, with so many accusers about, he was bound to
believe their charges. The *equites* earned his constant displeasure for spending their time, or so he complained, at the
plays or the games. On one occasion the people cheered the
wrong team; he cried angrily, 'I wish all you Romans had only
one neck!' When a shout arose in the amphitheatre for Tetrinius
the bandit to come out and fight, he said that all those who
called for him were Tetriniuses too. A group of net-and-trident
gladiators, dressed in tunics, put up a very poor show against
the five men-at-arms with whom they were matched; but when
he sentenced them to death for cowardice, one of them seized
a trident and killed each of his opponents in turn. Gaius then
publicly expressed his horror at what he called 'this most bloody
murder', and his disgust with those who had been able to
stomach the sight.

31. He went about complaining how bad the times were, and
particularly that there had been no public disasters like the
Varus massacre under Augustus or the collapse of the amphitheatre at Fidenae under Tiberius.[24] The prosperity of his own
reign, he said, would lead to its being wholly forgotten, and he
often prayed for a great military catastrophe or for famine,
plague, fire or at least an earthquake.

32. Everything that Gaius said and did was marked with
equal cruelty, even during his hours of rest and amusement
and banquetry. He frequently had trials by torture held in his
presence while he was eating or otherwise enjoying himself,
and kept an expert headsman in readiness to decapitate the
prisoners brought in from jail. When the bridge across the sea
at Puteoli was being dedicated, he invited a number of spectators from the shore to inspect it and then abruptly tipped
them into the water; some clung to the ships' rudders, but he
had them dislodged with boathooks and oars and left to drown.
At a public dinner in Rome he sent to his executioners a slave
who had stolen a strip of silver from a couch; they were to lop

off the man's hands, tie them around his neck so that they hung on his breast, and take him for a tour of the tables, displaying a placard in explanation of his punishment. On another occasion a gladiator against whom he was fencing with a wooden sword fell down deliberately, whereupon Gaius drew a real dagger, stabbed him to death, and ran about waving the palm branch of victory. Once, while serving at an altar in the role of sacrificial assistant, he swung his mallet as if at the victim, but instead felled his fellow assistant, whose duty it was to slit its throat. At one particularly extravagant banquet he burst into sudden peals of laughter. The consuls, who were reclining next to him, politely asked whether they might share the joke. 'What do you think?' he answered. 'It occurred to me that I have only to give one nod and both your throats will be cut on the spot!'

33. He played a prank on Apelles, the tragic actor, by striking a pose beside a statue of Jupiter and asking, 'Which of us two is the greater?' When Apelles hesitated momentarily, Gaius had him flogged, commenting on the musical quality even of his groans for mercy. He never kissed the neck of his wife or mistress without saying, 'And this beautiful throat will be cut whenever I please.' Sometimes he even threatened to torture Caesonia as a means of discovering why he was so devoted to her.

34. In his insolent pride and destructiveness he made malicious attacks on men of almost every epoch. Needing more room in the Capitol courtyard, Augustus had once shifted the statues of certain famous men to the Campus Martius; these Gaius dashed to the ground and shattered so completely that they could not possibly be restored, even though their bases were intact. After this no statue or bust of any living person could be set up without his permission. He toyed with the idea of suppressing Homer's poems – for surely, he would say, he might claim Plato's privilege of banishing Homer from his republic.[25] As for Virgil and Livy, Gaius came very near to having their works and busts removed from the libraries, claiming that Virgil had little knowledge and less skill and that Livy was a wordy and inaccurate historian. It seems also that he

proposed to abolish the study of law; at any rate, he often swore by Hercules that no legal expert's advice would ever thwart his will.

35. Gaius deprived the noblest men at Rome of their ancient family emblems – Torquatus lost his golden torc, Cincinnatus his lock of hair, and Gnaeus Pompeius the famous cognomen Magnus.[26] He invited King Ptolemy to visit Rome, welcomed him with appropriate honours, and then suddenly ordered his execution – as mentioned above – because at Ptolemy's entrance into the amphitheatre during a gladiatorial show the fine purple cloak which he wore had attracted universal admiration. Any good-looking man with a fine head of hair whom Gaius ran across had the back of his scalp brutally shaved.[27] One Aesius Proculus, the son of a *primipilaris*, was so well built and handsome that people nicknamed him 'Colosseros'.[28] Without warning, Gaius ordered Aesius to be dragged from his seat in the amphitheatre into the arena and matched first with a Thracian net fighter, then with a man-at-arms. Though Aesius won both combats, he was thereupon dressed in rags, led fettered through the streets to be jeered at by women, and finally strangled. In short, however low anyone's fortune or condition might be, Gaius always found some cause for envy. Thus he sent a stronger man to challenge the current King of the Grove,[29] simply because he had held his priesthood for a number of years. A chariot fighter called Porius drew such tremendous applause for freeing his slave in celebration of a victory at the games that Gaius indignantly rushed from the amphitheatre. In so doing he tripped over the fringe of his robe and pitched down the steps, at the bottom of which he complained that the most powerful race in the world seemed to take greater notice of a gladiator's trifling gesture than of all their deified emperors, even the one still among them.

36. He had not the slightest regard for chastity, either his own or others', and is said to have had sexual relations, both active and passive, with Marcus Lepidus, Mnester the pantomime dancer, and various foreign hostages; moreover, a young man of consular family, Valerius Catullus, publicly announced that Gaius had been his passive sexual partner and had com-

pletely exhausted him with his demands. Besides incest with his sisters, and a notorious passion for the prostitute Pyrallis, Gaius made advances to almost every well-known married woman in Rome; after inviting a selection of them to dinner with their husbands, he would slowly and carefully examine each in turn while they passed his couch, as a purchaser might assess the value of a slave, and even stretch out his hand and lift up the chin of any woman who kept her eyes modestly cast down. Then, whenever he felt so inclined, he would send for whoever pleased him best and leave the banquet in her company. A little later he would return, showing obvious signs of what he had been about, and openly discuss his bedfellow in detail, dwelling on her good and bad physical points and criticizing her sexual performance. To some of these unfortunates he issued, and publicly registered, divorces in the name of their absent husbands.

37. No parallel can be found for Gaius' far-fetched extravagances. He invented new kinds of baths and the most unnatural dishes and drinks – bathing in hot and cold perfumes, drinking valuable pearls dissolved in vinegar, and providing his guests with golden bread and golden meat; he would remark that Caesar alone could not afford to be frugal. For several days in succession he scattered large sums of money from the roof of the Basilica Julia, and he built Liburnian galleys with ten banks of oars, jewelled poop decks, multicoloured sails, and huge baths, colonnades and banqueting halls aboard – not to mention growing vines and fruit trees of different varieties. In these vessels he used to take day-long cruises along the Campanian coast, reclining on his couch and listening to songs and choruses. Villas and country houses were run up for him regardless of expense. In fact Gaius seemed interested only in doing the apparently impossible, which led him to construct moles in deep, rough water far out to sea, drive tunnels through exceptionally hard rocks, raise flat ground to the height of mountains, and reduce mountains to the level of plains – and all at immense speed, because he punished delay with death. But why give details? Suffice it to record that in less than a year he squandered Tiberius' entire fortune of 2,700 million sesterces, and an enormous amount of other treasure besides.

38. When bankrupt and in need of funds, Gaius concentrated on wickedly ingenious methods of raising funds by false accusations, auctions, and taxes. He ruled that no man could inherit the Roman citizenship acquired by any ancestor more remote than his father, and when confronted with certificates of citizenship issued by Divus Julius or Divus Augustus he rejected them as obsolete. He also disallowed all property returns to which, for whatever reason, later additions had been appended. If a *primipilaris* had bequeathed nothing either to Tiberius or himself since the beginning of the former's reign, he would rescind the will on the ground of ingratitude, and he likewise voided the wills of all other persons who were said to have intended making him their heir when they died but had not done so. This caused widespread alarm, so that people would openly declare that he was one of their heirs, with strangers listing him among their friends and parents among their children; but if they continued to live after the declaration he considered himself tricked, and sent several of them presents of poisoned sweets. Gaius conducted these cases in person, first announcing the sum he meant to raise, and not stopping until he had raised it. The slightest delay nettled him; he once passed a single sentence on a batch of more than forty men charged with various offences, and then boasted to Caesonia, when she woke from her nap, that he had done very good business since she dozed off.

He would auction whatever properties were left over from a theatrical show, driving up the bidding to such heights that many of those present, forced to buy at fantastic prices, found themselves ruined and committed suicide by opening their veins. A famous occasion was when Aponius Saturninus fell asleep on a bench, and Gaius warned the auctioneer to keep an eye on the senator of praetorian rank who kept nodding his head. Before the bidding ended Aponius had unwittingly bought thirteen gladiators for a total of 9 million sesterces.

39. While in Gaul, Gaius did so well by selling the furniture, jewellery, slaves and even the freedmen of his condemned sisters at a ridiculous overvaluation that he decided to do the same with the furnishings of the old palace. So he sent to Rome,

where his agents commandeered public conveyances and even draught animals from the bakeries to fetch the stuff north; this led to a bread shortage in Rome and to the loss of many lawsuits, because litigants who lived at a distance were unable to appear in court and meet their bail. He then used all kinds of tricks for disposing of the furniture: scolding the bidders for their avarice or for their shamelessness in being richer than he was, and pretending grief at this surrender of family property to commoners. Discovering that one wealthy provincial had paid his stewards 200,000 sesterces to be smuggled into a banquet, Caligula was delighted that the privilege of dining with him should be valued so highly, and when next day the same man turned up at the auction he made him pay 200,000 sesterces for some trifling object – but also sent him a personal invitation to dinner.

40. The publicans were ordered to raise new and unprecedented taxes, and found this so profitable that he detailed the tribunes and centurions of the praetorian guards to collect the money instead. No goods or services now avoided duty of some kind. He imposed a fixed tax on all foodstuffs sold in any quarter of the city, and a charge of 2½ per cent on the money involved in every lawsuit and legal transaction whatsoever, and also devised special penalties for anyone who settled out of court or abandoned a case. Porters had to hand over an eighth part of their day's earnings, and prostitutes their standard fee for a single act of intimacy, even if they had quitted their profession and were respectably married; pimps and ex-pimps also became liable to this public tax.

41. These new regulations having been announced by word of mouth only, many people failed to observe them through ignorance. At last he acceded to the urgent popular demand by posting the regulations up, but in an awkwardly cramped spot and written so small that no one could take a copy. He never missed a chance of making profits: setting aside a suite of rooms on the Palatine, he decorated them worthily, opened a brothel, stocked it with married women and freeborn boys, and then sent his pages around the squares and public places, inviting men of all ages to come and enjoy themselves. Those who

appeared were lent money at interest, and clerks wrote down their names under the heading 'Contributors to Caesar's Revenue'.

Even when Gaius played at dice he would always cheat and lie. Once he interrupted a game by giving up his seat to the man behind him and going out into the courtyard. A couple of rich *equites* passed; he immediately had them arrested and confiscated their property, and then resumed the game in high spirits, boasting that his luck had never been better.

42. His daughter's birth gave him an excuse for further complaints of poverty. 'In addition to the burden of sovereignty,' he said, 'I must now shoulder that of fatherhood' – and he promptly took up a collection for her education and dowry. He also announced that good-luck gifts would be welcomed on the Kalends of January, and then sat in the palace porch, grabbing the handfuls and capfuls of coins which a mixed crowd of all classes pressed on him. At last he developed a passion for the feel of money and, spilling heaps of gold pieces on an open space, would walk over them barefoot or else lie down and wallow.

43. Gaius had only a single taste of warfare, and even that was unpremeditated. At Mevania, where he went to visit the river Clitumnus and its sacred grove, he was reminded that he needed Batavian recruits for his bodyguard, and this suggested the idea of a German expedition.[30] He wasted no time in summoning legions and auxiliaries from all directions, levied troops with the utmost strictness, and collected military supplies on an unprecedented scale. Then he marched off with such rapidity that the praetorian cohorts could not keep up with him except by breaking tradition and tying their standards on the pack mules. Yet later he became so lazy and self-indulgent that he travelled in a litter borne by eight bearers, and whenever he approached a town he made the inhabitants sweep the roads and lay the dust with sprinklers.

44. After reaching the camp, Gaius showed how keen and severe a commander he intended to be by ignominiously dismissing any legate who was late in bringing along the auxiliaries he required. Then, when he reviewed the legions, he discharged

several veteran *primipilares* on grounds of age and incapacity, though some had only a few more days of their service to run, and, calling the remainder a pack of greedy fellows, scaled down their retirement bonus to 6,000 sesterces each.

All that he accomplished in this expedition was to receive the surrender of Adminius, son of the British king Cynobellinus, who had been banished by his father and come over to the Romans with a few followers. Gaius nevertheless wrote an extravagant dispatch which might have persuaded any reader that the whole island had surrendered to him, and ordered the couriers to drive their chariots all the way to the Forum and the Senate House[31] and to deliver his letter to the consuls in the Temple of Mars in the presence of the entire Senate.

45. Since the chance of military action appeared very remote, he soon ordered a few German prisoners to be taken across the Rhine and hidden among the trees. After lunch, scouts hurried in to tell him excitedly that the enemy were upon him. He at once galloped out at the head of his staff and part of the praetorian cavalry to halt in the nearest thicket, where they chopped branches from the trees and dressed them like trophies; then, riding back by torchlight, he taunted as cowards all who had failed to follow him and awarded his fellow heroes a novel fashion in crowns – he called it 'The Ranger's Crown' – ornamented with sun, moon and stars. On another day he took some German hostages from a school where they were being taught the rudiments of Latin and secretly ordered them on ahead of him. Later he left his dinner in a hurry and took his cavalry in pursuit of them, as though they had been fugitives. He was no less melodramatic about this foray: when he returned to the hall after catching the hostages and bringing them back in irons, and his officers reported that the army was marshalled, he made them recline at table, still in their corselets, and quoted Virgil's famous advice: 'Be steadfast, comrades, and preserve yourselves for happier occasions.'[32] He also severely reprimanded the absent Senate and People for enjoying banquets and festivities and for hanging about the theatres or their luxurious country houses while their Caesar was exposed to all the hazards of war.

46. In the end, he drew up his army in battle array on the shore of the Ocean[33] and moved the siege engines into position as though he intended to bring the campaign to a close. No one had the least notion what was in his mind, when suddenly he gave the order 'Gather seashells!' He referred to the shells as 'plunder from the sea, due to the Capitol and to the Palatine', and made the troops fill their helmets and the folds of their clothes with them; he commemorated this victory by the erection of a tall lighthouse, not unlike the one at Pharos,[34] in which fires were to be kept going all night as a guide to ships. Then he promised every soldier a bounty of 100 denarii, and told them, 'Go rich, go happy!', as though he had surpassed every standard of generosity.

47. He now concentrated his attention on the imminent triumph. To supplement the few prisoners taken in frontier skirmishes and the deserters who had come over from the barbarians, he picked the tallest Gauls of the province – 'those worthy of a triumph', as he himself said – and some of their leaders as well, for his supposed train of captives. These had not only to grow their hair and dye it red, but also to learn Germanic speech and adopt Germanic names. The triremes used in the Ocean were carted to Rome, overland for most of the way. He sent a letter ahead instructing his agents to prepare a triumph more lavish than any hitherto known, but at the least possible expense, and added that everyone's property was at their disposal.

48. Before leaving Gaul he planned, in a sudden access of cruelty, to massacre the legionaries who, at news of Augustus' death, had mutinously besieged both his father Germanicus, their commander, and himself, still only a baby. His friends barely restrained him from carrying out this plan, and could not at all dissuade him from deciding on a decimation.[35] And so he summoned the troops to assemble without any arms, even their swords, and surrounded them with armed horsemen. But when he noticed that a number of legionaries, scenting trouble, were slipping away to fetch their weapons, he hurriedly absconded and headed straight for Rome. There, to distract attention from his inglorious exploits, he vengefully threatened the Senate, who

he said had cheated him of a well-earned triumph – though in point of fact he had expressly stated a few days before that they must do nothing to honour him, on pain of death.

49. So, when the distinguished senatorial delegates met him with an official plea for his immediate return, he shouted, 'I am coming, never fear, and this' – tapping the hilt of his sword – 'is coming too!' He proclaimed that he was returning only to those who would really welcome him, namely the *equites* and the people; so far as the senators were concerned, he would never again consider himself their fellow citizen or their *princeps*, and he even forbade any more of them to meet him. Having cancelled or at least postponed his triumph, he entered the city on his birthday and received an ovation. Within four months he was dead.

Gaius had dared commit fearful crimes and contemplated even worse ones, such as murdering the most distinguished of the senators and *equites* and then moving the seat of government first to Antium and afterwards to Alexandria. If at this point my readers become incredulous, let me record that two notebooks were found among his private papers entitled *Dagger* and *Sword*, each of them containing the names and particulars of men whom he had planned to kill. A huge chest filled with poisons also came to light. It is said that when Claudius later threw this into the sea, quantities of dead fish, cast up by the tide, littered the neighbouring beaches.

50. Gaius was tall, with a pallid complexion; he had a large body, but a thin neck and spindly legs; his eyes were sunken and his temples hollow, although his forehead was broad and forbidding. In contrast to his noticeably hairy body, the hair on his head was thin, and his crown was completely bald. Because of his baldness and hairiness, he announced that it was a capital offence for anyone either to look down on him as he passed or to mention goats in any context. He worked hard to make his naturally uncouth face even more repulsive by practising fearful grimaces in front of a mirror.

As to his health, Gaius was sick both physically and mentally. As a boy, he suffered from epilepsy, and, although his resistance to the disease gradually strengthened, there were times in his youth when he could hardly walk, stand, think or hold up his head, owing to sudden fits. He was well aware that he had mental trouble, and sometimes proposed taking a leave of absence from Rome to clear his brain; Caesonia is reputed to have given him an aphrodisiac which drove him mad. Insomnia was his worst torment. Three hours a night of fitful sleep were all that he ever got, and even then terrifying visions would haunt him – once, for instance, he dreamed that he had a conversation with the sea. He tired of lying awake the greater part of the night, and would alternately sit up in bed and wander through the long corridors, invoking the day which seemed as if it would never break.

51. I am convinced that this mental illness accounted for his two contradictory vices – overconfidence and extreme timorousness. Here was a man who despised the gods, yet shut his eyes and buried his head beneath the bedclothes at the most distant sound of thunder; and if the storm came closer he would jump out of bed and crawl underneath. In his travels through Sicily he poked fun at the miraculous stories associated with the various locales, yet on reaching Messana he suddenly fled in the middle of the night, terrified by the smoke and noise which came from the crater of Aetna. Despite his fearful threats against the barbarians, he showed so little courage after he had crossed the Rhine and gone riding in a chariot through a defile that when someone happened to remark 'What a panic there would be if the enemy unexpectedly appeared!' he leaped on a horse and galloped back to the bridges. These were crowded with army transport, but he had himself passed from hand to hand over the men's heads in his haste to regain the further bank. Even when safely home he was alarmed by reported revolts in Germany and decided to escape by sea. He fitted out a large fleet for this purpose, finding comfort only in the thought that, should the enemy be victorious and occupy the Alpine passes, as the Cimbri had done, or Rome, as the Senones had done,[36] he would at least be able to hold his overseas provinces. This was probably what later gave his assassins the idea of quieting his vengeful German bodyguard with the story that rumours of a defeat had scared him into sudden suicide.

52. Gaius paid no attention to traditional or current fashions in his dress, but ignored masculine and even human conventions. Often he made public appearances in a cloak covered with embroidery and encrusted with precious stones, a long-sleeved tunic, and bracelets, and at other times in silk or even a woman's gown; and he came shod sometimes with slippers, sometimes with buskins, sometimes with military boots, sometimes with women's shoes. Occasionally he affected a golden beard and carried Jupiter's thunderbolt, Neptune's trident or Mercury's caduceus.[37] He even dressed up as Venus, and long before his expedition he wore the uniform of a triumphant general, often embellished with the breastplate which he had stolen from the tomb of Alexander the Great.

53. Though no man of letters, Gaius took pains to study oratory, and showed remarkable eloquence and quickness of mind, especially when prosecuting. Anger incited him to a flood of verbiage; he moved about excitedly while speaking, and his voice carried a great distance. At the start of every speech he would threaten to 'draw the sword which he had forged in his midnight study'; yet he so despised more elegant and melodious styles that he discounted Seneca, then at the height of his fame, as a 'mere textbook orator' and 'sand without lime'. He often published confutations of speakers who had successfully pleaded a case, or composed speeches for both the prosecution and the defence of important men who were on trial by the Senate – the verdict depending entirely on the caprice of his pen – and would invite the *equites* by proclamation to attend and listen.

54. Gaius practised many other arts – most enthusiastically too. He made appearances as a Thracian gladiator and a charioteer, as a singer and a dancer; he would fight with real weapons and drive chariots in the circuses that he had built in many places. Indeed, he was so proud of his singing and dancing that he could not resist the temptation of supporting the tragic actors at public performances, and would repeat their gestures by way of praise or criticism. On the very day of his death he seems to have ordered an all-night festival so that he could take advantage of the free-and-easy atmosphere to make his stage debut.

He often danced even at night, and once, at the close of the second watch, summoned three senators of consular rank to the palace; arriving half-dead with fear, they were conducted to a stage upon which, amid a tremendous racket of flutes and castanets, Gaius suddenly burst, dressed in a shawl and an ankle-length tunic; he performed a song and dance, and disappeared as suddenly as he had entered. Yet with all these gifts he could not swim a stroke!

55. On those whom he loved he bestowed an almost insane passion. He would shower kisses on Mnester the pantomime dancer even in the theatre, and if anyone made the slightest noise during his performances Gaius had the offender dragged from his seat and beat him with his own hands. To an *eques* who created some disturbance while Mnester was on the stage, Gaius sent instructions by a centurion to sail from Ostia and convey a sealed message to King Ptolemy in Mauretania. The message read, 'Do nothing at all, either good or bad, to the bearer.'

He chose Thracian gladiators to officer his German bodyguard. Disliking the men-at-arms, he reduced their defensive armour; and when a gladiator of this sort, called Columbus, won a fight but was lightly wounded, Gaius treated him with a virulent poison which he afterwards called 'Columbinum' – at any rate that was how he described it in his catalogue of poisons. Gaius supported the Green faction[38] with such ardour that he would often dine and spend the night in their stables, and on one occasion he gave the driver Eutychus presents worth 2 million sesterces. To prevent Incitatus, his favourite horse, from growing restive he always picketed the neighbourhood with troops on the day before the races, ordering them to enforce absolute silence. Incitatus owned a marble stable, an ivory stall, purple blankets and a jewelled collar, as well as a house, furniture and slaves – to provide suitable entertainment for guests whom Gaius invited in its name. It is said that he even planned to award Incitatus a consulship.

56. Such frantic and reckless behaviour roused murderous thoughts in certain minds. One or two plots for his assassination were discovered; others were still maturing when two tribunes

of the praetorian guard put their heads together and succeeded in killing him, thanks to the cooperation of his most powerful freedmen and the praetorian prefects. Both these tribunes had been accused of being implicated in a previous plot and, although innocent, realized that Gaius hated and feared them. Once, in fact, he had subjected them to public shame and suspicion, taking them aside and announcing, as he waved a sword, that he would gladly kill himself if they thought him deserving of death. After this he accused them again and again, each to the other, and tried to make bad blood between them. At last they decided to kill him about noon at the conclusion of the Palatine Games, the principal part in this drama of blood being claimed by Cassius Chaerea. Gaius had persistently teased Cassius, who was no longer young, for his supposed effeminacy. Whenever he demanded the watchword, Gaius used to give him 'Priapus' or 'Venus';[39] and if he came to acknowledge a favour he always stuck out his middle finger for him to kiss, and wiggled it obscenely.

57. Many omens of Gaius' approaching death were reported. While the statue of Jupiter at Olympia was being dismantled before removal to Rome at his command, it burst into such a roar of laughter that the scaffolding collapsed and the workmen took to their heels, and a man named Cassius appeared immediately afterwards saying that Jupiter had ordered him in a dream to sacrifice a bull. The Capitol at Capua was struck by lightning on the Ides of March, which some interpreted as portending another death of the same sort that had previously occurred on that day. At Rome, the Palatine steward's lodge was likewise struck, and this seemed to mean that the master of the house stood in danger of attack by his own guards. On asking the astrologer Sulla for his horoscope, Gaius learned that he must expect to die very soon. The oracle of the goddesses of Fortune at Antium likewise warned him, 'Beware of Cassius!'; whereupon, forgetting Chaerea's nomen, he ordered the murder of Cassius Longinus, the consular governor of Asia. On the night before his assassination he dreamed that he was standing beside Jupiter's heavenly throne, when the god kicked him with the great toe of his right foot and sent him tumbling down to earth.

Some other events that occurred on the day of his death were read as portents. For instance, blood splashed Gaius as he was sacrificing a flamingo; Mnester danced the same tragedy that had been performed by the actor Neoptolemus during the games at which King Philip of Macedonia was assassinated; and a farce called *Laureolus*, at the close of which the leading character, a highwayman, had to die while escaping and vomit blood, was immediately followed by a humorous epilogue – the comedians were so anxious to display their proficiency at dying that they flooded the stage with blood. An evening performance by Egyptians and Ethiopians was also in rehearsal – a play staged in the underworld.

58. On 24 January then, at just about the seventh hour, Gaius could not make up his mind whether to rise for lunch; he still felt a little queasy after too heavy a banquet on the previous night. However, his friends persuaded him to come out with them along a covered walk, and there he found some boys of noble family, whom he had summoned from Asia to perform on stage, rehearsing their presentation. He stopped to watch and encourage them, and would have taken them back to the theatre and held the performance at once had their principal not complained of the cold. Two different versions of what followed are current. Some say that Chaerea came up behind Gaius as he stood talking to the boys and, with a cry of 'Take this!', gave him a deep sword wound in the neck, whereupon Gaius Sabinus, the other conspirator, stabbed him in the breast. The other version makes Sabinus tell certain centurions implicated in the plot to clear away the crowd and then ask Gaius for the day's watchword. He is said to have replied 'Jupiter', whereupon Chaerea, from his rear, yelled 'So be it!' and split his jawbone as he turned his head. Gaius lay twitching on the ground: 'I am still alive!' he shouted, but word went round, 'Strike again!', and he succumbed to further wounds, including sword thrusts through the genitals. Gaius' bearers rushed to help him at the first alarm, using their litter poles as spears, and soon his German bodyguard appeared – too late to be of any service, though they killed several of the assassins and a few innocent senators into the bargain.

59. He died at the age of twenty-nine, after ruling for three years, ten months and eight days. His body was moved secretly to the Lamian Gardens, half-cremated on a hastily built pyre, and then buried beneath a shallow covering of sods. Later, when his sisters returned from exile, they exhumed, cremated and entombed it. But all the city knew that the gardens had been haunted until then by his ghost, and that something horrible appeared every night at the scene of the murder until at last the building burned down.

His wife Caesonia died at the same time as he, stabbed with a sword by a centurion, and his little daughter's brains were dashed out against a wall.

60. The terror inspired by Gaius' reign could be judged by the sequel: everyone was extremely reluctant to believe that he had really been assassinated, and suspected that the story was invented by himself to discover what people thought of him. The conspirators had not planned to bestow power on anyone in particular, and most senators were so bent on restoring the republic that the consuls summoned the first assembly not to the Senate House, because it was named the Julian Hall, but to the Capitol. Some wanted all memory of the Caesars obliterated and their temples destroyed. People commented on the fact that every Caesar named Gaius had died by the sword, beginning with the one murdered in Cinna's day.[40]

DIVUS CLAUDIUS

1. When, three months after her marriage to Augustus, Livia gave birth to Decimus (later Nero) Drusus, the father of Claudius Caesar, people suspected that Augustus, not her ex-husband, was the father. This provoked the following epigram:

> How fortunate those parents are for whom
> Their child is only three months in the womb![1]

Drusus commanded an army against the Raeti and then against the Germans, while holding the successive ranks of quaestor and praetor. He was the first Roman general to navigate the northern Ocean, and also constructed the canals across the Rhine that still bear his name, a remarkable and demanding task. After defeating the local tribes in a series of battles, Drusus drove them far back into the wild interior, until checked by an apparition: a barbarous woman of phenomenal size, who warned him in Latin to venture no further.

These campaigns earned Drusus an ovation and triumphal decorations, and he became consul directly the praetorship ended. On resuming the war, he died at his summer headquarters, thenceforth known as 'The Accursed Camp'. His body was carried to Rome in a coffin by relays of leading citizens from the various free towns and colonies which lay along the route. There a waiting deputation of magistrates' clerks took it to a pyre on the Campus Martius. The army voluntarily built a cenotaph for him, at which on a fixed day every year the soldiers were to perform a ceremonial drill and the cities of Gaul offer sacrifice. The Senate voted Drusus many honours, among them a marble arch on the Via Appia decorated with trophies and the surname Germanicus to be held by himself and his descendants in perpetuity.

Drusus was, they say, no less eager for personal glory than he was unassuming and restrained in his personal style. Not content with gaining victories over the enemy, he had a long-standing ambition to win what were called 'the Noblest Spoils',[2] and used to chase the German leaders across the battlefield at great risk to his life. He also openly announced that, as soon as he came to power, he would restore the republic. This must be why some writers allege that Augustus was suspicious of him, recalled him from his province, and, when he did not come back at once, had him poisoned. I think it right not to suppress what seems to me a most improbable view; in point of fact, Augustus felt so deep a love for Drusus that, as he admitted to the Senate on one occasion, he made him co-heir with his adopted sons, and his public funeral speech not only eulogized Drusus but included a prayer that the gods would make these young Caesars closely resemble him and would grant them as honourable a death. Nor did he think it enough to have an adulatory inscription carved on Drusus' tomb: he also wrote his biography.

Antonia the younger bore Drusus several children, three of whom survived him: Germanicus, Livilla and Claudius.

2. Claudius was born at Lugdunum in the consulship of Iullus Antonius and Fabius Africanus on the Kalends of August, the very day when the altar was first dedicated there to Augustus, and was given the name Tiberius Claudius Drusus; he took Germanicus' cognomen after his brother had been adopted into the Julian family.[3] He was orphaned as a baby, and nearly the whole of his childhood and youth was so troubled by various diseases that he grew dull-witted and had little physical strength; and on reaching the age at which he should have won a magistracy or chosen a private career he was considered by his family incapable of doing either.

Even after coming of age he remained under the supervision of a tutor, about whom he later wrote, 'The man was a barbarian, an ex-transport officer who had been assigned the task

of punishing me savagely whatever I might do.' Claudius' weak
health also accounted for his being muffled in a mantle – an
unprecedented sight – while presiding at the gladiatorial games
given by Germanicus and himself to honour their father's
memory; on assuming the toga of adulthood he was taken up
to the Capitol in a litter, about midnight, without the customary
solemn procession.

3. Nevertheless, he applied himself seriously to literature
while still a child, and published several samples of his proficiency in its various departments. Yet even this did not
advance him to public office or inspire the family with brighter
hopes for his future. His mother Antonia often called him 'a
monster: a man whom Nature had begun to work upon but
then flung aside'; and if she ever accused anyone of stupidity
she would exclaim, 'He is a bigger fool even than my son
Claudius!' Livia Augusta, his grandmother, never failed to treat
him with the deepest scorn, and seldom addressed him personally; her reproofs came in the form of brief, bitter letters or oral
messages. When his sister Livilla heard someone predict that he
would one day hold power, she prayed aloud that the Roman
people might be spared so cruel and undeserved a misfortune.
Finally, to show what his great-uncle Augustus thought of him,
I quote the following extracts from his correspondence.

4. 'As you suggested, my dear Livia, I have now discussed
with Tiberius what we should do about your grandson Tiberius
Claudius at the coming festival of Mars. We both agreed that
a decision ought to be taken for once and all regarding our
plans for him. The question is whether he has, so to speak, full
command of his five senses. If so, I can see nothing against
sending him through the same degrees of office as his brother
Germanicus; but should he prove physically and mentally
deficient, the public (which is always amused by trifles) must
not be given a chance of laughing at him and us. I fear that we
shall find ourselves in constant trouble if the question of his
fitness to officiate in this or that capacity keeps cropping up. We
should therefore decide in advance whether he can or cannot be
trusted with public offices generally.

'As regards the immediate question in your last letter, I have no objection to his taking charge of the priests' banquet at the festival, if he lets his brother-in-law, young Silvanus, stand by to see that he does not make a fool of himself. But I am against his watching the games in the Circus from the gods' platform, where the eyes of the whole audience would be on him. I am also against his going to the Alban Mount or being in Rome for the Latin Festival; for why should he not be made prefect of the city if he can accompany his brother to the mountain?[4] There, my dear Livia, you have my views: it seems to me that we must reach a decision on this matter once and for all, to save us from further alternations of optimism and anxiety. You are at liberty to show this part of the letter to Antonia.'

Augustus wrote to Livia on another occasion: 'While you are away, I shall certainly invite young Tiberius Claudius to dine every afternoon, rather than leave him to the exclusive company of his pals Sulpicius and Athenodorus. I wish he would carefully and thoughtfully choose someone to imitate! Someone who holds himself up properly, walks well, and has graceful gestures. I am sorry for the poor little fellow, because in serious matters, when not wool-gathering, he shows considerable nobility of principle.'

And again, in a third letter, 'I'll be damned, my dear Livia, if your grandson Tiberius Claudius hasn't given me a very pleasant surprise! How on earth anyone who talks so confusedly can nevertheless declaim so well – with such clearness, saying all that needs to be said – I simply do not understand.'

However, it is clear what decision Augustus eventually took, because he gave Claudius no honours except a seat in the college of augurs, and listed him in his will among heirs in the third degree[5] – people so distant as to be practically strangers – and even at that level left him only a sixth part of his estate; the only legacy Claudius got in hard cash was a mere 800,000 sesterces.

5. When his uncle Tiberius succeeded Augustus, Claudius asked to be given some public office; Tiberius sent him the consular insignia. Claudius then pressed for the duties as well as the empty title of a consul. Tiberius' reply ran, 'I'm sending you forty aurei to be spent on trinkets for the Saturnalia and

Sigillaria.'⁶ After that, Claudius renounced all hopes of a political career, spending an obscure and idle life between his suburban mansion and a villa in Campania. Since several of his intimates were men of the lowest class, Claudius' reputation for worthlessness was further enhanced by stories of his drunkenness and love of gambling. Yet even so he never lost people's respect or public esteem.

6. The *equites* twice chose Claudius as their official representative to the consuls:⁷ the first time was when they requested the privilege of carrying Augustus' body back to Rome on their shoulders; the second, when Sejanus' conspiracy had been suppressed and they were offering felicitations; in fact when Claudius appeared at public shows, the entire equestrian order would rise and take off their cloaks as a mark of honour. The Senate, for their part, voted that he should be made an extraordinary member of the Augustan priesthood, who were as a rule chosen by lot; and when one day his mansion burned down they decreed that it should be rebuilt at public expense and that he should have the honour of addressing the Senate among men of consular rank. Tiberius, however, vetoed this decree on the ground that Claudius' ill health prevented him from participating in debates, and undertook that the cost of rebuilding the mansion would be defrayed at his own expense. When he died, Claudius was again listed only with heirs of the third degree, this time to a third part of the estate; but he did secure a legacy of 2 million sesterces and a commendation (in a list of Tiberius' relatives) to the army and the Senate and People of Rome.

7. As soon as Claudius' nephew Gaius became emperor and tried every means of gaining popularity, Claudius entered on his belated public career as his colleague in a two months' consulship; and when he first entered the Forum with the fasces, an eagle swooped down and perched on his shoulder. He also drew lots for a second consulship, and won one that would fall due four years later. Claudius sometimes presided as Gaius' substitute at the games, where the audience greeted him with 'Long live the emperor's uncle!' and 'Long live Germanicus' brother!'

8. Nevertheless, these honours did not protect him from

frequent insults. If ever he arrived a little late in the dining hall, there was nothing for it but to tour the tables in search of a vacant couch; and whenever he nodded off after dinner, as he usually did, the company would pelt him with olives and date stones. Some jokesters exercised their wit by putting slippers on his hands as he lay snoring, and then gave him a sudden blow of a whip or cane to wake him, so that he rubbed his eyes with them.

9. At times he even found himself in real danger. He was nearly removed from his first consulship for having taken so long to set up statues of Gaius' brothers Nero and Drusus, and later he had a variety of vexatious accusations brought against him, not only by strangers but by his own servants. When the Senate sent him with other envoys to felicitate Gaius, then in Germany, on the detection of a conspiracy headed by Lepidus and Gaetulicus,[8] Gaius felt so annoyed that his uncle, of all people, had been entrusted with this mission – as if to a child in need of a guardian – that he nearly killed him. According to one account, Claudius was thrown fully dressed into the Rhine as soon as he arrived. Afterwards, by way of humiliation, Gaius gave orders that Claudius should be the last man of consular rank called upon to speak in any debate. The Senate even found that a will witnessed by him was a forgery. As a climax, when he was obliged to pay a fee of 8 million sesterces for entering Gaius' new priesthood, he had to borrow the sum from the public treasury, pledging his property as security; but he then could not meet the obligation, and so his goods were formally advertised for sale in accordance with the law.

10. Having spent the better part of his life in circumstances like these, Claudius became emperor, at the age of fifty, by an extraordinary accident. When the assassins ordered Gaius' courtiers to disperse, pretending that he wished to be alone, Claudius went off with the rest and retired to a room called the Hermaeum; but he soon heard about the murder and slipped away in alarm to a nearby balcony, where he hid trembling behind the door curtains. A common soldier who happened to be running past noticed a pair of feet beneath the curtain, pulled their owner out for identification, and recognized him. Claudius

dropped on the floor and clasped the soldier's knees, but found himself acclaimed emperor. The man took him to his fellow soldiers, who were angry, confused and at a loss what to do; they placed him in a litter and, because his own bearers had scattered, took turns at carrying him to the praetorian camp. Claudius looked the picture of terror and despair; in his passage through the streets, everyone cast him pitying glances as if he were an innocent man being hurried to execution. Once safely within the camp, he spent the night among the sentries, confident now that no immediate danger threatened, but feeling little hope for the future since the consuls, with the approval of the Senate and the aid of the urban cohorts, had seized the Forum and Capitol and were determined on restoring the republic. When the tribunes of the people summoned him to visit the Senate House and there clarify the situation, Claudius replied that he was being forcibly detained and could not come. The next day, however, the Senate proved far from unanimous on questions of practical policy, but prolonged the debate with tiresome recriminations that prevented the passing of any decree; meanwhile, crowds surrounded the building and demanded a single ruler, expressly calling for Claudius. At last he allowed the soldiers to swear allegiance to him and promised every man 15,000 sesterces, which made him the first of the Caesars to purchase the loyalty of his troops.

11. No sooner had Claudius' power been established than he gave priority to the task of obliterating all records of those two days when there had been talk of a new constitution. He ordered a general amnesty and observed it himself, apart from executing a few of the tribunes and centurions who had conspired against Gaius – both to make an example of them and because they had, he knew, planned his own murder as well. Next, to show his family devotion, he always used 'By Augustus' as the most sacred and frequent of his oaths; he made the Senate decree his grandmother Livia divine honours, as well as an elephant-drawn carriage for her image, to match Augustus', during ritual processions around the Circus; and he instituted public commemorative rites for his parents, and in addition annual Circus games on his father's birthday, during which the

image of his mother – now posthumously given the title of Augusta, which she had refused while alive – was paraded in a carriage. He also never missed a chance of keeping green the fame of his brother Germanicus; he entered a Greek comedy written by him for a theatrical contest at Neapolis, and had the satisfaction of announcing that the judges awarded it first prize. He did not even fail to honour Mark Antony; in one proclamation he begged the people 'to celebrate my father Drusus' birthday all the more heartily because it happens likewise to have been that of my maternal grandfather Antony'. For Tiberius, he completed the marble arch near Pompey's Theatre voted some years before by the Senate, but neglected by Gaius; and, while annulling all Gaius' edicts, he would not allow the day of his assassination to be proclaimed a public festival, even though it marked the beginning of his own reign.

12. Claudius did not presume to accept excessive honorifics, even refusing the praenomen Imperator, and let the betrothal of his daughter and the birthday of his grandson be celebrated only privately. He recalled no exile from banishment without senatorial permission, and when wishing to bring the praetorian prefect and some military tribunes into the Senate House or to have the judicial decisions of his procurators ratified, would ask the Senate for these privileges as a favour; he actually approached the consuls for leave to hold market fairs on his private estates. Often he sat on the advisory council of magistrates when they were conducting trials, and when they presided over public games he would rise with the audience and show his appreciation by hailing them and clapping. When the tribunes of the people appeared before his judge's chair, he apologized for not offering them seats – only lack of room on the platform, he said, condemned them to stand. This sort of behaviour endeared him to the people so soon that, when a rumour went around of his having been ambushed and assassinated on the Ostia road, everyone was aghast and began accusing the troops of treachery and the senators of murder. The magistrates had to bring two or three witnesses forward on the Rostra, followed by several more, to assure the people that he was safe and on the way home.

13. Nevertheless, various attempts were made on his life: by individuals, by a group of conspirators, and by a full-scale rebellion. To be precise: a plebeian with a dagger was arrested about midnight near Claudius' bedroom. Two *equites* were found waiting to kill him in public – one with a sword cane, as he left the theatre, the other with a hunting knife, as he sacrificed in the Temple of Mars. Then Asinius Gallus and Statilius Corvinus, grandsons respectively of the orators Pollio and Messala, brought some of Claudius' own freedmen and slaves into a plot for his deposition.[9] Lastly, Furius Camillus Scribonianus,[10] governor of Dalmatia, persuaded his legions to revolt; but, on being ordered to march off and rally around their new emperor, they found that some divine intervention prevented them from adorning the Eagles and from pulling up and moving the standards. Because of a superstitious fear engendered by these portents, the rebellion was smothered in less than five days.

14. Claudius held four more consulships:[11] the first two in successive years, the others at four-yearly intervals. The fourth lasted for six months, the remainder only for two; and he took over the third from a consul who had just died – a thing which no other emperor has ever done, before or since. During these terms of office, and indeed at all times, Claudius was a most conscientious judge, sitting in court even on his own birthday and those of his family, sometimes actually on ancient popular holidays or days of ill omen. Instead of always observing the letter of the law, he let himself be guided by his own sense of equity, and when he thought the punishments prescribed were either too lenient or too severe he changed them accordingly. Thus, should plaintiffs have lost their cases in a civil suit by demanding more damages than the law sanctioned, he allowed them to modify the plea and ordered a retrial. But if anyone were found guilty of some really shocking crime, Claudius went beyond the lawful punishment and condemned him to the wild beasts.

15. However, his behaviour in court varied unpredictably: sometimes he was careful and keen-witted, sometimes thoughtless and hasty, sometimes downright foolish and apparently out of his senses. One man had presented himself for jury

service without disclosing that he was exempt, as a father of three children; Claudius, revising the roster, expunged his name, remarking that he showed an unwholesome liking for jury duty.[12] Another juror, challenged by his opponents with a lawsuit, responded that the matter was one for the civil courts and did not need to be brought before Caesar; Claudius intervened, instructing him to bring the case before him at once, noting that the way he handled his own case would show how far he might be trusted while judging those of others. A woman once refused to admit that she was the mother of a young man produced in court, and a conflict of evidence arose; but the truth came out when Claudius ordered her to marry the man.

He had a tendency to decide against whichever party in a suit happened to be absent, without troubling to ask whether or not this might have been unavoidable. After a man was found guilty of forgery, a bystander shouted, 'He ought to have his hands cut off!' Claudius immediately sent for an executioner, with block and cleaver, to act on this suggestion. Again, during a wrangle between counsel as to whether a man accused of wrongfully posing as a Roman citizen should wear a Roman toga or a Greek mantle in court, Claudius, as if to demonstrate his fair-mindedness, made him keep changing his clothes so as to appear in a mantle when being accused and a toga when being defended. In one case, it is said, he wrote out the following verdict: 'I decide in favour of the party which has told the truth.'

Such erratic behaviour brought Claudius into open and widespread contempt – so much so that when an advocate kept apologizing for the non-appearance of a provincial witness whom Claudius had summoned, but would not explain it, Claudius had to browbeat him before at last eliciting the answer 'He is dead; I trust the excuse is legitimate.' Another thanked Claudius for letting him defend a client, and added, 'though this is, of course, established practice'. Old people I know have told me that litigants imposed so rudely on his good nature that they would not only call him back after he had closed the court, but would catch at the hem of his toga and even at his foot in their efforts to detain him. Though all this may sound incredible, I can also record that one party to a lawsuit, a little Greek, lost his temper with Claudius and burst out, 'You're an old man too, and an idiot to boot!' It is a matter of common knowledge that when a Roman *eques* was being falsely accused of obscene behaviour against women – the charge had been framed by private enemies who would stop at nothing – and saw that Claudius was admitting the evidence of common prostitutes, he hurled a stylus and set of wax tablets in his face, shouting, 'A curse on your stupid, cruel ways!' Claudius' cheek was badly gashed.

16. Claudius also assumed the office of censor, which had been allowed to lapse since the days of Plancus and Paulus, sixty years previously; but here again he proved inconsistent, as much in his general principles as in his particular decisions. He kept the name of a young reprobate on a list of *equites* which he was reviewing, and set no black mark against it, simply because the father asserted that he was extremely well behaved: 'This young man has a censor in his own home' was Claudius' judgement. Another *eques*, though a notorious seducer of girls and married women, escaped with a caution: 'Restrain your passions, or at least go more carefully in future. Why should it be any business of mine who your mistress may be?' Once a man's friend persuaded Claudius to remove the black mark which stood against his name; 'but I want the erasure to show,' he insisted. Then there was the Greek nobleman struck from the roster of jurymen and actually deprived of his rights as a Roman citizen because he did not know Latin, for Claudius would not let anyone employ an advocate, when asked to give an account of his life, but made him speak for himself as best he could. Several *equites* were also struck from the list, much to their surprise, on the novel charge of leaving Italy without a formal demand for leave of absence; since one of them had been acting as adviser to a provincial ruler, Claudius brought up the classical case of Rabirius Postumus,[13] who had followed King Ptolemy to Alexandria in the hope of recovering a loan and was charged with *maiestas* when he came back.

His attempts to remove still other names failed, the information collected by his agents proving so inaccurate. He found

to his great shame that most of those charged with being bachelors or childless or too poor to sustain their rank were in fact
married or fathers of families or quite comfortably off; and one
eques, accused of having attempted suicide with a dagger, tore
off his clothes and cried, 'Then show me the scar!' Among
Claudius' memorable acts as censor was the purchase of a
beautiful silver chariot, offered for sale in the Sigillaria; he then
had it hacked to pieces before his eyes.[14] He also published
twenty edicts in a single day, of which two were the following:
'This year's vintage is unusually abundant, so everyone must
pitch his wine jars well'; 'The sap of the yew tree is sovereign
against snake bite.'

17. Claudius' sole campaign was of no great importance. The
Senate had already voted him triumphal decorations, but he
thought it beneath his dignity to accept these, and decided that
Britain was the country where a real triumph could be most
readily earned. Its conquest had not been attempted since the
days of Divus Julius, and the Britons were now threatening
vengeance because the Romans had refused to return some
fugitives. Sailing from Ostia, Claudius was nearly wrecked off
the Ligurian coast and again near the Stoechades islands, but
made port safely at Massilia. Thence he marched north through
Gaul until reaching Gesoriacum; crossed over to Britain without incident; and was back in Rome six months later. He had
fought no battles and suffered no casualties, but reduced a
large part of the island to submission. His triumph was a very
splendid one, and among those whom he allowed to travel to
Rome to witness it were his provincial governors, and several
exiles as well. The emblems of his victory included the naval
crown – representing the crossing and conquest, so to speak, of
the Ocean – which he set on the gable of his Palatine home next
to the civic crown. His wife Messalina followed the chariot in
a covered carriage, and behind her marched those who had
won triumphal decorations in Britain. All these wore purple-
bordered togas and came on foot, except Marcus Crassus Frugi:
having earned this same honour on a previous occasion, he
now came dressed in a palm-embroidered tunic and rode a
caparisoned charger.

18. Claudius always interested himself in the proper upkeep of the city and the regular arrival of grain supplies. When an obstinate fire ravaged the Aemilian quarter, he lodged at the Diribitorium for two nights running; because a force of soldiers and slaves proved insufficient to cope with the blaze, he made the magistrates summon people from every district and then sat, with bags of coin piled before him, recruiting firefighters, whom he paid on the spot whatever seemed a suitable fee for their services. Once, after a series of droughts had caused a scarcity of grain, a mob stopped Claudius in the Forum and pelted him so hard with curses and stale crusts that he had difficulty in regaining the palace by a side door; as a result, he took all possible steps to import grain, even during the winter months – insuring merchants against the loss of their ships in stormy weather (which guaranteed them a good return on their ventures) and offering a bounty for every new grain transport built, proportionate to its tonnage.

19. The shipowner, if he happened to be a Roman citizen, was exempted from the Papian–Poppaean Law; if only a Latin, he acquired full Roman citizenship; if a woman, she enjoyed the privileges granted to mothers of four children. These regulations have never since been modified.

20. Claudius' public works, though not numerous, were important. They included the draining of the Fucine Lake and the building of the harbour at Ostia – though he knew that Augustus had turned down the frequent requests of the Marsi for emptying the lake and that Divus Julius, while often on the point of excavating the harbour at Ostia, had always abandoned the project as impractical. Claudius also completed a task begun by Gaius: he brought the cool and abundant springs called the Caerulean and the Curtian or Albudignan, as well as the New Anio, into Rome; the water ran along a stone aqueduct, with lofty arches, now known by his name, and was then distributed into a number of ornamental reservoirs. He undertook the Fucine drainage scheme as much for profit as for glory: a group of businessmen had offered to shoulder the expense if he awarded them the reclaimed land. The outlet took eleven years to dig, although 30,000 men were kept continuously at

work; it was three miles long, and his engineers had to level part of a hill and tunnel through the remainder. At Ostia, Claudius threw out curved breakwaters on either side of the harbour and built a deep-water mole by its entrance. For the base of this mole he used the ship in which the great obelisk had been brought from Egypt; it was first sunk, then secured with piles, and finally crowned with a very tall lighthouse – like the Pharos at Alexandria – that guided ships into the harbour at night by the beams of a lamp.[15]

21. Claudius often distributed largesse to the people and gave numerous magnificent public shows: not only the traditional ones in the customary places, but others, including novelties and ancient revivals and ones in places where nobody had ever seen them staged before. When he held games at the rededication of Pompey's Theatre, which had been damaged by fire, he first sacrificed in the shrines built above the auditorium and then walked down the aisle between packed and silent tiers to inaugurate the games from a raised seat in the orchestra. He also celebrated Saecular Games,[16] on the excuse that Augustus had staged them before they were really due, although he himself describes in his own histories how much trouble Augustus took to reckon the intervals separating their occurrences in the past and to recommence the series, after the tradition had long been broken, when the correct year came round once more. Therefore, when the herald invited the people, in the ancient formula, to 'attend games which nobody present has ever seen or will ever see again', a great shout of laughter arose. Not only had many persons present witnessed Saecular Games, but some actors were even billed to take part in them for the second time. Claudius often gave chariot races in the Vatican quarter, sometimes introducing wild-beast shows between every five events.

In the Circus Maximus, he replaced the old tufa starting gates with new marble ones, and the old wooden turning posts with new gilded ones, and also reserved seats for the senators, who had hitherto sat among the common people. Besides the chariot races he staged the Troy Game; a panther hunt by a squadron of praetorian cavalry under their tribunes and the praetorian

prefect in person; and a show in which Thessalian horsemen
drove wild bulls across the arena, tired them out, leaped on
them, seized hold of their horns, and then threw them to the
ground.

He presented many different kinds of gladiatorial games in a
variety of places: an annual one in the praetorian camp, without
wild beasts or fancy equipment, to celebrate his accession;
another of the usual kind in the Saepta; and a third, also in the
Saepta, but not with a regular programme. This last show ran
for a few days only and he himself called it a 'Picnic', because
the first time he presented one he invited the people by his
heralds 'to take pot luck, as it were'. Claudius never behaved
less formally than at these Picnics – passing out the gold pieces
to the winners with his left arm extended[17] and counting along
with the crowd: 'One, two, three,' he would shout. He urged
the audience to enjoy themselves, addressing them all indiscriminately as 'my lords', and cracking stupid and far-fetched
jokes. Once, on hearing the cry 'Bring on the Dove!', he yelled
back, 'Certainly, but he'll take a bit of catching!'[18] Yet when
four brothers pleaded for the discharge of their father, a chariot
fighter, Claudius presented him with the customary wooden
sword amid resounding cheers, and then wrote a note for the
herald to read aloud: 'You now see the great advantage of
having a large family; it can win favour and protection even for
a gladiator.'

He also staged, on the Campus Martius, the realistic storm
and sack of a fortified town, with a tableau of the British kings'
surrender, at which he presided in his commander's cloak.
Before allowing the water to escape from the Fucine Lake, he
arranged to have a sham sea fight on it; but when the gladiators
shouted, 'Hail, Caesar, we who are about to die salute you!',
he answered sarcastically, 'Or not, as the case may be.' They
took him up on this and refused to fight, insisting that his words
amounted to a pardon. Claudius grew so angry that he was on
the point of sending troops to massacre them or burn them all
in their ships; however, he changed his mind, jumped from his
seat and, hobbling ridiculously down to the lakeside, threatened
and coaxed the gladiators into battle. Twelve Rhodian triremes

then engaged twelve Sicilian ones, the signal for the fight being given by a mechanical silver Triton which emerged from the lake bottom and blew a conch.

22. In matters of religious ritual, civil and military customs, and the social status of all ranks at home and abroad, Claudius not only revived obsolescent traditions but invented new ones. He never admitted a priest into a college without first taking a personal oath that he thought him worthy of the honour, and whenever an earthquake shock was registered at Rome he required the praetor to call an assembly and proclaim a public holiday. If a bird of evil omen perched on the Capitol, Claudius would go to the Rostra in his capacity as pontifex maximus, order labourers and slaves to withdraw, and then read out the customary formula of supplication, which the people repeated after him.

23. The court sessions, hitherto divided into summer and winter terms, he joined together into one. Another of his changes was to institute permanent courts, both at Rome and in the provinces, for judging fiduciary cases, instead of entrusting them to the annually appointed Roman magistrates. He cancelled Tiberius' supplement to the Papian–Poppaean Law which implied that men over sixty years of age could not beget children, authorized the consuls to choose guardians for orphans, and ruled that no person who had been exiled from a province might enter Italy. A new form of punishment which forbade a man to go more than three miles outside Rome was likewise introduced by Claudius. Whenever any business of peculiar importance came up in the Senate, he would take his seat either between the two consuls or else on the bench kept for tribunes of the people. Hitherto, when public officials wished to travel abroad, the Senate had considered their applications; Claudius reserved the right to deal with these himself.

24. He awarded consular insignia even to procurators of the second class; if anyone declined senatorial rank,[19] he deprived him of his equestrian rank as well. At the beginning of his reign Claudius undertook to create no new senator unless he could prove that his ancestors had been Roman citizens for five generations; eventually, however, he granted senatorial

standing to the son of a freedman on the sole condition that he should get himself adopted by an *eques*. Then, to forestall criticism, he gave out that his own ancestor Appius Caecus had as censor admitted freedmen's sons into the Senate; yet this was to misread the word 'freedmen', which in the days of Appius, and for quite a while afterwards, meant the freeborn sons of freed slaves, not the freed slaves themselves.

Claudius relieved the quaestors of their obligation to keep the roads paved, expecting them to stage gladiatorial shows instead; he also withdrew those on duty at Ostia and in Gaul and gave them back their custodianship of the public treasury in the Temple of Saturn, which at that point was, as now once more, held by praetors or men of praetorian status.

After he awarded triumphal decorations to Silanus (the fiancé of his daughter Octavia) while he was still a boy and to older men in great numbers, all on the slightest of excuses, the legions sent him a joint letter begging that he would issue the same honour to all his consular legates at the same time as he appointed them – otherwise they would try to win it in the field by provoking frontier incidents. He granted Aulus Plautius an ovation, going out to meet him when he entered the city and courteously giving him the place of honour on his way up to the Capitol and down again. Moreover, Gabinius Secundus was permitted to adopt the cognomen Cauchius for his victory over the Cauchi, a German tribe.

25. Claudius made new regulations for the military careers of *equites*: after commanding an infantry cohort, they were promoted to a cavalry squadron, and only then became military tribunes. He also introduced a so-called 'supernumerary' army service for performance in name only, though it counted as effective, and persuaded the Senate to issue a decree forbidding soldiers to pay complimentary calls on senators. Any freedman who tried to pass himself off as a *eques* found his property confiscated, and if one proved ungrateful to his former master and caused him annoyance, back he went to slavery; Claudius told advocates representing freedmen of this sort that he would not hear any cases which they might bring against their own freedmen. Finding that a number of sick or worn-out slaves had been

abandoned by their owners on the Island of Aesculapius, to avoid the trouble of giving them proper medical attention, Claudius freed them all and ruled that none who got well again should return to the control of his former owner; furthermore, that any owner who made away with a sick slave for the same mean reason should be charged with murder. One of his edicts banned travel through any Italian town except on foot, in a sedan chair or in a litter.[20] He also stationed fire brigades at Puteoli and Ostia.

It now became illegal for non-citizens to adopt the names of Roman families, and any who usurped the rights of Roman citizens were executed on the slopes of the Esquiline Hill. Tiberius had transferred the provinces of Achaia and Macedonia to his own jurisdiction; Claudius restored them to the Senate. He deprived the Lycians of self-governance to punish their love of savage vendettas, but restored that of the Rhodians to express his pleasure at their recent moral improvement. In granting the Trojans, as founders of the Roman race, perpetual exemption from tribute, he supported his act by reading aloud an ancient letter written in Greek to King Seleucus from the Senate and People of Rome, with a promise of loyal friendship on condition that Seleucus should 'keep their Trojan kinsfolk free from all imposts'. Because the Jews at Rome caused continuous disturbances at the instigation of Chrestus, he expelled them from the city.[21] When the German envoys first visited the theatre, they were seated among the common people, but, noticing the Parthian and Armenian envoys seated with the Senators in the orchestra, went to join them – were they not just as brave and nobly born? Claudius admired their simple confidence and let them remain there. Augustus had been content to prohibit any Roman citizen in Gaul from taking part in the savage and terrible Druidic cult; Claudius abolished it altogether. On the other hand, he attempted to transfer the Eleusinian Mysteries from Athens to Rome, and had the ruined temple of Venus on Mount Eryx in Sicily restored at the expense of the public treasury. Whenever he concluded a treaty with foreign rulers, he sacrificed a sow in the Forum, using the ancient formula of the Fetial priests.[22] Yet all these acts, and

others like them – indeed, one might say everything that Claudius did throughout his reign – were dictated by his wives and
freedmen: he practically always obeyed their whims rather than
his own judgement.

26. Claudius was twice betrothed while still a boy: to Augustus' great-granddaughter Aemilia Lepida, and to Livia Medullina Camilla, a descendant of the famous dictator Camillus.
However, when Aemilia Lepida's parents offended Augustus
her engagement was broken off,[23] and Livia Medullina died of
some illness on what should have been her wedding day. His
first wife, Plautia Urgulanilla, whose father had won a triumph,
he divorced for scandalous misbehaviour and the suspicion of
murder; his next, Aelia Paetina, daughter of a former consul,
he also divorced, for slighter offences. Then he married Valeria
Messalina, daughter of his cousin Messala Barbatus.[24] Among
other disgraceful crimes, she went so far as to commit bigamy
with Gaius Silius and even to sign a formal marriage contract
before witnesses; when Claudius discovered this, he had her
executed and told the praetorians that, having been unfortunate
in his wives, he was resolved to live a celibate life in future –
they could kill him if he did not keep his word!

Almost at once, however, he planned either to marry Lollia
Paulina, Gaius' widow, or to remarry his divorced wife Aelia
Paetina; but it was Agrippina, daughter of his brother Germanicus, who hooked him. She had a niece's privilege of kissing
and caressing Claudius, and exercised it with a noticeable effect
on his passions: when the Senate next met, he persuaded a
group of senators to propose that a union between him and her
should be compulsorily arranged in the public interest, and
that other uncles should likewise be free to marry their nieces,
though this had hitherto counted as incest. The wedding took
place without delay, but no other uncle cared to follow Claudius' example, except one freedman and one *primipilaris*,
whose marriage he and Agrippina both attended.

27. He had children by three of his wives. Urgulanilla bore
him Drusus and Claudia. Drusus died just before he came of
age, choked by a pear which he had playfully thrown up and
caught in his open mouth; since he had been betrothed only a

few days previously to Sejanus' daughter, the tradition that Sejanus murdered him becomes still less plausible. Claudia's real father was Claudius' freedman Boter; Claudius disavowed paternity and, though she was born nearly five months after the divorce, had her laid naked outside Urgulanilla's house door. Aelia Paetina bore him Antonia, who was twice married: first to Gnaeus Pompeius Magnus and then to Faustus Sulla, both young noblemen of distinction. Messalina's children were Octavia, who was betrothed to Lucius Silanus before marrying Claudius' stepson Nero, and Germanicus, afterwards called Britannicus,[25] born on the twentieth day of his father's reign, during his second consulship. Claudius would often pick little Britannicus up and show him to the troops or to the audience at the games, either seated in his lap or held at arms' length. His cry 'Good luck to you, my boy!' was loudly echoed on all sides. Of his three sons-in-law, Claudius adopted Nero; Pompeius and Silanus he not only rejected but put to death.

28. Among Claudius' favourite freedmen was Posides the eunuch, to whom at his British triumph he actually awarded an honorary spear, along with soldiers who had fought in the field. For Felix he had an equally high regard, giving him command of infantry cohorts and cavalry squadrons and the governorship of Judaea; this Felix married three princesses.[26] Then there was Harpocras, who earned the privileges of riding through Rome in a litter and of staging public entertainments as though he were an *eques*. Claudius had an even higher regard for Polybius, his cultural adviser, who often walked between the two consuls. But his firmest devotion was reserved for Narcissus, his secretary, and Pallas, his bookkeeper, whom he encouraged the Senate to honour with large gifts of money and the insignia of quaestors and praetors as well. They were able to acquire such riches, by legitimate and illegitimate means, that when one day Claudius complained about the lack of funds in the imperial exchequer, someone answered neatly that he would have heaps of pocket money if only his two freedmen took him into partnership.

29. As I mentioned above, Claudius fell so deeply under the influence of these freedmen and wives that he seemed to be their servant rather than their emperor; he distributed public

offices, army commands, pardons and punishments according to their wishes, however capricious, seldom even aware of what he was about. I need not dwell on matters of lesser importance: how grants were revoked, edicts cancelled, letters of appointment replaced or even brazenly amended. Suffice it to record that he executed his father-in-law Appius Silanus and the two Julias, the daughter of Tiberius' son Drusus and the daughter of his own brother Germanicus, all on uncertain charges and without the right to plead in self-defence. Gnaeus Pompeius, who had married his daughter Antonia, was stabbed to death while in bed with a young male favourite, and Lucius Silanus, whom Claudius had betrothed to his daughter Octavia, was forced to resign his praetorship four days before the Kalends of January and then to commit suicide on the very day that Claudius married Agrippina. He executed thirty-five senators and 300 Roman *equites* with so little apparent concern that once, when a centurion reported that so-and-so the former consul was now duly dispatched and Claudius denied having given any such command, his freedmen satisfied him that the soldiers had done right not to wait for instructions before taking vengeance on behalf of their emperor. It is very difficult, however, to believe that they tricked Claudius into signing the marriage contract between Messalina and her lover Silius by an assurance that the marriage was a mere fiction: a transference of portended dangers threatening 'Messalina's husband' from himself to someone else.

30. Claudius had a certain dignity of presence, which showed to best advantage when he happened to be standing or seated, and especially when he was expressing no emotion. This was because, though tall, well built and handsome, with a fine head of white hair and a firm neck, he stumbled as he walked owing to the weakness of his knees, and also because, if excited by either play or serious business, he had several disagreeable traits. These included an uncontrolled laugh, a horrible habit under the stress of anger of slobbering at the mouth and running at the nose, a stammer, and a persistent nervous tic – which grew so bad under emotional stress that his head would toss from side to side.

31. His health was wretched until he succeeded to the throne, when it suddenly became excellent, except for violent stomach aches which often, he said, made him think of suicide.

32. He gave many splendid banquets, usually in large public venues, and at times invited no fewer than 600 guests. One banquet was held close to the outlet of the Fucine Lake on the day it was emptied; but the water came rushing out in a deluge and almost drowned him. His sons and daughters, along with those of other leading citizens, were always expected to dine with him, sitting in old-fashioned style at the ends of the couches on which their parents reclined. Once, when a guest was believed to have pocketed a golden bowl, Claudius invited him again the next evening, this time setting a small earthenware basin in front of him. Some say that he planned an edict to legitimize breaking wind at dinner, either silently or noisily – after hearing about a man who was so modest that he endangered his health by an attempt to restrain himself.

33. No matter where Claudius happened to be, he always felt ready for food or drink. One day, while he was judging a case in the Forum of Augustus, the delicious smell of cooking assailed his nostrils. He descended from the tribunal, adjourned the court, and went to the dining room of the Salii[27] in the nearby Temple of Mars, where he immediately took his place at the meal he had scented. It was seldom that Claudius left a dining hall except gorged and sodden; he would then go to bed and sleep supine with his mouth wide open – thus allowing a feather to be put down his throat, which would bring up the superfluous food and drink as vomit. He slept in short snatches, being usually awake before midnight; but let him begin to nod in court and the advocates had difficulty in rousing him, however loud they shouted. His feelings for women were extremely passionate, but the male sex left him cold. So fervent was his devotion to dice that he published a book on the subject, and used to play even while out driving, on a special board fitted to his carriage which kept the dice from rolling off capriciously.

34. His bloodthirstiness appeared equally in great and small matters. For instance, if evidence had to be extracted under torture, or parricide punished, he allowed the law to take its

course without delay and in his own presence. Once, when an execution in ancient style[28] had been ordered at Tibur and the criminals had been tied to their stakes, nobody could be found capable of carrying it out; but Claudius summoned a specialist from Rome and was so set on witnessing the procedure that he waited until dusk for the man's arrival. At gladiatorial shows, whether or not they were staged by himself, he ruled that all combatants who fell accidentally should have their throats cut – above all net fighters, the death agony on whose faces was not hidden by any helmets. When a pair of gladiators mortally wounded each other he immediately sent for their swords and had pocket knives made from them for his personal use. He so greatly enjoyed wild-beast shows and the fencing matches during the lunch interval that, after he had spent the whole morning in the amphitheatre from daybreak until noon, he would dismiss the audience, keep his seat, and not only watch the regular combats but extemporize others between the stage carpenters and similar members of the theatre staff, as a punishment for the failure of any mechanical device to work as it should. He even forced one of his attendants to enter the arena and fight in his toga.

35. Above all, he was so timid and suspicious that, though making a show of restraint in the early days of his reign, as I mentioned above, he never attended a banquet unless with an escort of javelin-bearing bodyguards, and waited upon by soldiers. Before entering a sickroom he always had it carefully gone over: pillows and mattresses were prodded and bedclothes shaken out. Later, he even required all visitors to be thoroughly searched when they came to pay him a morning call, and excused no one. Indeed, it was not until the end of his reign that he reluctantly gave up the practice of having women, boys and girls pawed about during these routine examinations, and of removing the stylus case from every caller's attendant or secretary. Camillus the rebel felt sure that Claudius could be frightened into abdication merely by insolent threats, without the need of engaging in actual warfare; and Claudius did in fact seriously ask his advisers whether he should comply with Camillus' demands.

36. Baseless rumours of conspiracies caused Claudius such alarm that he tried to step down. After the arrest of the man with the dagger, he sent out heralds to call an immediate meeting of the Senate, at which he protested tearfully that no place was safe for him any longer, and for a long time he failed to appear in public. Nor did Messalina's insulting behaviour destroy the extravagant love he bore her so much as terror that she planned to turn over power to her lover Silius; and when the news of their marriage reached him he fled ignominiously to the praetorian camp, asking again and again as he went, 'Am I still emperor?'

37. At the slightest hint of danger he would take instant action against his supposed enemy. Once a morning caller drew Claudius aside and whispered, 'In my dreams last night you were murdered; I would recognize your assailant if I saw him.' A little later he shouted, 'Look! There he is, handing in a petition!' Claudius had the petitioner arrested as if caught in the act and hurried away to execution, unaware that the two men were at odds over a lawsuit. Appius Silanus is said to have been the victim of a similar ruse, for when Messalina and Narcissus decided to get rid of him they agreed that Narcissus should run in alarm to Claudius' bedroom just before dawn and pretend that he had dreamed of a violent attack on him by Appius. Messalina would then awake and exclaim with pretended astonishment, 'Why, it comes back to me now! I have dreamed the same dream for the last few nights.' They would have already sent Appius a summons to visit Claudius, so that when someone else announced that he was forcing his way in, Claudius would take this as positive proof that the dreams were true, accuse Appius of attempted murder, and sentence him to death. The plan worked, and the next day Claudius blandly told the Senate what had happened, incidentally thanking Narcissus for exercising such vigilance even while asleep.

38. In one edict he confessed to the faults of anger and resentment, but undertook that his anger would never last long nor his resentment be unjustified. Then there was his bitter letter reprimanding the citizens of Ostia because they had sent

no ships to meet him when he sailed up the Tiber, which made him feel 'reduced to the ranks'; yet he as suddenly forgave them and sent what amounted to an apology for the warmth of his remarks. If pestered in public by applicants of every sort, Claudius used to push them away with his own hands. Among the innocent people whom he banished without a hearing were a quaestor's clerk who had once treated him contemptuously in a court case before his accession and a senator of praetorian rank who, while aedile, had fined Claudius' tenants for illegally selling cooked food and then whipped his bailiff because he protested. The same resentment made Claudius deprive the aediles of their control over the cookshops.

Instead of keeping quiet about his stupidity, Claudius explained in a few short speeches that it had been a mere mask assumed for the benefit of Gaius, and that he owed both his life and his position to it. Nobody, however, believed him, and soon a book was published entitled *The Fool's Rise to Power*, the thesis being that no one would act the fool unless he were a fool already.

39. Claudius' scatter-brainedness and shortsightedness – or, if you prefer the Greek terms, his *meteoria* and *ablepsia* – were truly remarkable. After executing Messalina, he went in to dinner, and presently asked, 'Why is her ladyship not here?' On several occasions he sent for men to give him advice or throw dice with him and, when they did not appear, followed this up with a reproachful message calling them slugabeds – quite unaware that he had just sentenced them to death. While planning his incestuous marriage with Agrippina, he made certain most unsuitable public references to her, such as 'my daughter and foster child, born and bred in my lap, so to speak'. And shortly before adopting his stepson Nero – as though this were not wrong enough, when he already possessed a grown-up son – he gave out with pride more than once that nobody had ever yet been adopted into the Claudian family.

40. Often, in fact, Claudius showed such absent-mindedness in speech and action that it might have been thought that he neither knew nor cared to whom, or in whose hearing, or when or where, he was speaking. He intervened in a senatorial debate

on the subject of butchers and wine-sellers with the sudden question, 'But I ask you, how can anyone live without an occasional snack?' Then he rambled off into a speech about the abundance of taverns in his youth and how he often used to go the round of them himself. One of his reasons for supporting the candidature of a would-be quaestor was 'His father brought me a cool drink of water, long ago, when I was sick and very thirsty.' Of a witness who had been presented before the Senate, he said, 'Though in fact my mother's freedwoman and personal maid, she always treated me as her patron; I stress this point because even now certain members of my household staff refuse to do so.' Once, when the men of Ostia made a public petition, he lost his temper and shouted from the tribunal that he owed them no consideration, and that surely he was free, if anyone was! Every day, and almost at every hour and minute of the day, he would let fall such remarks as 'What? Do you take me for Telegenius?' and 'Talk but don't touch,'[29] along with other more inept ones, such as would have come ill even from a private citizen, let alone a *princeps* who, far from lacking eloquence and education, had devoted his whole life to liberal studies.

41. While still a boy, Claudius had started work on a Roman history, encouraged by Livy and assisted by Sulpicius Flavus. But when he gave his first public reading, to a packed audience, he found it difficult to pay proper attention because at the very beginning of his performance a very fat man came in, sat down, and broke a bench – which sent several of his neighbours sprawling and excited considerable merriment. Even when silence had been restored, Claudius could not help recalling the sight and going off into peals of laughter.

As *princeps* he continued to write, and through a professional reader gave frequent recitations. His history opened with the murder of the dictator Caesar, then skipped a few years and started again at the close of the civil wars, because he realized, from his mother's and grandmother's hectoring, that he would not be allowed to publish a free and unvarnished report on the intervening period. Of the first part he produced two volumes; of the second, forty-one. Moreover, he wrote eight volumes of

an autobiography, which are criticizable more for their lack of
taste than for a lack of style, as well as *A Defence of Cicero
against the Writings of Asinius Gallus*[30] – quite a learned work.
Claudius also added three new letters of his own invention to
the alphabet, maintaining that they were most necessary; he
had written a book on the subject before his accession, and
afterwards met with no obstacle in getting the letters officially
adopted. They may still be found in a number of books and in
public records and inscriptions.[31]

42. Claudius also studied Greek with great application and
took every opportunity of professing his love for this language,
which he declared to be the finest of all. Once, when a barbarian
addressed him first in Latin and then in Greek, he replied, 'You
come armed with both our languages.' Also, while eulogizing
Achaia to the senators, he called it a province which had endeared itself to him by a devotion to the same studies as he
pursued himself; often in the Senate he would answer Greek
envoys with a carefully composed oration in their own tongue.
Claudius used to quote Homer from the tribunal and, after
punishing a personal enemy or conspirator, made a habit of
giving the following line as a watchword to the officer of his
guards: 'Let him be first to attack, but be sure that you counter
him boldly.'[32] To conclude, he even wrote books in Greek:
twenty volumes of Etruscan history and eight of Carthaginian.
The city of Alexandria acknowledged these works by adding a
new wing to the Museum called 'the Claudian' in his honour,
and by having the Etruscan history publicly recited from end
to end once a year by relays of readers in the old wing and the
Carthaginian history, likewise, in the new.

43. In his last years Claudius made it pretty plain that he
repented of having married Agrippina and adopted Nero. For
example, when his freedmen congratulated him on having
found a certain woman guilty of adultery, he remarked that he
himself seemed fated to marry wives who 'were unchaste but
remained unchastened'; and when he came across Britannicus
he embraced him repeatedly with deep affection. 'Grow up
quickly, my boy,' he said, 'and I will then explain what my
policy has been.' With that he quoted the Greek saying 'The

hand that wounded you shall also heal,'[33] and declared his intention of letting Britannicus come of age because, although immature, he was tall enough to wear a toga, adding 'which will at last provide the Roman people with a true-born Caesar'.

44. Soon afterwards he composed his will and made all the magistrates put their seals to it as witnesses; but Agrippina, being now accused of many crimes by informers as well as her own conscience, prevented him from doing anything further.

Most people think that Claudius was poisoned, but when and by whom is disputed. Some say that the eunuch Halotus, his official taster, administered the drug while he was dining with the priests on the Capitoline Hill; others, that Agrippina did so herself at a family banquet, poisoning a dish of mushrooms, his favourite food. An equal discrepancy exists between the accounts of what happened next. Many authorities assert that he immediately lost his power of speech, suffered frightful pain all night long, and died shortly before dawn. A variant version is that he fell into a coma but vomited up the entire contents of his stomach and was then poisoned a second time, either by a gruel, the excuse being that he needed food to revive him, or by means of an enema, the excuse being that his bowels must be emptied too.

45. Claudius' death was not revealed until all the arrangements had been completed for his successor. As a result, people made vows for his safety as though he still lived, and a troop of comic actors were summoned, under the pretence that he had asked to be diverted by their antics. He died on 13 October, during the consulship of Asinius Marcellus and Acilius Aviola,[34] in the sixty-fourth year of his life and the fourteenth of his reign. He was given a princely funeral and officially deified, an honour which Nero later neglected and then cancelled but which Vespasian restored.

46. The main omens of Claudius' death included a comet, lightning that struck his father Drusus' memorial, and an unusual mortality among magistrates of all ranks. There is also evidence that he foresaw his end and made no secret of it: while choosing the consuls, he provided for no appointment after the month in which he died, and on his last visit to the Senate he

offered an earnest plea for harmony between Britannicus and
Nero, begging the senators to guide both of them with great
care through the difficult years of their youth. During a final
appearance on the tribunal he said more than once that he had
reached the close of his mortal career, though everyone present
cried, 'The gods forbid!'

NERO

1. Two branches of the Domitian family distinguished themselves – the Calvini and the Ahenobarbi. The Ahenobarbi were
named after their founder, Lucius Domitius; according to tradition, he was once returning to Rome from the country when
he met a pair of twins looking more like gods than men, who
told him to inform the Senate and the people that a battle,
whose outcome was as yet unknown, had now been won. In
proof of their divinity, the twins stroked him on both sides of
his chin and thereby turned his beard from black to the colour
of bronze – a physical peculiarity which became dominant
among his descendants.[1] Having gained seven consulships, a
triumph and two censorships, and been raised to patrician rank,
they all continued to use the same cognomen, with no other
praenomina than Gnaeus and Lucius. They gave an interesting
twist to this practice by sometimes having successive members
of the family known by the same praenomen and sometimes
varying the two – for instance, we know that each of the first
three Ahenobarbi was a Lucius, each of the second three was a
Gnaeus, and after this Lucius alternated with Gnaeus. A closer
study of the Domitian family history will reveal that, although
Nero made a ghastly caricature of his ancestors' virtues, many
of his vices were inherited.

2. Let me go back quite a long way to Nero's great-great-
great-grandfather, Gnaeus Domitius. While tribune of the
people, he deprived the pontifical college of their power to fill
vacancies in the priesthood and awarded it to the people; he
hated the college for not having appointed him to succeed his
father. As consul, he subdued the Allobroges and the Arverni,

and then rode through the province on an elephant with an escort of soldiers as though he were celebrating a triumph. Licinius Crassus, the orator, remarked, 'Should his bronze beard really surprise us? After all, he has an iron face and a heart of lead.'

Gnaeus' son Lucius, while praetor, summoned Julius Caesar before the Senate at the close of his consulship to be examined on the charge of having defied the laws and auspices. Afterwards, when consul, he tried to remove Caesar from the command in Gaul, and had himself named as his successor by Caesar's opponents. Then the civil war broke out and he was soon taken prisoner at Corfinium, but set free; whereupon he went to Massilia and supported the inhabitants during the difficult days of their siege. However, he abruptly deserted them, and fell a year later in the battle of Pharsalus. This Lucius was both harsh and remarkably indecisive. Once, in a fit of desperation, he attempted suicide by poison, but the prospect of immediate death so terrified him that he changed his mind and vomited up the dose – the family physician knew him well enough to have made it a mild one, which earned the wise fellow his freedom. Early in the civil war, when Pompey raised the question of how neutrals should be treated, Lucius was the sole senator who wanted them classified as enemies.

3. Lucius left one son, Gnaeus, without any doubt the best member of the family. Although aware of the conspiracy against Caesar, he took no part in the actual assassination; but he was condemned under the Pedian Law when he threw in his lot with his relatives Brutus and Cassius. After their deaths he continued to command and even to enlarge their fleet, which he would not surrender to Mark Antony until his associates had been everywhere routed, and then did so as though he were granting an immense favour. Of all those sentenced under the Pedian Law he alone was granted repatriation, and once home again he held all the highest offices in succession. When civil war broke out once more he became Antony's legate and was later offered the supreme command by those who were embarrassed by Cleopatra's presence; but a sudden illness made him wary of accepting it, although he never gave a definite refusal. Instead,

he transferred his allegiance to Augustus, and died a few days afterwards. But even he had a slight stain on his reputation, since Antony declared that his real motive in changing sides was to be with Servilia Nais, his mistress.

4. His son, the Lucius Domitius who became Augustus' chief executor, had been a famous charioteer in his youth and gained triumphal decorations for his part in the German campaign; but he was notorious for his arrogance, extravagance and extreme rudeness. While holding the office of aedile, he ordered Lucius Plancus, then censor, to make way for him in the street. As praetor and again as consul, he made *equites* and respectable married women act in stage farces. The cruelty of the wild-animal hunts presented by him in the Circus and elsewhere at Rome, and likewise of his gladiatorial contest, obliged Augustus – whose private warnings he had disregarded – to issue a cautionary edict.

5. Gnaeus Domitius, his son by Antonia the elder, became Nero's father, and was a wholly despicable character. As a young man he served in the east on the staff of Augustus' adopted son Gaius,[2] but forfeited his friendship by killing one of his own freedmen for refusing to drink as much as he was told. Yet even then he behaved no better. Once, driving through a village on the Via Appia, he whipped up his horses and deliberately ran over a boy, and when an *eques* criticized him rather freely in the Forum he gouged out his eye there and then. He was also remarkably dishonest, cheating his bankers of payment for goods they had bought him and, while praetor, even swindling victorious charioteers of their prize money. His sister openly teased him about this, and when the managers of the teams complained he decreed that in future all prizes must be paid on the spot. Just before Tiberius died he was charged with treason, adultery and incest with his sister Domitia Lepida; however, Gaius' accession saved him, and he died of dropsy at Pyrgi, after the birth of Nero, his son by Germanicus' daughter Agrippina.

6. Nero was born at Antium on 15 December, nine months after Tiberius' death; the sun was rising and its earliest rays touched the newly born boy almost before he could be laid

on the ground.³ People at once made a number of ominous predictions, and regarded as significant a comment made by his father Domitius in reply to friendly congratulations: namely that any child born to himself and Agrippina was bound to have a detestable nature and become a public danger. Another promise of ill luck occurred on the day of his ritual purification: when Agrippina asked her brother Gaius to give the boy whatever name he pleased, he glanced at his uncle Claudius (later emperor, and Nero's adoptive father) and said with a grin, 'I give him Claudius' name.'⁴ Since Claudius was then the butt of the court, Agrippina was not amused and ignored the suggestion.

At the age of three Nero lost his father and inherited one-third of the estate; but Gaius, who was also named in the will, not only took everything, but banished Agrippina. Nero therefore grew up in very poor circumstances under the care of his aunt Domitia Lepida, who chose a dancer and a barber to be his tutors. However, when Claudius succeeded Gaius, Nero had his inheritance restored to him in full, and a legacy from his stepfather, Crispus Passienus,⁵ left him well off. His mother's recall from banishment allowed him to enjoy once more the benefits of her powerful influence, so much so that the story got about that Claudius' wife Messalina, realizing that Nero would become a rival to her son Britannicus, had sent assassins to strangle him during his afternoon nap. They were driven away in terror, people said, by a snake which suddenly darted from beneath Nero's pillow; but this was a mere surmise based on the discovery of a sloughed snakeskin close by. Agrippina persuaded him to have this skin set in a golden bracelet, which he wore for a long time on his right wrist. After she died he threw it away because it reminded him too vividly of her, but when his situation grew desperate he hunted for it in vain.

7. While still very young he gave an exceptionally good performance in the Troy Game at the Circus and earned loud applause. When he reached the age of eleven⁶ Claudius adopted him and appointed Annaeus Seneca, who was already a senator, as his tutor. On the following night, the story goes, Seneca dreamed that his pupil was really Gaius; and, indeed, Nero soon made sense of the dream by giving signs of a naturally

cruel heart. Since Britannicus continued to call him 'Ahenobarbus' even after his adoption, he took revenge by trying to
convince Claudius that Britannicus was a supposititious child;
he also testified in public against his aunt Domitia Lepida just
to please his mother, who had engineered the trial.[7]

Nero celebrated his formal introduction into public life by
giving largesse to the people and a bounty to the troops, and
leading a ceremonial parade of the praetorians, shield in hand.
Afterwards, in the Senate, he made a speech of thanks to
Claudius. While Claudius was consul, Nero pleaded two cases
before him: one in Latin on behalf of the people of Bononia,
the other in Greek on behalf of the Rhodians and Trojans. He
first appeared on the tribunal as city prefect during the Latin
Festival;[8] eminent advocates brought him a number of important cases to try, instead of the dull and trivial ones that normally come up on such occasions – although Claudius had
expressly forbidden this. Next, Nero married Octavia, and
held games and a wild-beast hunt in the Circus on behalf of
Claudius' good health.

8. He had reached the age of sixteen when the news of
Claudius' death was made known, and he presented himself to
the guards that day between the sixth and seventh hours – ugly
omens having ruled out an earlier appearance. After being
acclaimed *imperator* on the palace steps, he was taken in a litter
to the praetorian camp, where he briefly addressed the troops.
He then visited the Senate House, where he remained until
nightfall, refusing only one of the many high honours voted
him, namely the title Father of His Country, and this because
of his youth.

9. Nero started off with a parade of virtue, giving Claudius
a lavish funeral, at which he delivered the oration in person,
and then deifying him. He also exalted the memory of his father
Domitius, and turned over all his public and private affairs
to Agrippina's management. On the day of his accession the
password he gave to the military tribune on duty was 'The Best
of Mothers', and she and he often rode out together through
the streets in her litter. Nero founded a colony at Antium
consisting of praetorian veterans, augmented by a group of rich

retired *primipilares*, whom he had move from their previous homes; he also built a harbour there, at great expense.

10. As a further guarantee of his virtuous intentions, he promised to model his rule on the principles laid down by Augustus, and never missed an opportunity of being generous or merciful or of showing what a good companion he was. He lowered, if he could not abolish, some of the heavier taxes, and reduced by three-quarters the fee for denouncing evasions of the Papian Law. Moreover, he presented the people with 400 sesterces each, settled annual salaries on distinguished but impoverished senators – to the amount of 500,000 sesterces in some cases – and granted the praetorian cohorts a free monthly issue of grain. If asked to sign the usual execution order for a felon, he would sigh, 'Ah, how I wish that I had never learned to write!' He seldom forgot a face, and would greet men of whatever rank by name without a moment's hesitation. Once, when the Senate passed a vote of thanks to him, he answered, 'Wait until I deserve them!' He allowed even the common people to watch him taking exercise on the Campus Martius, and often gave public declamations. Also, he recited his own poems, both at home and in the theatre – a performance which so delighted everyone that a special thanksgiving was voted him, as though he had won a great victory, and the passages he had chosen were printed in letters of gold on plaques dedicated to Jupiter Capitolinus.

11. He gave an immense variety of entertainments – youth games, chariot races in the Circus, stage plays, a gladiatorial show – persuading even old men of consular rank, and old ladies too, to attend the youth games. He reserved seats for the *equites* at the Circus, and actually raced four-camel chariots! At the Great Games, as he called the series of plays devoted to the hope of his reigning for ever, parts were taken by men and women of both orders, and one well-known *eques* rode an elephant down a sloping tightrope. When he staged *The Fire*, a Roman play by Afranius, the actors were allowed to keep the valuable furnishings they rescued from the burning house. Throughout the games all kinds of gifts were scattered to the people – 1,000 assorted birds daily, and quantities of food

parcels, besides vouchers for grain, clothes, gold, silver, precious stones, pearls, paintings, slaves, transport animals, and even trained wild beasts – and finally for ships, blocks of tenements, and farms.

12. Nero watched from the top of the proscenium. The gladiatorial show took place in a wooden theatre near the Campus Martius, which had been built in less than a year, but no one was allowed to be killed during these combats, not even criminals. He did, however, make 400 senators and 600 *equites*, many of them rich and respectable, do battle in the arena, and some had to fight wild beasts and perform various duties about the ring. He staged a naval engagement on an artificial lake of salt water which had sea monsters swimming in it; also ballets by certain young Greeks, to whom he presented certificates of Roman citizenship when their show ended. In one of these an actor disguised as a bull actually mounted another who played Pasiphae and occupied a hollow wooden heifer – or that, at least, was the audience's impression. In another, the actor who played Icarus,[9] while attempting his first flight, fell beside Nero's couch and spattered him with blood.

Nero rarely presided at shows of this sort, but would recline in an enclosed platform and watch through a window; later, however, he opened it up. He was the first to establish in Rome a festival of competitions in music, athletics and horsemanship, modelled on the Greek ones and held every four years, which he called the Neronia; and he simultaneously opened his baths, which had a gymnasium attached, and provided free oil for *equites* and senators. Men of consular status, drawn by lot, organized the Neronia, and occupied the praetors' seats. At the prize-giving, Nero descended to the orchestra stalls where the senators sat to accept the laurel wreath for Latin oratory and verse, which had been reserved for him by the unanimous vote of all the distinguished competitors. The judges also awarded him the wreath for a lyre solo, but he bowed reverently to them and said, 'Pray lay it on the ground before Augustus' statue.' At an athletic competition held in the Saepta, oxen were sacrificed on a lavish scale; that was when he shaved his chin for the first time, put the hair in a pearl-studded gold box, and dedicated it to Jupiter Capitolinus. He had invited the Vestal Virgins to watch the athletics, explaining that the priestesses of Ceres were accorded the same privilege at Olympia.

13. The welcome given Tiridates when he visited Rome deserves inclusion in the list of Nero's spectacles. Tiridates was an Armenian king whom he had lured to Rome with wonderful promises. Cloudy weather prevented Tiridates from being displayed to the people on the day fixed by edict; however, Nero brought him out as soon as possible afterwards. The praetorian cohorts were stationed in full armour around the temples of the Forum, while Nero occupied his curule chair on the Rostra, wearing triumphal dress and surrounded by military insignia and standards. Tiridates had to walk up a ramp and then prostrate himself in supplication; whereupon Nero stretched out his hand, drew him to his feet, kissed him, and replaced his turban with a diadem. When Tiridates' supplication had been translated into Latin by an interpreter and publicly recited, he was taken to the theatre (where he made a further supplication) and offered a seat on Nero's right. The people then hailed Nero as *imperator* and, after dedicating a laurel wreath in the Capitol, he closed the double doors of the Temple of Janus, as a sign that all war was at an end.

14. The first of Nero's four consulships[10] lasted for two months, the third for four, the second and the last for six. He let a year elapse between the first and second and between the third and fourth, but not between the second and third.

15. When he judged a case, he preferred to defer his judgement until the following day, and then give it in writing; and he ruled that, instead of a case being presented as a whole, first by one side and then by the other, every relevant charge should be debated separately. On withdrawing to study a problem of law, he never consulted openly with his judicial advisers, but made each of them write out an opinion, then mulled over these documents in private, came to his own conclusion, and passed it off as a majority opinion.

For a long time Nero excluded the sons of freedmen from the Senate, and forbade those who had held magistracies under his predecessors to do so again. If too many candidates competed for any high office, he kept the unsuccessful ones employed by giving them legions to command. It became his practice to appoint consuls for a period of six months, and when a consul died shortly before the Kalends of January he made no substitute appointment, to mark his disapproval of Caninius Rebilus' one-day consulship.[11] He awarded triumphal decorations to men of quaestorian rank and even to some *equites*, though their services had not been of a military nature. The consuls were ordered to read certain of his speeches sent for the Senate's information, thereby going over the heads of the quaestors, whose business it should have been.

16. Nero introduced his own new style of architecture: he had porches built out from the fronts of tenements and private houses to serve as firefighting platforms, subsidizing the work himself. He also considered a scheme for extending the city wall as far as Ostia, and cutting a canal which would allow ships to sail straight up to Rome.

During his reign a great many public abuses were suppressed by the imposition of heavy penalties, and among the novel enactments were sumptuary laws limiting private expenditure, the substitution of a simple cash distribution for public banquets, and a decree restricting the food sold in wine shops to green vegetables, dried beans and the like – whereas before all kinds of tasty snacks had been displayed. Punishments were inflicted on the Christians,[12] a sect professing a new and mischievous superstition. Nero also ended the licence which the charioteers had enjoyed for so long that they claimed it as a right: to wander merrily down the streets, swindling and robbing the populace. He likewise expelled from the city all pantomime actors and their hangers-on.

17. A new and effective check on forgery was discovered about this time. Every signed tablet now contained three leaves: the contract was written on the first, which was open, and also on the third, which had to be linked with the second by a linen thread passed through three holes bored in both and then sealed. If the contract on the first page appeared to have been tampered with, it was checked against that on the third, the seals which hid it being broken in the presence of a magistrate.

Provisions were also made that the first two pages of every will offered for witnesses to sign should bear only the testator's name, and that no one drafting a will for signature by anyone else might insert in it a legacy for himself. Moreover, litigants were ordered to pay their advocates at a fixed, reasonable rate, and no charge was to be made for seats in court. Further, all treasury suits, which had previously been settled by the treasury officials themselves, were in future to come before a board of arbitration in the Forum, and every appeal from the verdict of a jury was to be addressed to the Senate.

18. Nero felt no ambition to extend the Roman empire; he even considered withdrawing his forces from Britain, yet kept them there because such a decision might have reflected on the glory won by his adoptive father Claudius. The sole additions made during his reign to the list of provinces were the kingdom of Pontus, ceded to him by Polemon, and that of the Cottian Alps on the death of Cottius.

19. Nero planned only two tours: one to Alexandria, the other to Achaia. A warning portent made him cancel the Alexandrian voyage on the very day when his ship should have sailed: during his farewell round of the temples he had sat down in the shrine of Vesta, but when he rose to leave, the hem of his toga caught fire and then a temporary blindness overcame him. While in Achaia he tried to have a canal cut through the Isthmus of Corinth; he addressed a gathering of praetorians, urging them to undertake the task, and then took a mattock himself and, at a trumpet blast, broke the ground and carried off the first basket of earth on his back. He had also planned an expedition to the Caspian Gates,[13] enrolling a new legion of Italian-born recruits, all six feet tall, which he called 'The Phalanx of Alexander the Great'.

I have assembled this catalogue of Nero's acts – some forgivable, some even praiseworthy – in order to segregate them from his follies and crimes, which I must now begin to list.

20. Music formed part of his childhood curriculum, and he early developed a taste for it. Soon after his accession, he summoned Terpnus, the greatest lyre player of the day, to sing to him when dinner had ended, for several nights in succession,

until very late. Then, little by little, he began to study and practise himself, and conscientiously undertook all the usual exercises for strengthening and developing the voice. He would also lie on his back with a slab of lead on his chest, use enemas and emetics to keep down his weight, and refrain from eating apples and every other food considered deleterious to the vocal cords. Ultimately, though his voice was still feeble and husky, he was pleased enough with his progress to nurse theatrical ambitions, and would quote to his friends the Greek proverb 'Unheard melodies are never sweet.' His first stage appearance was at Neapolis, where, disregarding an earthquake which shook the theatre, he sang his piece through to the end. He often performed at Neapolis, for several consecutive days too, and even while giving his voice a brief rest he could not stay away from the theatre, but went to dine in the orchestra, where he promised the crowd in Greek that, when he had downed a drink or two, he would give them something to make their ears ring. So captivated was he by the rhythmic applause of some Alexandrian sailors from a fleet which had just put in that he sent to Egypt for more. He also chose a few young *equites* and more than 5,000 ordinary youths, whom he divided into claques to learn the various Alexandrian methods of applause – they were known respectively as 'Bees', 'Roof tiles' and 'Brickbats' – and to provide it liberally whenever he sang. It was easy to recognize them by their pomaded hair, splendid dress and absence of rings on their left hands. The *equites* who led them earned 400,000 sesterces a performance.

21. Appearances at Rome meant so much to Nero that he held the Neronia again before the scheduled date. When the crowd clamoured to hear his heavenly voice, he answered that he would perform in the gardens later if anyone really wanted to hear him; but when the guards on duty seconded the appeal, he delightedly agreed to oblige them. He wasted no time in getting his name entered on the list of competing lyre players, and dropped his ticket into the urn with the others. Praetorian prefects carried his lyre as he went up to play, and a group of military tribunes and close friends accompanied him. After taking his place and briefly begging the audience's kind attention,

he announced through Cluvius Rufus, a man of consular rank, that he was going to sing Niobe,[14] which he did, until almost the tenth hour. He then put off the rest of the competition and the award of the prize to the following year, which would give him another opportunity to sing. But, since a year was a long time to wait, he continued to make frequent appearances. He toyed with the idea of playing opposite professional actors in private shows, because a praetor had offered him 1 million sesterces if he would consent. And he did actually appear in tragedies, taking the parts of heroes and gods, sometimes even of heroines and goddesses, wearing masks modelled on his own face or that of whatever woman happened to be his current mistress. Among his performances were Canace in childbirth, Orestes the matricide, Oedipus blinded and Hercules raving.[15] There is a story that a young recruit on guard in the wings recognized him in the rags and fetters demanded by the part of Hercules and dashed boldly to his assistance.

22. Horses had been Nero's main interest since childhood; whatever his tutors might do, they could never stop his chatter about the chariot races at the Circus. When scolded by one of them for telling his fellow pupils about a Green charioteer who had the misfortune to get dragged by his team, Nero untruthfully explained that he had been discussing Hector.[16] At the beginning of his reign he used every day to play with model ivory chariots on a board, and came up from the country to attend all the races, even minor ones, at first in secret and then without the least embarrassment, so that there was never any doubt at Rome when he would be in residence. He frankly admitted that he wished the number of prizes increased; as a result, the races were multiplied so that the contests now lasted until a late hour and the faction managers no longer thought it worthwhile to bring out their teams except for a full day's racing. Very soon Nero set his heart on driving a chariot himself in a regular race, and after a preliminary trial in the palace gardens before an audience of slaves and *hoi polloi* he made a public appearance at the Circus Maximus; on this occasion one of his freedmen replaced the magistrate who dropped the napkin as the starting signal.

However, these amateur incursions into the arts at Rome did not satisfy him, and he headed for Achaia, as I mentioned above. His main reason was that the cities which regularly sponsored musical contests had adopted the practice of sending him every available prize for lyre playing; he always accepted these with great pleasure, giving the delegates the earliest audience of the day and invitations to private dinners. They would beg Nero to sing when the meal was over, and applaud his performance to the echo, which made him announce, 'The Greeks alone are worthy of my genius; they really listen to music.' So he sailed off hastily, and as soon as he arrived at Cassiope he gave his first song recital before the altar of Jupiter Cassius, after which he went the round of all the contests.

23. He ordered those contests which normally took place only at long intervals to be held during his visit, even if it meant repeating them, and broke tradition at Olympia by introducing a musical competition into the athletic games. When his freedman Helius advised him that he was urgently needed at Rome, he would not be distracted by official business, but wrote back, 'Yes, you have made yourself quite plain. I am aware that you want me to go home; you will do far better, however, if you encourage me to stay until I have proved myself worthy of my reputation.' No one was allowed to leave the theatre during his recitals, however pressing the reason, and the gates were kept barred. We hear of women in the audience giving birth and of men being so bored with the music and the applause that they furtively dropped down from the wall at the rear or shammed dead and were carried away for burial. Nero's stage fright and general nervousness, his jealousy of rivals, and his awe of the judges were more easily seen than believed. He treated his fellow competitors as though they were his equals, and would fuss over them, pay court to them, abuse them behind their backs, and sometimes insult them to their faces; if any were particularly good singers, he would bribe them not to do themselves justice. Before every performance he would address the judges with the utmost deference: he had done what he could, he said, and the issue was now in Fortune's hands; but since they were men of judgement and experience, they would know

how to eliminate the factor of chance. When they told him not to worry he felt a little better, but still anxious, and mistook the silence of some for severity and the embarrassment of others for disfavour, admitting that he suspected every one of them.

24. He strictly observed the rules, never daring to clear his throat and even using his arm to wipe the sweat from his brow. Once, while acting in a tragedy, he dropped his sceptre and quickly recovered it, but was terrified of disqualification. The accompanist, however, swore that the slip had passed unnoticed amid the audience's enthusiastic shouts of approval, so he took heart again. Nero insisted on announcing his own victories, and this emboldened him to enter the competition for heralds. To destroy every trace of previous winners in these contests he ordered all their statues and busts to be taken down, dragged away with hooks, and hurled into public privies. On several occasions he took part in the chariot racing, and at Olympia he drove a ten-horse team, a novelty for which he had censured King Mithridates in one of his own poems. He lost his balance, fell from the chariot, and had to be helped in again; but, though he failed to stay the course and retired before the finish, the judges nevertheless awarded him the prize. On the eve of his departure, he presented the whole province with its freedom and conferred Roman citizenship as well as large cash rewards on the judges. It was during the Isthmian Games at Corinth that he stood in the middle of the stadium and personally announced these benefits.

25. Returning to Italy, Nero entered Neapolis with a team of white horses, since it was there that he had made his debut as a singer, and ordered part of the city wall to be razed – which is the Greek custom whenever the victor in any of the sacred games comes home. He repeated the same performance at Antium, at Alba Longa and finally at Rome. For his processional entry into Rome he chose the chariot which Augustus had used in his triumph nearly a hundred years previously, and wore a Greek mantle spangled with gold stars over a purple robe. The Olympian wreath was on his head, the Pythian wreath in his right hand, and the others were carried before him,[17] with placards explaining where and against whom he

had won them, what songs he had sung, and in what plays he had acted. Nero's chariot was followed by his regular claque, who shouted that they were Augustiani and the soldiers of his triumph.[18] The procession passed through the Circus Maximus (he had the entrance arch pulled down to allow more room), then by way of the Velabrum and the Forum to the Palatine Hill and the Temple of Apollo. Victims were sacrificed in his honour all along the route, which was sprinkled with perfume, and the people showered him with songbirds, ribbons and sweetmeats as compliments on his voice. He hung the wreaths above the couches in his sleeping quarters, and set up several statues of himself playing the lyre. He also had a coin struck with the same device. After this, it never occurred to him that he ought to refrain from singing or even sing a little less, but he saved his voice by addressing the troops only in written orders or in speeches delivered by someone else, and would attend no entertainment or official business unless he had a voice trainer standing by, telling him when to spare his vocal cords and when to protect his mouth with a handkerchief. Whether he offered people his friendship or plainly indicated his dislike for them often depended on how generously or how feebly they had applauded.

26. His insolence, lust, extravagance, greed and cruelty he at first revealed only gradually and secretly, to be sure, as though merely youthful mistakes; but even then there could be no doubt that these were the faults of his character, not of his age. As soon as night fell he would snatch a hat or cap and make a round of the taverns or prowl the streets in search of mischief – and not always innocent mischief either, because one of his games was to attack men on their way home from dinner, stab them if they offered resistance, and then drop their bodies down the sewers. He would also break into shops, afterwards opening a miniature market in his home with the stolen goods, dividing them up into lots, auctioning them himself, and squandering the proceeds. During these escapades he often risked being blinded or killed – once he was beaten almost to death by a senator whose wife he had molested, which taught him never to go out after dark unless an escort of military tribunes was following

him at a discreet distance. He would also secretly visit the theatre by day, in a sedan chair, and watch the quarrels among the pantomime actors, cheering them on from the top of the proscenium; then, when they came to blows and fought it out with stones and broken benches, he joined in the fun by throwing things on the heads of the crowd. On one occasion he fractured a praetor's skull.

27. Gradually Nero's vices gained the upper hand: he no longer tried to laugh them off or hide or deny them, but turned quite brazen. His feasts now lasted from noon till midnight, with an occasional break for diving into a warm bath or, if it were summer, into snow-cooled water. Sometimes he would drain the artificial lake in the Campus Martius or the other in the Circus, and hold public dinner parties there, with prostitutes and dancing girls from all over the city serving as waitresses. Whenever he floated down the Tiber to Ostia or cruised past Baiae, he had a row of temporary brothels erected along the shore, where a number of noblewomen, pretending to be madams, stood waiting to solicit his business. He also forced his friends to provide him with dinners; one of them spent 4 million sesterces on a turban party, and another even more on a rose banquet.

28. Not satisfied with seducing freeborn boys and married women, Nero raped the Vestal Virgin Rubria. He nearly contrived to marry the freedwoman Acte, by persuading some friends of consular rank to swear falsely that she came of royal stock. Having tried to turn the boy Sporus into a girl by castration, he went through a wedding ceremony with him – dowry, bridal veil and all – which the whole court attended, then brought him home and treated him as a wife. A rather amusing joke is still going the rounds: the world would have been a happier place had Nero's father Domitius married that sort of wife. He dressed Sporus in the fine clothes normally worn by an empress, and took him in his own litter not only to every Greek assize and fair, but eventually through the Sigillaria[19] at Rome, kissing him amorously now and then. The passion he felt for his mother Agrippina was notorious, but her enemies would not let him consummate it, fearing that, if he

did, she would become even more powerful and ruthless than
hitherto. So he found a new mistress who was said to be her
exact image; some say that he did, in fact, commit incest with
Agrippina every time they rode in the same litter – the state of
his clothes when he emerged proved it.

29. Nero was as prodigal with his own chastity as with that of
others, and after befouling every part of his body he at last
invented a novel game: he was released from a den dressed in the
skins of wild animals, and attacked the private parts of men and
women who stood bound to stakes. After working up sufficient
excitement by this means, he was finished off – shall we say – by
his freedman Doryphorus. Doryphorus now married him – just
as he himself had married Sporus – and on the wedding night
he imitated the screams and moans of a girl being deflowered.
According to my informants he was convinced that no one could
remain sexually chaste or pure in any respect, but that most
people concealed their secret vices; hence, if anyone confessed to
obscene practices, Nero forgave him all his other crimes.

30. He believed that fortunes were made to be squandered,
and whoever could keep track of his expenses seemed to him a
stingy miser; 'True gentlemen', he said, 'always throw their
money about.' He professed deep admiration for his uncle
Gaius merely because he had run through Tiberius' vast fortune,
and he never thought twice himself about giving away or wasting money. Believe it or not, he spent 800,000 sesterces a day
on King Tiridates, and made him a parting gift of more than
100 million. He presented Menecrates the lyre player and Spiculus the gladiator with houses and estates worthy of men who
had celebrated triumphs, and showed equal generosity to his
monkey-faced moneylender Paneros, whom he later buried in
almost royal style. Nero never wore the same clothes twice; he
would stake 400,000 gold pieces on each pip of the winning
throw at dice; and when he went fishing he used a golden net
strung with purple and scarlet thread. He seldom travelled, it
is said, with a train of fewer than 1,000 carriages; the mules
were shod with silver, the muleteers wore Canusian wool, and
he was escorted by Mazacian horsemen[20] and outriders with
jingling bracelets and medallions.

31. His wastefulness showed most of all in the architectural projects. He built a house stretching from the Palatine to the Esquiline which he called 'The Passageway', and when it burned down soon afterwards he rebuilt it under the new name of 'The Golden House'.[21] The following details will give some notion of its size and magnificence. A huge statue of himself, 120 feet high, stood in the entrance hall, and a threefold portico ran for a whole mile. An enormous pool, more like a sea than a pool, was surrounded by buildings made to resemble cities, and by a landscape garden consisting of ploughed fields, vineyards, pastures and woodlands – where every variety of domestic and wild animal roamed about. Parts of the house were overlaid with gold and studded with precious stones and mother-of-pearl. All the dining rooms had ceilings of fretted ivory, the panels of which could slide back and let a rain of flowers, or perfume from hidden sprinklers, shower upon his guests. The main dining room was circular, and its roof revolved slowly, day and night, just like the sky. Sea water or sulphur water was always on tap in the baths. When the palace had been decorated throughout in this lavish style, Nero dedicated it, and condescended to remark, 'Good, now I can at last begin to live like a human being!'

He also had men at work on a covered bath surrounded by porticoes and stretching from Misenum to Lake Avernus; all the hot springs in the Baiae district would be canalized to feed it. Another project would have connected Lake Avernus with Ostia by a ship canal 160 miles long and broad enough for two quinqueremes to pass. Prisoners from every part of the empire were to be used for this task, even those convicted of capital crimes.

Nero's confidence in the national resources was not the only cause of his furious spending; he had also been excited by tales of a great hidden treasure, vouched for by a Roman *eques* who swore that the hoard brought by Queen Dido to Carthage centuries before, when she fled from Tyre, still lay untouched in certain huge African caves and could easily be retrieved.

32. When this hope failed to materialize, Nero found himself bankrupt; his financial difficulties were such that he could not lay hands on enough money even for the soldiers' pay or the

veterans' benefits, and he therefore resorted to robbery and blackmail.

First he made a law that if a freedman died who had taken the name of a family connected with his own and could not show adequate reason, five-sixths of the estate, not merely one-half, should be forfeited to him. Next, he seized the estates of those who had shown ingratitude by not bequeathing him enough, and fined the legal specialists responsible for writing and dictating such wills. Moreover, any man whose words or deeds offered the least handle to an informer was charged with *maiestas*. He took back the presents he had given to Greek cities in acknowledgement of prizes won at musical or athletic contests. On one market day he sent an agent to sell a few ounces of the amethystine and Tyrian purple dyes which he had forbidden to be used, and then closed the businesses of the dealers who had bought them. It is said that he once noticed a lady wearing this illegal colour at one of his recitals, pointed her out to his assistants, and had her dragged off – whereupon she was stripped not only of her clothes but of her entire property. His invariable formula, when he appointed a magistrate, was, 'You know my needs, don't you? You and I must see that nobody is left with anything.' Finally he robbed numerous temples of their treasures and melted down the gold and silver images, among them the household gods of Rome – which Galba, however, had recast soon afterwards.

33. Claudius was the first victim of his murderous career: though Nero may not have been actually responsible for his poisoning, he knew all about it, as he later made clear by appreciatively quoting a Greek proverb which calls mushrooms (the source of the poison) 'the food of the gods'.[22] And he did his utmost to insult Claudius' memory, accusing him at some times of stupidity and at others of cruelty. It was a favourite joke of his that Claudius had ceased 'to linger on' among men, lengthening the initial syllable of the verb *morari* so that it meant 'to play the fool'. Nero annulled many of Claudius' decrees and edicts on the ground that he had been a doddering old idiot, and enclosed the place where he had been cremated with nothing better than a low rubble wall.

He tried to poison Britannicus, no less because he was jealous of his voice, which was far more musical than his own, than for fear that the common people might be less attached to Claudius' adopted son than to his real one. The drug came from an expert poisoner named Lucusta, and when its action was not so rapid as he expected – the effect was violently laxative – he called for her, complaining that she had given him medicine instead of poison, and beat her with his own hands. Lucusta explained that she had reduced the dose to make the crime less obvious; 'Oho!' he said. 'So you think that I am afraid of the Julian law?' Then he led Lucusta into his bedroom and stood over her while she concocted the fastest-working poison in her pharmacopoeia. This he administered to a kid, but when it took five hours to die he made her boil down the brew again and again. At last he tried it on a pig, which died on the spot, and that night at dinner he had what remained poured into Britannicus' cup. Britannicus dropped dead at the very first taste, but Nero lyingly assured the guests that the poor boy had 'long been subject to these epileptic seizures'. Britannicus was buried hastily and without ceremony on the following day during a heavy shower of rain, and Nero granted Lucusta, in return for her services, immunity and some sizeable estates, and actually supplied her with students.

34. The over-watchful, over-critical eye that Agrippina kept on whatever Nero said or did proved more than he could stand. He first tried to embarrass her by frequent threats to abdicate and go into retirement in Rhodes. Then, having deprived her of all honour and power, and even of her Roman and German bodyguard, he expelled her from the Palatine; after which he did everything possible to annoy her, sending people to pester her with lawsuits while she stayed in Rome, and when she took refuge on her country estates making them constantly drive or sail past the windows, disturbing her with jeers and catcalls. In the end her threats and violent behaviour terrified him into deciding that she must die. He tried to poison her three times, but she had always taken the antidote in advance; so he rigged up a machine in the ceiling of her bedroom which would dislodge the panels and drop them on her while she slept. How-

ever, someone gave the secret away. Then he had a collapsible cabin boat designed which would either sink or fall in on top of her. Under pretence of a reconciliation, he sent the most friendly note inviting her to celebrate the Quinquatrus with him at Baiae, and on her arrival he made one of his captains stage an accidental collision with the galley in which she had sailed. Then he protracted the feast until a late hour, and when at last she said, 'I really must get back to Bauli' he offered her his collapsible boat instead of the damaged galley. Nero was in a very happy mood as he led Agrippina down to the quay, and even kissed her breasts before she stepped aboard. He sat up all night, on tenterhooks of anxiety, waiting for news of her death. At dawn Lucius Agermus, her freedman, entered joyfully to report that, although the ship had foundered, his mother had swum to safety, and that he need have no fears on her account. For want of a better plan, Nero ordered one of his men to drop a dagger surreptitiously beside Agermus, whom he arrested at once on a charge of attempted murder. After this he arranged for Agrippina to be killed, and made it seem as if she had sent Agermus to assassinate him but committed suicide on hearing that the plot had miscarried. Other more gruesome details are supplied by reliable authorities: it appears that Nero rushed off to examine Agrippina's corpse, handling her legs and arms critically and, between drinks, discussing their good and bad points. Though encouraged by the congratulations which poured in from the army and the Senate and People, he was never thereafter able to free his conscience from the guilt of this crime. He often admitted that the Furies[23] were pursuing him with whips and burning torches, and he set Persian mages at work to conjure up his mother's ghost and make her stop haunting him. During his tour of Greece he dared not participate in the Eleusinian Mysteries when a herald ordered all criminals present to withdraw before the ceremonies began.

Having disposed of his mother, Nero proceeded to murder his aunt Domitia.[24] He found her confined to bed with severe constipation. The old lady stroked his downy beard affectionately – he was already full grown – murmuring, 'Whenever you celebrate your coming of age and present me with this, I shall die happy.' Nero turned to his courtiers and said laughingly, 'In that case I must shave at once' – which he did. Then he ordered the doctors to give her a laxative of fatal strength, seized her property before she was quite dead, and avoided all legal complications by tearing up the will.

35. After Octavia, he took two more wives – first Poppaea Sabina, a quaestor's daughter, at that time married to an *eques*, and then Statilia Messalina, great-great-granddaughter of Augustus' general Statilius Taurus, who had twice been consul and won a triumph. To marry Statilia he was obliged to murder her husband, the consul Atticus Vestinus. Life with Octavia had soon bored him, and when his friends criticized his treatment of her he retorted, 'The title of wife ought surely to be enough for her.' He tried to strangle her on several occasions, but finally announced that she was barren and divorced her. This act made him so unpopular and caused so great a scandal that he banished Octavia and finally had her executed on a charge of adultery. Her innocence was proved by the refusal of the witnesses to testify against her, even under torture; so he bribed his old tutor Anicetus to confess (falsely) that he had tricked her into infidelity. Though he doted on Poppaea, whom he married twelve days after his divorce from Octavia, he kicked her to death while she was pregnant and feeling very ill, because she dared complain that he came home late from the races. Poppaea had borne him a daughter, Claudia Augusta, who died in infancy.

There was no family relationship which Nero did not criminally abuse. When Claudius' daughter Antonia refused to take Poppaea's place, he had her executed on a charge of attempted rebellion; he likewise destroyed every other member of his family, including relatives by marriage. Among them was young Aulus Plautius, whom he raped before having him put to death, remarking, 'Now Mother may come and kiss my successor'; he claimed that Agrippina had been in love with Aulus and had induced him to make a bid for the throne. There was also his stepson, Rufrius Crispinus, Poppaea's child by her former husband. Nero had the boy's own slaves drown him on a fishing expedition simply because he was said to have played at being a general and an emperor. He banished Tuscus, the son of his wet nurse and now procurator of Egypt, for daring to use the baths which he had built in preparation for Nero's visit to Alexandria. When his teacher Seneca repeatedly asked leave to retire and had surrendered all his estates, Nero swore that he had no cause to suspect the old man, whom he would rather die than harm; but he drove him to commit suicide nevertheless. He promised Burrus, the praetorian prefect, a cough mixture, but sent poison instead, and he also poisoned the food and drink of the rich old freedmen who had originally arranged for him to be adopted as Claudius' heir and were now acting as his advisers.[25]

36. Nero was no less cruel to strangers than to members of his family. A comet, popularly supposed to herald the death of some person of outstanding importance, appeared several nights running and greatly disturbed him. His astrologer Balbillus observed that monarchs usually avoided portents of this kind by executing their most prominent subjects and thus directing the wrath of heaven elsewhere; so Nero resolved on a wholesale massacre of the nobility. What fortified him in this decision and seemed to justify it was that he had discovered two plots against his life. The earlier and more important of the two was the Pisonian conspiracy in Rome; the other was the Vinician conspiracy at Beneventum.[26] When brought up for trial, the conspirators were loaded with three sets of chains. Some, while admitting their guilt, claimed that the only way they could help a man so thoroughly steeped in evil as Nero was to kill him. All children of the condemned men were banished from Rome and then starved to death or poisoned; it is well known that a group of them were killed at a single lunch, along with their tutors and attendants, and that others were prevented from seeking sustenance.

37. After this, nothing could restrain Nero from murdering anyone he pleased, on whatever pretext. Here are a few instances only: Salvidienus Orfitus was charged with leasing three shops, which formed part of his house, close to the Forum, as offices for the representatives of certain allied states; and a blind legal expert, Cassius Longinus, with keeping a mask of Gaius Cassius, one of Julius Caesar's murderers, attached to the family tree; and Thrasea Paetus for looking like a cross old

schoolmaster. Those whom he ordered to commit suicide were never given more than an hour's grace. To insure against delays he made doctors 'take care' of any who were found still alive – which in Nero's vocabulary meant opening their veins. He was eager, it is said, to get hold of a certain Egyptian – a sort of ogre who would eat raw flesh and practically anything else he was given – and watch him tear live men to pieces and then devour them. These 'successes', as Nero called them, went to his head, and he boasted that no previous ruler had ever realized the extent of his power. Often he hinted broadly that it was not his intention to spare the remaining senators, but would one day wipe out the entire senatorial order and let *equites* and freedmen govern the provinces and command the armies instead. He certainly never gave senators the kisses they expected when he set out on a journey or returned from one, and never bothered to answer their greetings. In his announcement of the Isthmus-canal project to a huge crowd, he loudly voiced the hope that it might benefit himself and the Roman people, but made no mention of the Senate.

38. Nero showed no greater mercy to the common folk, or to the very walls of Rome. Once, in the course of a general conversation, someone quoted the line 'When I am dead, may fire consume the earth,' but Nero said that the first part of the line should read 'While I yet live', and soon converted this fancy into fact. Pretending to be disgusted by the drab old buildings and narrow, winding streets of Rome, he brazenly set fire to the city, and though a number of former consuls caught his attendants trespassing on their property with tow and blazing torches, they dared not interfere. He also coveted the sites of several granaries, solidly built in stone, near the Golden House; having knocked down their walls with siege engines, he set the interiors ablaze. This terror lasted for six days and seven nights, causing many people to take shelter in the tombs. Not only did a vast number of tenements burn down, but houses which had belonged to famous generals and were still decorated with their trophies; temples too, dating back to the time of the kingship, and others dedicated during the Punic and Gallic wars – in fact every ancient monument of historical interest that had hitherto

survived. Nero watched the conflagration from the tower in the Gardens of Maecenas, enraptured by what he called 'the beauty of the flames', then put on his tragedian's costume and sang *The Fall of Troy* from beginning to end. He offered to remove corpses and rubble free of charge, but allowed nobody to search among the ruins even of his own home; he wanted to collect as much loot as possible himself. Then he opened a fire-relief fund and insisted on contributions, which bled the provincials white and practically beggared all private citizens.

39. Fate made certain unexpected additions to the disasters of Nero's reign. In a single autumn, 30,000 deaths from plague were registered at the Grove of Libitina. Two important British garrison towns were taken by storm, and huge numbers of Romans and allies were massacred. The legions in Armenia were shamefully defeated and sent beneath the yoke, and Syria was almost lost at the same time.

Amid all this, it was strange and quite striking that there was nothing which Nero seemed to mind less than curses and insults, and that there was no one to whom he was more lenient than those who attacked him in jokes and lampoons. Many things of this sort, in both Greek and Latin, were posted up on walls or passed from mouth to mouth. Here are a few examples:

> Alcmaeon, Orestes and Nero are brothers,
> Why? Because all of them murdered their mothers.[27]

*

> Count the numerical values
>   Of the letters in Nero's name,[28]
> And in 'murdered his own mother':
>   You will find their sum is the same.

*

> Aeneas the Trojan hero
>   Carried off his aged father;
> His remote descendant Nero
>   Likewise carried off (or rather
> Let Death carry off) his mother:
> Heroes worthy of each other.[29]

*

> Though Nero may pluck the chords of a lyre,
> And the Parthian king the string of a bow,
> He who chants to the lyre with heavenly fire
> Is Apollo as much as his far-darting foe.
>
> *
>
> The palace is spreading and swallowing Rome!
> Let us all flee to Veii and make it our home.
> Yet the palace is growing so damnably fast
> That it threatens to gobble up Veii at last.

He never tried to trace the authors, and when an informer handed the Senate a short list of their names he gave instructions that they should be let off lightly. Once, as he crossed a street, Isidorus the Cynic loudly taunted him with 'In your song about Nauplius[30] you make good use of ancient ills, but in all practical matters you make ill use of modern goods.' Again, the comedian Datus, acting in an Atellan farce, illustrated the first line of the song 'Goodbye Father, goodbye Mother' with gestures of drinking and swimming – Claudius had been poisoned, Agrippina nearly drowned – and the last line, 'Hell guides your feet,' with a wave of his hand towards the senators whom Nero planned to massacre. Nero may have been impervious to insults of this sort or he may merely have pretended not to care, for fear of encouraging others to be equally witty; at any rate, he did no more than banish Datus and Isidorus from Italy.

40. At last, after nearly fourteen years of Nero's misrule, the earth rid herself of him. The first move was made by the Gauls under Julius Vindex, the praetorian governor of the province.

Nero's astrologers had told him that he would one day be removed from public office, and were given the famous reply 'A simple craft will keep a man from want.' This referred doubtless to his lyre playing, which, although it might be only a pastime for a *princeps*, would have to support him if he were reduced to earning a livelihood. Some astrologers forecast that, if forced to leave Rome, he would find another throne in the east; one or two even particularized that of Jerusalem.[31] Others assured him that he would recoup all his losses, a prediction on which he based high hopes, for when he seemed to have lost the provinces of Britain and Armenia, but managed to regain them both, he assumed that the disasters foretold had already taken place. Then the oracle of Apollo at Delphi warned him to beware the seventy-third year, and assuming that this referred to his own seventy-third year, not Galba's, he looked forward cheerfully to a ripe old age and an unbroken run of good luck – so much so that when he lost some very valuable objects in a shipwreck, he hastened to tell his friends that the fish would fetch them back to him.

Nero heard of the Gallic revolt on the anniversary of his mother's murder. He was in Neapolis at the time, and took the news so phlegmatically that everyone diagnosed satisfaction at finding a good excuse to declare war on such rich provinces and strip them clean. Going straight to the gymnasium, he was soon engrossed in watching the athletic contests, and when a far more serious dispatch reached him at dinner time he still showed no sign of disturbance beyond a threat to punish the rebels. In fact for eight days he wrote no orders and issued no special announcements, apparently trying to ignore the whole affair.

41. At last a series of insulting edicts signed by Vindex must have made some impression on him: in a letter to the Senate he urged them to avenge himself and the commonwealth, but pleaded an infected throat as an excuse for not appearing in person. Two taunts really went home: an insulting claim that he was a bad lyre player, and a reference to him as 'Aheno-barbus' rather than 'Nero'. Yet he told the Senate that he had already intended to renounce his adoptive name and resume that of his family; as for his lyre playing, he replied that he could hardly deserve Vindex's taunt (which proved the other accusations just as false) after his long and painstaking culti-vation of the art, and asked several senators whether they knew of any better performer than himself. When further urgent dispatches arrived in quick succession he hurried back to Rome in a state of terror. On the way, however, he happened to notice a group of monumental sculpture which represented a beaten Gaul being dragged along, head first, by a mounted Roman; this lucky sign sent him into a transport of joy, and he lifted his hands in gratitude to heaven. When, therefore, he arrived

in the city, he neglected to address either the Senate or the people; instead, he summoned the leading citizens to his home where, after a brief discussion of the Gallic situation, he devoted the remainder of the session to demonstrating a completely new type of water organ and explaining the mechanical complexities of several different models. He even remarked that he would have them installed in the theatre, 'if Vindex has no objection'.

42. But when news arrived of the revolt of Galba and the Spanish provinces, he fainted dead away and remained mute and insensible for a long while. Coming to himself, he tore his clothes and beat his forehead, crying that all was now over. His old nurse tried to console him by pointing out that many rulers in the past had experienced similar setbacks, but Nero insisted that to lose the supreme power while still alive was something that had never happened to anyone else before. Yet he made not the slightest attempt to alter his lazy and extravagant life. On the contrary, he celebrated whatever good news came in from the provinces with the most lavish banquets imaginable, and composed comic songs about the leaders of the revolt, which he set to bawdy tunes and sang with appropriate gestures; these have since become popular favourites. Then he stole into the theatre and sent a message to an actor who was being loudly applauded that he was taking advantage of his leader's absence from the stage on business of state by pushing himself forward.

43. At the first news of revolt Nero is said to have formed several appalling, though characteristic, schemes for dealing with the situation. Thus he intended to recall all army commanders and provincial governors and execute them on a charge of conspiracy, and to slaughter all exiles everywhere, for fear they might join the rebels, and all Gallic residents at Rome, because they might be implicated in the rising. He further considered giving the army free permission to pillage the Gallic provinces; poisoning the entire Senate at a banquet; and setting fire to the city again, but first letting wild beasts loose in the streets to hinder the citizens from coping with the blaze. However, he had to abandon these schemes, not because he scrupled to carry them out, but because he realized their impracticability in view of the military campaign soon to be forced on him. So

he dismissed the consuls from office before their term ended and took over both consulships himself, declaring, 'It stands to reason: only a consul can subdue Gaul.' But one day, soon after assuming the consular insignia, he left the dining room with his arms around two friends' shoulders, and remarked that when he reached Gaul he would at once step unarmed in front of the embattled enemy and weep, and weep. This would soften their hearts and win them back to loyalty, and on the next day he would stroll among his joyful troops singing paeans of victory, which he really ought to be composing now.

44. In his military preparations he was mainly concerned with finding enough wagons to carry his stage equipment and arranging for the concubines who would accompany him to have male haircuts and be issued with Amazonian shields and axes. When this was settled, Nero called the Roman people to arms; but since not a single eligible recruit came forward, he forcibly enlisted a number of slaves, choosing the best from each household and refusing exemption even to stewards or secretaries. All classes had to pay an income tax, and every tenant of a private house or flat was told that he owed a year's rent to the imperial exchequer. Nero insisted on being paid in none but newly minted coins, or in silver and gold of high standard; hence many people would not contribute anything, protesting that he would do much better if he reclaimed the fees from his informers.

45. He aggravated popular resentment by profiteering in grain, which was already priced far too high. And, unluckily for him, word went around during the general shortage of food that a ship from Alexandria had just unloaded a cargo of sand for the imperial wrestlers.

Nero was now so universally loathed that no abuse could be found bad enough for him. Someone tied a tress of hair to the head of one of his statues, with a note attached in Greek: 'This is a real contest for once, and you are going to lose!' A leather bag was draped around the neck of another statue, with a similar note reading, 'I have done what I could, but you deserve the sack.'[32] Insults were scrawled on columns about his crowing having aroused even the cocks, and many people played the trick of pretending to have trouble with their slaves at night and shouting out, 'Vengeance is coming!'[33]

46. The implications of auspices, of omens old and new, and of his own dreams began to terrify Nero. In the past he had never known what it was to dream, but after killing his mother he dreamed that he was steering a ship and that someone tore the tiller from his hands. Next, his wife Octavia pulled him down into thick darkness, where hordes of winged ants swarmed over him. Then the statues of the nations, which had been dedicated in the Theatre of Pompey, began to hem him in and prevent him from getting away, while his favourite Asturian horse turned into an ape, or all except the head, which whinnied a tune. Finally, the doors of the Mausoleum opened by themselves and a voice from inside called, 'Enter, Nero!'

On the Kalends of January the household gods, which had just been decorated, tumbled to the ground during preparations for the sacrifice, and as Nero was taking the auspices Sporus gave him a ring engraved with Proserpine's descent to the underworld.[34] Then a great crowd gathered to pay their annual vows to Nero, but the keys of the Capitol were mislaid. Again, while his speech against Vindex was being read in the Senate, a passage running 'the criminals will soon incur the punishment and die the death which they so thoroughly deserve' was hailed on all sides with cries of 'Augustus, you will do so!' People also noticed that Nero, at his latest public appearance, sang the part of Oedipus in exile and ended with the line 'Wife, mother, father, do my death compel!'[35]

47. When a dispatch bringing the news that the other armies had also revolted was brought him at lunch, he tore it up, pushed over the table, and sent smashing to the ground two of his 'Homeric' drinking cups – so called because they were engraved with scenes from Homer. He made Lucusta give him some poison, which he put in a golden box, and then crossed to the Servilian gardens, where he tried to persuade the tribunes and centurions of the praetorians to flee with him – because his most faithful freedmen had gone ahead to equip a fleet at Ostia. Some answered evasively, others flatly refused; one even shouted out the line 'Is it so terrible a thing to die?'[36]

Nero had no idea what to do. A number of alternatives offered – for example, throwing himself on the mercy of the Parthians or of Galba, or appearing pathetically on the Rostra to beg the people's pardon for his sins – they might at least make him prefect of Egypt, he thought, if they could not find it in their hearts to forgive him altogether. A speech to this effect was later found among the papers in his writing case, and the usual view is that only fear of being torn to pieces before he reached the Forum prevented him from delivering it.

Nero suspended his deliberations until the following day, but woke at midnight to find that his bodyguard had deserted him. He leaped out of bed and summoned his friends. When they did not appear, he went with a few members of his staff to knock at their doors. But nobody either opened or answered. He returned to his room. By now even the servants had absconded with the bed linen and the box of poison. He shouted for Spiculus the gladiator or any other trained executioner to end his misery at one blow. No one came. 'What? Have I then neither friends nor enemies left?' he cried, and dashed out, apparently intending to hurl himself into the Tiber.

48. Changing his mind once more, however, he said that all he wanted was some secluded spot where he could collect his thoughts at leisure. Phaon, an imperial freedman, suggested his own suburban villa, four miles away, between the Via Salaria and the Via Nomentana. Nero jumped at the offer. He was barefoot and wearing only a tunic, but he simply pulled on a faded cloak and hat, took horse, and trotted off, holding a handkerchief over his face. Only four companions went with him, including Sporus. Suddenly a slight earth tremor was felt and lightning flashed in their eyes, which terrified Nero. Then from the nearby camp he heard soldiers shouting about the defeat which Galba would inflict on him. He heard one man exclaim as they passed, 'Those fellows are in pursuit of Nero,' and another, 'What's the latest news of him in the city?' Then Nero's horse took fright at the smell of a dead body lying by the roadside, which made him expose his face. He was immediately recognized and saluted by a praetorian veteran. They reached a lane leading to Phaon's villa and, abandoning

their horses, followed a path which ran through a briar patch and a plantation of reeds to the rear wall of the house. Because the going was difficult Nero made them spread a cloak for him to walk on. When begged by Phaon to lie low for a while in a gravel pit, he answered, 'No, I refuse to go underground before I die.' While the servants tunnelled through the wall, he scooped up some water in his hands from a neighbouring pool and drank it, saying, 'This is Nero's own special brew.' Then he pulled out all the thorns from his ragged cloak and crawled into the villa by way of the tunnel. Finding himself in a slave's bedroom, beside a couch with a poor mattress over which an old cape had been thrown, he sank down on it and, although hungry, refused some coarse bread; but he confessed himself still thirsty, and sipped a little warm water.

49. Finally, when his companions unanimously insisted on his trying to escape from the miserable fate threatening him, he ordered them to dig a grave at once, of the right size for his body, and then collect any pieces of marble that they could find and fetch wood and water for the disposal of the corpse. As they bustled about obediently, he muttered through his tears, 'Dead! And so great an artist!'

A runner brought a letter to Phaon. Nero tore it from the man's hands and read that, having been declared a public enemy by the Senate, he would be punished in ancient style when arrested. He asked what 'ancient style' meant, and learned that the executioners stripped their victim naked, thrust his head into a wooden fork, and then flogged him to death with sticks. In terror, he snatched up the two daggers which he had brought along and tried their points, but threw them down again, protesting that the fatal hour had not yet come. Then he begged Sporus to weep and mourn for him, and also begged one of them to set him an example by committing suicide first. He kept moaning about his cowardice and muttering, 'How ugly and vulgar my life has become!'; 'This is certainly not fitting for Nero, not fitting at all'; 'I have to keep a stiff upper lip in all this'; 'Come, pull yourself together!' By this time the troop of cavalry who had orders to take him alive were coming up the road. Nero gasped, 'Hark to the sound I hear! It is hooves of galloping horses.'[37] Then, with the help of his secretary Epaphroditus, he stabbed himself in the throat and was already half-dead when a cavalry officer entered, pretending to have rushed to his rescue, and staunched the wound with his cloak. Nero muttered, 'Too late! But, ah, what fidelity!' So speaking, he died, with eyes glazed and bulging from their sockets, a sight which horrified everybody present. He had made his companions promise, whatever happened, not to let his head be cut off, but to have him buried all in one piece. Galba's freedman Icelus, who had been imprisoned when the first news came of the revolt and was now at liberty again, granted this indulgence.

50. They laid Nero on his pyre, dressed in the gold-embroidered white robes which he had worn on the Kalends of January; the funeral cost 200,000 sesterces. Ecloge and Alexandria, his old nurses, helped Acte, his mistress, to carry the remains to the Pincian Hill, which can be seen from the Campus Martius. His coffin, of white porphyry, stands there in the Domitian family tomb behind a rail of Thasian stone and over-shadowed by an altar of Luna marble.

51. Nero was of fairly average height, with a pustular and malodorous body and blondish hair; his face was pretty rather than handsome, his eyes blue-grey and rather weak; he had a squat neck, a protuberant belly, and spindly legs. His health was amazingly good: for all his extravagant indulgence, he had only three illnesses in fourteen years, and none of them serious enough to stop him from drinking wine or breaking any other regular habit. He did not take the least trouble to dress in an appropriate fashion, but always had his hair set in rows of curls, and when he visited Achaia he let it grow long and hang down his back. He often appeared in public wearing an unbelted silk dressing gown and slippers, with a scarf tied around his neck.

52. As a boy, Nero studied most of the usual subjects except philosophy, which Agrippina warned him was no proper pursuit for a future ruler. His teacher Seneca hid the works of the old orators from him, intending to be admired himself as long as possible. So Nero turned his hand to poetry, and would dash off verses without any effort. It is often claimed that he

published other people's work as his own, but notebooks and loose pages have come into my possession which contain some of Nero's best-known poems in his own handwriting and have clearly been neither copied nor dictated: many erasures and cancellations, as well as words substituted above the lines, prove that he was thinking things out for himself. Nero also took more than an average interest in painting and sculpture.

53. His greatest weaknesses were his thirst for popularity and his jealousy of men who caught the public eye by any means whatsoever. After he had swept the board of all public prizes offered for acting, most people expected him to compete as an athlete at the next Olympian games; he was in fact also an enthusiastic wrestler, and every time he watched a contest in the gymnasium during his tour of Greece he would squat on the ground in the stadium like the umpires, and if any pair of competitors worked away from the centre of the ring he would push them back himself. Figuring that he was already thought to rival Apollo in singing and the Sun in chariot racing, he now apparently planned to imitate the deeds of Hercules, for according to one story he had a lion so carefully trained that he could safely face it naked before the entire amphitheatre, and then either kill it with his club or else strangle it.[38]

54. Just before the end he even took a public oath that if he managed to keep his throne he would celebrate the victory with a music festival, performing successively on water organ, reed pipe and bagpipes, and on the last day would dance the role of Turnus from Virgil.[39] Some people say he killed the actor Paris because he considered him a serious professional rival.

55. Nero's unreasonable craving for immortal fame made him change a number of well-known names in his own favour. The month of April, for instance, became 'Neroneus', and Rome was on the point of being renamed 'Neropolis'.

56. He despised all religious cults except that of the Syrian Goddess, and one day he showed that he had changed his mind even about her by urinating on the divine image. He had come, instead, to rest a superstitious belief – the only one, as a matter of fact, to which he ever remained faithful – in the statuette of a girl sent him by an anonymous plebeian as a charm against

conspiracies. It so happened that a conspiracy came to light immediately afterwards; so he began to worship the girl as though she were a powerful goddess, and sacrificed to her three times a day, expecting people to believe that she gave him knowledge of the future. He did inspect some entrails once, a few months before his death, but they contained no omen at all favourable to him.

57. Nero died at the age of thirty-two, on the anniversary of Octavia's murder. In the widespread general rejoicing, citizens ran through the streets wearing caps of liberty.[40] But a few faithful friends used to lay spring and summer flowers on his grave for some years, and had statues made of him wearing his toga, which they put up on the Rostra; they even continued to circulate his edicts, pretending he was still alive and would soon return to confound his enemies. What is more, King Vologaesus of Parthia, on sending ambassadors to ratify his alliance with Rome, particularly requested the Senate to honour Nero's memory. In fact twenty years later, when I was a young man, a mysterious individual came forward claiming to be Nero,[41] and so magical was the sound of his name in the Parthians' ears that they supported him to the best of their ability and were most reluctant to concede Roman demands to hand him over.

GALBA

1. With Nero, the line of the Caesars became extinct. Among the many prophetic indications of this event, two outstanding ones are mentioned by historians. As Livia was returning to her villa at Veii after marrying Augustus, an eagle flew by and dropped into her lap a white hen which it had just pounced upon. Noticing a laurel twig in its beak, she decided to keep the hen for breeding and to plant the twig. Soon the hen raised such a brood of chickens that the house is still known as 'The Poultry'; moreover, the twig took root and grew so luxuriously that the Caesars always plucked laurels from it to wear at their triumphs. It also became an imperial custom to cut new slips and plant these close by, and, remarkably enough, the death of each emperor was anticipated by the premonitory wilting of his laurel. In the last year of Nero's reign, then, not only did every tree wither at the root, but the whole flock of poultry died. And, as if that were insufficient warning, a thunderbolt presently struck the temple of the Caesars, decapitated all the statues at a stroke, and dashed Augustus' sceptre from his hands.

2. Galba succeeded Nero. Though not directly related to the Julii, he came from a very ancient aristocratic house, and he used to amplify the inscriptions on his own statues with the statement that Quintus Catulus Capitolinus was his great-grandfather; as emperor, he even had a tablet set up in the forecourt of his house tracing his ancestry back to Jupiter on the male side, and to Pasiphae,[1] Minos' wife, on the female side.

3. It would be tiresome to reproduce this pedigree here in all its glory, but I shall touch briefly on Galba's immediate family.

Why the surname Galba was first assumed by a Sulpicius and where it originated must remain moot points. One suggestion is that after a tediously protracted siege of some Spanish town the Sulpicius in question set fire to it, using torches smeared with resin [*galbanum*]. Another is that he resorted to *galbeus*, a kind of poultice, during a long illness. Others are that he was very fat, the Gallic word for which is *galba*; or that, on the contrary, he was very small – like the *galba,* a creature which breeds in oak trees. The Sulpicii acquired a certain lustre during the consulship of Servius Galba, described as the most eloquent speaker of his time, and preserve a tradition that, while governing Spain as praetorian governor, he massacred 30,000 Lusitanians – an act which provoked the war with Viriatus.[2] Servius Galba's grandson, enraged when Julius Caesar, whose legate he had been in Gaul, passed him over for the consulship, joined the assassins Brutus and Cassius and was subsequently sentenced to death under the Pedian Law. The emperor Galba's father and grandfather were descended from this personage. The grandfather had a far higher reputation as a scholar than as a statesman, never rising above the rank of praetor but publishing a monumental, and not negligible, historical work. The father, however, won a consulship and, although so squat as to be almost a hunchback and a speaker of modest abilities, was extremely active as an advocate. He married first Mummia Achaica, granddaughter of Catulus and great-granddaughter of the Lucius Mummius who sacked Corinth, and then Livia Ocellina, a rich and beautiful woman, whose affections are said to have originally been stirred by his rank, but afterwards even more by his frankness – in reply to her bold advances he furtively stripped to the waist and revealed his hump as a proof that he wished to hide nothing from her. Achaica bore him two sons, Gaius and Servius. Gaius, the elder, left Rome owing to financial embarrassment and, because Tiberius crossed him off the list of proconsuls when he became due for a province, committed suicide.

4. On 24 December, when Marcus Valerius Messala and Gnaeus Lentulus were consuls,[3] Servius Galba, the future emperor, was born in a hillside house beside the road which links

Tarracina with Fundi. To please his stepmother Livia Ocellina, who had adopted him, he took the nomen Livius, the cognomen Ocellare and even the praenomen Lucius until becoming emperor. There is a widespread story that Augustus once singled Galba out from a group of small boys and chucked him under the chin, saying in Greek, 'You too will taste a little of my power, child,' and Tiberius, hearing that he would be emperor when an old man, grunted, 'Very well, let him live in peace; it has nothing at all to do with me.' One day, as Galba's grandfather was expiating a bolt of lightning, an eagle suddenly snatched the victim's intestines out of his hands and carried them off to an oak tree laden with acorns. A bystander suggested that this sign portended great honour for the family. 'Yes, yes, perhaps so,' the old man agreed, smiling, 'on the day that a mule foals.' When Galba later launched his rebellion, what encouraged him most was the news that a mule had, in fact, foaled. Although everyone else considered this a disastrous omen, Galba remembered the sacrifice and his grandfather's quip, and interpreted it in precisely the opposite sense.

On reaching adulthood, Galba dreamed that the goddess Fortuna announced that she was tired of waiting outside his door and would he please let her in quickly or she would be fair game for the next passerby. He awoke, opened the door, and found on the landing a bronze image of the goddess, more than a cubit tall. This he carried lovingly to Tusculum, his summer home, and consecrated a domestic shrine to Fortuna, worshipping her with monthly sacrifices and an annual vigil.

Even as a young man he faithfully observed the national custom, already obsolescent and maintained only in his home, of summoning the freedmen and slaves twice a day to wish him good morning and goodnight, one after the other.

5. Galba received a sound education of the usual sort, and also studied law. He took marriage seriously but, on losing his wife Lepida and the two sons she had borne him, remained single for the rest of his life. Nobody could interest him in a second match, not even Agrippina, who, when her husband Domitius died, made such shameless advances to him – though he had not yet become a widower – that his mother-in-law gave

her a public reprimand, going so far as to slap her before an entire gathering of married women.

Galba was always particularly attentive to Livia Augusta, who showed him considerable favour while she lived, and then left him 50 million sesterces, the largest bequest of all. But, because the amount was expressed in marks, not words, Tiberius, as her executor, reduced it to a mere 500,000, and Galba never handled even that modest sum.

6. He won his first public appointment while still underage. As praetor in charge of the games of the goddess Flora, he introduced the spectacular novelty of tightrope-walking elephants. Then he governed the province of Aquitania for nearly a year, and next held a consulship for six months. Curiously enough, Galba succeeded Nero's father, Gnaeus Domitius, and preceded Salvius Otho, father of Otho – a foreshadowing of the time when he should reign between these two consuls' sons. At Gaius' orders, Galba replaced Gaetulicus as governor of Upper Germany. The day after taking up his command he put a stop to applause at a festival by circulating a notice to the effect that 'hands will be kept inside cloaks on all occasions.' Very soon the following doggerel went the rounds:

> Soldier, soldier, on parade,
> You should learn the soldier's trade,
> Galba's now commanding us –
> Galba, not Gaetulicus!

Galba came down just as severely on requests for leave. In gruelling manoeuvres he toughened old campaigners as well as raw recruits, and he sharply checked a barbarian raid into Gaul. Altogether, he and his army made so favourable an impression when Gaius came to inspect them that they won more praise and prize money than any other troops in the field. Galba scored a personal success by not only directing the ceremonial drill but also running for twenty miles beside the emperor's chariot.

7. Although strongly urged to seize the occasion after Gaius' murder, Galba held back, thus earning Claudius' heartfelt

gratitude. Claudius, indeed, considered Galba so close a friend that, when a slight indisposition overtook him, the British expedition was postponed on his account. Later, Galba became proconsul in Africa for two years on an extraordinary appointment, with instructions to suppress the disturbance caused there by domestic rivalries and a native revolt. He executed his commission somewhat ruthlessly it is true, but showed scrupulous attention to justice. Discovering, for instance, that while rations were short a certain legionary had sold a surplus peck of wheat from his rations for 100 denarii, he forbade all ranks to feed the fellow when his stores were exhausted, and so let him starve to death. At a court of inquiry into the ownership of a transport animal, Galba found both the evidence and the pleadings unsatisfactory and, since the truth seemed to be anybody's guess, gave orders: 'Lead the beast blindfolded to its usual trough and let it drink. Then uncover its eyes and watch to whom it goes of its own accord. That man will be the owner.'

8. For these achievements in Africa and his previous successes in Germany, Galba won triumphal decorations and a triple priesthood, being elected to the Quindecimviri, the Sodales Titii and the Sodales Augustales.[4] But from then onward, until the middle years of Nero's reign, he lived almost exclusively in retirement, never going anywhere, even for a country drive, without the escort of a second carriage containing 1 million sesterces. At last, while living at Fundi, he was offered the governorship of Tarraconensian Spain, where, soon after his arrival, as he sacrificed in a temple, the boy who carried the incense went white-haired before his eyes – a sign shrewdly read as portending the succession of a young emperor by an old one. And presently, when a thunderbolt struck a Cantabrian lake, twelve axes, unmistakable emblems of high authority, were recovered from it.

9. He governed Tarraconensian Spain for eight years, beginning with great enthusiasm and energy, and even going a little too far in his punishment of crime. He sentenced a money-changer of questionable honesty to have both hands cut off and nailed to the counter, and crucified a man who had poisoned his ward to inherit the property. When this murderer begged

for justice, protesting that he was a Roman citizen, Galba recognized his status and ironically consoled him by saying, 'Let this citizen hang higher than the rest and have his cross whitewashed.' As time wore on, however, he grew lazy and inactive, but this was done purposely to deny Nero any pretext for disciplining him: in his own words, 'Nobody can be forced to give an account of how he spends his leisure hours.'

Galba was holding assizes at Carthago Nova when news reached him of the revolt in the Gallic provinces. It came in the form of an appeal for help sent by the governor of Aquitania, which was followed by another from Vindex asking whether he would take the lead in rescuing humanity from Nero. He accepted the suggestion, half hopefully, half fearfully, but without much delay, having accidentally come across Nero's secret orders for his own assassination; he took heart from certain very favourable signs and portents – especially the predictions of a nobly born girl which, according to Jupiter's priest at Clunia, matched the prophecies spoken in a trance by another girl two centuries before: the priest had just found a record of these in the temple vault, following directions given him in a dream. The gist of these prophecies was that the lord and master of the world would some day arise in Spain.

10. Accordingly, Galba took his place on the tribunal as though going about the business of freeing slaves, but before him were ranged statues and pictures of Nero's prominent victims. A young aristocrat, recalled from exile in the nearby Balearic Islands for this occasion, stood near while Galba deplored the present state of the empire. Galba was at once hailed as *imperator* and accepted the honour, announcing that he represented the Senate and People of Rome. He closed the courts and began raising legions and auxiliary troops from the native population to increase his existing command of one legion, two squadrons of cavalry and three infantry cohorts. Next he chose the most distinguished and intelligent provincials to serve in a kind of senate, to which matters of importance could be referred whenever necessary. He also picked certain young *equites* instead of ordinary troops to guard his sleeping quarters, and although these ranked as volunteer infantrymen

they still wore the gold rings proper to their condition. Then he called upon everyone in the provinces to unite energetically in the common cause of rebellion. At about this time a ring of ancient design was discovered in the fortifications of the city that he had chosen as his headquarters, the engraved gem representing Victory raising a trophy. Soon afterwards an Alexandrian ship drifted into Dertosa, loaded with arms, but neither helmsman, crew nor passengers were found aboard her – which left no doubt in anyone's mind that this must be a just and righteous war, favoured by the gods.

Suddenly, however, without the least warning, Galba's rebellion nearly collapsed. As he approached the station where one of his cavalry troops was quartered, the men felt a little ashamed of their defection and tried to go back on it; Galba kept them at their posts only by a great effort. Again, he was nearly murdered on his way to the baths: he had to pass down a narrow corridor lined by a company of slaves whom one of Nero's freedmen had presented to him, obviously with some treachery in view. But while they plucked up their courage by urging one another 'not to miss this opportunity', one of his staff took the trouble to ask, 'What opportunity is this?'; later they confessed under torture.

11. Galba's embarrassments were increased by the death of Vindex, a blow so heavy that it almost turned him to despair and suicide. Presently, however, messengers arrived from Rome with the news that Nero too was dead, and that the citizens had all sworn obedience to himself; so he dropped the title of governor and assumed that of Caesar. He now wore a commander's cloak, with a dagger hanging from his neck, and did not put on a toga again until he had accounted first for the men who were plotting further trouble: the praetorian prefect Nymphidius Sabinus in Rome, and Fonteius Capito and Clodius Macer, who commanded respectively in Germany and Africa.[5]

12. Stories of Galba's cruelty and greed preceded him: it was said that he punished townships in Spain and Gaul which had been slow to receive him by levying huge taxes and even dismantling their fortifications; that he executed not only local

officials and administrators, but their families too; and that, when the people of Tarraco offered him a golden crown from the ancient temple of Jupiter, described as weighing fifteen pounds, he had this melted down and made them supply the three ounces needed to tip the scales at the advertised weight. Galba more than confirmed this reputation on his entry into Rome. He sent back to rowing duty some sailors whom Nero had turned into soldiers, and when they stubbornly insisted on their right to the Eagle and the standards he not only scattered them with a cavalry charge but also decimated them.[6] Galba also disbanded the cohort of Germans who had served as body-guards for the Caesars and proved consistently loyal, repatriating them without a bounty on the ground that they had shown excessive devotion to Gnaeus Dolabella[7] by camping close to his estate. Other anecdotes to his discredit, possibly true, possibly false, went the rounds: when an especially lavish dinner was set before him he had groaned aloud; when presented with the usual abstract of treasury accounts, he had rewarded the treasurer's scrupulous labours with a bowlful of beans; delighted by Canus' performance on the flute, he had drawn the magnificent sum of five denarii from his purse and pressed them on him.

13. Galba's accession was not entirely popular, as became obvious at the first theatrical show he attended. This was an Atellan farce, in which occurred the well-known song 'Here comes Onesimus, down from the farm.' The whole audience took up the chorus with fervour, repeating that particular line over and over again.

14. His power and prestige were far greater while he was assuming control of the empire than afterwards: though affording ample proof of his capacity to rule, he won less praise for his good acts than blame for his mistakes. Three officials, nicknamed 'the imperial nursemaids', always hovered around Galba; he seemed to be tied to their apron strings. These were the greedy Titus Vinius, his former legate in Spain; the intolerably arrogant and stupid Cornelius Laco, an ex-assessor praetorian prefect; and his own freedman Icelus, who, having recently acquired the cognomen of Marcianus and the right to

wear a gold ring, now had his eye on the highest appointment available to a man of his rank.[8] Galba let himself be so continuously guided by these experts in vice that he was far less consistent in his behaviour – at one time meaner and more bitter, at another more wasteful and indulgent – than an elected *princeps* had any right to be in the circumstances.

He sentenced men of all ranks to death without trial on the scantiest evidence, and seldom granted applications for Roman citizenship. Nor would he concede the prerogatives which could in law be enjoyed by every father of three children except to an occasional claimant, and even then for a limited period only. When the judges recommended the formation of a sixth judicial division, Galba was not content simply to turn this down, but cancelled the privilege, which Claudius had allowed them, of being excused court duties in the winter months and at the beginning of the year.

15. It was generally believed that he intended to restrict all official appointments for both *equites* and senators to two-year periods, and to choose only men who either did not want them or could be counted on to refuse. He annulled all Nero's awards, letting the beneficiaries keep no more than a tenth part and enlisting the help of fifty *equites* to ensure that his order was obeyed; he further ruled that if any actor or other performer had sold one of Nero's gifts, spent the money and was unable to refund it, the missing sum must be recovered from the buyers. Yet he denied his friends and freedmen nothing, with or without payment – taxes here, exemptions there, an innocent party sentenced here, a culprit excused there. Moreover, when a popular demand arose for the punishment of Halotus and Tigellinus, undoubtedly the vilest of all Nero's assistants, Galba not only protected their lives but gave Halotus a lucrative procuratorship and published an imperial edict charging the people with undeserved hostility towards Tigellinus.

16. Thus he outraged all classes at Rome; but the most virulent hatred of him smouldered in the army. Though the officers had promised a larger bonus than usual to the soldiers who had pledged their swords to Galba before his arrival in the city, he would not honour this commitment, but announced,

'It is my custom to levy troops, not to buy them.' This remark infuriated the troops everywhere, and he earned the praetorians' particular resentment by his dismissal of a number of them suspected of being in Nymphidius' pay. The loudest grumbling came from camps in Upper Germany, where the men claimed that they had not been rewarded for their share in the operations against Vindex and the Gauls.[9] These, the first Roman troops bold enough to withhold their allegiance, refused on the Kalends of January to take any oath except in the name of the Senate; they informed the praetorians by messenger that they were fed up with this made-in-Spain emperor, and would the praetorians please choose one who deserved the approval of the army as a whole?

17. Galba heard about this message and, thinking that he was being criticized for his childlessness rather than his old age, singled out from a group of his courtiers a handsome young man of good family, Piso Frugi Licinianus, whom he already highly esteemed, and appointed him perpetual heir to his name and property. Calling him 'my son', he led Piso into the praetorian camp, and there formally and publicly adopted him – without, however, mentioning the word 'bounty', and thus giving Marcus Salvius Otho an excellent opportunity for his *coup d'état* five days later.

18. A succession of signs had been portending Galba's end in accurate detail. During his march on Rome, victims were being sacrificed right and left whenever he passed through a town, and once an ill-aimed axe blow made a frenzied ox break its harness and charge Galba's chariot, rearing up and drenching him with blood. Then, as he climbed out, one of his runners, pushed by the mob, nearly wounded him with a spear. When he first entered the city and then the palace, a slight earthquake shock was felt, and a sound arose as of bulls bellowing. Clearer presages followed. Galba had set aside from his treasures a necklace of pearls and precious stones to adorn his image of the goddess Fortuna at Tusculum. But, impulsively deciding that it was too good for her, he consecrated it to Venus Capitolina instead. The very next night Fortuna complained to him in a dream that she had been robbed of a gift intended for

herself and threatened to take back what she had already given him. At dawn, Galba hurried in terror towards Tusculum to expiate the fault revealed by his dream, having sent outriders ahead to prepare the sacrifices; but when he arrived he found only warm ashes on the altar and an old black-cloaked fellow offering incense in a glass bowl and wine in an earthenware cup.[10] It was noticed too that while he was sacrificing on the Kalends of January his garland fell off, and that the sacred chickens flew away when he went to read the auspices. Again, before Galba addressed the troops on the subject of Piso's adoption, his aides forgot to set a camp chair on the tribunal, and in the Senate House his curule chair was discovered facing the wall.

19. When attending an early-morning sacrifice, Galba was now repeatedly warned by a haruspex to expect danger – murderers were about. Soon afterwards news came that Otho had seized the praetorian camp. Though urged to hurry there in person, because his rank and presence could carry the day, Galba determined to stay where he was and rally to his standard the legionaries scattered throughout the city. He did, indeed, put on a linen corselet, although openly admitting that it would afford small protection against so many swords. But he was drawn out by false rumours, which the conspirators were diligently spreading about in order to entice him into the open: a few of his supporters rashly assured him that peace had been made and the rebels arrested – their troops were on the way to surrender and pledge loyal allegiance. Completely deceived, Galba went forward to meet them in the utmost confidence. When a soldier claimed with pride to have killed Otho, he snapped, 'On whose authority?', and hurried on to the Forum. There a party of cavalrymen, clattering through the streets and dispersing the mob, recognized him; these were his appointed assassins. They reined in for a moment, then charged at the solitary figure, abandoned now by all his followers, and cut him down.

20. Some people report that, just before his death, Galba shouted out, 'What is all this, comrades? I am yours; you are mine!', and went so far as to promise the bounty; but, according

to the more usual account, he realized the soldiers' intention, bared his neck, and encouraged them to go ahead and strike, since they thought it the right thing to do. It is amazing that no one present made any attempt to rescue the emperor, and that all the soldiers summoned to rally around him turned a deaf ear. Only a single company of soldiers from the troops in Germany rushed to his assistance, because he had once treated them with kindness while they were convalescents; not knowing the city well, however, they took a wrong turning and arrived too late.

Galba was murdered beside the Curtian Lake and left lying just as he fell. A private soldier returning from the grain issue set down his load and decapitated Galba's body. He could not carry the head by the hair and so stuffed it in his cloak, and soon brought it to Otho with his thumb thrust into the mouth. Otho handed the trophy to a crowd of servants and camp boys, who stuck it on a spear and carried it scornfully round the camp, chanting at intervals:

> Galba, Galba, Cupid Galba,
> Please enjoy your vigour still!

Apparently Galba had enraged them by quoting to someone who congratulated him on his robust appearance, 'So far my vigour undiminished is.'[11] A freedman of the Neronian Patrobius bought the head for 100 aurei, but only to hurl it to the ground exactly where Patrobius had been executed at Galba's orders. In the end his steward Argivus removed it, with the trunk, to the tomb in Galba's private gardens which lay beside the·Via Aurelia.

21. Galba was of medium height, with a completely bald head, blue eyes and a hooked nose. His hands and feet were twisted by arthritis or some such disease, which made him unable to unroll or even hold parchment scrolls or wear shoes. His body was badly ruptured on the right side, so that he required a truss for support.

22. He was a heavy eater, in winter always breakfasting before daylight, and with a habit at dinner of passing on

accumulated leavings to his attendants. In his sexual tastes he inclined to males, with a decided preference for mature, sturdy men. It is said that when Icelus, one of his trusty bedfellows, brought the news of Nero's death, Galba not only openly showered him with kisses, but begged him to strip without delay and led him off into his private quarters.

23. Galba died in his seventy-third year, before he had reigned seven months. The Senate, as soon as it was able, voted that a column decorated with ships' beaks should be set up in the Forum to accommodate his statue and mark the spot where he had fallen. Vespasian, however, subsequently vetoed this decree; he was convinced that Galba had sent agents from Spain to Judaea with orders for his assassination.

OTHO

1. The seat of Otho's ancient and distinguished family was the city of Ferentium; they could trace their origins back to an Etruscan royal house. His grandfather, Marcus Salvius Otho, the son of a Roman *eques* and a peasant girl – she may not even have been freeborn – owed his place in the Senate, where he never rose above praetor's rank, to the influence of his protectress Livia Augusta. He made a brilliant marriage, but his son, Lucius, was such a favourite of Tiberius' and so closely resembled him that many people believed Tiberius to be his actual father. This Lucius Otho (father of the emperor) had the reputation of being a strict disciplinarian, whether during his magistracies at Rome or his proconsulship in Africa, or when on special military missions. In Illyricum he went so far as to preside over the execution of certain soldiers because, in repentance for their role in Camillus' rebellion,[1] they had killed the officers whom they blamed for their betrayal of Claudius, even though he knew well enough that Claudius himself had rewarded these same men with promotion for the act. Lucius Otho's rough justice may have increased his reputation, yet it certainly decreased his standing at court, until by extorting information from a group of slaves he contrived to uncover a plot against Claudius' life. Thereupon the Senate paid Lucius the unique honour of setting up his statue on the Palatine, and Claudius, in raising him to patrician rank, is said to have panegyrized him as 'one whose loyalty I call hardly dare hope that my children will emulate'. Albia Terentia, his nobly born wife, bore him two sons: the elder named Lucius Titanius, and the younger Marcus Otho, like his grandfather; also a daughter,

who was betrothed in her girlhood to Germanicus' son Drusus.

2. Otho, the future emperor, was born on 28 April, when Camillus Arruntius and Domitius Ahenobarbus were the consuls.[2] From early youth he was wild and extravagant, earning many a beating from his father; he is said to have been in the habit of wandering about the city at night and tossing in a cloak any drunk or disabled person who crossed his path. After his father's death he advanced his fortunes by a pretended passion for an influential freedwoman at court, though she was almost on her last legs. With her help he insinuated himself into the position of Nero's leading favourite – understandably enough, since Nero and Otho were birds of a feather, although it has often been suggested that they also enjoyed each other's sexual favours. Otho grew so powerful that, having accepted a huge bribe to rehabilitate a man of consular status who had been convicted of extortion, he did not think twice about bringing the fellow before the Senate to make his formal speech of thanks even before he had actually effected his restitution.

3. As Nero's confidant he had a finger in all his schemes, and on the day chosen by him for murdering his own mother he threw everyone off the scent by inviting them both to an exceptionally elegant dinner party. Otho was asked to become the protector of Poppaea Sabina – who had been taken by Nero from her husband to be his mistress – and they went through a form of marriage together. However, he not only enjoyed Poppaea, but conceived so deep a passion for her that he would not tolerate even Nero as a rival; we have every reason to believe the story of his rebuffing first the messengers sent by Nero to fetch Poppaea, and then Nero himself, who was left on the wrong side of the bedroom door, alternately threatening and pleading for his rights in the lady. As a result, the marriage was dissolved, and Otho was sent off to Lusitania as Nero's legate; fear of scandal kept Nero from doing more. Even so, the following lampoon went the rounds:

> 'Otho in exile?' 'Yes and no;
> That is, we do not call it so.'

'And may we ask the reason why?'
'*They charged him with adultery.*'
'But could they prove it?' '*No and yes:*
It was his wife he dared caress.'

Otho, with the rank of quaestor, governed the province for ten years, with considerable moderation and restraint.

4. He seized the earliest opportunity of revenging himself on Nero by joining Galba as soon as he heard of the revolt, but the political atmosphere was so uncertain that he did not underrate his own chances of power. Seleucus,[3] an astrologer who encouraged these ambitions, had already foretold that Otho would outlive Nero, and he now arrived unexpectedly with the further prediction that he would soon also become emperor. After this Otho missed no chance of flattering or showing favour to anyone who might prove useful to him. When he entertained Galba at dinner, for instance, he would bribe the bodyguard with aurei and do everything possible to put the rest of the escort in his debt. Once a friend of Otho's laid claim to part of a neighbour's estate and asked him to act as arbitrator; Otho bought the disputed piece of land himself and presented it to him. As a result, there was hardly anyone who did not think and openly declare that he alone was worthy of becoming the next emperor.

5. Galba's adoption of Piso came as a shock to Otho, who had hoped to secure this good fortune himself. Disappointment, resentment and a massive accumulation of debts now prompted him to revolt. His one chance of survival, Otho frankly admitted, lay in becoming emperor, and he would add, 'I might as well fall to some enemy in battle as to my creditors in the Forum.' The 1 million sesterces just paid him for a stewardship by one of the emperor's slaves served to finance the undertaking. To begin with he confided in five of his personal guards, each of whom co-opted two others; they were paid 10,000 sesterces a head, and promised 50,000 more. These fifteen men recruited a certain number of assistants, but not many, since Otho counted on mass support as soon as he had raised the standard of revolt.

6. His first plan was to occupy the praetorian camp immediately after Piso's adoption and to capture Galba during dinner at the palace. But he abandoned this because the same cohort happened to be on guard duty as when Gaius had been assassinated and again when Nero had been left to his fate; he felt reluctant to deal their reputation for loyalty a further blow. Unfavourable omens and Seleucus' warnings delayed matters another five days. However, on the morning of the sixth, Otho posted his fellow conspirators in the Forum at the Golden Milestone near the Temple of Saturn while he entered the palace to greet Galba, who kissed him as usual, and attended his sacrifice. The haruspices had finished their report on the omens of the victim, when a freedman arrived with the message 'The architects are here.' This was the agreed signal. Otho excused himself to the emperor, saying that he had arranged to view a house that was for sale, then slipped out of the palace by a back door and hurried to the rendezvous. (Another account makes him plead a chill and leave his excuses with the emperor's attendants, in case anyone should miss him.) At all events, he went off in a closed sedan chair of the sort used by women and headed for the camp, but jumped out and began to run when the bearers' pace flagged. As he paused to lace a shoe, his companions hoisted him on their shoulders and acclaimed him emperor. The street crowds joined the procession as eagerly as if they were sworn accomplices, and Otho reached his headquarters to the sound of hurrahs and the flash of drawn swords. He then dispatched a troop of cavalry to murder Galba and Piso and, avoiding all rhetorical appeals, told the troops merely that he would welcome whatever powers they might give him but claim no others.

7. Towards evening Otho delivered a brief speech to the Senate, claiming to have been picked up in the street and compelled to accept the imperial power, but promising to respect the people's sovereign will. Hence he proceeded to the palace, where he received fulsome congratulations and flattery from all present, making no protest even when the crowd called him 'Nero'; indeed, some historians record that he even added the cognomen Nero to some of his first certificates and letters to

provincial governors.[4] He certainly replaced some of Nero's busts and statues and reinstated some of his procurators and freedmen; in addition, his first act as emperor was to make a grant of 50 million sesterces for the completion of the Golden House.

Otho is said to have been haunted that night by Galba's ghost in a terrible nightmare; the servants who ran in when he screamed for help found him lying on the bedroom floor. After this he did everything in his power to placate the ghost, but next day, while he was taking the auspices, a storm sprang up and caused him a bad tumble which made him mutter repeatedly, 'Playing long flutes is hardly my trade.'[5]

8. Meanwhile, the armies in Germany took an oath of loyalty to Vitellius. Otho heard of this and persuaded the Senate to send a deputation urging them to keep quiet, since an emperor had already been appointed. But he also wrote Vitellius a personal letter: an invitation to become his father-in-law and share the empire with him. Vitellius, however, had already sent troops forward to march on Rome under their generals, and war was inevitable. Then, one night, the praetorians gave such unequivocal proof of their faithfulness to Otho that it almost involved a massacre of the Senate. A detachment of sailors had been ordered to fetch some arms from the praetorian camp and take them aboard their vessels. They were carrying out their instructions at dusk when the praetorians, suspecting treachery on the part of the Senate, rushed to the palace in a leaderless mob and demanded that every senator should die. Having driven away or murdered the tribunes who tried to stop them, they burst into the banqueting hall, dripping with blood. 'Where is the emperor?' they shouted; but as soon as they saw him busy with his meal they calmed down.

Otho set out on his campaign very energetically, but haste prevented him from paying sufficient attention to the omens. The sacred shields used by the Salii had not yet been returned to the Temple of Mars – traditionally a bad sign – and this was the very day when the worshippers of the Mother of the Gods began their annual lamentation. Besides, the auspices were most unfavourable: at a sacrifice offered to Father Dis the victim's intestines had a healthy look, which was exactly what they should not have had.[6] Otho's departure was, moreover, delayed by a flooding of the Tiber, and at the twentieth milestone he found the road blocked by the ruins of a collapsed building.

9. Vitellius' forces being badly off for supplies and having little room for manoeuvre, Otho should have maintained the defensive, yet he rashly staked his fortunes on an immediate victory. Perhaps he suffered from nervousness and hoped to end the war before Vitellius himself arrived; perhaps he could not curb the offensive spirit of his troops. But when it came to the point he made Brixellum his headquarters and kept clear of the fighting. Although his army won three lesser engagements – in the Alps, at Placentia, and at a place called Castor's – they were tricked into a decisive defeat near Betriacum. There had been talk of an armistice, but Otho's troops, preparing to fraternize with the enemy while peace was discussed, found themselves suddenly committed to battle.

Otho immediately decided on suicide. It is more probable that his conscience prevented him from continuing to hazard lives and treasure in a bid for sovereignty than that his men had become demoralized and unreliable; fresh troops stood in reserve for a counter-offensive, and reinforcements came streaming down from Dalmatia, Pannonia and Moesia. What is more, his defeated army were anxious to redeem their reputation, even without such assistance.

10. My own father, Suetonius Laetus, served as a military tribune in the Thirteenth Legion in this campaign. He often said afterwards that Otho had so deeply abhorred the thought of civil war while still a private citizen that he would shudder if the fates of Brutus and Cassius were mentioned at a banquet, and that he would not have moved against Galba to begin with if he had not been confident of a bloodless victory. Otho had now ceased to care what happened to himself, my father added, because of the deep impression made on him by a soldier who arrived at Brixellum to report that the army had been defeated. When the garrison called him a liar and a cowardly deserter, the man fell on his sword at Otho's feet. Otho, greatly moved, issued a public statement that he would never again risk the

lives of such gallant fellows. After embracing his brother, his nephew and his friends, he dismissed them with orders to consult their own safety. Then he retired and wrote two letters: of consolation to his sister and of apology to Nero's widow, Statilia Messalina, whom he had meant to marry – at the same time begging her to bury him and preserve his memory. He next burned all his private correspondence to avoid incriminating anyone if it fell into Vitellius' hands, and distributed among his household staff whatever loose cash he had with him.

11. While making final preparations for suicide, Otho heard a disturbance outside, and was told that the men who had begun to drift away from camp were being arrested as deserters. He forbade his officers to award them any punishment, and saying, 'Let us add one extra night to life,' went to bed, but left his door open for several hours, in case anyone wished to speak with him. After drinking a glass of cold water and testing the points of two daggers, he put one of them under his pillow, closed the door, and slept soundly. He awoke at dawn and promptly stabbed himself in the left side. His attendants heard him groan and rushed in; at first he could not decide whether to conceal or reveal the wound, which proved fatal. They buried him at once, as he had ordered them to do. His age was thirty-seven, and he had reigned for ninety-five days.

12. Otho did not look like a very courageous man: he was of medium height, bow-legged and with splay feet, but almost as fastidious about appearances as a woman. His entire body had been depilated, and a well-made toupee covered his practically bald head. He shaved every day, and since boyhood had always used a poultice of moist bread to retard the growth of his beard. He used publicly to celebrate the rites of Isis, wearing the appropriate linen robe.

The sensation caused by Otho's end was, I think, largely due to its contrast with the life he had led. Several soldiers visited the deathbed, where they kissed his hands and feet, praising him as the bravest man they had ever known and the best emperor imaginable; afterwards they committed suicide themselves close to his funeral pyre. Stories are also current of men having killed one another in an access of grief when the news of his death reached them. Thus many who had hated Otho while alive loved him for the way he died; and he was even commonly believed to have killed Galba with the object not so much of becoming emperor as of restoring the free republic.

VITELLIUS

1. Vitellius' family may have been an old and noble one, or it may have been of undistinguished and even mean extraction. Both views are held, and either might reasonably be discounted as due to the prejudice excited by his reign, were it not that these origins had been hotly argued about many years previously.

Writing to Quintus Vitellius, one of Divus Augustus' quaestors, Quintus Elogius described the family as follows: 'You Vitellii are descended from Faunus, an aboriginal king of Italy, and Vitellia, who was widely worshipped as a goddess. At one time you ruled over the whole of Latium, but later the surviving members of the family moved from Sabine territory to Rome, where they became patricians. For centuries after, Vitellii were to be found along the Vitellian Way, which runs from the Janiculum to the sea, and the people of a settlement there of the same name demanded permission to defend themselves against the Aequiculi under their own officers. Another group of Vitellii, serving in the Roman army during the Samnite war, were dispatched to Apulia and established themselves at Nuceria, but eventually their descendants went back to resume senatorial privileges at Rome.'[1]

2. On the other hand, many people claim that the family had been founded by a freedman; Cassius Severus and a few others add that he was a cut-rate shoemaker, whose son made a comfortable living as professional litigant and a dealer in confiscated property, before marrying a low-class woman, the daughter of a baker named Antiochus, and fathering on her a Roman *eques*. We may leave undecided the question of which account is correct.

At all events, whether his ancestry should have inspired pride or shame, Publius Vitellius of Nuceria was certainly an *eques* and a procurator under Augustus. He passed on his name to four distinguished sons: Aulus, Quintus, Publius and Lucius. Aulus, an epicure and a famous host, died during his consulship, as partner to Nero's father Domitius. Quintus was degraded in a purge of subversive senators proposed by Tiberius. Publius was an aide-de-camp to Germanicus, whose murderer, Gnaeus Piso, he arrested and brought to justice. He attained the praetorship, but was himself arrested in the aftermath of Sejanus' conspiracy. When handed over to the custody of his own brother, Aulus, he cut his wrists with a penknife; yet he allowed them to be bandaged up, not through any fear of death, but because his friends begged him to stay with them. Later, he fell ill and died in prison.

Lucius became consul and then governor of Syria, where with masterly diplomacy he induced King Artabanus of Parthia to attend a parley and even to worship the legionary standards. Afterwards, Lucius shared two regular consulships with the emperor Claudius, held the office of censor, and took full charge of the empire while Claudius was away on the British expedition. Lucius' integrity and industry were outstanding; the only blot on his fame was a scandalous infatuation for a certain freedwoman, whose spittle he would mix with honey and use every day, quite openly, as a salve for his neck and throat. A skilful flatterer, he instituted the practice of worshipping Gaius as a god: on his return from Syria, he never dared enter the imperial presence without covering his head, turning around, and finally prostrating himself.[2] Since Claudius, Gaius' successor, was ruled by his wives and freedmen, Lucius, who lost no chance of advancement, begged Messalina to grant him the tremendous privilege of removing her shoes; thereafter he nursed the right shoe inside his toga, occasionally taking it out to kiss it. He placed golden images of Narcissus and Pallas among his household gods. He is also the one who said to Claudius, 'May you do this very often!' when he was congratulating him at the celebration of the Saecular Games.[3]

3. Lucius died of paralysis on the day after he had been

accused of treason, but lived to see his two sons by Sestilia – a noble-hearted woman of distinguished family – achieve the consulship in the same year,[4] the younger following the elder in the July appointment. The Senate awarded him a public funeral and a statue on the Rostra inscribed 'Steadfast in Loyalty to the Emperor'.

Lucius' son Aulus Vitellius, the future emperor, was born on 24 September, or perhaps on 7 September, while Drusus Caesar and Norbanus Flaccus were consuls.[5] The boy's horoscope read so appallingly that Lucius did everything in his power to prevent him from winning a provincial governorship, and when he was proclaimed emperor in Germany his mother gave him up for lost. Vitellius had spent his boyhood and adolescence on Capreae, among Tiberius' profligates. There he won the nickname 'Spintria', which clung to him throughout his life; by surrendering his chastity to Tiberius, the story goes, he secured his father's first advancement to public office.[6]

4. Vitellius, as he grew up, was notorious for every sort of vice and became a fixture at court: Gaius admired his skill in chariot driving, Claudius his skill at dice. Nero not only appreciated these talents, but was also indebted to him for one particular service. At the Neronia, Nero was anxious to compete in the lyre-playing contest, but did not dare do so even though the whole theatre clamoured for him enthusiastically; so he left his seat and disappeared until Vitellius, as president of the games, came in pursuit and on behalf of the audience persuaded him to reconsider his decision.[7]

5. Since he was the favourite of three emperors, Vitellius won the usual magistracies and several very distinguished priesthoods, and later served as governor of Africa and minister of public works. His reputation and energies, however, varied with the employment given him. He was exceptionally honest during his two-year administration of Africa, where he acted as legate for his brother, who succeeded him. But Vitellius' behaviour at Rome was by no means so commendable: he used to pilfer offerings and ornaments from the temples and replace gold and silver with brass and pewter.

6. He married Petronia, a consul's daughter, who in her will

made their one-eyed son Petronianus her heir, with the proviso that Vitellius renounce paternal rights. To this he consented, but then shortly thereafter, as most people think, killed the boy; Vitellius' story was that Petronianus, when accused of planning parricide, had been overcome by feelings of guilt and had himself drunk the poison which he had intended to use against his father. Next he married Galeria Fundana, whose father was a praetor; she bore him one daughter and a son who had so bad a stammer that he could hardly force out a word.

7. Galba's appointment of Vitellius to the governorship of Lower Germany was entirely unexpected; the accepted view today is that Titus Vinius arranged it. This Vinius, a man of very great influence at the time, was well disposed towards Vitellius because they were fellow supporters of the Blues in the Circus.[8] Yet, since Galba had openly stated that a glutton was the sort of rival whom he feared least and that he expected Vitellius to cram his belly with the fruits of the province, the appointment must have been made in contempt, not approval. Vitellius was so short of funds at the time and in such low water generally – this is common knowledge – that he rented an attic for his wife and children at Rome, let his own house for the remainder of the year, and financed his journey by pawning a pearl taken from his mother's earring. The only means by which he could shake off the huge crowd of creditors who were continuously waylaying him – these included the people of Sinuessa and Formiae, whose public revenues he had embezzled – was to scare them with false accusations. Thus he pressed an action for assault against a freedman who had dunned him once too often, claiming to have been struck and kicked, and demanding damages in the amount of 50,000 sesterces.

The army's dislike of Galba having now reached a stage little short of mutiny, they welcomed Vitellius with open arms as a gift from the gods. After all, here was the son of a man who had held three consulships – in the prime of life too, and of an easy, generous disposition. Vitellius' conduct further enhanced their initial good opinion of him. He would greet even private soldiers with an embrace, and at wayside inns he behaved most affably towards the muleteers and suchlike whom he met in the morning, enquiring whether they had yet breakfasted, and then belching loudly to prove that he had done so himself.

8. At his camp in Germany he granted every favour asked of him and cancelled all punishments whatsoever, whether the men concerned were in disgrace, awaiting trial, or undergoing sentence. Consequently, before a month had passed, a group of soldiers suddenly crowded into his bedroom, saluted him as emperor, and, late though the hour was, carried him around the larger villages without even giving him time to dress. In the first flush of congratulation someone presented Vitellius with a drawn sword, taken from a shrine of Mars, which had once been Julius Caesar's, and this he carried in his hand. During his absence a stove set fire to the dining room at headquarters, but when this unlucky portent caused general concern he told the troops, 'Courage, my men! Light is given us.' That was the only speech he made them. The army in Upper Germany, which had previously pledged its loyalty to the Senate rather than to Galba, now came out in his favour. Vitellius then assumed the cognomen Germanicus, which everyone eagerly pressed on him, but he hesitated to accept that of Augustus, and emphatically rejected that of Caesar.[9]

9. As soon as news reached Germany of Galba's murder, Vitellius put his affairs in order and split the army into two divisions, one of which stayed with him. He sent the other against Otho, and it was at once granted a lucky augury: an eagle, swooping down from the right hand, hovered over the standards and flew slowly ahead of the advancing columns. However, when he marched off with the second division, several equestrian statues raised in his honour collapsed because the horses' legs were weakly made; also, the laurel wreath which he had so ceremoniously bound on his head fell into a stream, and a few days later, while he was presiding over a court at Vienna, a rooster perched first on his shoulder, then on his hand.[10] These presages were confirmed by future events, for he proved unable to support the weight of power won for him by his legates.

10. The news of the victory at Betriacum and of Otho's suicide reached Vitellius before he had left Gaul. At once he

disbanded all praetorian cohorts in Rome by a comprehensive decree, accusing them of a disgraceful lapse in discipline: they must surrender their arms to the tribunes. He gave further orders for the arrest and punishment of 120 praetorians known to have demanded a bounty from Otho in respect of services rendered at Galba's assassination. These irreproachably correct acts raised the hope that Vitellius would make an admirable emperor, but the rest of his behaviour was instead in keeping with the character he had shown in the past, and fell far short of the imperial. At the outset of his march, for instance, he had himself carried through the main streets of the cities on his route, wearing triumphal dress; he crossed rivers in elaborately decorated barges wreathed in garlands; and he always kept a lavish supply of delicacies within reach of his hand. He let discipline go by the board, and would joke about the excesses committed by his men: not content with being wined and dined everywhere at public expense, they amused themselves by freeing slaves at random and then whipping, wounding and even murdering whoever tried to restrain them. When he reached one of the recent battlefields, where the stench of unburied corpses caused some consternation, Vitellius cheered his companions with the brazen remark 'Only one thing smells sweeter to me than a dead enemy, and that is a dead fellow citizen.' Nevertheless, he took a good swig of neat wine to counteract this perfume, and generously passed the flagon around. Equally offensive was his remark when he came across Otho's simple headstone: 'Well, he deserved this type of mausoleum.' Having sent the dagger with which Otho had killed himself to the temple of Mars at Colonia Agrippinensis, he staged an all-night religious festival on the slopes of the Apennines.

11. At last, amid fanfares of trumpets, Vitellius entered Rome wearing a commander's cloak and a sword, surrounded by standards and banners; his staff wore military cloaks, and his soldiers carried drawn swords.[11]

Paying less and less attention to all laws, human or divine, Vitellius next assumed the office of pontifex maximus – and chose to do so on the anniversary of the Allia defeat.[12] On the same occasion he announced his appointments for the ten years ahead, and elected himself consul for life. Then he dispelled any doubt as to what model he would follow in managing the commonwealth by making commemorative offerings to Nero in the middle of the Campus Martius, amid a crowd of public priests. At the subsequent banquet, while a popular lyre player was performing, Vitellius admonished him that he should also play 'something of the Master's'; when the player started in on one of Nero's solos, Vitellius jumped up delightedly and led the applause.

12. This was how his reign began. Later, he based many important political decisions on what the lowest performers in the theatre and circus told him, and relied particularly on the advice of his freedman Asiaticus. Asiaticus had been Vitellius' slave and sexual partner, but he soon grew tired of this role and ran away. After a while he was discovered selling cheap drinks at Puteoli, and was put in chains until Vitellius ordered his release and again made him his favourite. However, Asiaticus behaved so insolently, and so thievishly as well, that Vitellius sold him to an itinerant trainer of gladiators; but he impulsively bought him back when he was just about to take part in the final match of a gladiatorial contest. When sent to govern Lower Germany, Vitellius freed Asiaticus, and on his first day as emperor he presented him with the gold ring of equestrian status; this surprised everyone, because that very morning he had rejected a popular demand for this award with the statement that Asiaticus' appointment would disgrace the order.

13. Vitellius' ruling vices were gluttony and cruelty. He banqueted three and often four times a day, namely morning, noon, afternoon and evening – the last meal being mainly a drinking bout – and survived the ordeal well enough by vomiting frequently. What made things worse was that he used to invite himself out to private banquets at all hours, and these never cost his various hosts less than 400,000 sesterces each. The most notorious feast of the series was given him by his brother Lucius on his entry into Rome: 2,000 magnificent fish and 7,000 game birds are said to have been served. Yet even this hardly compares in luxuriousness with a single tremendously

large dish which Vitellius dedicated and named 'The Shield of Minerva the Protectress'. The recipe called for pike livers, pheasant brains, peacock brains, flamingo tongues and lamprey milt, and the ingredients, collected in every corner of the empire from the Parthian frontier to the Spanish straits, were brought to Rome by naval triremes. Vitellius paid no attention to place or time in satisfying his remarkable appetite. While a sacrifice was in progress, he thought nothing of snatching lumps of meat or cake off the altar, almost out of the sacred fire, and bolting them down, and on his travels he would devour cuts of meat fetched smoking hot from wayside cookshops, and even yesterday's half-eaten scraps.

14. His cruelty was such that he would kill or torture anyone at all on the slightest pretext – not excluding noblemen who had been his fellow students or friends, and whom he lured to court by promises of the highest advancement. One of them, with fever on him, asked for a glass of cold water; Vitellius brought it with his own hands, but added poison. As for all the moneylenders, creditors and tax collectors who had ever dunned him at Rome or demanded prompt payment for goods or services on the road, it is doubtful whether he showed mercy in a single instance. When one of these men paid a courtesy call at the palace, Vitellius sent him off to be executed, but a moment later countermanded the order. The courtiers praised this clemency, but Vitellius explained that he merely wished to give himself a treat by having the man killed before his eyes. Two sons came to plead for their father's life; he had all three of them dispatched. An *eques* who was being marched away to his death called out, 'You are my heir!' Vitellius granted a stay of execution until the will had been produced; then, finding himself named as joint heir with the man's freedman, ordered the two of them to die together. He even executed some of the common people for disparaging the Blues, on the suspicion that such criticism was directed against him. He particularly disliked lampoonists and astrologers, and made away at once with any who came up before him. This resentment dated from when an edict of his, forbidding any astrologers to remain in Italy after the Kalends of October, had been capped with a counter-edict:

> Decreed by all astrologers
> In blessing on our state:
> Vitellius will be no more
> On the appointed date.

According to some accounts, a prophetess of the Chatti, whom
Vitellius credited with oracular powers, had promised him a
long and secure reign if he outlived his mother; so when she fell
sick he had her starved to death. Another version of the story
is that his mother, grown weary of the present and apprehensive
of the future, begged him for a supply of poison – a request
which he was not slow to grant.

15. In the eighth month of Vitellius' reign the Moesian and
Pannonian legions repudiated him and swore allegiance to
Vespasian; those in Syria and Judaea followed suit and took
their oaths in person. To keep the goodwill of his remaining
troops, Vitellius embarked on a course of limitless public and
private generosity. He opened a recruiting campaign in Rome
and promised volunteers immediate discharge after victory,
with the full rights and privileges of regular service. When
the forces supporting Vespasian converged on Rome, he sent
against them the troops who had fought at Betriacum, under
their original officers, and put his brother in command of a fleet
manned by recruits and gladiators. Realizing, however, that he
was being beaten or betrayed on every side, he approached
Flavius Sabinus, Vespasian's brother, and asked, 'What is my
abdication worth?' Sabinus offered him his life and a fee of
100 million sesterces. Later, from the palace steps, Vitellius
announced his decision to the assembled soldiers, explaining
that the imperial power had, after all, been forced upon him.
When an uproar of protest greeted this speech, he put things
off; but next day he went in mourning to the Rostra and tearfully read it out again from a scroll. Once more the soldiers and
the crowds shouted 'Stand fast!' and outdid one another in
their expressions of loyalty. Suddenly taking heart, Vitellius
drove the unsuspecting Sabinus and the Flavian supporters into
the Capitol, set fire to the Temple of Jupiter Optimus Maximus,
and burned them alive; he watched the play of the flames and

his victims' struggles while banqueting in the mansion which had belonged to Tiberius. He was soon overcome by remorse and, blaming someone else for the murder, he called an assembly and forced all present to bear witness that peace was now his sole objective. Then, drawing his dagger, he tried in turn to make the consul, the other magistrates and the remaining senators accept it. When all refused, he went to lay it up in the Temple of Concord. However, they called him back by shouting, 'No, you yourself are Concord!' So back he came, saying, 'Very well, I will keep the dagger and adopt the divine name you have graciously awarded me.'

16. Vitellius also made the Senate send envoys, accompanied by the Vestal Virgins, to arrange an armistice or at least to gain time for deliberation. But on the following day, while he was waiting for a response, a scout arrived with news that enemy detachments were close at hand. Stowing himself furtively into a sedan chair and accompanied only by his pastrycook and chef, he hurried to his father's house on the Aventine, having planned an escape from there into Campania. But a faint rumour of peace tempted him back to the palace, which he found deserted, and when his two companions slipped away he strapped on a money belt full of gold pieces and hid in the doorkeeper's quarters, tethering a dog outside and jamming a mattress against the door.

17. The advance guard had entered Rome without opposition and at once began searching about, as was to be expected. They hauled Vitellius from his hiding place and, not recognizing him, asked who he was and whether he knew the emperor's whereabouts. Vitellius gave some lying answer, but was soon identified; so he begged to be placed in safe custody, even if that meant prison, on the ground that he had certain information crucial to Vespasian's safety. Instead, his hands were tied behind him, a noose was fastened round his neck, and amid cheers and abuse the soldiers dragged him, half-naked, with his clothes in tatters, along the Sacred Way to the Forum. They pulled his head back by the hair, as is done with criminals, and stuck a sword point under the chin, which exposed his face to public contempt. Dung and filth were hurled at him, also such

epithets as 'Greedy guts' and 'Fire-raiser', and his forlorn appearance occasioned loud laughter. Indeed, Vitellius looked queer enough even at his best, being unusually tall, with an alcoholic flush, a huge paunch and a limp, the result of a chariot crash – Gaius had been driving at the time. The soldiers put him through the torture of the little cuts before finally killing him near the Gemonian Stairs. Then they dragged his body to the Tiber with a hook and threw it in.

18. Vitellius died at the age of fifty-six; nor did his brother and son outlive him. The omen of the rooster at Vienna, noted above, had been interpreted as meaning that a Gaul would kill him. This proved correct: the general who dispatched him was Antonius Primus, a native of Tolosa, and his boyhood nickname had been Becco, which means 'rooster's beak'.[13]

DIVUS VESPASIAN

1. The Flavii, admittedly an obscure family, none of whose members had ever enjoyed high office, at last brought stable government to the empire; they had found it drifting uneasily through a year of revolution in the course of which three successive emperors lost their lives by violence. We have no cause to be ashamed of the Flavian record, though it is generally admitted that Domitian's cruelty and greed justified his assassination.

Titus Flavius Petro, a citizen of Reate, who fought for Pompey in the civil war as a centurion or perhaps a reservist, made his way back there from the battlefield of Pharsalus, secured an honourable discharge with a full pardon, and took up debt collecting. Although his son Sabinus is said either to have been a *primipilaris* or to have resigned a position as centurion on grounds of ill health, the truth is that he avoided military service and became a customs supervisor in Asia, where several cities honoured him with statues inscribed 'To an Honest Customs Officer'. He later turned banker among the Helvetii, and there died, leaving a wife, Vespasia Polla, and two sons, Sabinus and Vespasian. Sabinus, the elder, attained the rank of city prefect at Rome; Vespasian became emperor. Vespasia Polla belonged to a good family from Nursia. Vespasius Pollio, her father, had three times held the position of military tribune and been camp prefect; her brother was a senator of praetorian rank. Moreover, on a hilltop some six miles from Nursia along the road to Spoletium stands the village of Vespasiae, where a great many tombs testify to the family's antiquity and local renown. Some people admittedly claim that the emperor's great-grandfather, originally from the region beyond the Po, acted as a foreman of the labourers who come from Umbria every year to help the Sabines with their harvest, and that he married and settled in Reate, but my own careful researches have turned up no evidence whatsoever to substantiate this.

2. Vespasian was born in the evening on 17 November, in the hamlet of Falacrina just beyond Reate, during the consulship of Quintus Sulpicius Camerinus and Gaius Poppaeus Sabinus,[1] five years before the death of Augustus. His paternal grandmother, Tertulla, brought him up on her estate at Cosa, and as emperor he would often revisit the house, which he kept exactly as it had always been in an attempt to preserve his childhood memories intact. At religious festivals and holidays he made a practice of drinking from a little silver cup which had once belonged to his grandmother, so dear was her memory to him.

For years he postponed his candidature for the broad purple stripe of senatorial rank, already earned by his brother Sabinus, and in the end it was Vespasia Polla who drove him to take this step – not by pleading with him or commanding him as his mother, but by constant sarcastic use of the phrase 'your brother's footman'. Vespasian served as a military tribune in Thrace, and when quaestorships were being assigned by lot he drew that of Crete and Cyrenaica. His first attempt to win an aedileship came to nothing; at the second he scraped through in only the sixth place; however, as soon as he stood for the praetorship he was one of the most popular choices. The Senate then being at odds with Gaius, Vespasian, who never missed a chance of winning favour at court, proposed that special games should be held to celebrate the emperor's German victory. He also proposed that, as an additional punishment, the bodies of conspirators should be denied public burial, and during a full session of the Senate he acknowledged the emperor's graciousness in having invited him to dine.

3. Meanwhile, Vespasian married Flavia Domitilla, the former mistress of Statilius Capella, an *eques* from Sabrata in Africa. Her father, Flavius Liberalis, although only a humble quaestor's clerk from Ferentium, had appeared before a board of arbitration and established her claim to free birth and the

full Roman citizenship in place of only a Latin one.[2] Vespasian
had three children by Flavia, namely Titus, Domitian and
Domitilla, but he lost both his wife and his daughter even before
he held a magistracy. He then took up with Caenis, his former
mistress and one of Antonia's freedwomen secretaries, who
remained his wife in all but name even when he became
emperor.

4. On Claudius' accession, Vespasian was indebted to
Narcissus for the command of a legion in Germany; he then
proceeded to Britain, where he fought thirty battles, subjugated
two warlike tribes, and captured more than twenty towns,
besides the entire island of Vectis. In these campaigns he served
at times under Aulus Plautius, the consular legate, and at times
directly under Claudius, earning triumphal decorations; soon
afterwards he obtained a couple of priesthoods, as well as a
consulship for the last two months of the year. While waiting
for a consular appointment, however, he lived in retirement,
for fear of Agrippina's power over Nero and of the animosity
which she continued to feel towards any friend of Narcissus
even after his death.

In the distribution of provinces Vespasian drew Africa, where
his rule was characterized by justice and great dignity, except
on a single occasion when the people of Hadrumetum rioted
and pelted him with turnips. It is known that he came back no
richer than he went, because his credit was so nearly exhausted
that, in order to keep up his position, he had to mortgage all
his estates to his brother Sabinus and go into trade; this gave
him the nickname 'Mule Driver'. Vespasian is also said to have
earned a severe reprimand after getting a young man raised to
senatorial rank, against his father's wishes, for a fee of 200,000
sesterces.

He toured Achaia in Nero's retinue, but offended him deeply
by either leaving the room during his song recitals or staying
and falling asleep. In consequence he not only lost his favour
but was dismissed from court, and fled to a small out-of-the-way
township, where he hid in terror of his life until finally offered
the military command of a province.

An ancient superstition was current in the east that out of

Judaea would come the rulers of the world. This prediction, as it later proved, referred to Roman emperors, but the Jews, who read it as referring to themselves, rebelled; after murdering their procurator, they routed the consular governor of Syria when he came down to restore order, and captured an Eagle. To crush this uprising the Romans needed a strong army under an energetic commander, who could be trusted not to abuse his powers. The choice fell on Vespasian. He had given signal proof of energy, and nothing, it seemed, need be feared from a man of such modest antecedents. Two legions, with eight cavalry divisions and ten supernumerary cohorts, were therefore dispatched to join the forces already in Judaea, and Vespasian took his elder son Titus to serve on his staff. No sooner had they reached Judaea than he impressed the neighbouring provinces by his prompt tightening up of discipline and his audacious conduct in battle after battle. During the assault on one enemy city he was wounded on the knee by a stone and caught several arrows on his shield.

5. When Nero and Galba were both dead and Vitellius was disputing the rule with Otho, Vespasian began to remember his imperial ambitions, which had originally been raised by the following omens. An ancient oak tree, sacred to Mars, growing on the Flavian estate near Rome, put out a shoot for each of the three occasions when his mother gave birth, and these clearly had a bearing on the child's future. The first slim shoot withered quickly, and the eldest child, a girl, died within the year. The second shoot was long and healthy, promising good luck, but the third seemed more like a tree than a branch. Sabinus, the father, is said to have been greatly impressed by an inspection of a victim's entrails and to have congratulated his mother on having a grandson who would become emperor. She roared with laughter and said, 'Fancy your going soft in the head before your old mother does!'

Later, during Vespasian's aedileship, the emperor Gaius, furious because Vespasian had not kept the streets clean as was his duty, ordered some soldiers to load him with mud; they obeyed by stuffing into the fold of his senatorial toga as much as it could hold – an omen interpreted to mean that one day the soil of Italy would be neglected and trampled upon as the result of civil war, but that Vespasian would protect it and, so to speak, take it to his bosom.

Then a stray dog picked up a human hand at the crossroads, which it brought into the room where Vespasian was breakfasting and dropped under the table.[3] On another occasion a plough ox shook off its yoke, burst into Vespasian's dining room, scattered the servants, and then, as if suddenly exhausted, fell at his feet and lowered its neck. He also found a cypress tree lying uprooted on his grandmother's farm, though there had been no gale to account for the accident; yet by the next day it had taken root again and was greener and stronger than ever.

In Achaia, Vespasian dreamed that he and his family would begin to prosper from the moment when Nero lost a tooth, and on the following day, while he was in the imperial quarters, a doctor entered and showed him one of Nero's teeth which he had just extracted.

In Judaea, Vespasian consulted the god of Carmel and was given a promise that he would never be disappointed in what he planned or desired, however lofty his ambitions. Also, a distinguished Jewish prisoner of Vespasian's, Josephus by name, insisted that he would soon be released by the very man who had now put him in fetters and who would then be emperor.[4] Reports of further omens came from Rome: Nero, it seemed, had been warned in a dream shortly before his death to take the sacred chariot of Jupiter Optimus Maximus from the Capitol to the Circus, calling at Vespasian's house as he went. Soon after this, while Galba was on his way to the elections which gave him a second consulship, a statue of Julius Caesar turned of its own accord to face east; and at Betriacum, when the battle was about to begin, two eagles fought in full view of both armies, but a third appeared from the rising sun and drove off the victor.

6. Still Vespasian made no move, although his adherents were impatient to press his claims, until he was suddenly stirred to action by the fortuitous support of a distant group of soldiers whom he did not even know: 2,000 men belonging to the three legions in Moesia that had been sent to reinforce Otho. They

had marched forward as far as Aquileia, despite the news of
Otho's defeat and suicide which reached them on the way, and
had there taken advantage of the unsettled times to plunder at
pleasure. Pausing at last to consider what the reckoning might
be on their return, they hit on the idea of setting up their own
emperor. And why not? After all, the troops in Spain had
appointed Galba; the praetorians, Otho; the troops in Germany, Vitellius. So they went through the whole list of provincial governors, rejecting each name in turn for this reason or
that until finally choosing Vespasian – on the strong recommendation of some Third Legion men who had been sent to Moesia
from Syria just prior to Nero's death – and marking all their
standards with his name. Though they were temporarily recalled to duty at this point and did no more in the matter,
the news of their decision leaked out. Tiberius Alexander,
the prefect in Egypt, thereupon made his legions take the oath
to Vespasian, on the Kalends of July, later celebrated as
Vespasian's accession day, and on 11 July the army in Judaea
swore allegiance to Vespasian in person. Three things helped
him greatly: first, the copy of a letter (possibly forged) in which
Otho begged him most earnestly to save Rome and take vengeance on Vitellius; second, a persistent rumour that Vitellius
had planned, after his victory, to restation the legions, trans-
ferring those in Germany to the east, a much softer option;
lastly, the support of Licinius Mucianus, then commanding in
Syria, who swallowed the jealousy of Vespasian which he had
long made no effort to hide and promised to lend him the
whole Syrian army, and the support of Vologaesus, king of the
Parthians, who promised him 40,000 archers.

7. So Vespasian began a new civil war: having sent troops
ahead to Italy, he himself crossed over to Alexandria, so that
he might occupy this key to Egypt. There he dismissed his
companions and entered the Temple of Serapis, alone, to consult the auspices and discover how long he would last as
emperor. After many propitiatory sacrifices he turned to go, but
saw his freedman Basilides handing him the customary branches,
garlands and bread[5] – although Basilides had for a long time been
nearly crippled by rheumatism and was moreover far away.

Almost at once dispatches from Italy brought the news of Vitellius' defeat at Cremona and his assassination at Rome.

Vespasian, still rather bewildered in his new role of emperor, felt a certain lack of authority and of what might be called the divine spark; yet both these attributes were granted him. As he sat on the tribunal, two labourers, one blind, the other lame, approached together, begging to be healed. Apparently the god Serapis had promised them in a dream that if Vespasian would consent to spit on the blind man's eyes and touch the lame man's leg with his heel, both would be made well. Vespasian had so little faith in his curative powers that he showed great reluctance in doing as he was asked, but his friends persuaded him to try them, in the presence of a large audience too – and the charm worked. At the same time, certain soothsayers were inspired to excavate a sacred site at Tegea in Arcadia, where a hoard of very ancient vases was discovered, all painted with a striking likeness of Vespasian.

8. As a man of great promise and reputation, Vespasian celebrated a triumph over the Jews on his return to Rome, and added eight more consulships to the one he had already earned.[6] He also assumed the office of censor, and throughout his reign he made it his principal business first to shore up the foundations of the commonwealth, which were in a state of collapse, and then to embellish it artistically.

The troops, whose discipline had been weakened either by the exultation of victory or by the humiliation of defeat, had been indulging in all sorts of wild excesses; moreover, rumbles of internal dissension could be heard in the provinces and free cities as well as in certain of the subject kingdoms. This led Vespasian to discharge or punish a large number of Vitellius' men and, so far from showing his own troops any special favour, he was slow in paying them even the victory bonus to which they were entitled. He missed no opportunity of tightening discipline: when a young man, reeking of perfume, came to thank him for a promotion in rank, Vespasian turned his head away in disgust and cancelled the order, saying crushingly, 'I should not have minded so much if it had been garlic.' When the marine brigade, detachments of which had to be constantly

on the move between Ostia or Puteoli and Rome, applied for
a special shoe allowance, Vespasian not only turned down
the application, but instructed them in future to march barefoot, and this has been their practice ever since. He revoked
the privilege of self-governance from Achaia, Lycia, Rhodes,
Byzantium and Samos, and reduced the kingdoms of Trachian
Cilicia and Commagene to provincial status. He garrisoned
Cappadocia as a precaution against the frequent barbarian
raids, and appointed a governor of consular rank instead of a
mere *eques*.

Rome had become unsightly, since many buildings had
burned or collapsed, and so Vespasian authorized anyone who
pleased to take over vacant sites and build on them if the
original owners failed to come forward. He personally inaugur-
ated the restoration of the burned Capitol by collecting the first
basketful of rubble and carrying it away on his shoulders, and
undertook to replace the 3,000 bronze tablets which had been
lost in the fire, hunting high and low for copies of the inscriptions engraved on them. Those ancient, beautifully phrased
records of senatorial decrees and popular ordinances dealt with
such matters as alliances, treaties and the privileges granted to
individuals, and dated back almost to the foundation of Rome.

9. He also started work on several new buildings: the Temple
of Peace near the Forum; the Temple of Divus Claudius on
the Caelian Hill, begun by Agrippina but almost completely
destroyed by Nero; and an amphitheatre in the centre of the
city,[7] which he knew Augustus had always planned to construct.

He reformed the senatorial and equestrian orders, now weakened by frequent murders and long-term neglect, reviewing
their membership and replacing undesirables with the most
eligible Italian and provincial candidates available; in order to
define clearly the difference between these orders as one of
status rather than of privilege, he pronounced the following
judgement in a dispute between a senator and an *eques*: 'No
abuse must be offered a senator, although it may be returned
when given.'

10. Vespasian found a huge waiting list of lawsuits: old
ones left undecided because of interruptions in regular court

proceedings, and new ones due to the recent states of emergency. So he drew lots for a board of commissioners to settle war-compensation claims and make emergency decisions in the centumviral court, thus greatly reducing the number of cases. Most of the litigants would otherwise have been dead by the time they were summoned to appear.

11. Since nothing at all had been done to counteract the debauched and reckless style of living then in fashion, Vespasian induced the Senate to decree that any woman who had taken another person's slave as a lover should lose her freedom, and that nobody lending money to a minor should be entitled to collect the debt, even if the father died and the minor inherited the estate.

12. He was from first to last modest and restrained in his conduct of affairs, and more inclined to parade than to cast a veil over his humble origins. Indeed, when certain people tried to connect his ancestors with the founders of Reate and with one of Hercules' comrades whose tomb is still to be seen on the Via Salaria, Vespasian burst into a roar of laughter. He had anything but a craving for outward show; on the day of his triumph, the painful crawl of the procession so wearied him that he said frankly, 'What an old fool I was to demand a triumph, as though I owed this honour to my ancestors or had ever made it one of my own ambitions! It serves me right!' Moreover, he neither claimed the tribunician power nor adopted the title Father of His Country until late in his reign, and even before the civil war was over he discontinued the practice of having everyone who attended his morning audiences searched for concealed weapons.

13. Vespasian showed great patience if his friends took liberties with him in conversation, or advocates made innuendoes in their speeches, or philosophers affected to despise him, and great restraint in his dealings with Licinius Mucianus, a bumptious and immoral fellow who traded on his past services by treating him disrespectfully. Thus he complained only once about Mucianus, and then in private to a common acquaintance, his concluding words being 'I, at least, am a man.'[8] When Salvius Liberalis was defending a rich client, he earned a laugh

from Vespasian himself by daring to ask, 'Does the emperor really care whether Hipparchus is or is not worth a million in gold?'[9] And when Demetrius the Cynic, who had been banished from Rome, happened to meet Vespasian's travelling party, yet made no move to rise or salute him and barked out some rude remark or other, Vespasian merely commented, 'Good dog!'[10]

14. Not being the sort of man to bear grudges or pay off old scores, he arranged a splendid match for the daughter of his former enemy Vitellius, even providing her dowry and trousseau. Then there was the matter of the chief usher. When, long before, Vespasian had been dismissed from Nero's court and cried in terror, 'But what shall I do? Where on earth shall I go?', the chief usher answered, 'Oh, go to Plagueville!', and pushed him outside. He now came to beg for forgiveness, and Vespasian did no more than show him the door with an equally short and almost identically framed goodbye.

He felt so little inclination to execute anyone whom he feared or suspected that, warned by his friends against Mettius Pompusianus, who was believed to have an imperial horoscope, he saddled him with a debt of gratitude by making him consul.

15. My researches show that no innocent party was ever punished during Vespasian's reign except behind his back or while he was absent from Rome, unless by deliberate defiance of his wishes or by misinforming him about the facts in the case. He showed great leniency towards Helvidius Priscus, who on his return from Syria was the only man to greet him simply as 'Vespasian',[11] and who throughout his praetorship omitted all courteous mention of him from official orders. However, feeling himself, as it were, reduced to the ranks by Priscus' insufferable rudeness, Vespasian flared up at last, banished him, and eventually gave orders for his execution. Nevertheless, he meant to save him, and wrote out a reprieve; but this was not delivered, owing to a mistaken report that Priscus had already been executed. Vespasian never rejoiced in anyone's death, and would often weep when convicted criminals were forced to pay the extreme penalty.

16. His one serious failing was avarice. Not content with restoring the duties remitted by Galba, he levied new and

heavier ones, increased and sometimes doubled the tribute due from the provinces, and openly engaged in business dealings which would have disgraced even a private citizen – such as buying up certain commodities only to put them back on the market at higher prices. He thought nothing of exacting fees from candidates for public office or of selling pardons to the innocent and guilty alike, and is said to have deliberately raised his greediest procurators to positions in which they could fatten their purses satisfactorily before he came down hard on them for extortion. They were, at any rate, nicknamed his 'sponges' – he put them in to soak, only to squeeze them dry later.

Some claim that greed was in Vespasian's very bones – an accusation once thrown at him by an old slave of his, a cattle-man. When Vespasian became emperor the slave begged to be freed but, finding that he was expected to buy the privilege, complained, 'So the fox has changed his fur, but not his nature!' Still, the more credible view is that the emptiness alike of the public treasury and the imperial exchequer forced Vespasian into heavy taxation and unethical business dealings; he himself had declared at his accession that 40,000 million sesterces were needed to put the commonwealth on its feet again. Certainly he spent his income to the best possible advantage, however questionable its sources.

17. Vespasian behaved most generously to all classes: grant-ing subventions to senators who did not possess the property qualifications of their rank; securing impoverished men of consular rank an annual pension of 500,000 sesterces; rebuild-ing on a grander scale than before the many cities throughout the empire which had been burned or destroyed by earthquakes; and proving himself a devoted patron of the arts and sciences.

18. He was the first to pay teachers of Latin and Greek rhetoric a regular annual salary of 100,000 sesterces from the imperial exchequer; he also awarded prizes to leading poets, and to artists as well, notably the ones who refashioned the Venus of Cos and the Colossus.[12] An engineer offered to haul some huge columns up to the Capitol at moderate expense by a simple mechanical contrivance, but Vespasian declined his services: 'I must always ensure', he said, 'that the working

classes earn enough money to buy themselves food.' Nevertheless, he paid the engineer a very handsome fee.

19. When the Theatre of Marcellus opened again after
Vespasian had built its new stage, he revived the former musical
performances and presented Apelles the tragic actor with
400,000 sesterces, Terpnus and Diodorus the lyre players with
200,000 each, and several others with 100,000; his lowest
cash awards were 40,000, and he also distributed several gold
crowns. Moreover, he ordered a great number of formal dinners
on a lavish scale, to support the dealers in provisions. On
the Saturnalia he gave party favours to his male dinner guests,
and he did the same for women on the Kalends of March. But
even this generosity could not rid him of his reputation for
stinginess. Thus the people of Alexandria continued to call him
'Cybiosactes', after one of the meanest of all their kings. And
when he died the famous comedian Favor, who had been chosen
to wear his funeral mask in the procession and give the customary imitations of his gestures and words, shouted to the stewards, 'Hey! how much will all this cost?' 'Ten million sesterces,'
they answered. 'Then I'll take a hundred thousand down, and
you can just pitch me into the Tiber.'

20. Vespasian was square-shouldered, with strong, well-
formed limbs, but always wore a strained expression on his
face, so that once, when he asked a well-known wit who always
used to make jokes about people, 'Why not make one about
me?', the answer came, 'I will, when you have at last finished
relieving yourself.' He enjoyed perfect health and took no medical precautions for preserving it, except to have his throat and
body massaged regularly in the court for ball games, and to
fast one whole day every month.

21. Here follows a general description of his habits. After
becoming emperor he would rise early, before daylight even, to
deal with his correspondence and official reports. Next he would
invite his friends to wish him good morning while he put on his
shoes and dressed for the day. Having attended to any urgent
business, he would first take a drive and then return to bed for a
nap – with one of the several mistresses whom he had engaged
after Caenis' death. Finally he took a bath and went to dinner,

where he would be in such a cheerful mood that members of his household usually chose this time to ask favours of him.

22. Yet Vespasian was nearly always just as good-natured, cracking frequent jokes; he was in fact a man of considerable wit, although it often took such a low and vulgar form that he even indulged in schoolboy humour. All the same, some of his sayings are still remembered. Taken to task by Mestrius Florus, a man of consular status, for vulgarly saying *plostra* instead of *plaustra*, he greeted him the following day as 'Flaurus'.[13] Once a woman complained that she was desperately in love with him, and would not leave him alone until he consented to seduce her. 'How shall I enter that item in your expense ledger?' asked his steward later, on learning that she had got 400,000 sesterces out of him. 'Oh,' said Vespasian, 'just put it down to "love for Vespasian".'

23. With his knack of apt quotation from the Greek classics, he once described a very tall man whose genitals were grotesquely overdeveloped as 'Striding along with a lance which casts a preposterous shadow'.[14] And when, to avoid paying death duties into the imperial exchequer, a very rich freedman named Cerylus changed his name to Laches and announced that he had been born free, Vespasian quoted:

> O, Laches, when your life is o'er,
> Cerylus you will be once more.[15]

Most of his humour, however, centred on the way he did business; he always tried to make his swindles sound less offensive by passing them off as jokes. One of his favourite servants applied for a stewardship on behalf of a man whose brother he claimed to be. 'Wait,' Vespasian told him, and had the candidate brought in for a private interview. 'How much commission would you have paid my servant?' he asked. The man mentioned a sum. 'You may pay it directly to me,' said Vespasian, giving him the stewardship. When the servant brought the matter up again, Vespasian's advice was 'Go and find another brother. The one you mistook for your own turns out to be mine!'

Once, on a journey, his muleteer dismounted and began

shoeing the mules; Vespasian suspected a ruse to hold him up, because a friend of the muleteer's had appeared and was now busily discussing a lawsuit. Vespasian made the muleteer tell him just what his shoeing fee would be, and insisted on being paid half. Titus complained of the tax which Vespasian had imposed on urinals. Vespasian handed him a coin which had been part of the first day's proceeds: 'Does it smell bad, my son?' he asked. 'No, Father.' 'That's odd: it comes straight from the urinal!' When a deputation reported that a huge and expensive statue had been voted him at public expense, Vespasian held out his hand, saying, 'The pedestal is waiting.'

Nothing could stop this flow of humour, even the fear of imminent death. Among the many portents of his end was a yawning crevice in the Mausoleum of Augustus. 'That will be for Junia Calvina,' he said; 'she is one of his descendants.'[16] And at the fatal sight of a comet he cried, 'Look at that long hair! The King of Parthia must be going to die.'[17] His deathbed joke was 'Dear me! I must be turning into a god.'

24. During his ninth and last consulship Vespasian visited Campania and was bothered by slight attacks of fever. He hurried back to Rome, then went on to Cutiliae and his summer retreat near Reate, where he made things worse by bathing in cold water and irritating his stomach. Yet he carried on with his imperial duties as usual and even received deputations at his bedside, until he almost fainted after a sudden violent bout of diarrhoea; he struggled to rise, muttering that an emperor ought to die at least on his feet, and collapsed in the arms of the attendants who went to his rescue. This was 23 June, when he had lived sixty-nine years, seven months and seven days.[18]

25. All accounts agree on Vespasian's supreme confidence in his horoscope and those of his family. Despite frequent plots to murder him, he dared tell the Senate that either his sons would succeed him or no one would. He is said to have dreamed about a pair of scales hanging in the hall of the palace: Claudius and Nero in one pan were exactly balanced against himself, Titus and Domitian in the other. And this proved an accurate prophecy, since the families were destined to rule for an equal length of time.

DIVUS TITUS

1. Titus, whose cognomen was the same as his father's,[1] had such winning ways – whether inborn, cultivated subsequently, or conferred on him by fortune – that he became an object of universal love and adoration. Oddly enough, this happened only after his accession: both as a private citizen and later as his father's colleague, Titus had been not only unpopular but venomously loathed. He was born on 30 December, the memorable year of Gaius' assassination, in a small, dingy, slum bedroom close to the Septizonium.[2] The house, which is still standing, has lately been opened to the public.

2. He grew up at court with Britannicus, sharing his teachers and following the same curriculum. The story goes that when one day Claudius' freedman Narcissus called in a physiognomist to examine Britannicus' features and prophesy his future, he was told most emphatically that Britannicus would never be emperor, whereas Titus (who happened to be present) would. The two boys were such close friends that when Britannicus drank his fatal dose of poison, Titus, who was reclining at the same table, is said to have emptied the glass in sympathy and to have been dangerously ill for some time. He never forgot his friendship for Britannicus, but had two statues of him made: a golden one to be installed in the palace, and an ivory equestrian one which is still carried in the Circus procession and which he personally followed around the ring at its dedication.

3. When Titus came of age, the beauty and talents that had distinguished him as a child grew even more remarkable. Though not tall, he was both graceful and dignified, both muscular and handsome, except for a certain paunchiness. He had

a phenomenal memory, and displayed a natural aptitude alike for the arts of war and peace; handled arms and rode a horse as well as any man living; could compose speeches and verses in Greek or Latin with equal ease, and actually extemporized them on occasion. He was something of a musician too: he sang pleasantly, and had mastered the harp. It often amused him to compete with his secretaries at shorthand dictation, or so I have heard; and he claimed that he could imitate any handwriting in existence and might, in different circumstances, have been the most celebrated forger of all time.

4. Titus' reputation while an active and efficient military tribune in Germany and Britain is attested by the numerous busts and statues of him found in both provinces. After completing his military service he returned to Rome, where he spent a great deal of time at the law courts as an advocate – but only because it was a respectable occupation, not because he meant to make a career of it. The father of his first wife, Arrecina Tertulla, although only of equestrian rank, was a former prefect of the praetorian cohorts. When she died, Titus married the very well-connected Marcia Furnilla, whom he divorced as soon as she had borne him a daughter. When his quaestorship at Rome ended, he went to command one of his father's legions in Judaea, and there captured the fortified cities of Tarichaeae and Gamala. In the course of the fighting he had a horse killed under him, but mounted another belonging to a comrade who fell at his side.

5. Titus was sent to congratulate Galba on his accession, and all whom he met on the way thought that Galba had summoned him in order to adopt him as his heir. Seeing, however, that a new revolution threatened in Rome, Titus turned back from his journey, and while consulting the oracle of Venus at Paphos about his voyage he was confirmed in his hope of ruling. The prophecy grew much more credible after his father had been acclaimed emperor and left him to complete the conquest of Judaea. In the final assault on Jerusalem Titus managed to kill twelve of the garrison with successive arrows, and the city was captured on his daughter's birthday. Titus' prowess inspired such deep admiration in the troops that they hailed him as

imperator and, on several occasions, when he seemed on the point of relinquishing his command, begged him either to stay or to let them follow him, even threatening violence if he would not humour their wishes. Such passionate devotion aroused a suspicion that he planned to usurp his father's power in the east, especially since he had worn a diadem while attending the consecration of the Apis bull at Memphis on his way to Alexandria; but this was a gross slander on his conduct, which accorded with ancient ritual. Titus sailed for Italy at once in a naval transport, touching at Rhegium and Puteoli. Hurrying on to Rome, he exploded all the false rumours by greeting Vespasian, who had not been expecting him, with the simple words 'Here I am, Father, here I am!'

6. From that point on he became his father's colleague, almost his guardian, sharing in the Judaean triumph, in the censorship, in the exercise of tribunician power, and in seven consulships. He bore most of the burdens of government and, in his father's name, dealt with official correspondence, drafted edicts, and even took over the quaestor's task of reading his speeches to the Senate. Titus also assumed command of the praetorians, a post which had always before been entrusted to an *eques*, and in which he behaved somewhat violently and high-handedly. If anyone aroused his suspicion, detachments of praetorians would be sent into theatre or camp to demand the man's punishment in the name of every loyal citizen present, and he would then be executed on the spot. Titus disposed of Aulus Caecina, a former consul, by inviting him to dinner and having him stabbed on the way out of the dining room; yet here he could plead political necessity – the manuscript of a disloyal speech which Caecina intended for the troops had fallen into his hands. Actions of this sort, although an insurance against the future, made Titus so deeply disliked at the time that perhaps no more unwelcome claimant to the supreme power has ever won it.

7. He was believed to be profligate as well as cruel, because of the riotous parties which he kept going with his more extravagant friends far into the night; and lustful too, because he kept a troop of toy boys and eunuchs, and nursed a notorious passion for Queen Berenice, to whom he had allegedly promised

marriage. He also had a reputation for accepting bribes and not being averse to using influence to settle his father's cases in favour of the highest bidder. It was even prophesied quite openly that he would prove to be a second Nero. However, this pessimistic view stood him in good stead: as soon as everyone realized that here was no monster of vice but an exceptionally noble character, public opinion flew to the opposite extreme.

His dinner parties, far from being orgies, were very pleasant occasions, and the friends he chose were retained in office by his successors as key men for both their own affairs and those of the commonwealth. He immediately sent Berenice away from Rome, which was painful for both of them, and broke off all relations with some of his favourite boys; even though they danced well enough to make a name for themselves on the stage, he never attended their public performances.

No emperor could have been less of a robber than Titus, who showed the greatest respect for private property and would not even accept the gifts sanctioned by tradition. Nor had any of his predecessors ever displayed such generosity. At the dedication of the Amphitheatre and the Baths, which had been hastily built beside it, Titus provided a most lavish gladiatorial show; he also staged a sea fight on the old artificial lake, and when the water had been let out he used the basin for further gladiatorial contests and a wild-beast hunt, 5,000 beasts of different sorts dying in a single day.

8. Titus was naturally kind-hearted, and though no emperor, following Tiberius' example, had ever consented to ratify individual concessions granted by his predecessor unless these suited him personally, Titus did not wait to be asked but signed a general edict confirming all such concessions whatsoever. He also had a rule never to dismiss any petitioner without leaving him some hope that his request would be favourably considered. Even when warned by his staff how impossible it would be to make good such promises, Titus maintained that no one ought to go away disappointed from an audience with the emperor. One evening at dinner, realizing that he had done nobody any favour since the previous night, he spoke these memorable words: 'My friends, I have wasted a day.'

He took such pains to humour the people that on one occasion, before a gladiatorial show, he promised to forgo his own preferences and let the audience choose what they liked best; and he kept his word by refusing no request and encouraging everyone to tell him what each wanted. Yet he openly acknowledged his partisanship of the Thracian school of gladiators, and would gesture and argue vociferously with the crowd on this subject, though never losing either his dignity or his sense of justice. Sometimes he would use the new public baths, as a means of keeping in touch with the common people.

Titus' reign was marked by a series of catastrophes – an eruption of Mount Vesuvius in Campania, a fire at Rome which burned for three days and nights, and one of the worst outbreaks of plague that had ever been known. Throughout these frightful disasters, he showed far more than an emperor's concern: it resembled the deep love of a father for his children, which he conveyed not only in a series of comforting edicts but by helping the victims to the utmost extent of his purse. He set up a board of former consuls, chosen by lot, to relieve distress in Campania, and devoted the property of those who had died in the eruption and left no heirs to a fund for rebuilding the stricken cities. His only comment on the fire at Rome was 'This has ruined me!' He stripped his own mansions of their decorations, distributed these among the damaged temples and public buildings, and appointed a body of *equites* to see that his orders were promptly carried out. Titus attempted to control the plague by every imaginable means, human as well as divine – resorting to all sorts of sacrifices and medical remedies.

One of the worst features of Roman life at the time was the licence long enjoyed by informers and their managers. Whenever Titus laid his hands on any such he had them well whipped, clubbed, and then taken to the Amphitheatre and paraded in the arena, where some were put up for auction as slaves and the remainder deported to desert islands. In further discouragement of this evil, he allowed nobody to be tried for the same offence under more than one law, and limited the period during which inquiries could be made into the status of dead people.

9. He had promised before his accession to accept the office

of pontifex maximus as a safeguard against committing any crime, and he kept his word. Thereafter he was never directly or indirectly responsible for a murder, and, although often given abundant excuse for revenge, he swore that he would rather die than take life. Titus dismissed with a caution two patricians convicted of aspiring to the empire; he told them that, since this was a gift of destiny, they would be well advised to renounce their hopes. He also promised them whatever else they wanted, within reason, and hastily sent messengers to reassure the mother of one of the pair, who lived some distance away, that her son was safe. Then he invited them to dine among his friends, and the next day to sit close by him during the gladiatorial show, where he asked them to test the blades of the contestants' swords brought to him for inspection. Finally, the story goes, he consulted the horoscopes of both men and warned them what dangers threatened from unexpected quarters – quite correctly, as events proved.

Titus' brother Domitian caused him endless trouble: he took part in conspiracies, stirred up disaffection in the armed forces almost openly, and toyed with the notion of escaping from Rome and putting himself at their head. Yet Titus had not the heart to execute Domitian, dismiss him from court, or even treat him less honourably than before. Instead, he continued to repeat, as on the first day of his reign, 'Remember that you are my partner and chosen successor,' and often took Domitian aside, begging him tearfully to return the affection he offered.

10. Death, however, intervened, which was a far greater loss to the world than to Titus himself. At the close of the games he wept publicly; he then set off for Sabine territory in a gloomy mood because a victim had escaped when he was about to sacrifice it, and because thunder had sounded from a clear sky. He collapsed with fever at the first posting station, and on his way home in his litter he is said to have drawn back the curtains, gazed up at the sky, and complained bitterly that life was being undeservedly taken from him – since he had done nothing at all which he had cause to regret, save for one thing only. What that was he did not reveal, and it remains difficult to guess. Some people think that he was referring to an affair with

Domitian's wife Domitia, but she herself solemnly denied the allegation. And had the charge been true she would surely never have made any such denial but boasted of it – as she did of all her other misdeeds.

11. Titus died at the age of forty-two, in the same country house where Vespasian had also died. It was the Ides of September, and he had reigned two years, two months and twenty days.[3] When the news spread, the common people went into mourning as though they had suffered a personal loss. Senators hurried to the Senate House without waiting for an official summons, and even before the doors had been opened began speaking of him with greater thankfulness and praise than they had ever used while he was alive and still among them.

DOMITIAN

1. On 24 October, a month before Vespasian as consul-elect was due to take office, his son Domitian was born in Pomegranate Street, which formed part of the sixth district of Rome.[1] Later, he converted his birthplace into the Temple of the Flavians. Most people agree that Domitian spent a poverty-stricken and rather degraded youth, without even any silver on the family table. At all events, it is an established fact that Claudius Pollio, a man of praetorian rank and the target of Nero's satire *The One-eyed Man*, used to show his guests a letter in Domitian's handwriting, which he happened to have kept, offering to spend the night with him. It is also often insisted that Domitian was seduced by his eventual successor, the emperor Nerva.

During the war against Vitellius, Domitian with his uncle Flavius Sabinus and some of their supporters fled to the Capitol; but when the enemy set the temple on fire Domitian concealed himself all night in the caretaker's quarters and at daybreak, disguised as a devotee of Isis, took refuge among the priests of that rather questionable order. Presently he managed to escape with a friend across the Tiber, where the mother of one of his fellow students hid him so cleverly that she outwitted the agents who tracked him to her house and searched it from cellar to attic. Emerging after Vitellius' death, Domitian was hailed as Caesar and accepted an appointment as city praetor with consular powers – but in name only, because he left all judicial decisions to a junior colleague. However, the lawlessness with which he exploited his position as the emperor's son clearly showed what might be expected of him later. I shall not discuss this subject in any detail; suffice it to say that Domitian had affairs with several married women, and finally persuaded Domitia Longina to divorce her husband Aelius Lamia for his sake; and that once, when he had distributed more than twenty appointments at home and abroad in the course of a single day, Vespasian murmured, 'I wonder he did not name my successor while he was about it!'

2. To acquire a military reputation that would compare favourably with his brother Titus', Domitian planned a quite unnecessary expedition into Gaul and Germany from which, by luck, his father's friends managed to dissuade him. He earned a reprimand for this, and was made to feel a little more conscious of his youth and unimportance by being made to live with his father. Whenever Vespasian and Titus went out in their sedan chairs, he had to be content with following behind in a litter, and, although taking part in their Judaean triumph, rode on a white horse.[2] Of the six consulships enjoyed by Domitian before becoming emperor, only one was not a suffect appointment, and that came his way because Titus had resigned in his favour.[3]

Domitian pretended to be extremely modest, and though he displayed a sudden devotion to poetry, which he would read aloud in public, his enthusiasm was matched by a later neglect of the art. It is to his credit, however, that he did everything possible to get sent against the Alani when a request for auxiliary troops, commanded by one of Vespasian's sons, arrived from Vologaesus, king of the Parthians. And he subsequently tried by bribes and promises to coax similar requests from other eastern kings.

At Vespasian's death Domitian toyed for a while with the idea of offering the troops twice as large a bounty as Titus had given them, and he stated bluntly that his father's will must have been tampered with, since it originally assigned him a half share in the empire. He never once stopped plotting, secretly or openly, against his brother. When Titus fell suddenly and dangerously ill, Domitian told the attendants to presume his death by leaving the sickbed before he had actually breathed his last, and afterwards he granted him no recognition at all

beyond approving his deification. In fact he often slighted Titus'
memory by the use of ambiguous terms in speeches and edicts.

3. At the beginning of his reign Domitian would spend hours
alone every day doing nothing more than catching flies and
stabbing them with a needle-sharp pen. Once, on being asked
whether anyone was closeted with the emperor, Vibius Crispus
answered wittily, 'No, not even a fly.' Domitia presented
Domitian with a son during his second consulship, whom he
lost in the second year after becoming emperor, and she was
therefore awarded the title of Augusta; but he then divorced
her because she had fallen in love with Paris, the actor. This
separation, however, proved to be more than Domitian could
bear, and he very soon took her back, claiming that such was
the people's wish. For a while he governed in an uneven fashion:
that is to say, his vices were at first balanced by his virtues.
Later, he transformed his virtues into vices too – for I am
inclined to believe that, above and beyond his natural inclinations, lack of funds made him greedy, and fear of assassination
made him cruel.

4. Domitian presented many extravagant entertainments not
only in the Amphitheatre but also in the Circus, where besides
the usual two- and four-horse chariot races he staged a double
battle, with both infantry and cavalry; in the Amphitheatre he
presented a sea fight as well as wild-beast hunts and gladiatorial
shows, some by torchlight in which women as well as men took
part. Nor did he ever forget the Quaestorian Games which he
had revived, and he allowed the people to demand a combat
between two pairs of gladiators from his own troop, whom he
would bring on last in their gorgeous court livery. Throughout
every gladiatorial show Domitian would chat, sometimes in
very serious tones, with a little boy who had a grotesquely small
head and always stood at his knee dressed in red. Once he was
heard to ask the child, 'Can you guess why I have just appointed
Mettius Rufus governor of Egypt?' A lake was dug at his orders
close to the Tiber, surrounded with seats, and used for almost
full-scale naval battles, which he watched even in heavy rain.

He also held Saecular Games, fixing their date by Augustus'
old reckoning and ignoring Claudius' more recent celebration

of them; and for the Circus racing, which formed part of the festivities, he reduced the number of laps from seven to five, so that 100 races a day could be run. In honour of Jupiter Capitolinus he founded a festival of music, horsemanship and athletics to be held every five years, and awarded far more prizes than is customary nowadays. The festival included Latin and Greek public-speaking contests and competitions for choral singing to the lyre and for lyre playing alone, besides the usual solo singing to lyre accompaniment; he even instituted foot races for girls in the Stadium. When presiding at these functions he wore buskins, a purple Greek mantle, and a gold crown engraved with the images of Jupiter, Juno and Minerva; at his side sat the flamen of Jupiter and the college of the Flaviales,[4] wearing the same costume as he did, except for crowns decorated with his own image. Domitian also celebrated the Quinquatrus for Minerva at his Alban villa, and he founded in her honour a college of priests whose task it was to supply officers, chosen by lot, for producing lavish wild-beast hunts and stage plays and sponsoring competitions in rhetoric and poetry.

On three occasions Domitian distributed a popular bounty of 300 sesterces a head, and once, to celebrate the Feast of the Seven Hills, he gave a splendid banquet, picnic fashion, with large hampers of food for senators and *equites* and smaller ones for the common people, taking the inaugural bite himself. The day after, he scattered all kinds of gifts to be scrambled for, but since most of these fell in the seats occupied by the common people he had 500 tokens thrown into those reserved for senators and another 500 into those reserved for *equites*.

5. He restored many important buildings that had been gutted by fire, including the Capitol, which had burned down again; but he allowed no names to be inscribed on them except his own – not even the original builder's. He also raised a temple to Jupiter the Guardian on the Capitoline Hill, the Forum of Nerva (as it is now called), the Temple of the Flavians, the Stadium, the Odeum, and an artificial lake for sea battles – its stones later served to rebuild the two sides of the Circus Maximus which had been damaged by fire.

6. Some of Domitian's campaigns, that against the Chatti for instance, were quite unjustified by military necessity; but not so that against the Sarmatians, who had massacred a legion and killed its commander. And when the Dacians defeated first the former consul Oppius Sabinus and then his successor, the praetorian prefect Cornelius Fuscus, Domitian led two punitive expeditions in person. After several indecisive engagements he celebrated a double triumph over the Chatti and the Dacians, but did not insist on recognition for his Sarmatian campaign, contenting himself with the offer of a laurel wreath to Jupiter Capitolinus.

Only an amazing stroke of luck checked the rebellion which Lucius Antonius, the governor of Upper Germany, raised during Domitian's absence from Rome; the Rhine thawed in the nick of time, preventing the German barbarians in Antonius' pay from crossing the ice to join him, and the troops who remained loyal were able to disarm the rebels. Even before news of this success arrived, Domitian had wind of it from portents: on the critical day, a huge eagle embraced his statue at Rome with its wings, screeching triumphantly, and a little later rumours of Antonius' death came so thick and fast that a number of people claimed to have seen his head being carried into Rome.

7. Domitian made a number of social innovations: he cancelled the distribution of food parcels, restoring the custom of holding formal dinners; he added two new teams of chariot drivers, the Golds and the Purples, to the existing four in the Circus; and he forbade actors to appear on the public stage, though still allowing them to perform in private. Castration was now strictly prohibited, and the price of eunuchs remaining in slave dealers' hands was officially controlled. One year, when a bumper vintage followed a poor grain harvest, Domitian concluded that grain farming was being neglected in favour of vineyards. He therefore issued an edict that forbade the further planting of vines in Italy and ordered the acreage in the provinces to be reduced by at least half, if it could not be got rid of altogether; yet he took no steps to implement this edict. He divided certain important positions among freedmen and

equites. Another of his edicts forbade any two legions to share
a camp, or any individual soldier to deposit at headquarters a
sum in excess of 1,000 sesterces, because the large amount of
soldiers' savings laid up in the joint winter headquarters of the
two legions on the Rhine had provided Lucius Antonius with
the necessary funds for launching his rebellion. Domitian also
raised the legionaries' pay from 900 to 1,200 sesterces a year.

8. He was most conscientious in dispensing justice, and convened many extraordinary legal sessions in the Forum. He
annulled every decision of the centumviral court which seemed
to him unduly influenced, and continually warned the board of
arbitration not to grant any fraudulent claims for freedom. It
was his ruling that if a juryman were proved to have taken
bribes, all his colleagues must be penalized as well as himself.
He personally urged the tribunes of the people to charge a
corrupt aedile with extortion and to petition the Senate for a
special jury in the case, and kept such a tight hold on his city
magistrates and provincial governors that the general standard
of justice rose to an unprecedented high level – you need only
observe how many such personages have been charged with
every kind of corruption since his time!

As part of his campaign for improving public manners, Domitian made sure that the theatre officials no longer condoned the
appropriation by common people of seats reserved for *equites*,
and he came down heavily on authors who lampooned distinguished men and women. He expelled one former quaestor
from the Senate for being overfond of acting and dancing,
forbade women of notoriously bad character the right to use
litters or to benefit from inheritances and legacies, struck an
eques from the jury roll because he had divorced his wife on a
charge of adultery and then taken her back again, and sentenced
members of both orders under the Scantinian Law.[5] Taking a
far more serious view than his father and brother had done of
unchastity among the Vestals, he began by sentencing offenders
to execution and afterwards resorted to the traditional form of
punishment. Thus, though he allowed the Oculata sisters and
Varronilla to choose how they should die and sent their lovers
into exile, he later ordered Cornelia, a Chief Vestal – acquitted

at her first trial, but rearrested some years later and convicted – to be buried alive, and had her lovers clubbed to death in the Comitium. The only exception he made was in the case of a former praetor, who had the death sentence commuted to banishment for confessing his guilt after the interrogation of witnesses under torture had failed to establish the truth of the crime with which he was charged. As a lesson that the sanctity of the gods must be protected against thoughtless abuse, Domitian made his soldiers tear down a tomb built for the son of one of his own freedmen from stones intended for the Temple of Jupiter Capitolinus and fling the contents into the sea.

9. While still young, Domitian hated the idea of bloodshed; once, in his father's absence, he remembered Virgil's line 'Before an impious people took to eating slaughtered bullocks',[6] and drafted an edict forbidding the sacrifice of cattle. No one thought of him as in the least greedy or mean either before or for some years after his accession – in fact he gave frequent signs of self-restraint and even of generosity: he treated his friends with great consideration and always insisted that, above all, they should do nothing mean; he refused to accept bequests from men who had children; and he cancelled a clause in Rustius Caepio's will which required the heir to find an annual sum of money for distribution among newly appointed senators.

Moreover, if suits against debtors to the public treasury had been pending for more than five years, he quashed them and permitted a renewal of proceedings only within the same year, and on the condition that if the prosecutor should then lose his case he must go into exile. Although the Clodian Law restricted the private business activities of quaestors' scribes, Domitian now pardoned such of them as had broken it, and generously allowed former owners of commandeered land to farm whatever plots survived the assignment of smallholdings to veterans. He dealt severely with informers who had increased the public revenue by bringing false charges against property owners and getting their estates confiscated. A saying attributed to him runs, 'An emperor who does not punish informers encourages them.'

10. His goodwill and self-restraint were not, however, destined to continue long, although his cruel streak appeared more

quickly than his greed. He executed one sickly boy merely because he happened to be a pupil of the pantomime actor Paris and closely resembled him in looks and mannerisms. Then Hermogenes of Tarsus died because of some incautious allusions that he had introduced into a historical work, and the slaves who acted as his copyists were crucified. Because Domitian was always down on Thracian-style gladiators, a chance remark by one citizen to the effect that a Thracian might be 'a match for his Gallic opponent, but not for the patron of the games' was enough to have him dragged from his seat and – with a placard tied around his neck reading 'A Thracian supporter who spoke evil of his emperor' – torn to pieces by dogs in the arena.

Domitian put many senators to death, including some former consuls; three of these, Civica Cerealis, Salvidienus Orfitus and Acilius Glabrio, he accused of conspiracy – Cerealis was executed while governing Asia, Glabrio while in exile – but others were killed for the most trivial reasons. Aelius Lamia lost his life as a result of some ill-advised but harmless witticisms made several years previously: when someone praised his voice after he had been robbed of his wife by Domitian, he remarked drily, 'I'm in training';[7] and then, encouraged by Titus to marry again, he asked, 'What? You are not wanting a wife too, are you?' Salvius Cocceianus died because he continued to celebrate the birthday of the emperor Otho, his paternal uncle; Mettius Pompusianus because he was said to have an imperial horoscope, and because he always carried with him a parchment map of the world and a collection of speeches by kings and generals extracted from Livy – and because he had named two of his slaves Mago and Hannibal.[8] Sallustius Lucullus, governor of Britain, had equally offended Domitian by allowing a new type of lance to be called 'the Lucullan'; so had Junius Rusticus by his eulogies of Thrasea Paetus and Helvidius Priscus, whom he called the most virtuous of men – an incident which led Domitian to banish all philosophers from Italy – and the younger Helvidius by his farce about Paris and Oenone,[9] which seemed a reflection on Domitian's divorce; and Domitian's own cousin Flavius Sabinus by being mistakenly announced by the election-day herald as emperor-elect instead of consul-elect.

After the suppression of Antonius' rebellion, Domitian grew even more cruel. He hit on the novel idea of scorching his prisoners' genitals to make them divulge the whereabouts of other rebels still in hiding, and he cut off the hands of others. It is a fact that only two leaders of the revolt – a military tribune of senatorial rank and a centurion – earned his pardon, which they did by the simple expedient of proving themselves to have been so disgustingly immoral that they could have exerted no influence at all over either Antonius or the troops.

11. Domitian was not merely cruel, but devious and cunning into the bargain. He summoned a bookkeeper to his bedroom, invited him to share his couch, made him feel perfectly secure and happy, condescended to offer him portions of his dinner – yet had already given orders for his crucifixion on the following day! He was more than usually gracious to the former consul Arrecinus Clemens, one of his close associates and agents, just before his death sentence, and invited him out for a drive. As they happened to pass the man who had informed on Arrecinus, Domitian asked, 'Shall we listen to that utter scoundrel tomorrow?' And he impudently prefaced all his most savage sentences with the same little speech about mercy; indeed, this preamble soon became a recognized sign that something dreadful was on the way. Having brought a group of men before the Senate on a treason charge, he announced that this must be a test of his popularity with the senators, and thus easily got them condemned to an execution in ancient style.[10] However, he seems to have become all at once appalled by the cruelty involved, because he pleaded to have the sentence modified. His exact words are interesting: 'Gentlemen of the Senate, allow me to beg of you one thing that I know you will not readily grant: pray allow these men to choose the manner of their deaths! That will be easier on your eyes, and the world will know that I have played my part in the Senate.'

12. Unfortunately, his new building programme and expensive entertainments, added to the rise in army pay, were more than Domitian could afford, so he decided to reduce expenditure by cutting down on the number of soldiers. But then

realizing that this would expose his frontiers to barbarian attack without appreciably easing the financial situation, he resorted to every form of extortion. Any charge, however slight, might result in the confiscation of a man's property, even if he were already dead: it was enough to have said or done anything at all that might detract from the emperor's dignity. An unsupported claim that someone had been heard, before his death, to name the emperor as his heir, even though he were a perfect stranger, was sufficient pretext for taking over the estate. In addition, Domitian's agents collected the tax on Jews[11] with a peculiar lack of mercy, and took proceedings not only against those who kept their Jewish origins a secret in order to avoid the tax, but also against those who lived as Jews without professing it. As a boy, I remember once attending a crowded court where a steward had a ninety-year-old man stripped to establish whether or not he had been circumcised.

From his earliest years Domitian was consistently discourteous and presumptuous in both his speech and his actions. When Caenis, his father's former mistress, returned from Histria and, as usual, offered him her cheek to kiss, he held out his hand instead. He objected when his brother's son-in-law dressed his servants in white – Domitian's own servants wore white – and announced, 'Too many rulers are a dangerous thing.'[12]

13. On his accession, Domitian boasted to the Senate of having himself conferred the imperial power on Vespasian and Titus – it had now merely returned to him. He also spoke of his action in taking Domitia back, after the divorce, as 'a recall to my divine bed', and on the day of his public banquet he delighted to hear the audience in the Amphitheatre shout, 'Long live our Lord and Lady!'[13] At the festival of Jupiter Capitolinus, when the people unanimously implored him to reinstate Palfurius Sura, who had been expelled from the Senate but had won the prize for public speaking, Domitian did not deign to reply but merely sent a public crier to silence them. Just as arrogantly, he began a letter, which his stewards were to circulate, with the words 'Our Lord God instructs you to do this.' Thereafter, 'Lord God' became his regular title both in

writing and in conversation. His images in the Capitol had to
be of either gold or silver, and not below a certain weight; and
he raised so many arcades and arches, decorated with chariots
and triumphal insignia, in various city districts, that someone
scribbled *arci* on one of them – but used Greek characters.[14] He
held seventeen consulships,[15] which was a record. The seven
middle ones formed a series, and all were held in title only: he
relinquished all of them before the Kalends of May, and most
before the Ides of January. Having adopted the title Germanicus
after his two triumphs, he renamed September and October, the
months of his accession and birth, respectively, as 'Germanicus'
and 'Domitianus'.

14. All this made him everywhere hated and feared. Finally, his
friends and freedmen conspired to murder him, with Domitia's
connivance. He had a pretty good idea of what would be the
last year and day of his life, and even of the hour and the way
he would die: Chaldaean astrologers had foretold everything
when he was just a boy. Also, Vespasian had once teased him
openly at dinner for refusing a dish of mushrooms, saying that
it would be more in keeping with his destiny to be afraid of
swords. As a result, Domitian was such a prey to anxiety that
the least sign of danger unnerved him. The real reason for his
reprieving the vineyards, which he had ordered to be rooted
up, is said to have been the publication of this stanza:

> You may tear up my roots, goat,
>   But what good will that do?
> I shall still have some wine left
>   For sacrificing you.

Though he loved honours of all kinds, this same anxiety made
him veto a senatorial decree that, whenever he held the consulship, a group of *equites* should be picked by lot to walk, dressed
in purple-striped togas and armed with lances, among the lictors
and attendants who preceded him.

As the critical day drew near, his nervousness increased.
The portico where he took his daily exercise was now lined
with plaques of highly polished moonstone, which reflected

everything that happened behind his back, and no imperial audiences were granted to prisoners unless Domitian were alone with them and had tight hold of their fetters. To remind his staff that even the best of intentions could never justify a freedman's complicity in a master's murder, he executed his secretary Epaphroditus, who had reputedly helped Nero to commit suicide after everyone else had deserted him.

15. The occasion of Domitian's murder was that he had executed on some trivial pretext his extremely lazy cousin Flavius Clemens, just after the completion of a consulship, though he had previously designated Clemens' two small sons as his heirs and changed their names to Vespasian and Domitian.

There had been so much lightning during the past eight months that Domitian cried out, 'Now let the Almighty strike whomever he pleases!' The Almighty did in fact strike the Temple of Jupiter Capitolinus, the Temple of the Flavians, the palace, even Domitian's own bedroom; and a tempest wrenched the inscription plate from the tile base of a triumphal statue of his and hurled it into a nearby tomb. The famous cypress tree,[16] which had been blown down but had then taken root again while Vespasian was still a private citizen, now collapsed a second time. Throughout his reign Domitian had made a practice of commending each new year to the care of the goddess Fortuna at Praeneste, and every year she had granted him the same favourable omen; but this year the omen was a dreadful one, portending bloodshed. Domitian also dreamed that Minerva, whom he worshipped fervently, emerged from her shrine to tell him that she had been disarmed by Jupiter and could no longer protect him. What disturbed him most, however, was a prediction by the astrologer Ascletarion, and its sequel. This man, when charged, made no secret of having revealed the future, which he had foreseen by his skill. Domitian at once asked whether he could prophesy the manner of his own end, and upon Ascletarion's replying that he would very soon be torn to pieces by dogs he had him executed on the spot, and gave orders for his funeral rites to be conducted with the greatest care, in order to refute the claims of astrology. But

while the funeral was in progress a sudden gale scattered the
pyre and a pack of stray dogs mangled the astrologer's half-
burned corpse. Latinus, the comic actor, who happened to
witness this incident, mentioned it at dinner when he brought
Domitian the latest gossip.

16. On the day before Domitian's assassination someone
brought him a present of medlars. 'Serve them tomorrow,' he
told the servants, adding, 'if I'm still here to enjoy them.' Then,
turning to his companions, he remarked, 'There will be blood
on the moon tomorrow as she enters Aquarius, and a deed will
be done for everyone to talk about.' With the approach of
midnight Domitian became so terrified that he jumped out of
bed, and at dawn he condemned to death a haruspex from
Germany who was charged with having said that the lightning
portended a change of government. He then scratched an
inflamed wart on his forehead and made it bleed, muttering, 'I
hope this is all the blood required.' Presently he asked for
the time. As had been prearranged, his freedmen answered
untruthfully, 'The sixth hour,' because they knew it was the
fifth he feared. Convinced that the danger had passed, Domitian
went off quickly and happily to take a bath, whereupon his
head valet, Parthenius, met him with the news that a man had
called on very important business that could not be put off.
So Domitian, having dismissed his attendants, hurried to his
bedroom and there was killed.

17. The following details of the plot and the assassination
are pretty well known. While the conspirators were spending
time debating whether it would be better to murder Domitian
in his bath or at dinner, Stephanus, his niece Domitilla's steward, who at the time stood accused of embezzlement, approached them and offered his services. To divert suspicion, he
feigned an injury and went around for several days with his left
arm in woollen bandages. Into these, just before the appointed
hour, he slipped a dagger; he then claimed to have discovered
a plot, and was admitted to Domitian's bedroom; he produced
a list of names, and then suddenly stabbed Domitian in the
groin while he was reading it. Domitian put up a good fight,
but succumbed to seven further stabs, his assailants being a

subaltern named Clodianus, Parthenius' freedman Maximus, the head chamberlain Satur, and one of the imperial gladiators. The boy who was as usual attending to the household gods in the bedroom witnessed the murder and later described it in some detail. On receiving the first blow, Domitian screamed at the boy to hand him the dagger which was kept under his pillow and then call for the servants; the dagger, however, proved to have no blade, and all the doors were locked. Domitian grabbed Stephanus and pulled him to the ground, and after cutting his own fingers in a prolonged effort to disarm him he began clawing at his eyes.

He died on 18 September at the age of forty-four, after reigning not much more than fourteen years.[17] The body was carried away on a common litter by the public undertakers, as though he were a pauper, and was cremated by his old nurse Phyllis in her garden on the Via Latina. She secretly took the ashes to the Temple of the Flavians and mixed them with those of Titus' daughter Julia, who had also been one of her charges.

18. Domitian was tall, with a ruddy complexion, large and rather weak eyes, and not at all an imperious expression. He was moreover handsome and comely, especially in his youth, in all parts of his body except for his feet, which had hammer toes. Later on he became disfigured by a bald head, a paunchy stomach and thin legs, which as a result of protracted illness grew spindly. He was so conscious of his handsome features that he once told the Senate, 'Hitherto my intentions and my face have been equally acceptable to you.' He was so distressed by his baldness that he took it as a personal insult if anyone, whether they were joking or not, brought up the subject even when talking of someone else. All the same, in his manual *Care of the Hair*, which he dedicated to a friend, he quoted by way of mutual consolation, 'Cannot you see that I too have a tall and beautiful person?',[18] and added the following comment: 'Yet my hair will go the same way, and I am resigned to having an old man's head before my time. How pleasant it is to be elegant, yet how quickly that stage passes!'

19. Domitian hated to exert himself. While in Rome he hardly ever went for a walk, and during campaigns and travels he

seldom rode a horse, but almost always used a litter. Weapons did not interest him, though he was an exceptionally keen archer. He shot hundreds of wild animals on his Alban estate, and many eyewitnesses report that he sometimes brought down a quarry with two successive arrows so dexterously placed in the head as to resemble horns. Occasionally he would tell a slave to post himself at a distance and hold out one hand; he then shot arrows between his fingers with amazing skill.

20. At the beginning of his reign he abandoned the study of literature, even though he went to a great deal of trouble and expense in restocking the burned-out libraries, hunting all over for lost volumes and sending people to Alexandria to transcribe and correct them. No longer bothering with either history or poetry or even the rudiments of a style, he now read nothing but Tiberius' notebooks and official memoirs, and let secretaries polish his own correspondence, edicts and speeches. Still, Domitian had a lively turn of phrase, and some of his remarks are well worth recording. Once he said, 'Ah, to be as good-looking as Maecius thinks he is!', and on another occasion he compared a friend's red hair, which was turning white, to 'mead spilt on snow'.

21. He also claimed that all emperors are necessarily wretched, since only their assassination can convince the public that the conspiracies against their lives are real. His chief relaxation at all hours, even in the morning and on working days, was to throw dice. He used to bathe before noon, and then eat such an enormous lunch that a Matian apple and a small pitcher of wine generally contented him at dinner. His many large banquets were never prolonged past sunset or allowed to develop into drinking bouts, and he spent the rest of the day strolling idly by himself in a quiet part of the palace.

22. Domitian was extremely lustful, and called his sexual activities 'bed wrestling', as though they were a sport. Some say that he would depilate his concubines himself and go swimming with the commonest of common prostitutes. He had been offered the hand of his brother's daughter Julia when she was still a virgin, but persistently refused to marry her on account of his infatuation for Domitia. Later, when she was married to

another, he seduced her, though Titus was still alive, and after both her father and her husband[19] were dead he demonstrated his love for her so openly and ardently that in the end she became pregnant by him and died as the result of an abortion which he forced on her.

23. Though the general public greeted the news of Domitian's fate with indifference, it deeply affected the troops, who at once began to speak of him as Divus – they would have avenged him had anyone given them a lead – and insisted that his assassins should be brought to justice. The senators, on the other hand, were delighted, and thronged to denounce Domitian in the Senate House with bitter and insulting cries. Then, sending for ladders, they had his images and the votive shields engraved with his likeness brought smashing down, and ended by decreeing that all inscriptions referring to him must be effaced and all records of his reign obliterated.

A few months before the murder, a raven perched on the Capitol and croaked out the words 'All will be well!' – a portent which some wag explained in the following verse:

> There was a raven, strange to tell,
>   Perched upon Jove's own gable, whence
> He tried to tell us 'All is well!' –
>   But had to use the future tense.

Domitian is said to have dreamed that a golden hump sprouted from his back, deducing from this that the standing of the commonwealth would be far richer and happier when he had gone; and soon the wisdom and restraint of his successors proved him right.

Glossary of Terms

advocate A trained orator who spoke on behalf of the plaintiff or defendant in trials.

aedile A Roman civic official, concerned especially with the upkeep of the city, regulation of markets, oversight of the water and grain supply, and similar issues; aediles ranked above quaestors and below praetors.

amphora A large two-handled jar normally used for the transport and storage of wine, oil and other goods.

Atellan farce A traditional genre of native Italian plays that featured stock characters in slapstick situations.

augur An official diviner in the Roman tradition, trained in the interpretation of auspices; augurs constituted one of the chief colleges of public priests.

aureus Plural, aurei; see 'coins'.

auspices A form of divination based on the observation of birds and used to determine whether the gods approved or disapproved of a proposed action. Roman magistrates took the auspices before every major decision affecting the Roman people: elections, political assemblies, and battles. Auspices originally were taken from the flight patterns of birds, but by the historical period they were normally based on the eating patterns of chickens that were kept on hand for this purpose: it was a good omen if they ate greedily, and a bad omen if they refused their food.

auxiliaries Non-citizen troops serving with the Roman army; from the reign of Augustus on, they constituted a formal and permanent supplement to the citizen legions.

bireme See 'trireme'.

censor In the republican period, two censors were elected every five years to conduct a census, review the membership of the Senate and the equestrian order, and oversee public morals. The election of censors became very irregular in the late republic and ceased entirely after 22 BC; thereafter the emperors gradually assumed their functions.

centumviral court Literally, 'the court of 100 men', even though it numbered 105 men in the late republic and 180 in the empire; it dealt with cases of inheritance and other aspects of property rights.

centurion The commander of a century, a military unit of eighty men; centurions were the main professional officers of the Roman army, often promoted from the ranks.

civic crown A wreath of oak leaves, used as a Roman military decoration; awarded for saving the life of a fellow citizen in battle.

cognomen Plural, cognomina; see 'names'.

cohort A general word for a military unit, especially a subdivision of a legion; there were ten cohorts in a legion, each notionally comprising 480 men.

coins The sestertius was the basic Roman monetary unit used for expressing sums of money. In the mid first century BC, three sesterces a day was the normal wage for an unskilled labourer (Cicero, *Pro Roscio* 28); in the early empire, the annual salary for an ordinary legionary was 900 sesterces. There were four sesterces to a silver denarius, and twenty-five denarii (or 100 sesterces) to a gold aureus.

colony A new foundation of Roman citizens established under the authority of officials in Rome; in the imperial period, it became increasingly common for pre-existing settlements to be given colonial status, sometimes with the addition of new settlers, so that their inhabitants acquired Roman citizenship. Both Caesar and Augustus used colonial foundations as a way to settle their veterans.

consul The chief executive official in the Roman republican constitution; traditionally, two consuls were elected each year, so that the annual consulships could be used for dating purposes: 'in the consulship of so-and-so and so-and-so'. This practice continued in the imperial period, although the position of consul became largely honorary; it also became customary for the initial consuls of the year to resign before the end of their terms in favour of replacements ('suffect consuls'). Provincial governorships were normally held by men of either consular or praetorian rank.

curule chair The official Roman chair of state, inlaid with ivory and used by the higher magistrates on formal occasions.

denarius Plural, denarii; see 'coins'.

dictator Traditionally, a single executive official in the Roman republican constitution, appointed for a term of six months in times of crisis; Sulla and Caesar, by holding the dictatorship for years at a time, transformed the office into something approaching a monarchy.

divus A Latin word meaning 'god', an alternative to the more common word *deus*; in the imperial period, used almost exclusively as a title for emperors who were officially deified after their deaths.

Eagle The standard of a Roman legion.

edict A formal proclamation issued by a Roman civic official.

Eleusinian Mysteries Secret initiations in honour of the goddesses Demeter and Kore, held at the town of Eleusis near Athens.

empire A word used in three distinct but overlapping senses. Geographically, it describes the territory ruled by Rome; constitutionally, it denotes the system of government in which supreme power lay in the hands of one man; chronologically, it refers to the period of Roman history in which this system of government was operative (conventionally said to start in 31 BC, with the defeat of Antony by Augustus).

eques Literally, 'horseman' or 'knight' (plural, *equites*); the term designated a member of the equestrian order, the second tier of the Roman elite. Although in the republican period *equites* by definition did not hold political office, in the early imperial period they began to fill an increasing number of administrative positions and military commands. *Equites* had to possess property worth at least 400,000 sesterces, and had the right to wear a gold ring as a sign of their status.

fasces The bundle of rods that symbolized the authority of the senior Roman civic officials.

flamen A traditional Roman priest; unlike pontifices and augurs, flamens were assigned to the worship of individual gods – Jupiter especially.

freedman A slave freed by his owner, to whom he then owed various obligations and for whom he often worked as an agent or representative.

genius A man's divine alter ego or guardian spirit; the *genius* of the head of a household traditionally received offerings from that man's dependants.

grammaticus A professional teacher of language and literature, especially poetry; *grammatici* were particularly known for their mastery of minute details of linguistic usage and mythology.

haruspex A diviner of Etruscan origin who specialized in the interpretation of thunder, omens (unusual happenings of any sort) and especially the entrails of sacrificed animals; plural, haruspices.

Ides See 'time-reckoning'.

imperator A Latin word meaning literally 'commander'. It was originally bestowed on a victorious general by the acclamation of his troops, but was granted to Caesar as a permanent title and adopted by Octavian as his praenomen. It gradually came to function as one of the imperial titles, whence its modern derivative 'emperor'.

Kalends See 'time-reckoning'.

legate A representative of a Roman official who exercised command under that official's authority. Legates served most often as army commanders, but from Augustus on emperors governed their personal provinces through legates as well.

legion The largest division of the Roman army. Only Roman citizens could serve in a legion; non-citizens served in the auxiliaries. By the late republic, a legion notionally consisted of ten cohorts, each containing six centuries of eighty men, for a total strength of 4,800. Each legion had its own commander and title, which consisted of a number and a name, e.g. Legio V Alauda.

lictor An attendant of Roman public officials, who normally carried the fasces.

Lupercalia An ancient Roman festival celebrated on 15 February by an association of men called the Luperci; after sacrificing goats, they would race through the city, naked except for a covering of goatskin, striking the bystanders with goatskin thongs.

maiestas A Latin word meaning 'majesty'; in legal terminology, an abbreviation for the phrase *maiestas minuta*, 'the diminution of the majesty of the Roman people', a criminal category that covered any sort of treason or dereliction of duty. In the imperial period, it also came to cover disrespect towards the emperor.

master of the horse In the Roman republican constitution, the second-in-command to a dictator.

military tribune The senior officers of the Roman army, serving just below the legionary commander; there were normally six to a legion.

names Traditional Roman names for men had three elements: first, the praenomen or personal name (e.g. Gaius); second, the nomen or family name (e.g. Julius); third, the cognomen, which usually distinguished a particular branch of the larger family (e.g. Caesar). The number of traditional praenomina was very small, and they were therefore normally abbreviated; the standard abbreviations are provided in the List of Abbreviations. Women traditionally had only one name, the nomen with the feminine ending (e.g. Julia). Slaves had only a personal name; when freed, they adopted the praenomen and nomen of their former masters, and retained their personal name as a cognomen. Among the aristocrats of the early imperial period, especially in the imperial family itself, it became fashionable to deviate from these norms in order to include more family names; thus, for example, the emperor Tiberius' younger brother was given the name Nero, the cognomen of his paternal grandfather, in the place of a traditional praenomen. Similarly, elite women began to have two names, the second derived from a cognomen (e.g. Livia Drusilla) or some other family name (e.g. Domitia Lepida).

nomen Plural, nomina; see 'names'.

Nones See 'time-reckoning'.

optimates A term loosely used for political leaders in the first century BC who supported the political dominance of the Senate and the ascendancy of the established elite; defined in opposition to *populares*.

ovation A victory procession of a lower grade than a triumph.

pantomime A sophisticated art form in which a solo dancer enacted stories from myth to musical accompaniment; introduced at Rome in 22 BC, it became widely popular in the imperial period.

Papian–Poppaean Law A law passed in AD 9 which modified and supplemented Augustus' original marriage legislation of 18 BC (see *Aug.* 34); it granted certain benefits and privileges to people with three (or in some cases four) children.

patrician An elite hereditary status in Rome, contrasted with plebeian status. In archaic Rome patricians monopolized the most powerful public offices, but by the late republic only a few largely ceremonial positions were reserved for them, and the ruling elite consisted of both patrician and plebeian families.

Pedian Law A law passed in 43 BC, sponsored by Q. Pedius but promoted by Octavian, that set up a special court to try the assassins of Julius Caesar (see *Aug.* 10); all were condemned *in absentia*.

plebeian A hereditary status in Rome; traditionally, plebeians were subordinate to patricians, but by the late republic the legal distinction was for most purposes no longer significant; the term came instead to denote 'lower class' or 'common'.

pontifex A member of one of the main colleges of public priests in Rome; the pontifices had general oversight of public cult, the calendar and burial law. The president of the college was the pontifex maximus, a position always held by the emperor from Augustus on.

populares A term loosely used for political leaders in the first century BC who appealed to the interests of groups outside the Senate and used popular support to further their political careers (singular, *popularis*); defined in opposition to optimates.

praenomen Plural, praenomina; see 'names'.

praetor The second highest of the civic officials in the Roman republican constitution; praetors had particular oversight over judicial matters. From 81 BC on, eight praetors were elected every year; Augustus raised the number to first ten and then twelve. Provincial governorships were normally held by men of either consular or praetorian rank.

praetorians Members of a permanent military force (originally nine cohorts, but the number increased over the years) established by Augustus to serve as his bodyguard and suppress disturbances in the city of Rome. They were under the command of either one or two equestrian officers known as praetorian prefects.

prefect of the city A senatorial officer, first appointed by Augustus, with the duty of maintaining peace and order in the city of Rome; he presided over his own court, and had command of the urban cohorts.

primipilaris In a Roman legion, the centurion of the first century of the first cohort; the position brought with it enough pay and benefits that a *primipilaris* was often able on retirement to obtain equestrian status.

princeps Latin word meaning 'first', especially 'first in authority, chief'; by Suetonius' time, used as a term for the emperor.

procurator A Latin word simply meaning 'supervisor', used for a variety of officials; the most important were the non-senatorial governors of certain provinces (including Egypt) and the emperor's financial agents in provinces with senatorial governors.

publicans The collection of taxes in republican Rome was contracted out to the highest bidders, who would make their profits out of the funds that they collected; such businessmen were called 'publicans', because they were in charge of public revenues.

quaestor The lowest ranked of the major civic officials in the Roman republican constitution; from 81 BC on there were normally twenty quaestors elected each year. Quaestors generally served as assistants to senior officials.

Quindecimviri See 'Sibylline Books'.

Quinquatrus A five-day festival in honour of the goddess Minerva, held on 19–23 March.

quinquereme See 'trireme'.

republic The conventional name given to the Roman system of government in which popularly elected annual officials held the chief executive power and the Senate acted as the chief policy-making body. 'The republic' is also used to denote the period of Rome's history during which this system of government was operative, conventionally 510–31 BC; the period 133–31 BC is known as the 'late republic'.

Saturnalia An ancient festival in honour of the god Saturn. The chief rituals took place on 17 December, but the holiday continued for three days thereafter; Caligula added a fourth day, and Claudius a fifth. The festival was marked by the exchange of gifts and the relaxation of normal standards of propriety.

Senate A deliberative body in Rome consisting in practice of all current and former civic officials. In the republican constitution, although the Senate's role was in theory merely advisory, it acted in effect as the chief policy-making body; under the emperors its effective power was considerably reduced, although senators continued individually and collectively to play a major role in the administration of the empire. Senators had the right to wear certain distinctive items of clothing, most notably togas bordered with purple stripes.

sesterces See 'coins'.

Sibylline Books An official collection of Greek oracles that was consulted at times of crisis; the priests in charge were called the Quindecimviri ('the Fifteen Men').

talent A Greek unit of weight; a talent of silver (approximately 26 kg according to one standard) was used as a currency unit for very large sums.

time-reckoning The Romans designated years not by reference to a fixed point but by the names of the annual consuls; for example, the emperor Claudius was in Roman reckoning born not 'in 10 BC' but 'in the consulship of Iullus Antonius and Fabius Africanus'. The days of the month were not numbered sequentially, but were reckoned from three fixed days: the Kalends, which always fell on the 1st, the Nones, which fell in some months on the 5th and in others on the 7th, and the Ides, which fell in some months on the 13th and in others (including March) on the 15th. The Kalends of January was the start of the new year; the consuls who took office on that date were the ones who gave their name to the year. The Roman day from sunrise to sunset was divided into twelve hours, the seventh hour beginning at noon; the hours were of varying length depending on the length of the day. The night was similarly divided into four watches.

tribe A division of the Roman citizen body that served as the voting unit in political elections as well as the basis for the census. Every Roman citizen had to belong to a tribe, even after tribes lost their chief political function with the abolition of popular elections in AD 15.

tribune of the people A civic official in the Roman republican constitution, charged especially with upholding the rights of the people; a tribune could veto any proposed legislation that he considered harmful to the people, and his person was sacrosanct: that is, no physical force was to be brought against him. Ten tribunes were elected each year. See also 'military tribune'.

trireme The standard warship of antiquity, with three banks of oars arranged so that there were three men to an oar. The bireme similarly had two men to an oar, the quadrireme four, and the quinquereme five.

triumph A major Roman ceremony in which a general who had won an important victory processed with his troops through the city to the temple of Jupiter on the Capitoline Hill. In the imperial period, when the right to celebrate a triumph was limited to emperors and members of their immediate families, it became customary to award other victorious commanders the decorations worn by a triumphing general, in lieu of an actual triumph.

Troy Game A traditional pageant in the form of a sham fight performed by young boys on horseback; it was thought to have been established by the Trojan hero Aeneas.

urban cohorts The police force of Rome, established by Augustus and placed under the command of the prefect of the city.

Vestal Virgins The six priestesses of the goddess Vesta, who enjoyed a significant public role and important privileges.

Glossary of Place Names in Rome

Numbers in parentheses refer to Map 9.

Aemilian quarter A poor residential district in the southern Campus Martius.

Amphitheatre An oval arena with banks of seats on all sides, used especially for gladiatorial performances. The first permanent amphitheatre in Rome was built by T. Statilius Taurus in 29 BC, probably in the southern Campus Martius; it burned down in the fire of AD 64. The Flavian Amphitheatre (18), better known as the Colosseum, was begun by Vespasian in the 70s and dedicated by Titus in AD 80.

Atrium of Liberty A building north of the Forum of Caesar, containing the offices of the censors; the original structure was rebuilt and enlarged by C. Asinius Pollio, who added a public library.

Aventine The southernmost hill of Rome.

Basilica Julia (6) A large colonnaded hall on the south side of the Forum, begun by Julius Caesar and rebuilt by Augustus, who dedicated it in the names of his adopted sons Gaius and Lucius in AD 12.

Baths of Nero (33) The second public baths in Rome, built in the early 60s AD on the Campus Martius; the first baths (31), built by Agrippa, were nearby.

Baths of Titus (19) Built near the Flavian Amphitheatre in AD 80.

Caelian One of the hills of Rome, on the south-eastern side of the city.

Campus Martius A large level area north-west of the Capitoline Hill, subject to flooding, and so relatively undeveloped until the mid first century BC.

Capitol (21) The great temple on the Capitoline Hill, dedicated to the chief patron deities of Rome, Jupiter Optimus Maximus ('Best and Greatest'), Juno and Minerva; also known as the Temple of Jupiter Capitolinus. The original archaic temple was burned down in the civil wars of 83 BC; its replacement was similarly burned down in the civil wars of AD 69, and again in a fire of AD 80.

Capitoline One of the hills of Rome, just east of the Forum.

Carinae A district on the south-western end of the Esquiline Hill, where many prominent citizens lived during the republic.

Circus An arena used for chariot races; Suetonius normally means the Circus Maximus, south of the Palatine.

Comitium (10) The chief place for political assemblies in Rome, off the western end of the Forum in front of the Senate House.

Curtian Lake A sacred site in the Forum; by the time of Augustus it was apparently a sort of pit.

Diribitorium (30) A large roofed building in the Campus Martius, at the south end of the Saepta, used for the sorting of votes; begun by Agrippa and completed by Augustus in 7 BC.

Esquiline One of the hills of Rome, on the eastern side of the city.

Forum The Forum Romanum, low ground between the Capitoline, Palatine and Quirinal hills; the traditional centre of public life.

Forum of Augustus (15) A colonnaded square centring on the Temple of Mars Ultor, north-east of the Forum of Caesar; begun probably in the mid 20s BC, and dedicated in 2 BC.

Forum of Caesar (14) A colonnaded square centring on the Temple of Venus Genetrix, just north of the Forum Romanum; dedicated by Caesar in 46 BC, but only completed by Augustus.

Forum of Nerva (13) A long rectangular colonnaded square, filling in the space between the Forum of Augustus and the Temple of Peace; built by Domitian, but dedicated by Nerva early in AD 97.

Gardens of Maecenas An estate on the Esquiline Hill laid out by Maecenas and bequeathed to the imperial family.

Gemonian Stairs A flight of steps on the Capitoline Hill on which the bodies of executed criminals were flung; the name was popularly connected with the Latin verb *gemere*, 'to moan'.

Grove of Libitina A sacred grove containing the shrine of Libitina, the goddess of funerals, which served as a sort of funeral parlour for Rome; apparently on the Esquiline, although the exact location is unknown.

Island of Aesculapius (25) A shrine of the healing god on an island in the Tiber; it functioned as a quasi-hospital, where the ill or injured went for cures.

Janiculum A hill on the west bank of the Tiber.

Lamian Gardens An estate on the Esquiline Hill, imperial property since the reign of Tiberius.

Lesser Codeta A marshy region in the Campus Martius.

Mausoleum of Augustus A monumental tomb near the Via Flaminia, at the northern end of the Campus Martius; constructed by Augustus between 28 and 23 BC.

Odeum of Domitian (32) A theatre-like structure for musical performances, built by Domitian to the north of the Theatre of Pompey.

Palatine One of the hills of Rome, in the centre of the city; in the late republic it was a well-to-do residential neighbourhood, but over the course of the first century AD the steadily expanding imperial residences gradually took over. As a result, the name Palatium (whence the modern 'palace') came to denote the whole complex of buildings used by the emperors and their families.

Pincian A hill north of the city, east of the Via Flaminia.

Portico of Gaius and Lucius (2) A double arch on the eastern end of the Forum, connecting the Temple of Divus Julius with the Basilica Aemilia to the north.

Portico of Livia A colonnade on the Esquiline, dedicated in 7 BC.

Portico of Octavia (26) A colonnaded square south of the Campus Martius, enclosing two earlier temples; dedicated sometime after 27 BC.

praetorian camp The barracks of the praetorian guard, built by Tiberius in AD 21–3 at the instigation of Sejanus; on the far north-eastern edge of the city.

Quirinal One of the hills of Rome, on the northern side of the city.

Regia (1) The 'Royal House' at the eastern end of the Forum, which served as the official residence of the pontifex maximus.

Rostra (8) The speaker's platform in the western end of the Forum, adjacent to the Comitium; a new speaker's platform was later built in front of the temple of Divus Julius.

Sacred Way A street adjacent to the Forum.

Saepta (34) Literally, 'Enclosures'; originally a structure in the Campus Martius where elections took place, but replaced by an elaborate rectangular portico planned by Caesar and completed by Agrippa in 26 BC.

Senate House (11) The usual meeting place of the Senate, north of the Forum.

Stadium of Domitian A racetrack on the Campus Martius.

Subura A low-lying region north-east of the Forum.

Tarpeian Rock A cliff on the Capitoline Hill.

Temple of Apollo (23) A temple south of the Campus Martius, built in the 430s BC.

Temple of Apollo Palatine (17) A temple built by Augustus adjacent to his home on the Palatine; dedicated in 28 BC.

Temple of Castor and Pollux (5) A temple on the south side of the

Forum, originally built in the early fifth century BC and rebuilt by Tiberius in AD 6.

Temple of Concord (9) A temple on the north-west corner of the Forum; built originally in the mid fourth century BC, restored and rededicated by Tiberius in AD 10.

Temple of Diana An ancient temple on the Aventine Hill, restored under Augustus by L. Cornificius.

Temple of Divus Augustus A temple located somewhere on the north-west side of the Palatine Hill; begun by Tiberius, but left either uncompleted or undedicated.

Temple of Divus Claudius (20) A temple on the Caelian Hill; begun by Agrippina the younger and completed by Vespasian.

Temple of Divus Julius (3) A temple dedicated in 29 BC at the eastern end of the Forum, adjacent to the Regia.

Temple of the Flavians A structure on the Quirinal built by Domitian in the early 90s AD, apparently for use as a family tomb.

Temple of Hercules and the Muses (27) A temple south of the Campus Martius; originally built in the 180s BC, restored and surrounded with a portico by L. Marcius Philippus in 29 BC.

Temple of Janus Quirinus (12) An ancient temple north of the Forum, whose gates were closed as a sign that Rome was at peace.

Temple of Jupiter Capitolinus See 'Capitol'.

Temple of Jupiter Optimus Maximus See 'Capitol'.

Temple of Jupiter Tonans (22) A temple on the Capitoline Hill built by Augustus in honour of Jupiter 'the Thunderer' (see *Aug.* 29); dedicated in 22 BC.

Temple of Mars Ultor (15) A temple built by Augustus in honour of Mars 'the Avenger' and dedicated in 2 BC; the centrepiece of the Forum of Augustus.

Temple of Peace (16) A temple with an attached colonnade north-east of the Forum; built by Vespasian and dedicated in AD 75.

Temple of Saturn (7) An ancient temple on the south-west corner of the Forum, used as a public treasury; rebuilt in 42 BC by L. Munatius Plancus.

Temple of Venus Genetrix (14) A temple built by Julius Caesar in honour of Venus 'the Ancestress' (see *Jul.* 6 with the note) and dedicated in 46 BC; the centrepiece of the Forum of Caesar.

Temple of Vesta (4) A small round shrine of the goddess of the hearth fire at the eastern end of the Forum.

Theatre of Balbus (28) A theatre on the southern Campus Martius built by L. Cornelius Balbus the younger and dedicated in 13 BC.

Theatre of Marcellus (24) A theatre built by Augustus in memory of his nephew Marcellus adjacent to the Capitoline Hill; dedicated in 13 BC.

Theatre of Pompey (29) The first permanent theatre in Rome, constructed on the Campus Martius in 55 BC; a large colonnaded square was attached to its rear.

Triumphal Gate The gate through which generals celebrating triumphs entered Rome; its location is unknown, but it seems to have been in the vicinity of the Campus Martius.

Vatican quarter A region of Rome across the Tiber from the main part of the city, the site of a circus constructed by Gaius.

Velabrum A low-lying area between the Capitoline and Palatine hills.

Via Appia A road leading south-east from Rome to Capua, later extended to Brundisium.

Via Aurelia A road leading west from Rome and then north along the west coast of Italy.

Via Flaminia A road leading north from Rome to Ariminium on the Adriatic coast of Italy; within the city, it ran along the eastern edge of the Campus Martius.

Via Latina A road branching east off the Via Appia.

Via Nomentana A local road branching east off the Via Salaria.

Via Salaria A road leading north from Rome to Reate, and then on to the Adriatic coast.

Key to Maps

The ancient name (with brief identifications and, where appropriate, modern equivalents in parentheses) is followed by the map number.

Achaia (province; S. Greece) 5, 8
Actium (promontory; W. Greece) 5, 8
Aenaria (island; Ischia) 2
Aetna (volcano; Etna) 1
Aetolia (region; W. Greece) 5
Africa (province; Tunisia and W. Libya) 1, 8
Alani (people; north of the Caucasus) 8
Alban Mount (Monte Cavo) 2
Alexandria (city; El Iskandariya) 7, 8
Allobroges (people; S. France) 3
Anio (river; Aniene) 2
Anticyra (town; Antikyra) 5
Antioch (city; Antakya) 7, 8
Antium (town; Anzio) 2
Apennine Mountains 1
Apollonia (town; in Albania) 5
Apulia (region of S.E. Italy; Puglia) 1
Aquileia (town; near Venice) 1
Aquitania (province; S.W. France) 3, 8
Arcadia (region; S. Greece) 5
Arelate (town; Arles) 3
Aricia (town; Arricia) 2

Ariminum (town; Rimini) 1
Armenia (kingdom and province; E. Turkey, Armenia) 7, 8
Arverni (people; S. France) 3
Asia (province; W. Turkey) 6, 8
Astura (town; Astura) 2
Asturia (region; N.W. Spain) 3
Athens (city) 5, 8
Avernus (lake) 2

Baiae (town; Baia) 2
Balearic Islands 3
Batavi (people; S. Netherlands) 4
Bauli (town) 2
Beneventum (town; Benevento) 2
Betriacum (town, also spelled 'Bedriacum'; near Calvatone) 1
Bithynia (kingdom, province from 75 BC; N.W. Turkey) 6, 8
Bononia (town; Bologna) 1
Bovillae (town; near Frattochie) 2
Breuci (people; Croatia) 1
Britain (province from AD 43) 3, 8

Brixellum (town; Bescello) 1
Bructeri (people; N.W.
  Germany) 4
Brundisium (town; Brindisi) 1, 8
Byzantium (town; Istanbul) 6

Calagurris (town; Calahorra) 3
Campania (region) 1, 2
Cantabria (region; N. Spain) 3
Canusium (town; Canosa) 1
Cappadocia (kingdom, province
  from AD 17; central Turkey)
  6, 8
Capreae (island; Capri) 2
Capua (city; Santa Maria Capua
  Vetere) 2, 8
Carrhae (town; S. Turkey) 7
Carthage (city) 1, 8
Carthago Nova (town;
  Cartagena) 3
Caspian Gates (mountain pass;
  Dariel Pass) 7
Cassiope (town; on N. coast of
  Corfu) 5
Cauchi (people; N.W. Germany)
  4
Ceraunian Mountains (S.
  Albania) 5
Chatti (people; W. Germany) 4
Chios (island) 6
Cilicia (province; S.E. Turkey) 6,
  8
Circeii (town; Circeo) 2
Cisalpine Gaul (province to
  42 BC; N. Italy) 1, 8
Clunia (town; Coruña del
  Conde) 3
Colonia Agrippinensis (town;
  Cologne) 4
Commagene (kingdom, province
  from AD 42; S. Turkey) 7
Confluens (town; Koblenz) 4

Corduba (town; Cordova) 3, 8
Corfinium (town; Corfinio) 1
Corinth (city) 5, 8
Cosa (town) 1
Cottian Alps (W. Alps) 3
Cremona (town) 1, 8
Crete (island) 8
Cutiliae (town; Bagni di
  Paterno) 2
Cyrenaica (region; N.E. Libya) 8
Cyzicus (town; Bal Kiz) 6

Dacia (region, province from AD
  106; Romania) 5, 8
Dalmatia (region; coast of
  Croatia) 1
Danube (river) 4, 5, 8
Delphi (sanctuary and town) 5
Dertosa (town; Tortosa) 3
Dyrrhachium (town; Durrës) 5,
  8

Egypt (kingdom, province from
  30 BC) 7, 8
Elbe (river) 4, 8
Eleusis (sanctuary and town) 5
Eryx (mountain) 1
Etruria (region; Tuscany) 1
Euphrates (river) 7, 8

Ferentium (town) 2
Fidenae (town; Castel Giubileo)
  2
Formiae (town; Formia) 2
Forum Appii (town) 2
Fucine Lake (Fucino) 2
Fundi (town; Fondi) 2
Further Spain (province; S.W.
  Spain) 3, 8

Gadara (town; Umm Keis) 7
Gades (town; Cadiz) 3, 8

Pandataria (island; Pantelleria)
2
Pannonia (province from AD 9;
W. Hungary, Croatia, N.
Serbia) 4, 8
Paphos (town; west coast of
Cyprus) 7
Parthia (kingdom; Iran, E. Iraq)
7, 8
Parthini (people; Albania) 5
Patavium (town; Padua) 1
Peloponnese (peninsula; S.
Greece) 5
Pergamum (city; Bergama) 6
Perusia (town; Perugia) 1
Pharmacussa (island) 6
Pharsalus (town) 5, 8
Philippi (town) 5
Picenum (region; central Italy)
1
Placentia (town; Piacenza) 1
Po (river) 1
Pollentia (town) 1
Pomptine Marshes 2
Pontia (island; Ponza) 2
Pontus (kingdom, province from
63 BC; N. Turkey) 8
Praeneste (town; Palestrina) 2
Puteoli (town; Pozzuoli) 2, 8
Pyrgi (town) 2

Raetia (province from 15 BC; E.
Switzerland) 4, 8
Ravenna (town) 1, 8
Reate (town; Rieti) 2
Rhegium (town; Reggio di
Calabria) 1
Rhine (river) 3, 4, 8
Rhodes (island; Rodos) 6
Rhône (river) 3
Rome (city) 1, 2, 8
Rubicon (river) 1

Sabines (people; central Italy) 2
Sabrata (town) 8
Salassi (people; N.W. Italy) 1
Samos (island) 6
Sardinia (island) 1, 3, 8
Sarmatians (people) 4
Scythia (region; north of the
Black Sea) 8
Sicily (island) 1, 8
Sinuessa (town; near
Mondragone) 2
Sparta (town; Sparti) 5
Spoletium (town; Spoleto) 2
Stoechades (islands; Iles
d'Hyères) 3
Surrentum (town; Sorrento) 2
Syracuse (city; Siracusa) 2
Syria (province) 7, 8

Tarichaeae (town) 7
Tarracina (town; Terracina) 2
Tarraco (town; Tarragona) 3, 8
Tarraconensian Spain (province;
E. and N. Spain) 3, 8
Tarsus (town) 6
Tegea (town) 5
Thasos (island) 5
Thessaly (region; central Greece) 5
Thrace (kingdom, province from
AD 46; N.E. Greece, S.E.
Bulgaria) 5, 6, 8
Thurii (town) 1
Thyatira (town; Akhisar) 6
Tiber (river) 1, 2
Tibur (town; Tivoli) 2
Tigris (river) 7, 8
Tolosa (town; Toulouse) 3
Tralles (town; Aydin) 6
Transalpine Gaul, *see* Gaul
Trebiae (town; Trevi) 1
Treveri (people; around Trier) 4
Troy (town; Hisarlik) 6

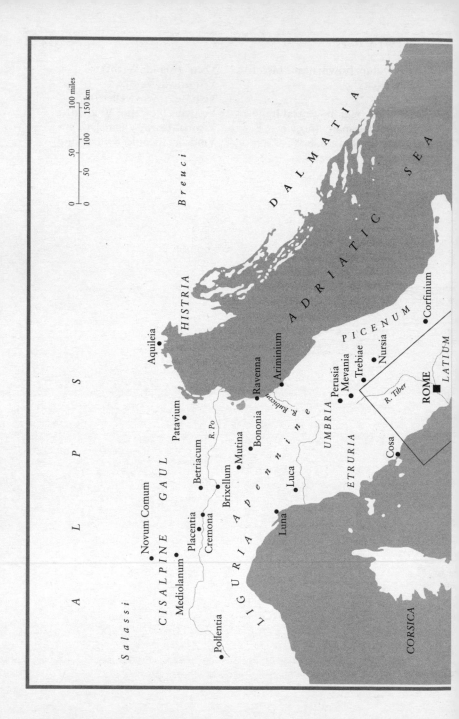

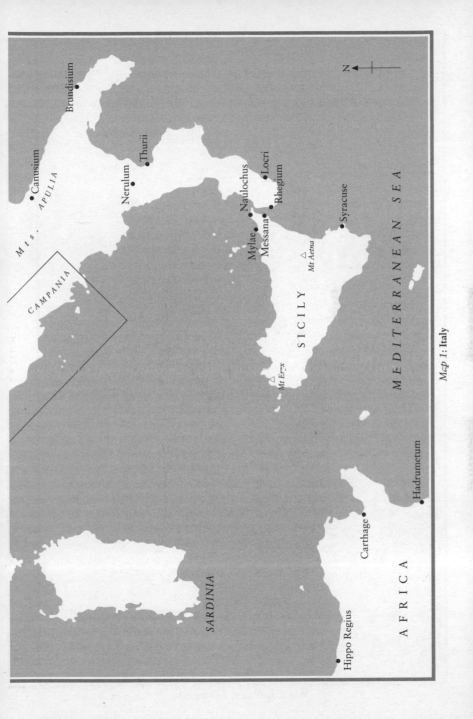

Map 1: Italy

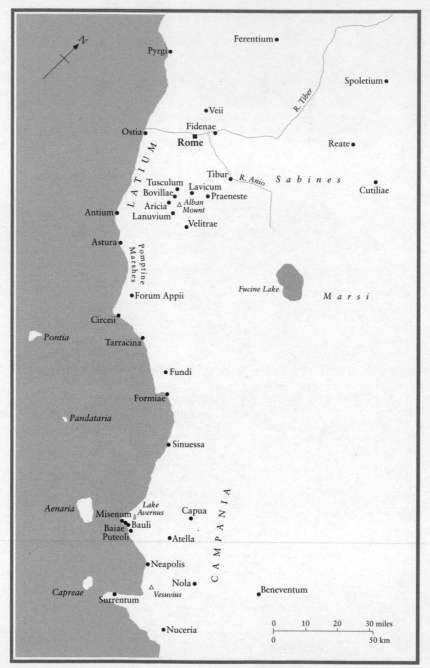

Map 2: Latium and Campania

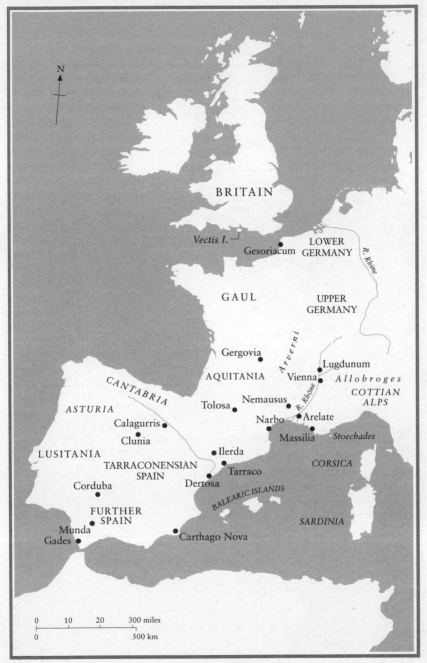

Map 3: **Western Europe**

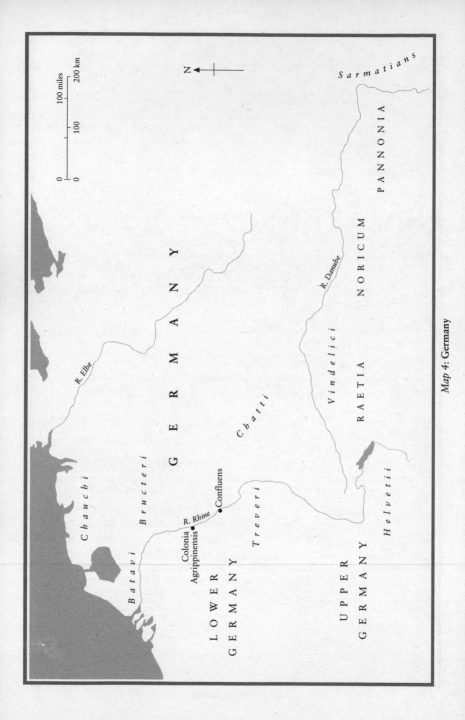

Map 4: Germany

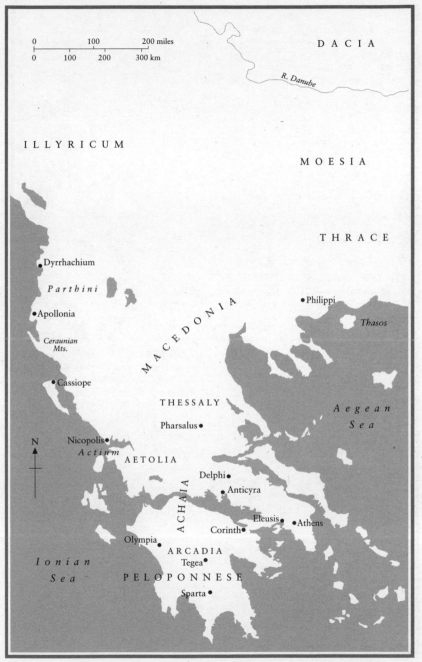

Map 5: **The Balkans**

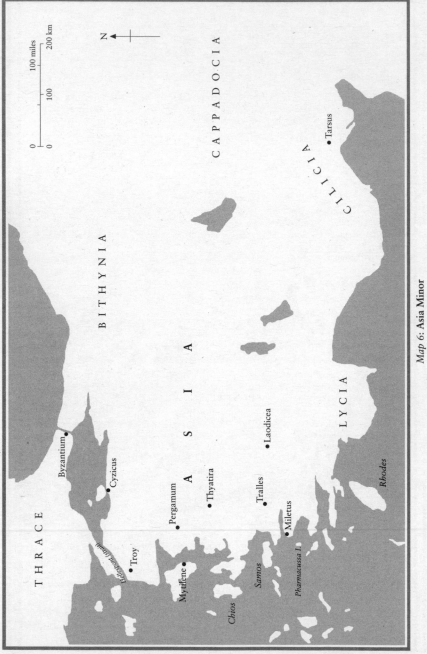

Map 6: **Asia Minor**

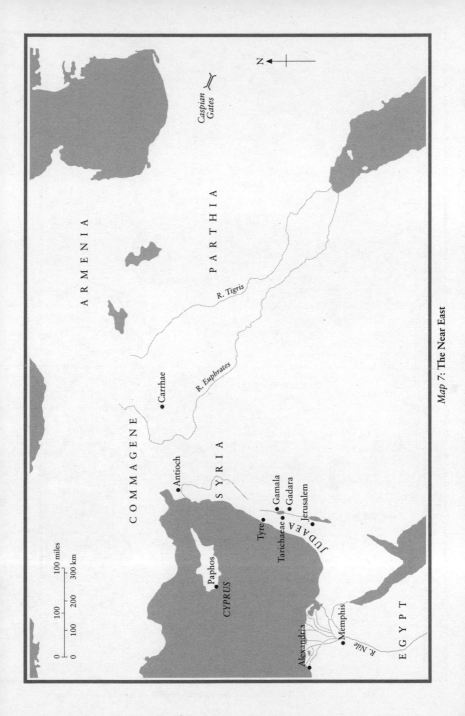

Map 7: The Near East

Map 8: **The Roman Empire at the death of Augustus**

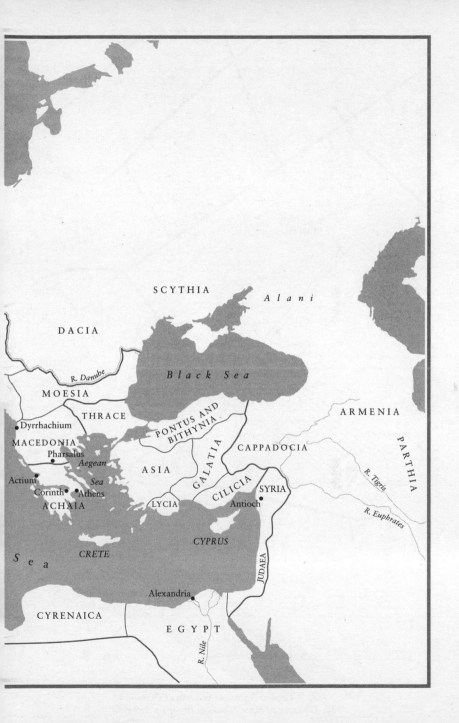

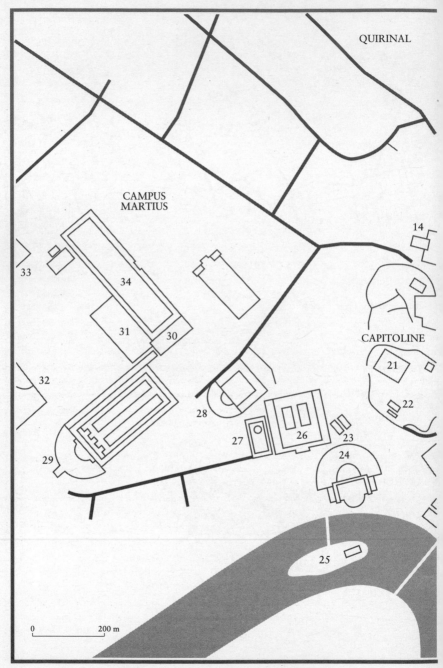

QUIRINAL

CAMPUS
MARTIUS

CAPITOLINE

14

33

34

31

30

32

21

28

22

27

26

23

29

24

25

0   200 m

Map 9: **Central Rome at the death of Domitian**
See Glossary of Place Names in Rome pp 319–323

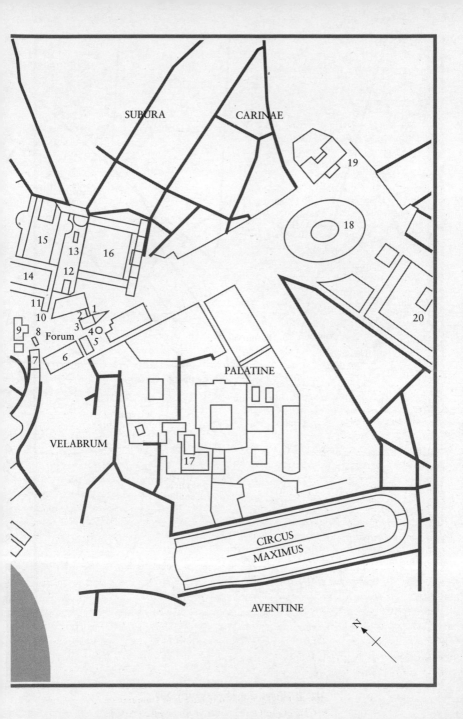

SUBURA

CARINAE

19

18

15

13

16

14

12

11

10

1

2

9

8

3

4

5

Forum

6

7

VELABRUM

PALATINE

17

20

CIRCUS
MAXIMUS

AVENTINE

N

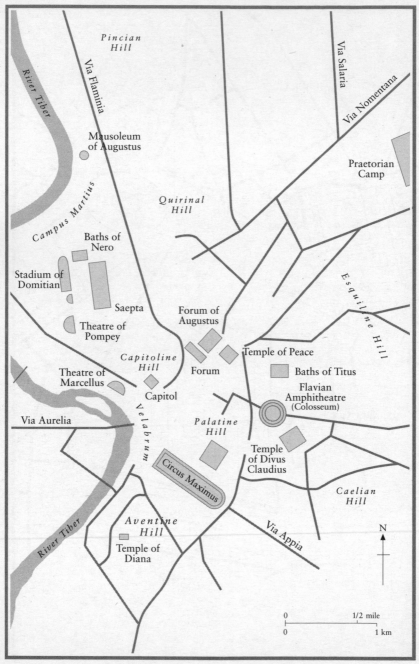

Map 10: **Rome in the first century A D**

A: The Family of Julius Caesar

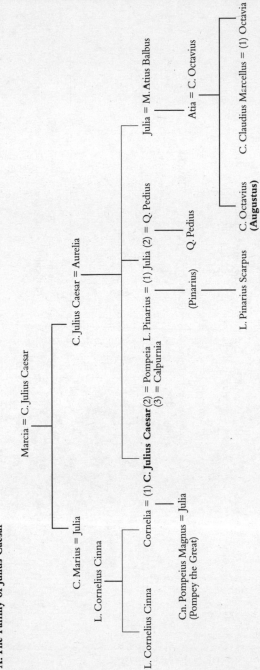

B: The Family of Augustus

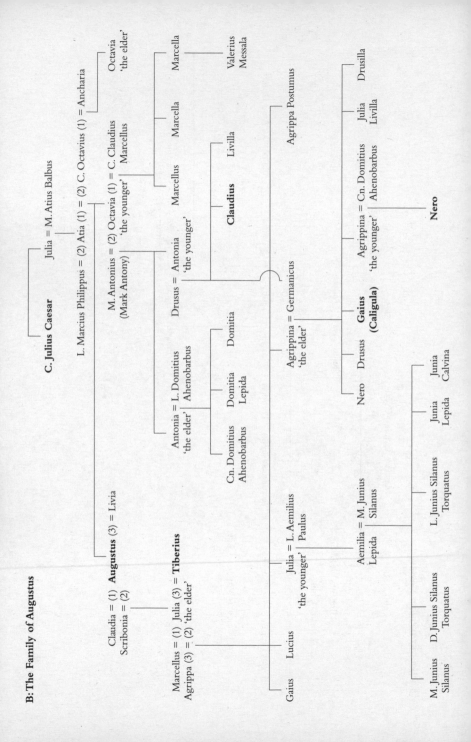

C: The Julio-Claudian Emperors

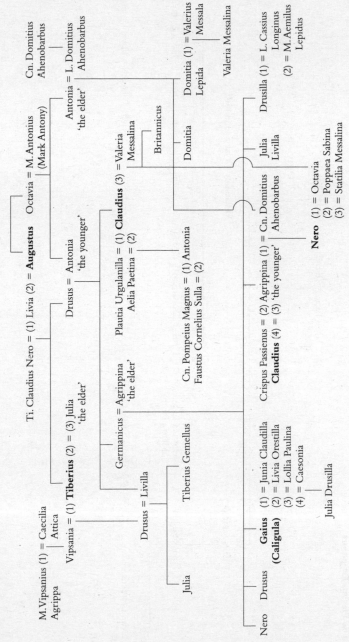

D: The Flavian Emperors

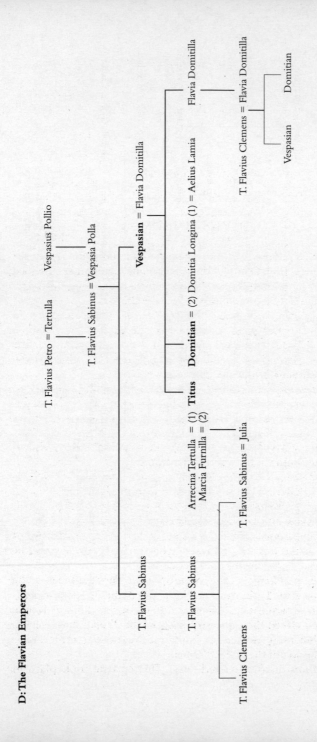

Notes

DIVUS JULIUS

1. *He lost his father . . . fifteen*: The beginning of the life is lost; see the Introduction, section 3. In it, Suetonius would have provided information about Caesar's family background, his full name (C. Julius Caesar), and his birth and childhood.

2. *opposing party*: L. Cornelius Sulla on the optimate side and L. Cornelius Cinna on the *popularis* side were the two leading figures in the Roman civil conflicts of the 80s BC; Sulla was the eventual victor, and as dictator (82–79 BC) he reformed the constitution to favour the optimates.

3. *many Mariuses . . . Caesar*: C. Marius, a great general and *popularis* leader, was one of the main instigators of the civil conflicts of the 80s BC; his wife was Julia, Caesar's aunt on his father's side.

4. *storming of Mytilene*: In 79 BC; Mytilene had supported Mithridates of Pontus in his war against Rome.

5. *a revolt headed by Marcus Lepidus*: M. Aemilius Lepidus, as consul in 78 BC, tried to overturn the political reforms of Sulla, and in 77 BC he led an armed revolt against the Senate; the revolt was crushed, and Lepidus died shortly thereafter.

6. *joined Sertorius*: From 80 to 72 BC Q. Sertorius, a supporter of Cinna in the 80s BC, led a guerrilla war in Spain against the senatorial government.

7. *descendant of kings . . . the goddess Venus*: The cognomen of the Marcii was the Latin word for 'king' (*rex*; plural, *reges*); according to tradition, Ancus Marcius was the fourth king of Rome. The Julii traced their ancestry back to the Trojan hero Aeneas through his son Ascanius or Julus, and Aeneas was according to myth the son of the godess Venus.

8. *desecration of these sacred rites*: This episode took place in

62–61 BC; the ceremony was in honour of Bona Dea, the 'Good Goddess', from which all men were strictly prohibited. See further section 74 below.

9. *the Latin colonies . . . citizenship*: The people living north of the Po, part of the province of Cisalpine Gaul, were given Latin rights, a sort of partial Roman citizenship, in 89 BC; after all the peoples south of the Po were given full Roman citizenship in the late 80s BC, those north of the Po began to demand the same status.

10. *cancelled the plan*: Since Caesar was aedile in 65 BC, these alleged conspiracies must date to late 66 and early 65 BC (Autronius' praenomen was in fact Publius, not Lucius). None of the writings mentioned by Suetonius survives, and the facts are very uncertain; according to Sallust (*Conspiracy of Catiline* 18–19), the two plots mentioned here were part of one conspiracy, masterminded by Cicero's great enemy Catiline.

11. *the heavenly twins . . . 'Castor's'*: In Greek myth, Castor and Pollux were the twin sons of Zeus; although the temple in the Forum was dedicated to both of them equally, people usually referred to it simply as the Temple of Castor.

12. *deposed their king . . . friend of Rome*: The king in question was Ptolemy XII Auletes, but Suetonius is mistaken about the events: although Crassus floated a proposal to annex Egypt at this time, Ptolemy's recognition by the Senate and expulsion from Alexandria did not take place until 59–58 BC.

13. *proscriptions . . . Cornelian laws*: After Sulla defeated his enemies in 82 BC, he outlawed ('proscribed') all those who had opposed him; the Cornelian laws are those he sponsored as dictator.

14. *the Catilinarian conspiracy*: A conspiracy under the leadership of L. Sergius Catilina that aimed at a violent change to the status quo; economic and social grievances were apparently the chief concerns of the conspirators, although their exact goals are unclear. For the main ancient accounts, see Cicero, *Against Catiline* 1–4, and Sallust, *The Conspiracy of Catiline*.

15. *a triple pact*: This is the so-called 'First Triumvirate', which as Suetonius makes clear was simply an informal political alliance between these three powerful and ambitious men.

16. *transferred from patrician to plebeian rank*: Clodius wanted the transfer in order to stand for the office of tribune of the people, which was open only to plebeians.

17. *Semiramis . . . Asia*: In Greek legend, Semiramis was a great Syrian queen of the distant past; the character derived from a

historical Assyrian queen of the late ninth century BC, Sammu-ramat. The Amazons were a mythic race of female warriors, usually located deep in Asia Minor.

18. *the following results*: Caesar was in Gaul from 58 to 50 BC; the seven books of his own account, *The Gallic War*, cover the first seven years; an eighth book by his officer A. Hirtius covers 51 BC, the last year of active campaigning. For his crossing of the Rhine (55 BC), see *Gallic War* 4.16–19; invasion of Britain (55 and 54 BC), 4.20–36 and 5.8–23; Gergovia (52 BC), 7.36–53; Titurius and Aurunculeius (54 BC), 5.24–37.

19. *offered him the hand . . . marry Pompey's daughter*: Pompey rejected both these proposals, which would have restored the marriage connection between the two men that had been lost with the death of Julia (54 BC).

20. *since Pompey . . . public treasury*: Subsequent to the popular decree granting Caesar the right to stand for the consulship in his absence (see above, section 26), Pompey, as consul in 52 BC, had sponsored another law requiring all candidates to stand in person; when Caesar's friends pointed out how damaging this law was to him, Pompey added a clause exempting Caesar, although it had no force since the law had already been passed and publicly recorded. M. Claudius Marcellus was consul in 51 BC.

21. *like Milo . . . armed men*: T. Annius Milo's men had killed P. Clodius Pulcher in a clash in 52 BC; Pompey had taken the unusual step of having soldiers stationed at the trial in order to prevent further disturbances.

22. *Cicero himself translated as follows*: Cicero, *On Duties* 3.82; the lines are Euripides' *Phoenician Women* 524–5. A more literal translation: 'If the law is to be violated, then it should be violated for the sake of ruling; in other matters cultivate piety.'

23. *The die is cast*: For a provincial governor to lead his troops out of his province without the authorization of the Senate was in effect an act of insurrection. Caesar himself does not mention this episode in his own account of the civil war, but later writers lay great stress on it; the story of his famous remark may go back to the history of C. Asinius Pollio, who was with him. Greek writers (Plutarch, *Caesar* 32.8; Appian, *Civil War* 2.35) quote it in a slightly different form, 'Let the die be cast,' which is surely correct; it is in fact a quotation from the Greek comic playwright Menander (see Athenaeus, *Deipnosophistae* 13.559e).

24. *subsequent movements*: For more detailed accounts of these

events, see the three books of Caesar's own *Civil War*, and the three anonymous works preserved in the manuscripts along with it: *The Alexandrian War, The African War* and *The Spanish War*.

25. *the first fourteen rows*: Laberius performed at Caesar's command, but in doing so he forfeited his equestrian status, since acting was a socially disreputable profession; Caesar's gifts restored his status. The first fourteen rows of the theatre were reserved for the equestrian order.

26. *the intercalary month*: In the Roman calendar of the republican period, a year consisted of 355 days; in order to keep it synchronized with the solar year, the pontifices would insert an additional ('intercalary') month as needed, normally after February.

27. *disqualifying the treasury tribunes*: The make-up of juries had been a major political issue for much of the late republic. The treasury tribunes were originally men who managed the pay of the troops; by the late republic the term designated a formal status comparable to that of *eques*, but probably with a lower property requirement.

28. *purple robes*: 'Purple' refers to a dye – produced from certain species of Mediterranean shellfish – that was very costly to manufacture (the actual colour ranged from scarlet to a deep violet); purple-dyed cloth was thus a luxury good, associated with high status.

29. *called 'Aegisthus'*: In Greek myth, Aegisthus was the lover of Clytemnestra, the wife of the great general Agamemnon.

30. *the son whom she had borne him*: His official name was Ptolemy XV Caesar, but the sources usually refer to him by his nickname Caesarion, 'Little Caesar'; he was eventually put to death by Augustus (see *Aug.* 17).

31. *prosecution of Dolabella . . . exact*: For the prosecution of Dolabella, see section 4 above; for Cicero's views, see *Brutus* 248–62 (the citation is from 261). Cicero's letters to Cornelius Nepos do not survive, nor do any of Caesar's speeches.

32. *no one knows . . . final book*: Many modern scholars are inclined to accept Hirtius as the author of *The Alexandrian War*, but the authors of the other two works remain unknown.

33. *Cicero . . . Hirtius . . . Pollio . . . revision*: The quotation from Cicero is at *Brutus* 262; that from Hirtius at *Gallic War* 8, praef. 5–6; the works of Asinius Pollio do not survive.

34. *literary remains . . . The Journey*: None of these works survives. The *Essay on Analogy* was a grammatical treatise advocating the standardization of conjugations and the like; the *Answers to*

Cato (literally, 'Anticatos') were a response not to Cato himself, who had committed suicide after Caesar's victory in Africa in April 46 BC and so was dead by the time of his final victory at Munda in March 45 BC, but rather to a pamphlet that Cicero wrote in praise of Cato.

35. *victim escaped . . . disgraceful life*: Three incidents from Caesar's African campaign. It was considered a very bad omen if the animal at a sacrifice bolted, or if a person stumbled at the start of a venture. P. Cornelius Scipio Africanus was the great hero of the Second Punic War (see *Aug.* 2 with the note), who decisively defeated the Carthaginian general Hannibal at Zama in Africa in 202 BC; his adoptive grandson P. Cornelius Scipio Aemilianus destroyed Carthage at the end of the Third Punic War in 146 BC. Other writers who refer to this incident give the name of Caesar's Scipio as 'Salutio' instead of 'Salvito', but the elder Pliny (*Natural History* 7.54) mentions a Cornelius Scipio who was nicknamed 'Salvitto' after a performer in popular farces.

36. *Cynegirus among the Greeks*: In the battle of the Athenians against the Persians at Marathon in 490 BC; the story is found in Herodotus, *History* 6.114.

37. *He supported . . . father*: For the context of Memmius' attack on Caesar, see section 23 above, and section 49 for a sample of his invective; Memmius stood for the consulship in 54 BC, but was involved in an electoral scandal and condemned for bribery. Suetonius quotes from one of Calvus' epigrams in section 49, but they are otherwise lost. The works of Calvus' friend Catullus do survive; he refers to Mamurra by name in poems 29 and 57, and more indirectly in 41, 43, 94, 105, 114 and 115; poems 54 and 93 also concern Caesar.

38. *imitate this treachery*: This incident took place in Spain during the first year of the civil war (49 BC); see further Caesar, *Civil War* 1.73–7.

39. *a new college of Luperci, and the renaming of a month after him*: There were traditionally two groups of Luperci (see 'Lupercalia' in the Glossary of Terms), to which a third was added in honour of Caesar. The seventh month in the Roman calendar was (for complex historical reasons) originally called Quintilis, 'Fifth', but was changed to Julius, whence modern 'July'.

40. *Caesar granted his request*: The man's name was C. Caninius Rebilus; compare *Nero* 15.

41. *the Latin Festival . . . statue*: The Latin Festival was an ancient festival in honour of Jupiter Latiaris (see *Calig.* 22 with the note),

presided over by the consul, which celebrated the union of all the towns of Latium; it took place on the Alban Mount south of Rome (compare *Claud.* 4). A white fillet was one of the insignia of kingship.

42. *I am Caesar, not king*: There is a possible pun here, since the Latin word *rex*, 'king', was also the cognomen of a noted family in Rome, of which Caesar's paternal grandmother was a member (see above, section 6); his reply could thus be translated as 'My name is Caesar, not King.'

43. *a purple gown*: I have here retained Graves's translation of 'toga' as 'gown' in order to preserve his verse; 'purple' refers to the distinctive purple stripe on the edge of senatorial togas. Gauls and other northern-European peoples wore breeches, although the people of the Mediterranean world did not; breeches were thus seen as stereotypical 'barbarian' garments.

44. *Brutus*: According to Roman tradition, L. Junius Brutus was the man who had led the movement to expel the last king and establish the republic at the end of the sixth century BC; the Caesarian conspirator M. Brutus was considered his descendant.

45. *the Assembly Hall of Pompey*: A room off the portico attached to the Theatre of Pompey; it was not the usual meeting place of the Senate.

46. *a descendant of his*: The Julian family claimed descent from the Trojan hero Aeneas (see section 6 above, with the note); according to Homer (*Iliad* 20.239), Capys was Aeneas' grandfather, although Virgil, who mentions Capys as the founder of Capua (*Aeneid* 10.145), describes him as one of Aeneas' companions (*Aeneid* 1.183, 2.35, 9.576). The alleged inscription apparently conflated these two figures.

47. *the pediment of their house*: Pediments were normally found only on temples; the honour of placing a pediment on his house had been voted to Caesar by the Senate.

48. *You too, my son*: This anecdote reflects the story found in later writers that Brutus was Caesar's illegitimate son. Caesar evidently did have a long-term affair with Brutus' mother Servilia (see above, section 50), but the story of Brutus' paternity cannot be true: he was born probably in 85 BC, when Caesar was only fifteen, and long before he began his affair with Servilia.

49. *heirs in the second degree*: Those who would inherit if the heirs in the first degree were unable to accept the legacy; D. Junius Brutus had served under Caesar in Gaul as well as throughout the civil war.

50. *read in Xenophon ... deathbed*: See Xenophon, *Cyropaedia* (*Education of Cyrus*) 8.7.

DIVUS AUGUSTUS

1. *Second Punic War*: The second of three major wars between Rome and the North African city of Carthage (218–201 BC); all three ended in Roman victories.

2. *letters survive from Cicero ... allies*: see Cicero, *Letters to his Brother Quintus* 1.1.21 and 1.2.7.

3. *Augustus was born ... district*: In 63 BC; nothing further is known about 'Ox Heads'.

4. *the emperor*: That is, Hadrian; Suetonius' phrasing here clearly indicates that he wrote this passage before his fall from favour.

5. *Thurinus ... Gaius Caesar ... Augustus ... by Munatius Plancus*: Augustus' original name was C. Octavius; Thurinus must have been a personal cognomen. In Roman tradition, adopted sons assumed the name of their adoptive fathers, sometimes using an adjectival form of their original nomen as an additional cognomen. Thus C. Octavius Thurinus, as a result of his testamentary adoption by Caesar (see *Jul.* 83), would have become C. Julius Caesar Octavianus; in fact he seems to have called himself 'Caesar' and never to have used the name Octavianus, although it has become conventional among modern scholars to refer to him during this period as 'Octavian' as a way of distinguishing him from Caesar. He assumed the praenomen Imperator in 40 BC, and was granted the title Augustus in 27 BC; thereafter the usual form of his name was Imperator Caesar Augustus.

6. *known as 'august' ... (or gustus)*: The Latin adjective *augustus* meant 'venerable, august'. Suetonius offers two derivations: from the participle *auctus*, 'increased, augmented', or from the phrase *avium gestus* or *avium gustus*, 'the deeds/feedings of birds', i.e. what augurs observed as the basis for their divination.

7. *twelve years ... forty-four years*: The twelve years are 43–31 BC: the triumvirate with Antony and Lepidus lasted officially from 42 to 33 BC, although Lepidus was ousted in 36 BC; despite the lapse of the triumvirate, Antony and Augustus continued to dominate the Roman world in 32 and 31 BC. The forty-four years of sole rule are 30 BC–AD 14.

8. *a patrician but not yet a senator*: Candidates for the tribuneship

were required to be of plebeian status, and would normally have already held the quaestorship and thus entered the Senate.

9. *honoured and then removed*: The person who said this was Cicero (see his *Letters to his Friends* 11.20); the original Latin involves a pun, since the second of the two verbs (*tollere*) could mean both 'to exalt' and 'to remove'.

10. *an alliance with Antony and Lepidus*: That is, the triumvirate: in late 43 BC, by popular vote, Augustus, Antony and Lepidus were appointed to a five-year term as 'the Commission of Three for Organizing the Republic'.

11. *The Sicilian war*: After being defeated by Caesar at the battle of Munda in 45 BC, the elder son of Pompey the Great was killed, but the younger, Sex. Pompey, escaped and was later given command of a fleet by the Senate. From 43 BC on he used this to occupy Sicily, which he made his power base; Sicily was at this time the chief source of grain for the city of Rome. He was finally defeated and killed in 36 BC.

12. *proscribed the father of Aemilius Paulus*: The father was L. Aemilius Paulus, the older brother of the triumvir Lepidus, who joined the Senate in declaring Lepidus and the other triumvirs public enemies in 43 BC; the name of the son, who was also proscribed but had by this time joined Augustus, was in fact Paulus Aemilius Lepidus.

13. *Titus Domitius*: His praenomen was in fact Gnaeus; he eventually sided with Augustus, and his great-grandson was the emperor Nero (see *Nero* 3).

14. *he actually summoned Psylli . . . asp*: The Psylli lived on the coast of what is now central Libya, and were reputed to be immune to poisonous snakes and to have the power of curing their bites (Pliny the Elder, *Natural History* 7.14).

15. *Nicopolis . . . games there every five years*: 'Nicopolis' is Greek for 'Victory-City'; the games were modelled on those at Olympia.

16. *leaders of the conspiracies . . . granddaughter*: M. Aemilius Lepidus was the son of the triumvir, and allegedly planned to kill Augustus on his return from Alexandria (Velleius 2.88). A. Terentius Varro Murena, the brother-in-law of Augustus' friend Maecenas, apparently plotted with Fannius Caepio in 23 BC to restore the republic (Velleius 2.91.2, Dio 54.3.4–8). M. Egnatius Rufus was executed in 19 BC (Velleius 2.91.3; cf. Dio 53.24.4–6). The conspiracy of Plautius Rufus and L. Aemilius Paulus (husband of the younger Julia) is otherwise almost unknown; Dio (55.27.1–3) mentions a scheme of P. Rufus, perhaps the same man, in AD 6.

17. *In addition . . . as well as Augustus*: All these episodes are otherwise unknown; the Parthini were a tribe of Illyricum; for the banishments of Julia and Agrippa Postumus, see section 65 below.

18. *while he was still in his teens*: Suetonius has his dates wrong: Augustus campaigned against the Dalmatae in 35–33 BC, when he was in his late twenties, although he was in his late teens when he stayed at Apollonia in the same region (see above, section 8).

19. *the Eagles captured from Marcus Crassus and Mark Antony*: The Parthians inflicted a major defeat on the Romans under M. Licinius Crassus at the battle of Carrhae in 52 BC; they won further battles against legates of Mark Antony in 40 BC and 36 BC. The recovery of the Eagles in 20 BC was achieved through diplomacy rather than war.

20. *Lollius and Varus . . . to a man*: In 16 BC German tribes crossed the Rhine and inflicted a defeat on M. Lollius (Dio 54.20.4–6); in AD 9 P. Quinctilius Varus, who was charged with reducing the newly conquered territory between the Rhine and the Elbe to a Roman province, was ambushed by a German revolt and massacred at the Teutoberg Forest (Velleius 2.117–20, Dio 56.18–22).

21. *the Cimbric and Marsic wars*: The Cimbri were a migrating Germanic tribe poised to invade Italy in the late second century BC; they were finally defeated by C. Marius in 101 BC. The Marsic War, better known as the Social War, was fought between Rome and its Italian allies in 91–87 BC.

22. *he decimated it and fed the survivors on barley*: Decimation was a traditional Roman military punishment in which every tenth (*decimus*) man in a unit, chosen by lot, was executed; barley was generally regarded as inferior to wheat, which was the normal ration for soldiers.

23. *The first . . . in force*: The first was the Illyrian revolt in AD 6 (see *Tib.* 16); the second was the defeat of P. Quinctilius Varus in AD 9 (see above, section 23).

24. *vallar or mural garlands*: These were military decorations awarded to the first soldier who crossed the palisade (*vallum*) or city wall (*murus*) of the enemy.

25. *his sons . . . came of age*: Gaius and Lucius were by blood the sons of Agrippa and Augustus' daughter Julia, but were adopted by Augustus in 17 BC. Augustus was consul in 43, 33, 31–23, 5 and 2 BC.

26. *secretly harboured his patron . . . proscribed*: Philopoemen was

a freedman of T. Vinius; the story is told in more detail by Dio (47.7.4–5).

27. *renamed the month of Sextilis ... victories*: Just as Caesar had changed the name of the seventh month from Quintilis to Julius (see *Jul.* 76), so now his successor changed the name of the eighth month from Sextilis to Augustus. Although later emperors similarly renamed months after themselves or their family members (see *Calig.* 15, *Nero* 55, *Dom.* 13), these were the only two renamings that stuck.

28. *certain obsolescent rites ... flowers*: The Saecular Games, held over a period of three nights, marked the transition from one era of a hundred years (*saeculum*) to another, and had last been held in 146 BC; a contemporary inscription recording Augustus' celebration of them in 17 BC survives largely intact, as does the hymn (*Carmen Saeculare*) written by the poet Horace for the occasion. The Compitalia were traditionally celebrated in honour of the Lares Compitales, the local gods of the crossroads; in their revived form the household gods of Augustus himself were the chief focus.

29. *increased the legal term ... claims*: The courts were closed on public holidays, but the magistrates who oversaw the games celebrated on those occasions tended to extend them for additional days at their own expense; these unofficial holidays were the ones that Augustus made available for legal business. Caesar had limited jury service to two panels, one of senators and one of *equites* (see *Jul.* 41 with the note), to which Antony had added a third panel; *ducenarii* were men whose property was worth 200,000 sesterces, half that of *equites*.

30. *committed parricide ... sack*: The traditional punishment for parricide was to be sewn up in a sack with a dog, a snake, a rooster and a monkey, and then drowned.

31. *'Orcus Men'*: Orcus was the god of the underworld, and the term 'Orcus Men' (*orcini*) was traditionally applied to slaves freed in their master's will, i.e. by a dead man; in this case it presumably refers to the claim that the papers of Julius Caesar found after his death contained instructions for these men's enrolment in the Senate.

32. *revived the traditional privilege of elections ... Scaptian*: Julius Caesar had set the precedent of appointing all the consuls himself and nominating half of the other magistrates (*Jul.* 41), a precedent that the triumvirs took even further. Augustus belonged to the Fabian tribe as a Julius by adoption, and to the Scaptian as an Octavius by birth.

33. *Behold them . . . Romans*: The line is a quotation from Virgil's *Aeneid*, 1.282.

34. *He records . . . expense*: Suetonius is here citing Augustus' *Res gestae* 22.

35. *No women . . . fifth hour*: Women were probably barred because the competitors in Greek athletic events were naked; the pontifical games were perhaps held to celebrate Augustus' assumption of the office of pontifex maximus in 12 BC, but they are otherwise unattested.

36. *the gods' platform*: Chariot races were normally held as part of a festival in honour of the gods, whose images were placed on couches on a special platform in the Circus so that they could 'watch' the proceedings.

37. *'Lord'*: The Latin word *dominus* meant literally 'master of a household', i.e. a person with proprietary power over others, especially slaves.

38. *Aesculapius*: The god of healing; see also *Claud.* 25.

39. *founded a city . . . Olympian Jupiter at Athens*: Examples are the cities refounded or renamed 'Caesarea' by Juba II of Mauretania (modern Cherchel in Algeria), Herod of Judaea (between Tel Aviv and Haifa on the coast of Israel) and Archelaus of Cappadocia (modern Kayseri in central Turkey). Jupiter is the Latin name for Zeus; the temple was begun by the tyrant Pisistratus in the late sixth century BC; it was finally completed by the emperor Hadrian in AD 132.

40. *According to Mark Antony . . . in exchange*: The Getae were a Thracian tribe, often confused with the Dacians. The context is presumably Augustus' pacification of Illyricum in 35–33 BC (see above, section 20), but whether there is any truth to the story is very uncertain: it is more likely an attempt by Antony to get back at Augustus for attacking his own relationship with Cleopatra.

41. *buying them . . . in a symbolic sale*: Literally, 'buying them by coin and scale'; this was an ancient procedure for adoption, in which the adopter struck a scale with a coin in the presence of the birth-father and claimed the son as his own.

42. *a curiate law*: Because Tiberius was already an independent head of a household (see *Tib.* 15), he could be adopted only through a special procedure involving a law passed by the curiate assembly, an archaic body represented at this time by thirty lictors.

43. *Ah, never to have married . . . to have died*: The line is a quotation from Homer's *Iliad*, 3.40.

44. *Salvidienus Rufus and Cornelius Gallus . . . suicide*: Q. Salvidienus Rufus was one of Augustus' earliest supporters and, along with Agrippa, one of his chief generals; in 40 BC, however, Augustus denounced him for plotting against him with Antony. C. Cornelius Gallus had erected boastful inscriptions and set up statues of himself throughout Egypt; he killed himself in 27 or 26 BC.

45. *confiding a secret to his wife Terentia . . . disclosed*: The problem here was that Terentia was Murena's sister, and so could have warned him that the plot had been discovered (see above, section 19).

46. *some of his freedmen . . . intimacy*: Celadus is otherwise unknown, but Licinus served as his financial officer in Gaul, where his corruption led the provincials to request his removal (Dio 54.21).

47. *see how this cinaedus regulates the sphere with his finger*: The Latin word *cinaedus* denoted a man who took the passive role in intercourse with another man, an activity popularly associated with the eunuch priests of Cybele, the Mother of the Gods. The line quoted involves a complicated Latin pun: the noun *orbis* meant any kind of circular or spherical object, such as a round drum, but could also denote the world; the verb *temperare* could mean 'to temper' a musical tone, but also to 'to control'.

48. *Corinthian bronzes*: 'Corinthian bronze' was an alloy of gold, silver and copper used especially for deluxe tableware and art objects.

49. *he diced openly . . . scooped the lot*: Gambling at dice was generally frowned upon at Rome, except during the festival of the Saturnalia in December. There were two sorts of dice: one with four faces and one with six. The game described in the letter involved four dice of the first sort, whose sides were marked with one, three, four and six dots; the side with one dot was called the 'dog', and a throw of all four dice with different faces was called 'Venus' (usually treated as a winning throw).

50. *Ajax . . . sword*: According to Greek myth, Ajax, one of the heroes of the Trojan War, felt himself so dishonoured when Achilles' arms were presented to Odysseus rather than to himself that he committed suicide by falling on his sword.

51. *the Greek Kalends . . . this Cato*: In the Roman calendar, the Kalends was the date on which debts were usually due; this way of reckoning the days of the month did not exist in the Greek calendar. M. Porcius Cato 'the elder', a great statesman of the

early second century BC, here represents a past standard that can no longer be attained.

52. *unusual synonyms . . . lachanizare*: The sense of some of these words is no longer clear. *Stultus* means 'fool'; *baceolus* is otherwise unattested, but may be connected with the Greek word *bakêlos*, a term for a eunuch priest of Cybele. *Pullus* means 'dark or drab-coloured', but *pulleiaceus* is unexplained. *Cerritus* is a colloquial word meaning 'frenzied' or 'insane'; *vacerrosus* is an adjective formed from the noun *vacerra*, 'fence post', and so may mean something like 'thick as a post'. *Male se habere* means 'to feel poorly'; *vapide* is an adverb formed from the adjective *vapidus*, 'flat' (in reference to wine that has turned bad). *Languere* means 'to feel faint or unwell'; *betizare* is a verb formed from the noun *beta*, 'beet', just as the Greek verb *lachanizare* is formed from the Greek noun *lachanon*, 'vegetable', and presumably means something like 'to veg out'.

53. *Old Comedy*: The customary term for the works of the Greek comic playwrights of the fifth century BC, notably Aristophanes, characterized by obscenity, political and social satire, and wild flights of fantasy.

54. *Attic Ceres' priests . . . Apis*: The reference here is to the Eleusinian Mysteries; Ceres was the Roman name for Demeter. Apis was a sacred bull worshipped at Memphis.

55. *Publius Nigidius . . . born*: P. Nigidius Figulus was a Roman scholar with particular interests in divination, later famous as an astrologer; this story is unlikely to be true, since Augustus was born on 23 September and the debates in the Senate regarding the Catilinarian conspiracy did not begin until November.

56. *Eutychus . . . Nicon*: The two names in Greek mean 'Good Fortune, Success' and 'Victorious, Conquering'; significant names encountered by chance were often taken as omens.

57. *ephebes . . . conservative settlement*: In traditional Greek cities, young men in their eighteenth year received a year of publicly sponsored athletic and civil training; they were known as ephebes (Greek *ephêboi*, 'youths').

58. *the consuls . . . Sextus Pompeius and Sextus Appuleius*: In AD 14.

59. *heirs in the second degree . . . heirs in the third degree*: These inherited only if those before them were unable to.

60. *a record of his accomplishments*: This document, known as the *Res gestae Divi Augusti*, 'The Accomplishments of Divus Augustus', survives in inscribed copies; see the on Further Reading section.

TIBERIUS

1. *the expulsion of the kings*: Rome was originally a monarchy; according to tradition, the last king was driven out in 510 BC and the republic was then established.
2. *Claudius Regillianus ... devices*: His name is usually given as Ap. Claudius Crassus Inregillensis Sabinus; for a full version of the story, see Livy 3.33–58.
3. *Mother Goddess ... did so*: The goddess Cybele, whose cult was officially introduced into Rome from Asia Minor in 204 BC; for a more detailed version of this story, see Ovid, *Fasti* 4.291–328.
4. *sons of Appius Caecus*: The founders of the two main branches of the Claudian family in the later republican period; Claudius Pulcher, whose praenomen was in fact Publius and not Appius, was the consul who threw the sacred chickens into the sea; nothing more is known of Tiberius Claudius Nero.
5. *paid to the Senones ... Camillus*: According to Roman tradition, in 390 BC Rome was sacked by a band of Gauls; the Romans agreed to pay a ransom of gold for their city, but at the last moment the hero Camillus appeared on the scene and forbade it to be handed over; for a full account, see Livy 5.33–55. These Gauls were later identified with the Senones, who settled in northern Italy and were wiped out by the Romans in 283 BC; the Gaul of which the first Drusus was governor is clearly meant to be Cisalpine Gaul, but he is not otherwise attested.
6. *'the Senate's patron' ... similar circumstances*: The elder Drusus, as tribune in 122 BC, was a staunch opponent of the reformer C. Sempronius Gracchus; his son, as tribune in 91 BC, put together a package of reforms meant to diffuse unrest, but was opposed by a range of interests and finally assassinated.
7. *The elder son ... Drusus*: Tiberius' full name was originally Ti. Claudius Nero, like that of his father; on his adoption by Augustus in AD 4, he became Ti. Julius Caesar; on the death of Augustus in AD 14 he acquired the name Augustus (see *Aug.* 101 and section 17 below); his formal name as emperor was Tiberius Caesar Augustus. The full name of his younger brother was Nero Claudius Drusus, with the cognomen of his mother's family and his father's cognomen as his praenomen; he was posthumously given the additional cognomen Germanicus in honour of his military exploits (see *Claud.* 1).

8. *the consuls as Marcus Aemilius Lepidus ... Lucius Munatius Plancus*: In 42 BC.

9. *one of Augustus' political opponents*: M. Gallius was the brother of Q. Gallius, who had been executed by Augustus (see *Aug.* 27).

10. *Caecilius Atticus*: His original name was T. Pomponius Atticus, and it is under this name that he is usually known; he was later adopted by his uncle Q. Caecilius, and as a result the name of his daughter, Agrippa's wife, was Caecilia Attica.

11. *captured from Marcus Crassus*: At the battle of Carrhae in 52 BC; see further *Aug.* 21 with the note.

12. *ceased to act as the head of a household ... peculium*: According to the letter of Roman law, sons remained under paternal authority as long as their fathers lived, and could not, among other things, legally possess property of their own; the father could, however, allot them the use of a certain amount of property, which was called *peculium*. Tiberius had been the head of his own household since the death of his father in 38 BC, but on adoption by Augustus he reverted back to the status of a dependant.

13. *the one he would acquire after he himself had died*: That is, 'Augustus'. *Invictus* means 'unconquered'; *pius*, 'pious', especially towards one's parents.

14. *'Alone he saved his by his cautious ways'*: A quotation from the now-lost *Annals* of Q. Ennius, referring to the tactics of Q. Fabius Maximus, a Roman general who in the early stages of the Second Punic War avoided pitched battles with the invading Carthaginian general Hannibal and instead pursued a successful policy of attrition.

15. *'If he came ... fire'*: A quotation from the *Iliad*, 10.246–7, in which Diomedes chooses Odysseus as his companion for a nocturnal sortie.

16. *Lucius Scribonius Libo ... Germany*: Libo's praenomen was in fact Marcus; Suetonius has mistakenly assigned him the praenomen held by his older brother, father and grandfather. For a more detailed account of this episode, see Tacitus, *Annals* 2.27–32; for Clemens, ibid. 2.39–40; for the mutinies, ibid. 1.16–49.

17. *the Plebeian Games*: A festival in honour of Jupiter; at their height they lasted from 4 to 17 November, with chariot races held on the last three days (including Tiberius' birthday on 16 November).

18. *three consulships*: In AD 18, 21 and 31; at the time of the last,

he had already retired to Capreae. He had previously been consul twice, in 9 and 7 BC.

19. *Biberius Caldius Mero*: Biberius is a play on the verb *bibere*, 'to drink'; Caldius on the adjective *calidus* or *caldus*, 'hot' (wine was sometimes mixed with hot water); Mero on the noun *merum*, 'unmixed' in the sense of 'straight, neat' (wine was normally mixed with water).

20. *'Caprineum'*: A play on the name of the island and the Latin adjective *caprinus*, 'goatish'; goats were proverbial for their sexual appetite.

21. *Atalanta . . . Meleager*: Figures from Greek myth. Atalanta was a virgin huntress who refused to marry unless a man could defeat her in a foot-race; Meleager was the hero of one of the great mythic exploits, the Calydonian boar hunt, in which Atalanta took part.

22. *Hector*: The great hero on the Trojan side of the Trojan War, killed by Achilles.

23. *a letter of complaint . . . famine*: Because of its strategic importance as the chief source of grain for Rome, Egypt was administered as an imperial possession; no senator was allowed to visit it without explicit imperial permission, which Germanicus had not obtained.

24. *Saturn's golden age*: According to Roman myth, the god Saturn ruled over Italy during the golden age, when nature provided for all human needs and people did not have to work to feed, clothe or house themselves.

25. *'Let them hate me, so long as they approve'*: An adaptation of a famous line from a tragedy by the Roman playwright Accius (170–*c*.86 BC), 'Let them hate me, so long as they fear me'; Suetonius elsewhere reports that Gaius quoted it in its original form (*Calig.* 30).

26. *A poet . . . the Romans*: Agamemnon was the mythical king of Mycenae and the leader of the Greek forces in the Trojan War; criticism of him in a tragedy could be taken as indirect criticism of the emperor, but nothing more is known of this particular case. The name of the historian was A. Cremutius Cordus, and his trial took place in AD 25; for a more detailed account, see Tacitus, *Annals* 4.34–5.

27. *little girls . . . violating them*: Suetonius is here probably generalizing from a single known instance, the execution of Sejanus' young daughter in AD 31: see Tacitus, *Annals* 5.9.

28. *Priam . . . family*: Priam, the mythical king of Troy, was killed only after all his sons had died fighting the Greeks.

29. *the Praenestine lots*: The Temple of Fortuna Primigenia, the chief
     deity of the town of Praeneste, was the site of an ancient and
     well-known oracle that people consulted by means of lots.

30. *Who was Hecuba's mother? ... Sirens sing*: These are the sort
     of recherché questions in which *grammatici* specialized. Hecuba
     was the queen of Troy during the Trojan War, the mother of
     Hector and Paris; Achilles' mother, aware that he was fated to
     die if he joined the Greek expedition to Troy, disguised him as a
     girl and hid him on the island of Scyros; the Sirens' song lured
     sailors to their destruction.

31. *Minos ... pipe players*: According to Greek myth, Minos was
     king of Crete, and his son was killed in Attica. In the Roman
     tradition, sacrifice always involved an offering of wine and
     incense, while an assistant played the pipes to mask any inaus-
     picious sounds.

32. *the consuls of the year ... Gaius Pontius Nigrinus*: In AD 37.

33. *statue of Apollo Temenites*: This was a famous statue of Apollo
     erected in the *temenos*, or sacred precinct, of the goddesses
     Demeter and Kore at Syracuse.

34. *Di Manes*: Gods of the underworld, identified with the spirits of
     the dead.

35. *'Take him to Atella! Give him a half-burning in an amphi-
     theatre!'*: The point here is not entirely clear: Atella gave its name
     to Atellan farces, and a partial cremation was presumably an
     insult, but more than that cannot be said.

GAIUS CALIGULA

1.   *Germanicus ... paternal uncle*: Germanicus' name derived from
     the honorific cognomen awarded posthumously to his father
     (see *Claud.* 1); his original name was Nero Claudius Drusus
     Germanicus. Tiberius adopted him at the same time that he
     himself was adopted by Augustus (see *Aug.* 65, *Tib.* 15), where-
     upon Germanicus became Germanicus Julius Caesar.

2.   *Piso ... lynching*: Tacitus provides a full account of Germanicus
     and Piso (*Annals* 2.43, 53–61 and 69–83, 3.8–18); in the late
     1980s an inscription was discovered that provides the full text
     of the Senate's decree in the case of Piso: see the Further Reading
     section.

3.   *the consulship shared by his father with Gaius Fonteius Capito*:
     In AD 12. Gaius' full name was originally C. Julius Caesar

Germanicus, although Julius does not appear in any extant source; on becoming emperor, he took the name C. Caesar Augustus Germanicus. 'Caligula' was a nickname (see below, section 9, with the note) and is the name by which he is now generally known; Suetonius, however, normally refers to him as 'Gaius Caesar'.

4. *puerae . . . pueri*: The masculine noun *puer* meant 'boy', and its feminine equivalent *puera* meant 'girl'; by the late republic, however, the diminutive feminine *puella* had effectively replaced *puera*, which almost disappeared, and the diminutive masculine *puellus*, which had previously been fairly common, also became extremely rare. Suetonius is here evidently drawing on his earlier work *On the Institution of Offices*, in which, as we learn from a citation by the fifth-century AD grammarian Priscian, he made precisely the same point.

5. *his cognomen Caligula . . . soldier*: The standard dress of soldiers included boots called *caligae* in Latin; 'Caligula' is a diminutive, and hence meant 'Bootikin' or 'Little Boot'.

6. *educating a Phaethon for the whole world*: In Greek myth, Phaethon was the son of the sun god Helios; he borrowed his father's fiery chariot, but lost control of the horses so that he came too near the earth and scorched it.

7. *a mere eques . . . Youth Leader*: Any man of wealth and high social status who had not held any of the traditional Roman magistracies (the quaestorship or higher) was technically an *eques*, not a senator, regardless of the status of his father or brothers. 'Youth Leader' (*princeps iuventatis*) was a semi-official title, first given by Augustus to his grandsons Gaius and Lucius on their coming of age, used to honour intended successors.

8. *spintrian perverts*: See *Tib.* 43.

9. *Titus Labienus, Cremutius Cordus and Cassius Severus*: These were orators and historians active in the reign of Augustus; for Cremutius Cordus, see *Tib.* 61 with the note; for Cassius Severus, see *Aug.* 56.

10. *the Parilia . . . born again*: The Parilia, on 21 April, was originally an agricultural festival, but by the late republic had come to be identified as the anniversary of Rome's foundation.

11. *Only the last two were in sequence*: Suetonius makes a slip here, since Gaius was consul in AD 37, 39, 40 and 41; the first was only a suffect consulship, because the ordinary consuls for the year were already in place when Tiberius died.

12. *Xerxes' famous feat . . . Hellespont*: The Persian king Xerxes built a bridge across the Hellespont in 480 BC in order to lead

his army against the Greeks of the mainland; for the classic account of this episode, see Herodotus, *Histories* 7.34–6.

13. *Optimus Maximus*: Literally, 'Best and Greatest', a title that belonged to Jupiter in his role as patron god of Rome.

14. *'Nay, let there be one master, and one king!'*: A quotation from Homer's *Iliad*, 2.204–5, where Odysseus is rallying the Greek soldiers to support the leadership of Agamemnon; Domitian would later quote the half-line that immediately precedes this (see *Dom.* 13).

15. *'Jupiter Latiaris'*: The chief god of the ancient league of Latin cities, worshipped on the Alban Mount south of Rome.

16. *'Either you throw me or I will throw you!'*: Another line from Homer's *Iliad*, 23.724, where Ajax is challenging Odysseus in a wrestling match at the funeral games of Patroclus.

17. *'Ulysses in petticoats'*: Ulysses (the Roman name for Odysseus) was renowned in Greek myth for his schemes and stratagems; although in earlier sources (for example, Homer's *Odyssey*) he was portrayed as an admirable figure, in later times he was regarded as deceitful, unreliable and treacherous.

18. *Aufidius Lurco ... high office at Rome*: Suetonius has made a mistake here, since the name of Livia's grandfather was in fact Alfidius, and he may very well have been a town councillor in Fundi (see *Tib.* 5 for the family connection); the Aufidius Lurco who held high office in Rome was a different person.

19. *placed them all in turn below him*: Gaius put his sisters in the place that his wife would normally take, and put his wife in the place usually given to the guest of honour.

20. *Aemilius Lepidus' trial ... kill him*: Little is known of this episode. M. Aemilius Lepidus was Drusilla's second husband, whom Gaius at one point evidently considered as a possible successor; Gaius had him tried for treason and executed in the autumn of AD 39, and exiled his sisters at the same time (Seneca, *Letters* 4.7; Dio 59.22.6–8); compare *Claud.* 9.

21. *Lollia Paulina, wife of Gaius Memmius*: She was later considered a possible wife for Claudius (*Claud.* 26); the praenomen of her previous husband, Memmius, who at the time commanded the armies in Moesia, Macedonia and Achaia, was not Gaius but Publius.

22. *Gallograecia*: That is, the area of Galatia in what is now central Turkey, which had been settled by invading Gauls in the third century BC but had become largely Greek in culture.

23. *'Let them hate me, so long as they fear me'*: A quotation from a

lost tragedy by the Roman playwright Accius (170–*c*.86 BC); compare *Tib.* 59.

24. *the Varus massacre or the collapse of the amphitheatre ... under Tiberius*: For these disasters, see *Aug.* 23 and *Tib.* 40.

25. *banishing Homer from his republic*: The reference is to Plato's argument that traditional myths of the gods, such as those found in the Homeric poems, were untrue and hence had no place in an ideal society (*Republic* 2.377–93).

26. *their ancient family emblems ... Magnus*: A torc was a metal collar used as a military decoration, and the name Torquatus was sometimes assumed as a hereditary cognomen by someone who had won one (see *Aug.* 43); the Torquatus mentioned here was probably one of the Junii Silani, descendants of Augustus through his granddaughter Julia and hence potential rivals to Gaius: perhaps D. Junius Silanus, consul in AD 19, or his brother L. Junius Silanus. Cn. Pompeius Magnus was a descendant through his mother of Pompey the Great, whose name he adopted. L. Quinctius Cincinnatus, one of the heroes of the early republic, was traditionally said to have earned his cognomen because of his curly hair (*cincinnus* means 'ringlet'); there were still Quinctii in the early empire, but they no longer used the cognomen Cincinnatus, and it is not clear whom Suetonius had in mind.

27. *a fine head of hair ... brutally shaved*: Gaius himself was balding (see section 50 below), hence his hostility.

28. *Colosseros*: The name is a combination of the Greek words *colossus*, 'giant', and *eros*, 'cupid'.

29. *King of the Grove*: In Latin, *rex Nemorensis*; the priest of Diana at her sacred grove (*nemus*) near Aricias south-east of Rome. The position was held by an escaped slave, who killed his predecessor and would in turn be killed by his successor.

30. *Batavian recruits ... German expedition*: The Batavi were a German tribe who lived at the mouth of the Rhine; the Julio-Claudian emperors used Germans as their personal bodyguard since, as foreigners, they had no other ties to Rome and so would be loyal to the emperor alone.

31. *drive their chariots all the way ... Senate House*: Wheeled traffic was ordinarily prohibited during daylight hours within the city of Rome, so that Gaius' instructions to his couriers constituted another example of his arrogance.

32. *'Be steadfast, ... happier occasions'*: A paraphrase of Virgil, *Aeneid* 1.207, the climax of a speech in which Aeneas encourages his followers to bear up under their troubles.

33. *the Ocean*: In Greek and Roman tradition, the Ocean was the body of water that encircled the world; the Romans applied the name to the seas beyond the mainland of Europe.

34. *the one at Pharos*: Pharos was a small island in the harbour of Alexandria, the location of a famous lighthouse.

35. *a decimation*: For this practice, see *Aug.* 24 with the note.

36. *the Cimbri ... the Senones had done*: Two barbarian tribes associated with attacks on Rome; for the Cimbri see *Aug.* 23 with the note, and for the Senones see *Tib.* 3 with the note.

37. *Jupiter's thunderbolt ... Mercury's caduceus*: The particular insignia, or attributes, associated with these gods; the thunderbolt signified Jupiter's power over storms, the trident Neptune's power over the sea, and the caduceus, or herald's staff, Mercury's role as messenger of the gods.

38. *the Green faction*: The chariots that raced in the Circus competed under different colours; these defined different factions or 'teams', each with its own supporters. The chief factions in the early empire were the Greens and the Blues.

39. *'Priapus' or 'Venus'*: The god Priapus was always depicted with a large erect phallus and was in literature associated with humorous obscenity; Venus was the goddess of sexual desire.

40. *the one murdered in Cinna's day*: C. Julius Caesar Strabo, the great-uncle of Julius Caesar, who was killed in 87/86 BC after Marius and Cinna seized control in Rome.

DIVUS CLAUDIUS

1. *How fortunate ... womb*: The verse is in Greek, and is thought to come from a now-lost comedy of the fourth century BC.

2. *'the Noblest Spoils'*: Latin, *spolia opima*; a military honour awarded to a Roman commander who killed an enemy commander in single combat; only three instances from all previous Roman history are cited in our sources.

3. *Claudius was born ... Julian family*: Claudius was born in 10 BC, the year before his father's death. His brother was adopted in AD 4 by Tiberius at the same time as Tiberius was adopted by Augustus (see *Tib.* 15 and *Calig.* 1), and so became a Julius; Claudius thereupon assumed the traditional Claudian cognomen Nero, which his brother lost on his adoption, and became Ti. Claudius Nero Germanicus. His official name as emperor was Ti. Claudius Caesar Augustus Germanicus.

4. *the gods' platform . . . the Latin Festival*: For the gods' platform, see *Aug.* 45 with the note. For the Latin Festival, see *Jul.* 79 with the note; during the few days' absence of the magistrates from Rome, the consul (in this case Germanicus) appointed a young man of good birth to the largely ceremonial position of prefect of the city (compare *Nero* 7); the reference to Germanicus as consul dates this letter to AD 12.

5. *heirs in the third degree*: They inherited only if those in the first and second degree did not; compare *Aug.* 101 with the note.

6. *for the Saturnalia and Sigillaria*: The Latin word *sigillaria* means in the first place small decorative items made of pottery; the word was also used for the market street in Rome where such items were typically sold, and (as here) for the final day of the Saturnalia, on which gifts of this sort were exchanged.

7. *The equites twice chose Claudius . . . consuls*: The *equites* looked to Claudius as one of the few leading members of the imperial family who was not a member of the Senate; see *Calig.* 15 with the note.

8. *conspiracy headed by Lepidus and Gaetulicus*: In the autumn of AD 39, Cn. Cornelius Lentulus Gaetulicus, then in command of the Roman army in Upper Germany, was detected in a planned coup against Gaius (Dio 59.22.5); for M. Aemilius Lepidus, see *Calig.* 24 with the note. This is the only reference to the two men acting together.

9. *Asinius Gallus and Statilius Corvinus . . . deposition*: Asinius Gallus was not only the grandson of C. Asinius Pollio, but also the half-brother of Tiberius' son Drusus: his mother was Vipsania, who after being divorced from Tiberius (see *Tib.* 7) had married Pollio's son C. Asinius Gallus. On the conspiracy, see further Dio 60.27.5. T. Statilius Taurus Corvinus is named as a conspirator only here.

10. *Furius Camillus Scribonianus*: He had been born M. Furius Camillus, but after being adopted took the name L. Arruntius Camillus Scribonianus; as governor of Dalmatia in AD 41/42, he made a short-lived attempt at a coup (see Dio 60.15.1–3).

11. *four more consulships*: Claudius' first consulship had been with Gaius in AD 37 (above, section 7, and compare *Calig.* 15); he held the others in AD 42, 43, 47 and 51.

12. *an unwholesome liking for jury duty*: Exemption from jury duty was evidently one of the benefits granted under the Papian–Poppaean Law (see the Glossary of Terms).

13. *the classical case of Rabirius Postumus*: He was defended by Cicero, whose speech on his behalf still survives.

14. *hacked to pieces before his eyes*: Among the duties of the censor
     was the obligation to curb extravagance; as with other censorial
     duties, this was assumed by the emperors (see for example *Tib.*
     34 and *Nero* 16).
15. *the great obelisk . . . lamp*: Gaius had brought from Egypt an
     obelisk to serve as one of the turning posts in the Circus that he
     built in the Vatican quarter (compare section 21); it now stands
     in front of St Peter's in Rome. On Pharos, see *Calig.* 46 with the
     note.
16. *Saecular Games*: See *Aug.* 31 with the note.
17. *with his left arm extended*: On formal occasions, a man's left
     arm would be bound up by the fold of his toga.
18. *the Dove . . . catching*: Well-known gladiators often had nick-
     names, just as some sports celebrities do today.
19. *declined senatorial rank*: Senatorial status involved sometimes
     onerous and expensive obligations, as well as restrictions, since
     senators were barred from engaging in the kinds of business
     activity that were open to *equites*.
20. *banned travel . . . except on foot . . . or in a litter*: This extended
     to the other towns of Italy the ban on vehicular traffic that
     already existed in Rome (see *Calig.* 44 with the note).
21. *at the instigation of Chrestus . . . from the city*: It is generally
     thought that Suetonius has here confused the common slave
     name 'Chrestus' with 'Christus', and that the disturbances he
     mentions were the result of Christian missionizing among the
     Jewish population of Rome. For the expulsion of the Jews, com-
     pare Acts 18:2, where Paul's associates Aquila and Priscilla are
     said to have left Rome and come to Corinth as a result of Clau-
     dius' decree.
22. *the Fetial priests*: Members of an ancient Roman priestly associ-
     ation, traditionally responsible for the rituals associated with
     declarations of war and the striking of peace treaties; it had more
     or less disappeared before being revived by Augustus.
23. *Aemilia Lepida's parents offended Augustus . . . broken off*: She
     was the daughter of the younger Julia and L. Aemilius Paulus;
     Julia was exiled in AD 8 for adultery (*Aug.* 65), and Paulus
     was executed, perhaps in the same year, for allegedly conspiring
     against Augustus (*Aug.* 19).
24. *his cousin Messala Barbatus*: M. Valerius Messala Barbatus was
     the son of Marcella, a daughter of Augustus' sister Octavia by
     her first husband, Marcellus; Claudius' mother Antonia was the
     daughter of Octavia and her second husband, Mark Antony, and

thus half-sister to Marcella. Messalina's mother, Domitia Lepida, was also Claudius' cousin, being the daughter of the elder Antonia, his mother's full sister.

25. *afterwards called Britannicus*: Claudius at first gave his son the traditional family name of Ti. Claudius Germanicus, but later marked his conquest of Britain by giving him the honorific name Britannicus.

26. *this Felix married three princesses*: Felix was governor of Judaea in AD 52–60, and married Drusilla, the daughter of Herod Agrippa I (Josephus, *Jewish War* 2.247–70, *Jewish Antiquities* 20.137–44 and 160–82); he was the governor before whom Paul defended himself (Acts 23:23–24:27).

27. *the dining room of the Salii*: The Salii were members of an ancient priestly college who in spring and autumn processed through Rome carrying shields of archaic design and performing ritual war dances; they afterwards enjoyed banquets that were proverbial for their luxury.

28. *an execution in ancient style*: See Nero 49.

29. *'What? Do you take me for Telegenius?' and 'Talk but don't touch'*: In the first phrase, Telegenius is otherwise unknown, although the context suggests that he was a byword for a stupid or incompetent person; the second phrase was a Greek saying equivalent to the English 'Sticks and stones may break my bones but words will never hurt me.'

30. *A Defence of Cicero ... Asinius Gallus*: C. Asinius Gallus, a prominent senator during the reign of Tiberius (and father of the Asinius Gallus who conspired against Claudius: see section 13), wrote a treatise unfavourably comparing the style of Cicero with that of his father C. Asinius Pollio. None of Claudius' writings is extant, although a few stray quotations survive from his history.

31. *three new letters ... inscriptions*: The three letters were an upside-down F, used to represent the sound 'w'; one that resembled the first half of H, apparently used to represent the sound of the Greek upsilon; and probably a backwards C, used for the combination 'bs'. Examples of the first two letters survive in a few inscriptions, although they all quickly fell out of use after Claudius' death.

32. *'Let him be first ... boldly'*: A line found several times in the Homeric epics: *Iliad* 24.369, *Odyssey* 16.72 and 21.133. Graves rendered it into an English hexameter; a more literal but less metrical translation would be 'Ward off the man who becomes angry unprovoked.'

33. *'The hand that wounded you shall also heal'*: A reference to the myth of Telephus, who was wounded by Achilles in the Trojan War and then told by an oracle that only Achilles could heal him.

34. *during the consulship of Asinius Marcellus and Acilius Aviola*: In AD 54.

NERO

1. *a pair of twins . . . descendants*: Suetonius is referring to the story that Castor and Pollux (see *Jul.* 10 with the note) announced the victory of the Romans over their Latin neighbours at the battle of Lake Regillus in the early fifth century BC; for a more detailed but different version, see Dionysius of Halicarnassus, *Roman Antiquities* 6.13; the story of Domitius and his beard is elsewhere mentioned only by Plutarch (*Aemilius Paulus* 25). The name Ahenobarbus derives from the Latin words *aeneus* (or *aheneus*), 'bronze-coloured', and *barba*, 'beard'.

2. *on the staff of Augustus' adopted son Gaius*: Suetonius has made a mistake here, since Cn. Domitius was much too young to have accompanied Gaius to the east in 1 BC; he perhaps meant Germanicus, who was sent to the east in AD 17.

3. *Nero was born . . . on the ground*: The year was AD 37. It was traditional to lay a newborn on the ground; the father then acknowledged the child by lifting him or her up.

4. *'I give him Claudius' name'*: The point here is that Nero eventually did in fact take Claudius' name. His original name was L. Domitius Ahenobarbus; after his adoption by Claudius, he became Nero Claudius Caesar Drusus Germanicus (although there is also evidence that he used the praenomen Tiberius); his official name as emperor was Nero Claudius Caesar Augustus Germanicus. The ritual purification to which Suetonius refers took place nine days after the birth, which was thought to bring pollution on both the mother and the child.

5. *his stepfather, Crispus Passienus*: C. Sallustius Crispus Passienus was a distinguished orator who first married Domitia, Nero's paternal aunt, and then his mother Agrippina; Suetonius included a biography of him in his section on orators in *On Illustrious Men*, of which an abbreviated version survives.

6. *the age of eleven*: Suetonius has made a slip with Nero's age here, since other evidence shows that he must recently have turned twelve at the time of his adoption (25 February AD 50).

7. *Domitia Lepida ... the trial*: According to Tacitus, *Annals* 12.64–5, Agrippina viewed Lepida as a rival and in AD 53 had her accused of using magic against the emperor's wife and endangering the peace in southern Italy by not keeping the slaves on her estates under control.

8. *city prefect during the Latin Festival*: See *Claud.* 4 with the note.

9. *Pasiphae ... Icarus*: The two ballets presented Greek myths associated with Crete. Minos, the king, angered the god Poseidon, who retaliated by causing his wife, Pasiphae, to develop a passion for a bull; the inventor Daedalus devised an artificial heifer in which she could hide in order for the bull to mate with her. Daedalus later escaped from Minos' service by creating wings made of wax and feathers for himself and his son Icarus; despite Daedalus' warnings, Icarus flew too high, so that the heat of the sun melted the wax and caused him to plunge to his death.

10. *Nero's four consulships*: In AD 55, 57, 58 and 60; in AD 68 he also briefly took the position of sole consul during the revolt of Vindex and Galba (see section 43 below).

11. *Caninius Rebilus' one-day consulship*: See *Jul.* 76.

12. *Punishments were inflicted on the Christians*: For a fuller account of this episode, see Tacitus, *Annals* 15.44, who says that Nero used the Christians as scapegoats for the great fire of AD 64.

13. *a canal ... an expedition to the Caspian Gates*: Neither of these schemes was realized: the former was a typically grandiose project allegedly contemplated by other rulers (for example, *Jul.* 44 and *Calig.* 21); the latter may have had a serious strategic purpose, but was apparently seen (by Nero or by others) as an attempt to rival the exploits of Alexander the Great.

14. *Niobe*: A famous figure from Greek myth; as the mother of seven sons and seven daughters, she boasted that she was superior to the goddess Leto, the mother of Apollo and Artemis; in retaliation, Leto had her children kill the children of Niobe. Niobe's subsequent lament was presumably the subject of Nero's performance.

15. *Canace ... Hercules raving*: More figures from Greek myth. Canace was impregnated by her brother; when she gave birth, the affair came to light and both she and her brother committed suicide. Orestes killed his mother Clytemnestra to avenge her murder of his father Agamemnon; Oedipus blinded himself after discovering that he had unknowingly killed his father and married his mother; Hercules, driven mad by the goddess Hera, killed his wife and children. Ancient readers would no doubt have been

struck that Nero's favourite roles involved the same themes of incest and parricide that appear in his own life story (compare section 46 below).

16. *a Green charioteer . . . Hector*: For the Circus teams of Greens and Blues, see *Calig.* 55 with the note. In Greek myth, after Achilles killed the Trojan hero Hector, he tied his body to the back of his chariot and dragged it through the dust (Homer, *Iliad* 22.395–404).

17. *The Olympian wreath . . . carried before him*: Wreaths were the prizes at the great traditional Greek games, of which the most prestigious were the Olympian games in honour of Zeus and the Pythian games at Delphi in honour of Apollo.

18. *Augustiani and the soldiers of his triumph*: According to Tacitus, *Annals* 14.15, 'Augustiani' was the name given to Nero's professional applauders (see section 20). Nero's ceremonial entrance into Rome after his victories in the Greek games was evidently meant to be a version of the traditional Roman triumph, with his fans in the place of the soldiers, and Apollo, the god of music, taking the place of Jupiter.

19. *the Sigillaria at Rome*: A market street; see *Claud.* 5 with the note.

20. *Canusian wool . . . Mazacian horsemen*: The town of Canusium was famous for the high quality of its wool; the Mazaces were a North African people noted as horsemen.

21. *'The Golden House'*: A massive complex (some 125 acres), incorporating extensive parklands as well as buildings, that extended from the Palatine to the Esquiline and Caelian hills; although largely dismantled by Vespasian, enough remains to give some sense of it.

22. *'the food of the gods'*: The joke was that Claudius was formally installed as a god (see section 9 above) after the mushrooms had caused his death (compare *Claud.* 44).

23. *the Furies*: In Greek myth, goddesses of vengeance who tormented those guilty of crimes against family members, especially matricide.

24. *his aunt Domitia*: Not Domitia Lepida, who had been put to death under Claudius (see section 7 above), but her sister.

25. *the rich old freedmen . . . advisers*: Suetonius presumably has in mind Claudius' freedman Pallas (see *Claud.* 28) and Nero's own freedman Doryphorus, who are said by Tacitus (*Annals* 14.65) to have been killed in the same year as Octavia (AD 62).

26. *the Pisonian conspiracy . . . Beneventum*: Tacitus provides an extensive account of the conspiracy headed by C. Calpurnius

Piso, which was revealed in AD 65 (*Annals* 15.48–74). In contrast, there is no other literary reference to the Vinician conspiracy, which took place probably in AD 66 or 67 and was perhaps headed by a man named Annius Vinicianus.

27. *Alcmaeon, Orestes and Nero . . . mothers*: This verse is in Greek. In Greek myth, Alcmaeon killed his mother Eriphyle, who had betrayed his father Amphiaraus after being bribed with a necklace; for Orestes, see above, section 21 with the note.

28. *Count the numerical values . . . Nero's name*: Also in Greek; the ancient Greeks used the letters of their alphabet to indicate numbers.

29. *Aeneas the Trojan hero . . . each other*: The remaining passages are in Latin. This one involves a pun on the verb *tollere*, which mean both 'to lift up' and 'to remove'; Aeneas famously carried his father out of Troy when it was being sacked by the Greeks.

30. *your song about Nauplius*: In Greek myth, Nauplius was the father of Palamedes, whom Odysseus framed on a charge of treason; to avenge him, Nauplius lit false beacons to wreck the Greek fleet on its return from Troy.

31. *another throne in the east . . . Jerusalem*: This is perhaps connected with the prophecy that a new ruler would arise in Judaea (see *Vesp.* 4). For the false Neros who later appeared in the east, see below, section 57, with the note.

32. *you deserve the sack*: Presumably a reference to the traditional punishment for parricides (see *Aug.* 33 with the note).

33. *aroused even the cocks . . . 'Vengeance is coming!'*: Both these jokes depend on Latin puns. The word *galli* means both 'cocks' and 'Gauls'; the word *vindex* means 'defender' or 'avenger', so that the nocturnal pranksters could justifiably shout out the name of Vindex when pretending to threaten their slaves.

34. *Proserpine's descent to the underworld*: In Greek myth, Hades, god of the underworld, abducted Persephone (called Proserpine in Latin), the daughter of Demeter, to be his wife.

35. *'Wife, mother, father, do my death compel!'*: The idea is that the ghosts of Oedipus' father and mother are driving him to his death as a result of his crimes against them (see section 21 above, with the note); so too the ghosts of those whom Nero killed.

36. *'Is it so terrible a thing to die?'*: Virgil, *Aeneid* 12.646.

37. *'Hark to the sound I hear! It is hooves of galloping horses'*: Homer, *Iliad* 10.535.

38. *Apollo . . . the Sun . . . Hercules . . . strangle it*: Nero's interest in Apollo as the god of music is noted above (section 25 with the

note); the Sun was said in traditional myth to drive a fiery chariot through the sky (see the note at *Calig.* 11); the first of Hercules' twelve labours was to kill a lion with his bare hands.

39. *Turnus from Virgil*: The great Italian hero who opposes Aeneas in the second half of Virgil's *Aeneid*.

40. *caps of liberty*: Traditionally worn by ex-slaves immediately after being freed by their owners.

41. *twenty years later ... claiming to be Nero*: There were in fact at least two men before this who appeared in the eastern part of the empire claiming to be Nero, the first in AD 69 (Tacitus, *Histories* 2.8–9) and the second in AD 79 or 80 (Dio 66.19.3b–c); this passage points to a third around the year AD 88, to which Tacitus, *Histories* 1.2, perhaps also refers.

GALBA

1. *Pasiphae*: See *Nero* 12 with the note.

2. *the war with Viriatus*: Viriatus was one of the few survivors of Galba's massacre in 150 BC, and by 147 BC he had become the war leader of the Lusitanians; he defeated a series of Roman commanders and maintained Lusitanian independence until 138 BC, when the Romans had him assassinated.

3. *when Marcus Valerius Messala and Gnaeus Lentulus were consuls*: In 3 BC; other evidence, however, indicates a date of 5 BC for Galba's birth. His original name was Ser. Sulpicius Galba; on his adoption by his stepmother Livia, he became L. Livius Ocella Sulpicius Galba; as emperor he seems to have used the name Ser. Galba Imperator Caesar.

4. *Quindecimviri ... Sodales Augustales*: The Quindecimviri were the board of fifteen men in charge of the Sibylline Books; the Sodales Titii were members of an ancient college revived by Augustus, about which little is known; the Sodales Augustales were responsible for the cult of Divus Augustus (and later Divus Claudius).

5. *Nymphidius Sabinus ... Africa*: C. Nymphidius Sabinus was praetorian prefect at the end of Nero's reign, and before Galba's arrival in Rome he tried to stage a coup by presenting himself to the praetorians; they refused to support him, and he was killed. C. Fonteius Capito was commander of the legions in Lower Germany, killed by some of his officers for reasons that are not entirely clear. L. Clodius Macer was governor of Africa; he seems

to have a followed a policy similar to Galba's but with less success, and was eventually killed on Galba's orders.

6. *decimated them*: For the practice of decimation, see *Aug*. 24 with the note.

7. *excessive devotion to Gnaeus Dolabella*: Cn. Cornelius Dolabella (his praenomen may in fact have been Publius) was at one point proposed to Galba as a possible successor, although Galba decided against him; it was in the wake of this episode that he dismissed the German guards.

8. *the right to wear a gold ring . . . man of his rank*: A gold ring was sign of equestrian status; by the highest office for men of this rank Suetonius presumably means that of praetorian prefect.

9. *the operations against Vindex and the Gauls*: It was the army in Upper Germany, under its commander L. Verginius Rufus, that in May of AD 68 had defeated Vindex and put an end to his rebellion.

10. *warm ashes . . . earthenware cup*: The point here is that these preparations are poor, or even contrary to normal practice, and therefore ill-omened for a person trying to expiate a fault.

11. *'So far my vigour undiminished is'*: Homer, *Iliad* 5.254 and *Odyssey* 21.426.

OTHO

1. *Camillus' rebellion*: See *Claud*. 13.

2. *when Camillus Arruntius and Domitius Ahenobarbus were the consuls*: In AD 32; Suetonius elsewhere (*Claud*. 13) calls Camillus Arruntius by his birth name, Furius Camillus.

3. *Seleucus*: Suetonius appears to be wrong about this man's name: Tacitus says that Seleucus was Vespasian's astrologer (*Histories* 2.78), while both Tacitus (*Histories* 1.22) and Plutarch (*Galba* 23.4) say that Otho's astrologer was named Ptolemaeus.

4. *he even added the cognomen Nero . . . governors*: No other evidence supports Otho's use of the name Nero; his official title as emperor seems instead to have been Imperator Marcus Otho Caesar Augustus.

5. *'Playing long flutes is hardly my trade'*: A Greek proverbial expression used of those doing something for which they were not suited.

6. *the Salii . . . should not have*: For the Salii, see *Claud*. 33 with the note; the March rituals of Cybele, the Mother of the Gods,

focused on the death of her consort Attis; Dis was the god of the underworld.

VITELLIUS

1. *Quintus Elogius described ... at Rome*: The Quintus Elogius mentioned here is completely unknown, and the name in fact seems to result from a mistake in the transmission of Suetonius' text. Almost none of this material can be corroborated from any other source: Faunus is an ancient but obscure figure from Italic tradition, but the goddess Vitellia and the Vitellian Way are otherwise unattested; there are a few references to a town called Vitellia in Latium, but the spelling of the name varies. The Aequiculi (or Aequi) were an Italian people who periodically threatened Rome in the fifth and fourth centuries BC. The Samnite Wars were fought with the peoples of central southern Italy in the late fourth and early third centuries BC; they did involve the establishment of Roman colonies, but the reference to Nuceria here is simply an error: Nuceria was in the Bay of Naples, while the Apulian town was called Luceria.

2. *covering his head ... prostrating himself*: A Roman who presided over a sacrifice normally covered his head with a fold of his toga; a covered head thus became a standard visual marker of piety and respect for the gods. Vitellius seems to have adopted his other actions from the east, where they were traditional ways of showing respect to a ruler.

3. *'May you do this very often' ... Saecular Games*: This was presumably a joke, since the Saecular Games were supposed to occur only once in a lifetime (compare *Claud.* 21), although a joke seems a little out of place in a discussion of his skill as a flatterer.

4. *his two sons ... achieve the consulship in the same year*: A. Vitellius, the future emperor, was regular consul in AD 48, followed by his younger brother L. Vitellius as suffect consul.

5. *while Drusus Caesar and Norbanus Flaccus were consuls*: In AD 15; yet below (section 18) Suetonius gives Vitellius' age at his death in December AD 69 as fifty-six, which implies that he was born in AD 12; various considerations suggest that the latter is correct.

6. *'Spintria' ... public office*: For Tiberius' *spintriae*, see *Tib.* 43; the story cannot be true, since L. Vitellius, as consul in AD 34,

must have been well along in his career by AD 27, when Tiberius went to Capreae.

7. *At the Neronia ... reconsider his decision*: On the Neronia, see *Nero* 12; for this episode, compare *Nero* 21.

8. *the Blues in the Circus*: On the different Circus factions, see *Calig.* 55 with the note.

9. *the cognomen Germanicus ... Caesar*: Documentary evidence confirms that as emperor he called himself A. Vitellius Germanicus Imperator, later adding the name Augustus.

10. *a rooster ... on his hand*: Suetonius explains the significance of this curious incident in section 18 below.

11. *wearing a commander's cloak ... drawn swords*: Vitellius' entrance into Rome takes the form of a quasi-triumph, a grossly offensive way to mark a victory over fellow citizens.

12. *the anniversary of the Allia defeat*: 18 July; according to tradition, it was on that day in 390 BC that the Romans were defeated by the Gauls in a battle at the Allia river, a defeat that paved the way for the Gallic sack of Rome (see further *Tib.* 3 with the note); the anniversary was always observed as a day of ill omen.

13. *The omen ... 'rooster's beak'*: The interpretation of the event is based not only on Antonius Primus' childhood nickname, but also the pun between *gallus* ('rooster') and *Gallus* ('Gaul'); compare *Nero* 45 with the note.

DIVUS VESPASIAN

1. *during the consulship of Quintus Sulpicius Camerinus and Gaius Poppaeus Sabinus*: In AD 9.

2. *full Roman citizenship in place of only a Latin one*: The Latin citizenship to which Suetonius refers was a limited form of Roman citizenship given to improperly freed slaves; these remarks about Flavia Domitilla suggest that she either was or was said to be a freedwoman.

3. *picked up a human hand ... under the table*: The point behind this macabre anecdote is that *manus*, the Latin word for 'hand', also signified the power that a husband had over a wife or a father over his children and slaves (hence 'to manumit' – literally, 'to send out of *manus*').

4. *who would then be emperor*: We have Josephus' own account of this incident: *Jewish War* 3.399–408.

5. *branches, garlands and bread*: Symbols of kingship in Hellenistic

Egypt; as Tacitus points out in his own account of this event (*Histories* 4.82), the name Basilides was itself an omen (since it is related to the Greek word *basileus*, 'king').

6. *eight more consulships to the one he had already earned*: Vespasian's first consulship had been in AD 51 (see above, section 4); on becoming emperor, he held the consulship in AD 70 and thereafter for every year of his reign except AD 73 and 78.

7. *an amphitheatre in the centre of the city*: This is the Flavian Amphitheatre, begun by Vespasian, dedicated by Titus (see *Tit.* 7), and finally completed by Domitian; it is better known today as the Colosseum, a name that it acquired in the Middle Ages after the colossal statue of Nero (see *Nero* 31 and section 18 below) had been moved there.

8. *immoral fellow . . . 'I, at least, am a man'*: The Latin word *impudicus*, which Graves translates here as 'immoral', carried the specific connotation of taking the passive role in homosexual intercourse.

9. *'Does the emperor really care . . . a million in gold?'*: This was a hint at Vespasian's greed, for which he was notorious (see section 16 below); other emperors had ensured that wealthy men were condemned simply so that they could confiscate their property (see, for example, *Calig.* 38 and *Nero* 32).

10. *'Good dog!'*: The Cynics were followers of a philosophical tradition that rejected all human conventions in favour of living in accordance with nature; the point of Vespasian's comment is that the name Cynic derived from the Greek word *kuôn*, 'dog'.

11. *simply as 'Vespasian'*: Vespasian's original name was T. Flavius Vespasianus; as emperor, however, he used the name Imperator Caesar Vespasianus Augustus.

12. *the Colossus*: The huge statue of himself that Nero erected (see *Nero* 31); according to the elder Pliny, Vespasian had it refashioned into an image of the sun god (*Natural History* 34.45).

13. *plostra . . . 'Flaurus'*: *Plaustra* is the Latin word for 'wagons'; the joke here involves not only the obvious play with the vowels, but also the allusion to the Greek word *phlauros*, 'petty'.

14. *'Striding along with a lance . . . shadow'*: Homer, *Iliad* 7.213.

15. *O, Laches . . . once more*: A quotation from a now lost comedy of Menander, with alterations by Vespasian.

16. *Junia Calvina . . . one of his descendants*: The daughter of Aemilia Lepida and granddaughter of the younger Julia; Junia Calvina was apparently the only one of Augustus' direct descendants to survive the reigns of Gaius, Claudius and Nero.

17. *'Look at that long hair . . . going to die'*: Comets were called 'long-haired stars' in antiquity, and were thought to portend disasters such as the death of a ruler (see *Nero* 36); Vespasian jokes that a long-haired star must refer to the death of a long-haired ruler.

18. *when he had lived sixty-nine years, seven months and seven days*: In AD 79.

DIVUS TITUS

1. *the same as his father's*: Titus' original name was T. Flavius Vespasianus; as emperor, he was called Imperator Titus Caesar Vespasianus Augustus.

2. *the memorable year . . . the Septizonium*: The year is AD 41, although the age that Suetonius assigns to Titus at his death (section 11 below) suggests that he was instead born in AD 39; the latter is usually considered correct. The Septizonium is otherwise unknown.

3. *the Ides of September, and he had reigned two years, two months, and twenty days*: On 13 September AD 81.

DOMITIAN

1. *Vespasian as consul-elect . . . the sixth district of Rome*: The year is AD 51; the sixth district was on the Quirinal Hill.

2. *rode on a white horse*: Vespasian and Titus rode in the triumphal chariot; Domitian's place on a horse is like that of the young Tiberius in Augustus' triumph (*Tib.* 6).

3. *six consulships . . . resigned in his favour*: Domitian was suffect consul in AD 71, 75, 76, 77 and 79; he held a regular consulship in 73, but there is no other evidence that Titus was originally designated for the position.

4. *the college of the Flaviales*: A board of priests who oversaw the cult of the deified Flavian emperors, Vespasian and Titus.

5. *Scantinian Law*: Directed against men who had sex with freeborn boys.

6. *'Before an impious people took to eating slaughtered bullocks'*: Virgil, *Georgics* 2.537.

7. *'I'm in training'*: The joke refers to the accepted wisdom that sexual activity was harmful to one's voice.

8. *Mago and Hannibal*: Hannibal was the great Carthaginian general who during the Second Punic War had invaded Italy and threatened the city of Rome; Mago was his younger brother.

9. *Paris and Oenone*: In Greek myth, Oenone was a nymph loved by Paris, the prince of Troy, whom he deserted for Helen; after he had been wounded, she refused to return to him and cure him.

10. *an execution in ancient style*: See *Nero* 49.

11. *the tax on Jews*: This had been imposed by Vespasian, who after the destruction of the Jerusalem Temple in AD 70 had redirected the ancient Temple tax (see Exodus 30:11–16) to a special fund in the Capitol in Rome (see Josephus, *Jewish War* 7.218).

12. *'Too many rulers are a dangerous thing'*: Homer, *Iliad* 2.204; Gaius had earlier quoted from the same passage (see *Calig.* 22 with the note).

13. *our Lord and Lady*: The Latin word *dominus*, which had connotations of 'master', had been firmly rejected by Augustus and Tiberius (see *Aug.* 53 with the note; compare *Tib.* 27).

14. *scribbled arci . . . but used Greek characters*: A bilingual pun: *arci* is the Latin word for 'arches', but spelled with Greek characters it becomes the Greek verb *arkei*, 'that's enough!'

15. *seventeen consulships*: Domitian held his first six consulships during the reign of his father (see section 2 above, with the note) and his seventh during that of his brother (AD 80); as emperor, he was consul every year from AD 82 to 88, and again in AD 90, 92 and 95.

16. *The famous cypress tree*: For this tree, see *Vesp.* 5.

17. *fourteen years*: The year was AD 96. Suetonius is wrong about the length of Domitian's reign, which began on 13 September AD 81 and so lasted a little more than fifteen years.

18. *'Cannot you see that I too have a tall and beautiful person?'*: Homer, *Iliad* 21.108.

19. *her husband*: Julia's husband was her cousin T. Flavius Sabinus, whom Domitian himself had executed (see section 10 above).

Index of Historical Persons

Apart from emperors, members of the imperial family and major authors, people are normally listed by their nomen; I have ordered identical names by date, since in most cases people of the same name belong to successive generations of the same family, and have omitted names that are known only from a single reference. Alphabetical references are to the family trees, and numerical references are to the section numbers of the lives; note that the entries for emperors include only references in biographies other than their own.

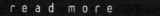
PENGUIN CLASSICS

THE REPUBLIC
PLATO

'We are concerned with the most important of issues, the choice between a good and an evil life'

Plato's *Republic* is widely acknowledged as the cornerstone of Western philosophy. Presented in the form of a dialogue between Socrates and three different interlocutors, it is an inquiry into the notion of a perfect community and the ideal individual within it. During the conversation other questions are raised: what is goodness; what is reality; what is knowledge? *The Republic* also addresses the purpose of education and the roles of both women and men as 'guardians' of the people. With remarkable lucidity and deft use of allegory, Plato arrives at a depiction of a state bound by harmony and ruled by 'philosopher kings'.

Desmond Lee's translation of *The Republic* has come to be regarded as a classic in its own right. The new introduction by Melissa Lane discusses Plato's aims in writing *The Republic*, its major arguments and perspective on politics in ancient Greece, and its significance through the ages and today.

Translated with an introduction by Desmond Lee

PENGUIN CLASSICS

THE RISE OF THE ROMAN EMPIRE
POLYBIUS

'If history is deprived of the truth,
we are left with nothing but an idle, unprofitable tale'

In writing his account of the relentless growth of the Roman Empire, the Greek statesman Polybius (*c*. 200–118 BC) set out to help his fellow-countrymen understand how their world came to be dominated by Rome. Opening with the Punic War in 264 BC, he vividly records the critical stages of Roman expansion: its campaigns throughout the Mediterranean, the temporary setbacks inflicted by Hannibal and the final destruction of Carthage in 146 BC. An active participant in contemporary politics, as well as a friend of many prominent Roman citizens, Polybius was able to draw on a range of eyewitness accounts and on his own experiences of many of the central events, giving his work immediacy and authority.

Ian Scott-Kilvert's translation fully preserves the clarity of Polybius' narrative. This substantial selection of the surviving volumes is accompanied by an introduction by F. W. Walbank, which examines Polybius' life and times, and the sources and technique he employed in writing his history.

Translated by Ian Scott-Kilvert

Selected with an introduction by F. W. Walbank

PENGUIN CLASSICS

THE POLITICS
ARISTOTLE

'Man is by nature a political animal'

In *The Politics* Aristotle addresses the questions that lie at the heart of political science. How should society be ordered to ensure the happiness of the individual? Which forms of government are best and how should they be maintained? By analysing a range of city constitutions – oligarchies, democracies and tyrannies – he seeks to establish the strengths and weaknesses of each system to decide which are the most effective, in theory and in practice. A hugely significant work, which has influenced thinkers as diverse as Aquinas and Machiavelli, *The Politics* remains an outstanding commentary on fundamental political issues and concerns, and provides fascinating insights into the workings and attitudes of the Greek city-state.

The introductions by T. A. Sinclair and Trevor J. Saunders discuss the influence of *The Politics* on philosophers, its modern relevance and Aristotle's political beliefs. This edition contains Greek and English glossaries, and a bibliography for further reading.

Translated by T. A. Sinclair
Revised and re-presented by Trevor J. Saunders

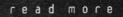

PENGUIN CLASSICS

THE BIRDS AND OTHER PLAYS
ARISTOPHANES

The Knights/Peace/The Birds/The Assemblywomen/Wealth

> 'Oh wings are splendid things, make no mistake:
> they really help you rise in the world'

The plays collected in this volume, written at different times in Aristophanes' forty-year career as a dramatist, all contain his trademark bawdy comedy and dazzling verbal agility. In *The Birds*, two frustrated Athenians join with the birds to build the utopian city of 'Much Cuckoo in the Clouds'. *The Knights* is a venomous satire on Cleon, the prominent Athenian demagogue, while *The Assemblywomen* considers the war of the sexes, as the women of Athens infiltrate the all-male Assembly in disguise. The lengthy conflict with Sparta is the subject of *Peace*, inspired by the hope of a settlement in 421 BC, and *Wealth* reflects the economic catastrophe that hit Athens after the war, as the god of riches is depicted as a ragged, blind old man.

The lively translations by David Barrett and Alan H. Sommerstein capture the full humour of the plays. The introduction examines Aristophanes' life and times, and the comedy and poetry of his works. This volume also includes an introductory note for each play.

Translated with an introduction by David Barrett and Alan H. Sommerstein

PENGUIN CLASSICS

THE PERSIAN EXPEDITION
XENOPHON

'The only things of value which we have at present are our arms and our courage'

In *The Persian Expedition*, Xenophon, a young Athenian noble who sought his destiny abroad, provides an enthralling eyewitness account of the attempt by a Greek mercenary army – the Ten Thousand – to help Prince Cyrus overthrow his brother and take the Persian throne. When the Greeks were then betrayed by their Persian employers, they were forced to march home through hundreds of miles of difficult terrain – adrift in a hostile country and under constant attack from the unforgiving Persians and warlike tribes. In this outstanding description of endurance and individual bravery, Xenophon, one of those chosen to lead the retreating army, provides a vivid narrative of the campaign and its aftermath, and his account remains one of the best pictures we have of Greeks confronting a 'barbarian' world.

Rex Warner's distinguished translation captures the epic quality of the Greek original and George Cawkwell's introduction sets the story of the expedition in the context of its author's life and tumultuous times.

Translated by Rex Warner with an introduction by George Cawkwell

Penguin Classics

THE CONSOLATION OF PHILOSOPHY
BOETHIUS

> 'Why else does slippery Fortune change
> So much, and punishment more fit
> For crime oppress the innocent?'

Written in prison before his brutal execution in AD 524, Boethius's *The Consolation of Philosophy* is a conversation between the ailing prisoner and his 'nurse' Philosophy, whose instruction restores him to health and brings him to enlightenment. Boethius was an eminent public figure who had risen to great political heights in the court of King Theodoric when he was implicated in conspiracy and condemned to death. Although a Christian, it was to the pagan Greek philosophers that he turned for inspiration following his abrupt fall from grace. With great clarity of thought and philosophical brilliance, Boethius adopted the classical model of the dialogue to debate the vagaries of Fortune, and to explore the nature of happiness, good and evil, fate and free will.

Victor Watts's English translation makes *The Consolation of Philosophy* accessible to the modern reader while losing nothing of its poetic artistry and breadth of vision. This edition includes an introduction discussing Boethius's life and writings, a bibliography, glossary and notes.

Translated with an introduction by Victor Watts

THE STORY OF PENGUIN CLASSICS

Before 1946 ... 'Classics' are mainly the domain of academics and students; readable editions for everyone else are almost unheard of. This all changes when a little-known classicist, E. V. Rieu, presents Penguin founder Allen Lane with the translation of Homer's *Odyssey* that he has been working on in his spare time.

1946 Penguin Classics debuts with *The Odyssey*, which promptly sells three million copies. Suddenly, classics are no longer for the privileged few.

1950s Rieu, now series editor, turns to professional writers for the best modern, readable translations, including Dorothy L. Sayers's *Inferno* and Robert Graves's unexpurgated *Twelve Caesars*.

1960s The Classics are given the distinctive black covers that have remained a constant throughout the life of the series. Rieu retires in 1964, hailing the Penguin Classics list as 'the greatest educative force of the twentieth century.'

1970s A new generation of translators swells the Penguin Classics ranks, introducing readers of English to classics of world literature from more than twenty languages. The list grows to encompass more history, philosophy, science, religion and politics.

1980s The Penguin American Library launches with titles such as *Uncle Tom's Cabin*, and joins forces with Penguin Classics to provide the most comprehensive library of world literature available from any paperback publisher.

1990s The launch of Penguin Audiobooks brings the classics to a listening audience for the first time, and in 1999 the worldwide launch of the Penguin Classics website extends their reach to the global online community.

The 21st Century Penguin Classics are completely redesigned for the first time in nearly twenty years. This world-famous series now consists of more than 1300 titles, making the widest range of the best books ever written available to millions – and constantly redefining what makes a 'classic'.

The Odyssey continues ...

The best books ever written

PENGUIN CLASSICS

SINCE 1946

Find out more at www.penguinclassics.com